Japanese/Korean Linguistics

Volume 21

Japanese/Korean Linguistics

Volume 21

edited by
Seungho Nam, Heejeong Ko, and Jongho Jun

Published for the Stanford Linguistics Association by

CSLI PUBLICATIONS
Center for the Study of
Language and Information
Stanford, California

CSLI Publications
Center for the Study of Language and Information
Leland Stanford Junior University
Printed in the United States
18 17 16 15 14   1 2 3 4 5

Library of Congress Cataloging-in-Publication Data

Conference on Japanese/Korean Linguistics (1st : 1989 : University of Southern California)

Japanese/Korean Linguistics / edited by Hajime Hoji.

Volume 21 / edited by Seungho Nam, Heejeong Ko, and Jongho Jun

p. cm.

Includes bibliographical references and index.
ISBN-13: 978-1-57586-653-6
ISBN-13: 978-1-57586-654-3 (pbk.)

1. Japanese language—Congresses. 2. Korean language—Congresses. 3. Japanese language—Grammar, Comparative—Korean—Congresses. 4. Korean language—Grammar, Comparative—Japanese—Congresses. 5. Linguistics—Congresses. I. Hoji, Hajime. II. Stanford Linguistics Association. III. Center for the Study of Language and Information (U.S.) IV. Title.
PL503.C6 1989
495.6–dc20 90-2550
CIP

∞ The acid-free paper used in this book meets the minimum requirements of the American National Standard for Information Sciences—Permanence of Paper for Printed Library Materials, ANSI Z39.48-1984.

For a list of volumes in this series, along with a cumulative table of contents, please visit

http://cslipublications.stanford.edu/site/JAKO.shtml

CSLI was founded in 1983 by researchers from Stanford University, SRI International, and Xerox PARC to further the research and development of integrated theories of language, information, and computation. CSLI headquarters and CSLI Publications are located on the campus of Stanford University.

CSLI Publications reports new developments in the study of language, information, and computation. Please visit our web site at
http://cslipublications.stanford.edu/
for comments on this and other titles, as well as for changes and corrections by the author and publisher.

Contents

Acknowledgments

The 21st Japanese/Korean Linguistics Conference was held at Seoul National University, Korea, on October 20-22, 2011. Forty-four papers were selected by blind review from the 142 abstracts submitted. There were twenty-eight oral presentations including four by invited speakers and twenty poster presentations although this volume contains only the papers presented in oral sessions. Paper presentations were balanced with respect to theory (formal and functional) and language data (Korean and Japanese), and covered a variety of topics. About 150 scholars and students from North America, Europe, Japan and Korea participated in the conference.

Paper presenters surely made a major contribution to the success of the conference. Our first thank should go to them for generously sharing their ideas and work. Among them, we were fortunate to have excellent invited speakers: Chai-song Hong (Seoul National University), David Pesetsky (MIT), Satosh Tomioka (University of Delaware), and Kie Zuraw (UCLA). We thank them for their inspiring presentations.

Each submitted abstract was reviewed by three to five experts. In total, seventy-nine linguists served as reviewers for this year's program. We would like to thank them for their time and effort.

It would be much more difficult for us to organize this conference if we have no information about the organization of the previous J/K conferences. We appreciate Sung-Ock Sohn (UCLA) for her advice and encouragement.

Many graduate and undergraduate students at Seoul National University participated as volunteers, helping with registration activities and other aspects of conference organization. Among them, Suzy Ahn and Songhee Kim played a main role in the conference organization. Although they as program coordinators dealt with many complicated things such as reviewer contact, abstract classification, reviewer assignment, etc., they handled them very well. They made a very important contribution to the success of the conference. We very much appreciate their help.

Finally, the 21st Japanese/Korean Linguistics Conference was supported by grants received from Department of Linguistics and Language Research Institute of Seoul National University. We are thankful to their support.

Seungho Nam, Heejeong Ko and Jongho Jun
Department of Linguistics
Seoul National University

Part I

Phonetics and Phonology

Analogy Effects on North Kyungsang Korean Accentuation of Novel Words

HYUN-JU KIM*
Stony Brook University

Patterns that emerge in the production of novel words have been generally assumed to reflect an abstract internalized grammar, though an alternative approach is that the production of novel words is influenced by analogy with existing words (e.g. Bybee 1985, 2001; Daelemans, Gillis, and Durieux 1994; Skousen 1989). North Kyungsang Korean (NKK), unlike standard Korean, is a pitch accent language where the tonal pattern of a given lexical word is not fully predictable, as illustrated in the following minimal triple *káci* 'kind', *kací* 'eggplant', *kácí* 'branch'. When lexical information for accent position is absent, how do NKK speakers decide to accent novel words? Will they consult the patterns of similar real words to determine the accent position? This study demonstrates that the accent patterns in novel words do not originate from analogy to phonetically similar familiar words. Rather, the accentuation of novel words reveals regular tendencies, which are sensitive to syllable structure.

* I am indebted to Ellen Broselow and Marie Huffman for their valuable input and help with my study. I would also like to thank the audience at the JK 21 conference, especially John Whitman, Hyang-sook Sohn, and Kie Zuraw, and anonymous reviewers for their helpful suggestions. All remaining errors are of my own.

Japanese/Korean Linguistics 21.
Edited by Seungho Nam, Heejeong Ko and Jongho Jun.

1. Previous findings and Hypothesis

This study investigates whether analogy to phonetically similar words crucially influences NKK accent placement in novel words. The effects of analogy to patterns in existing words have been found in several different studies using novel words (e.g. Baker and Smith 1976; Daelemans et al. 1994; Eddington 2000; Guion *et al.* 2003; Face 2004). Baker and Smith (1976) investigated English stress patterns in nonwords, testing the sometimes conflicting patterns predicted by SPE stress rules vs. analogy to real words. They found that in many cases, stress was assigned based on the stress of similar words, even when the resulting stress patterns were in conflict with the general rules. Guion *et al.* (2003) also showed that the location of stress on phonologically similar real words influenced stress placement in English nonwords, although they claimed that analogy is just one of the factors affecting stress patterns, others including syllable structure and lexical class. Investigating the factors determining the perception of stress, Face (2004) performed a study in which synthesized productions of Spanish nonwords were controlled so that all syllables were equal in acoustic prominence. Face examined several different factors including word similarity, syllable weight, and morphological category, and found that stress in phonetically similar words was one of the factors that influenced stress perception. On this view, language acquisition involves storing and categorizing linguistic experience, rather than generalizing from linguistic input to abstract rules or constraints, and novel words should be processed via analogy to existing words (Bybee 1985, 2001; Daelemans, Gillis, and Durieux 1994; Skousen 1989).

Because NKK lexical accent patterns are not predictable and therefore must be stored as part of a word's lexical entry, it seems reasonable to expect that accent patterns of existing similar words would play a major role in determining of the accent position that speakers assign in novel words. Therefore, the current study presents an experimental study to test the *Word Similarity Effect Hypothesis*, which predicts that in assigning accent to novel words, native speakers will be influenced by the accent patterns of phonetically similar existing words. The results suggest that this hypothesis is not supported: NKK speakers do not necessarily follow the accent patterns of analogous existing words when accenting novel words. Rather, they tend to accent novel words in accordance with syllable structure, even when an analogous existing word with the same syllable structure has a different accent pattern. The results clearly demonstrate that the effects of syllable structure outweigh the effects of word similarity in NKK accent patterns in novel words.

The rest of the paper is organized as follows: Section 2 presents an experimental study of NKK accentuation in novel words that have phonetically similar counterparts. Section 3 discusses the results and Section 4 remarks on effects of potential competing analogous counterparts. Section 5 concludes.

2. Experiment

A hypothesis which guided this study is that accent patterns in novel words will follow the patterns of existing words that are phonetically similar to the novel words. In order to test this hypothesis, the experiment employed novel words that were identical to existing words except for one consonant. If analogy to patterns of phonetically similar words crucially influences the accent placement in novel words, we expect that patterns emerging in novel words should not be significantly different from the patterns in the phonetically similar existing counterparts.

2.1 Experimental Design

2.1.1 Participants

30 subjects, ranging in age from 29 to 54 years (mean 39), participated in this study. Participants were born and grew up in Daegu or in the suburbs in the northern part of Kyungsang province, and most of them lived in the same area at the time of the experiments. 15 were male and 15 were female. They were paid for their participation, which took less than half an hour.

2.1.2 Procedure

Participants were asked to read a randomized list of words given in a Korean carrier sentence written in Korean characters, for example "*atöri* ________ *to satalla k*^{h}*atəra*" (My son asked me to buy ________ too) with 2 repetitions, and their production was recorded. Novel words were presented with pictures of unfamiliar cartoon characters as in (1) and introduced as the names of new cartoon characters which had recently become popular among children.

(1) Example sentence

atɨri  ***mucide*** to satalla k^{h}atəra

'My son asked me to buy ***mucide***, too'

Each speaker looked through the word list in order to familiarize himself/herself with all the words before recording. Speakers were asked to read in their own dialectal accent as natural conversational speech.

The second readings were analyzed and accent patterns in target words were judged by two native NKK speakers (the author and an undergraduate linguistics student at Stony Brook University). If disagreement occurred between the two judgments, the accent decision was made based on the pitch contour generated using Praat.

2.1.3 Materials

The stimulus set consisted of novel words, 24 bisyllabic words and 24 trisyllabic words. The novel words were identical to existing words except for one consonant in the final syllable.[1] In most cases, the corresponding consonants in the existing vs. the novel word differed in only one place feature: for example, novel word *kɨriŋ* vs. real word *kɨ́rím* 'picture'; novel word *mucide* vs. real word *múcíge* 'rainbow'. Liquid sounds were replaced by nasal sounds (e.g. novel word *tangoŋ* vs. real word *tángol* 'customer'). Following findings that the onset of a word activates a set of lexical candidates sharing that onset (e.g. Allopenna et al. 1998; Marslen-Wilson 1987), I assumed that the novel stimuli would activate neighboring lexical items. To determine whether analogy operates independently of syllable structure, each set of novel words corresponding to a particular syllable structure (e.g. CVCV) was balanced to ensure that each accent type was equally represented in the existing words that corresponded to the novel forms. The novel forms were separated into four different word types: for bisyllabic forms, LL, HL, LH, HH, and for trisyllabic forms, LLL, HLL, LLH, HHL (L=light syllable; H=heavy syllable). Six items were included for each word type: 2 corresponding to analogical real words with double accent, 2 corresponding to analogical real words with penultimate accent, and 2 corresponding to analogical real words with final accent. Due to the absence of final accent in existing HLL words, HLL novel forms targeting analogical final accent were not included. The novel stimuli and the analogical real counterparts are presented in Appendix.

2.2 Results

A total of 1434 tokens (48 items x 30 subjects, excluding six tokens from the analyses)[2] were collected for the analogy test: 719 bisyllabic and 715 trisyllabic tokens. Accent patterns of novel words were compared with tho-

---

[1] One item *paŋraŋi* was created by changing a consonant in the penultimate syllable of a word *paŋ.maŋ.i.* 'cudgel' because the existing word did not contain a consonant in the final syllable (*ŋ* is not a possible onset so *ŋ* in the second syllable would not be resyllabified as onset of the following syllable).

[2] Antepenultimate accent was rarely produced in novel words. Because only 5 of 720 trisyllabic tokens were produced with antepenultimate accent, these 5 tokens were omitted in the statistical analyses. In addition, one token was excluded due to production error.

se of existing analogous counterparts. Two types of statistical analysis were employed: a loglinear analysis for comparison of accent patterns between the two groups (novel words vs. existing words) and Pearson's Chi-square for the main effect of syllable structure and word similarity (analogical accent type). The independent variables were (i) accent position in novel words; (ii) syllable structure, e.g. LL, HL, LH, HH (H=heavy; L=light); and (iii) accent position in existing counterparts. The dependent variable was the number of tokens for each accent pattern (double; penultimate; final).

2.2.1 Overall results: analogy effects

The overall distribution of accent in novel words does not follow the distribution of accent in phonetically similar existing words. Only 46% of responses (661 out of 1434 tokens) followed analogical patterns: 39% in bisyllabic words and 53% in trisyllabic words.

In bisyllabic words, as Figure 1 illustrates, double accent was the most common pattern (40%: 288/719) and was actually more frequent in novel words than in phonetically similar real words (33%). In contrast, final accent was less frequent in novel words (25%:179/719) than in phonetically similar real words (33%).

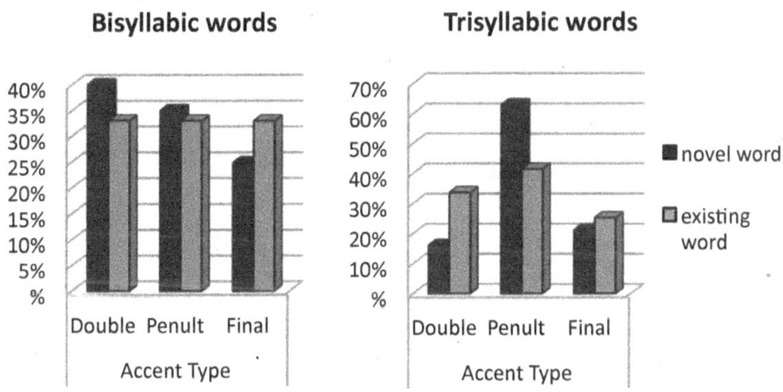

Figure 1. Accent distribution in novel words vs. phonetically similar existing words

In trisyllabic words, penultimate accent was the most frequent pattern in novel words (63%; 449/715), whereas penultimate accent occurred in only 41% of the analogical real words. Double accent assignment also did not match the analogical patterns: 16% (115/715) of novel words were produced with double accent, as opposed to 34% of phonetically similar existing words. Final accent was the only type showing a similar frequency in novel and phonetically similar real words: final accent was found in 21% (151/715) of novel words and 25% of existing words.

A loglinear analysis confirmed that the distribution of the accent patterns in novel vs. phonetically similar existing words was significantly different (χ^2 (3) = 84.28, p < .001). It also showed that interaction between syllable structure and accent type was significant (χ^2 (9) = 427.72, p < .001).

2.2.2 Effects of syllable structure

The number of novel word tokens produced with each accent pattern was counted according to syllable structure combinations. The results showed that accent patterns were not consistent across the syllable structure combinations.

In bisyllabic words, penultimate accent was the most frequent pattern in LL and HL (64%; 52%), but the least frequent pattern in LH and HH (11%; 14%). In contrast, final accent and double accent were the most common patterns in LH and in HH (58%; 63%), respectively. These results contradict the predictions of the hypothesis that speakers should accent novel words in accord with the accent pattern of phonetically similar existing words. Because the novel words were constructed so that their existing counterparts displayed equal distribution of accent type across different word types, analogy alone would predict equal proportions of each accent type. Contra the prediction, the accent placement of novel words displayed uneven distribution according to syllable structure, as illustrated in Figure 2.

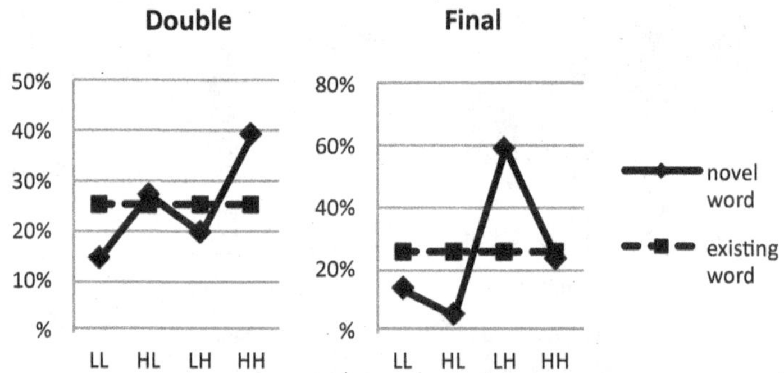

Figure 2. Accent distribution in novel words vs. phonetically similar existing words

As shown in Figure 2, the distribution of non-penultimate accent in novel forms did not parallel that in phonetically similar existing words. Double accent was more frequent in novel forms with initial heavy syllables (HL and HH) and final accent was more frequent in LH novel forms than in analogous real words. Therefore, distribution was skewed toward accenting heavy syllables in novel words, even where a phonetically similar existing word had accent on a non-heavy syllable. The main effects of syllable structure were significant for all the accent patterns in bisyllabic novel words: for penultimate accent, χ^2 (3)=169.9, p<.001, N=719; for double accent, χ^2 (3)=68.9, p<.001, N=719; and for final accent, χ^2 (3)=158.9, p<.001, N=719.

Results for trisyllabic words showed that preference for penultimate accent was fairly strong in all word types except LLH. Penultimate accent was the most frequent pattern in LLL, HLL, and HHL novel forms: 83% in LLL; 82% in HLL; 59% in HHL. Despite the overall tendency toward penultimate accent, final accent was the most frequent pattern in LLH (64%). The tendency toward final accent for LLH was fairly strong compared to the tendency toward final accent in other combinations (11% in LLL; 2% in HLL; 7% in HHL). Neither the predominant penultimate accent nor the strong final accent in LLH paralleled the analogical patterns of phonetically similar existing words. The following graphs in Figure 3 illustrate the mismatch between trisyllabic novel words and analogous existing words.

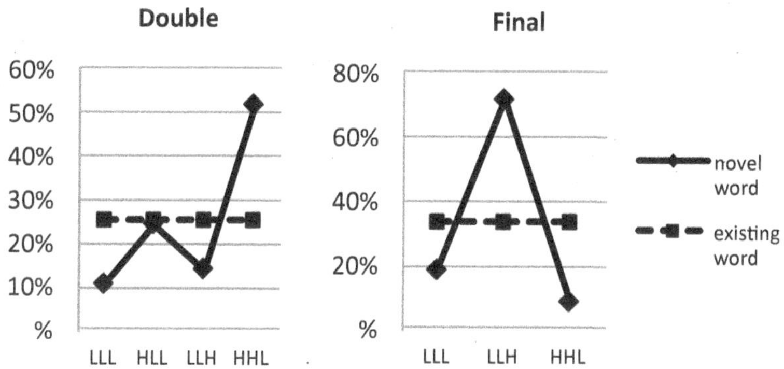

Figure 3. Proportion of each accent in novel words vs. existing counterparts

As shown in Figure 3, double accent was more frequent in HHL novel forms and final accent was more frequent in LLH novel forms than in analogous real words. Therefore, the analogical patterns of phonetically similar real words do not appear to serve as a major factor in the patterns of novel words. The main effects of syllable structure were significant for all the accent patterns in trisyllabic novel words: for penultimate accent, χ^2(3)=157.7, p<.001, N=715; for double accent, χ^2(3)=59.9, p<.001, N=715; and for final accent, χ^2(3)=267.8, p<.001, N=715.

2.2.3 Biased analogy effects

The results showed that the accentuation of novel words was affected by syllable structure, rather than the accent patterns of phonetically similar existing words. The patterns found in novel words are summarized as follows: (i) heavy syllables tended to attract accent in both bisyllabic and trisyllabic words: words with final heavy syllables (e.g. LH, LLH) tended to have final accent and words with initial heavy syllables (e.g. HH, HHL) tended to have double accent; (ii) in words without heavy syllables, penultimate accent was the most frequent pattern; and (iii) in trisyllabic novel words, penultimate accent was dominant across all the word types except LLH (words with final heavy syllables). These syllable structure-sensitive tendencies held even where analogy pulled in a different direction.

Nevertheless, effects of analogy with existing words were found in some cases. Interestingly, the analogy effects held only in the direction of the syllable structure-sensitive patterning. Namely, the assignment of analogical patterns was more likely when the analogical patterns matched the syllable structure-sensitive tendencies than when the patterns were in conflict with these tendencies. In consequence, the syllable structure-sensitive tendencies in novel words were never overridden by the analogy effects, but the two factors, analogy and syllable structure sensitivity, had a cumulative effect.

Figure 4 illustrates the biased analogy effects in bisyllabic novel words. The chart on the left-hand side represents different distribution of penultimate accent in novel words depending on accent type of existing analogous words. The chart on the right-hand side represents different assignment of double accent depending on analogical accent type.

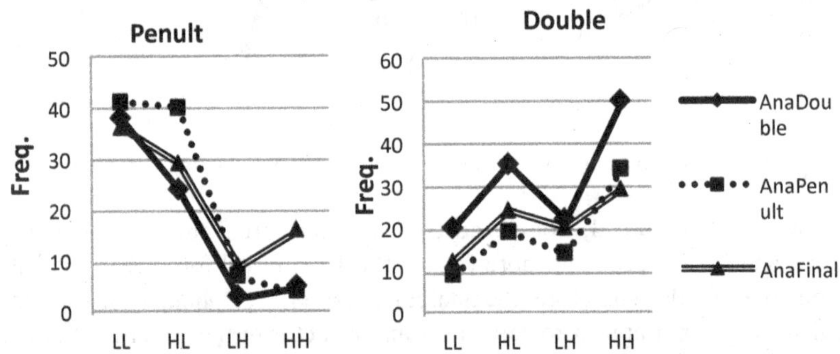

Figure 4. Raw frequency of each accent in bisyllabic novel words: (i)AnaDouble: the cases when existing counterparts carried double accent; (ii) AnaPenult: the cases when existing counterparts carried penultimate accent; and (iii) AnaFinal: the cases when existing counterparts had final accent.

As shown in the chart on the left-hand side in Figure 4, in LL and HL, penultimate accent was more frequent when the existing counterparts carried penultimate accent (AnaPenult) than when the existing counterparts carried non-penultimate accent patterns (AnaDouble; AnaFinal). The effect of analogical accent patterns was significant in HL words ($\chi^2(2)=8.94$, $p=.01$). It is interesting that the analogy effects were not consistent in LH and in HH. In LH forms, the assignment of penultimate accent was not much different according to analogical accent patterns. For HH forms, penultimate accent was actually produced more frequently when analogy predicted *final* accent than when analogy predicted penultimate accent. On the other hand, the chart on the right-hand side in Figure 4 shows that double accent was strikingly more frequent in HL and HH (but not in LL and LH forms) when analogy predicted double accent. The effects of analogical accent patterns were significant in HL and HH ($\chi^2(2)=9.1$, $p=.01$ in HL; $\chi^2(2)=18.6$, $p<.001$ in HH).

In trisyllabic words, the effects of analogical accent patterns were also significant in the assignment of double accent and final accent. Figure 5 shows that accent patterns in some cases were affected by analogical accent patterns. However, it is also notable that the effects were not consistent across the word types.

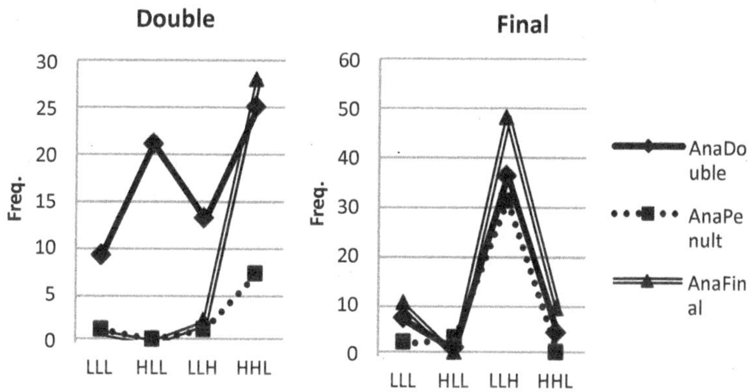

Figure 5. Raw frequency of each accent in trisyllabic novel words: (i)AnaDouble: the cases when existing counterparts carried double accent; (ii) AnaPenult: the cases when existing counterparts carried penultimate accent; and (iii) AnaFinal: the cases when existing counterparts had final accent.

As shown in the graph on the left-hand side in Figure 5, double accent was more frequent when analogous existing words had double accent than when analogous existing words had penultimate accent. Notably, in HLL and HHL, double accent was strikingly higher than in other word types. The statistical analyses confirmed that the effects of analogical accent patterns were significant ($\chi^2(1)=36.6$, $p<.001$ in HLL; $\chi^2(2)=19.4$, $p<.001$ in HHL). It is intriguing, however, that double accent in HHL was far more frequent even in cases when the accent was in conflict with the analogical patterns:

for example, double accent was more frequent even when the analogous existing word had *final* accent. On the other hand, the graph on the right-hand side in Figure 5 shows that final accent in LLH was even more frequent when the analogous existing word had final accent vs. other accent patterns ($\chi^2(2)=11.02$, $p=.004$), although the preference for final accent in LLH was strong in general regardless of analogical accent patterns. The analogy effect on final accent was notable in LLH but not in other word types.

I have shown that analogical patterns of existing words were relevant when the patterns were in accordance with the structure-sensitive tendencies. However, the analogy effects did not operate for the patterns which contradicted the structure-sensitive tendencies. In addition, there was a case in which analogy with existing words was not involved at all even for the patterns which were consistent with the structure-sensitive tendencies: assignment of final accent in bisyllabic words was totally independent of accent patterns in analogous existing words.

To summarize, accent patterns in novel words were significantly different from the patterns in analogous existing counterparts. On the other hand, syllable structure played a crucial role in accent assignment of novel words. The effect of syllable structure was independent of the analogical patterns because the existing counterparts displayed equal distribution of accent type across different word types. However, the frequency of the analogical patterns increased when analogical patterns matched the syllable structure-sensitive tendencies. Hence, the analogy effects were also dependent on syllable structure. Taken all together, analogy to patterns of phonetically similar existing words alone cannot explain NKK accent patterns in novel words.

3. Discussion

The previous section showed that the *Word Similarity Effect Hypothesis* did not hold in NKK accent patterns in novel words. Rather, NKK speakers accented the novel words in accord with the structure-sensitive tendencies. The syllable structure sensitivity was stronger than analogy even in the novel forms where the analogical patterns contradicted the structure-sensitive tendencies. The stronger effect of syllable structure is illustrated graphically in Figure 6:

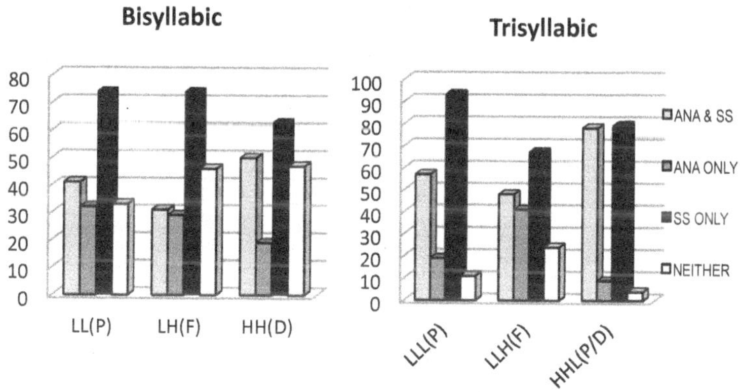

Figure 6. Patterns following analogy vs. Patterns following syllable structure
*As for responses following syllable structure, I counted responses with penultimate accent in LL/LLL; responses with final accent in LH/LLH; responses with double accent in HH; and responses with double/penultimate accent in HHL.

In Figure 6, the results were categorized into four different groups: (i) responses following both analogy and syllable structure (ANA&SS); (ii) responses following analogy rather than syllable structure (ANA ONLY); (iii) responses following syllable structure rather than analogy (SS ONLY); (iv) responses that follow neither (NEITHER). As shown in Figure 6, patterns following syllable structure rather than analogy (SS ONLY responses) were most frequent across all the word types both in bisyllabic and in trisyllabic novel forms, followed by patterns following both analogy and syllable structure (ANA&SS responses). In contrast, responses following analogy rather than syllable structure (ANA ONLY responses) were least frequent in bisyllabic novel forms and less frequent than SS ONLY and ANA&SS responses in trisyllabic novel forms. This clearly indicates that the effects of syllable structure outweigh analogy in NKK accent patterns in novel words.

The analogy effects were notable only when analogical accent patterns were in accordance with the syllable structure-sensitive tendencies, in that the assignment of analogical patterns was more likely when the analogical patterns matched the syllable structure-sensitive tendencies than when the patterns were in conflict with these tendencies. This suggests that NKK speakers must have implicit knowledge of the structure-sensitive patterning and that the analogy effect is constrained by this knowledge.

Given the fact that patterns in novel words are not attributable to analogy to phonetically similar familiar words, a question arises: where do these structure-sensitive tendencies come from? A corpus study of lexical statistics (H-J Kim, In press) showed that these tendencies have some support in the native language lexicon, where they are manifested as statistical preferences. This suggests that NKK speakers should have a stochastic grammar based on the lexical frequency (e.g. Zuraw 2000; Hayes and Londe 2006) and learning this grammar is also possible via the native lexicon. If this is the case, NKK speakers apply the grammar to newly adopted words, where there is no pressure to preserve lexically specified accent patterns. In addition, the syllable structure-sensitive tendencies in novel words are actually consistent with the regular patterns emerging in loanwords (Kenstowicz and Sohn 2001). This implies that the syllable structure effects emerging in online accent assignment in newly adopted words (novel words) persist in offline accent assignment in long-lasting loanwords.

4. Remark on Competing Analogous Counterparts

One possible confounding factor is that some of the bisyllabic novel forms in the experiment might have competing analogous existing counterparts with different accent patterns.[3] For example, for a novel form *cagu*, the real word *cigu* 'Earth' (with double accent) differs from the corresponding novel form in its initial vowel rather than in its final consonant, and therefore might compete with the existing counterpart *cadu* 'plum' (with final accent). Thus, in this section I considered accent patterns of competing analogous counterparts.

I collected additional analogous existing words which might compete with the base counterparts by asking three NKK informants to write as many existing words as they could think of that each novel form of the stimuli used in the experiment brought to mind. For most of the bisyllabic novel forms, one or two other existing words in addition to the base counterparts were produced and the list of the additional existing counterparts is presented in Appendix.[4] However, the accent patterns in bisyllabic novel forms did not consistently follow analogical patterns of the competing analogous words either: 29% (69/240) followed patterns of a nearly-identical group (identical to a novel form except for some other single segment): e.g. a real word *cígú* 'Earth' vs. a novel form *cagu*; 35% (107/300) followed patterns of a similar group (identical to a novel form except for two segments or share an identical final syllable): e.g. a real word *kkîni* 'meal' vs. a novel form *keni*. Recall that 39% of the responses (284/720) followed accent patterns of the base-existing counterparts in the experiment. The accent patterns of the competing counterparts were actually followed less frequently than those of the counterparts assumed in the original analysis. All these

[3] Potential effects of competing analogous counterparts were suggested by Hyang-sook Sohn and John Whitman.

[4] Non-phonetically related responses were excluded from the analyses.

together suggest that NKK speakers were not likely to follow analogical patterns even in the cases when they came up with alternative analogical words. Therefore, the overall results remain intact although other competing analogous counterparts were present.

Unlike bisyllabic novel forms, trisyllabic novel forms rarely had additional analogous counterparts. In the Korean lexicon, neighboring lexical words which share an identical onset in two or more syllables are not common. Actually, all three informants gave only the predicted analogous base words for 21 of the 24 trisyllabic novel forms.[5] Therefore, the trisyllabic novel forms in the experiment almost overwhelmingly reflect the target existing counterparts.

5. Conclusion

This study investigated analogy effects on NKK accent assignment of novel words, testing the *Word Similarity Effect Hypothesis*: analogy to patterns of phonetically similar words is a major factor in NKK accentuation of novel words. The results showed that word similarity did not play an important role in accent placement of novel words. Rather, NKK speakers accented novel words in accord with syllable structure: heavy syllables were likely to be accented; penultimate syllables were accented most frequently when the word did not have a heavy syllable, even when accent patterns in analogous existing words contradicted these syllable structure-sensitive tendencies. This indicates that structure sensitivity was stronger than analogy in NKK accentuation of novel words. There were cases where accent patterns of analogous existing words were relevant to accent patterns in novel forms, but even the analogy effects were not independent of syllable structure: the analogy effects were biased toward the structure-sensitive patterning. Therefore, I conclude that the effects of syllable structure emerging in novel words are indeed attributable to a phonologically-based source rather than an analogically-based process, and that the knowledge of relationship between syllable structure and accent also constrains the effects of analogy.

---

[5] Only three items of the 24 trisyllabic novel forms were given additional existing counterparts: *mudə́wi* 'sweltering heat'(c.f. base-counterpart *mudə́gi* 'pile') for a novel form *mudəbi*; *sasími* 'a loanword from Japanese, meaning raw fish' (c.f. base-counterpart *sadarí* 'ladder') for a novel form *sadami*; and *báŋráŋca* 'wanderer' (c.f. base-counterpart *baŋmáŋi* 'cudgel') for a novel form *baŋraŋi*. The competing accent patterns of these alternative analogous words were consistent with the syllable structure-sensitive tendencies (penultimate accent in words without heavy syllables; double accent in words beginning with a heavy syllable). Therefore, the presence of the competing analogous counterparts in trisyllabic novel forms should not be meaningful where analogical patterns compete with structure-sensitive patterning.

Appendix

1. Bisyllabic Stimuli

CV.CV.		CVC.CV.		CV.CVC.		CVC.CVC.	
NOVL	REAL	NOVL	REAL	NOVL	REAL	NOVL	REAL
suga	súdá	nɨkbe	nɨ́kdé	kɨriŋ	kɨ́rím	əkc^{h}əp	ə́kc^{h}ə́k
cop^{h}a	cók^{h}á	tamge	támbé	hobat	hóbák	pəpsət	pə́psə́k
keni	kémi	cipde	cípge	kasɨŋ	kásɨm	pancup	páncuk
nadi	nábi	kukda	kúkca	padap	pádak	tangoŋ	tángol
cagu	cadú	nemgi	nembí	kɨnɨm	kɨnɨ́l	əlgun	əlgúl
kubu	kudú	kamba	kamcá	kusət	kusə́k	hətgaŋ	hətgán

2. Trisyllabic Stimuli

CV.CV.CV.		CVC.CV.CV.		CV.CV.CVC.		CVC.CVC.CV.	
NOVL	REAL	NOVL	REAL	NOVL	REAL	NOVL	REAL
mucide	múcíge	simmami	símmáni	ərɨsiŋ	ə́rɨ́sin	caŋttangi	cáŋttánci
sat^{h}umi	sát^{h}úri	toŋc^{h}iri	tóŋc^{h}ími	jədɨnɨm	jə́dɨ́rɨm	kombaŋge	kómbáŋde
mudəbi	mudə́gi	talgugi	talgúci	arimaŋ	aríraŋ	paŋraŋi	paŋmáŋi
toragi	toráci	tanmugi	tanmúci	ttɨgegil	ttɨgécil	incəlri	incə́lmi
sadami	sadarí	coŋami	coŋári	susuttaŋ	susukkáŋ	cindamme	cindallé
nəsɨme	nəsɨré	nalc^{h}isi	nalc^{h}ígi	kədɨrɨŋ	kədɨrím	mindɨnne	mindɨllé

3. Additional analogous existing counterparts

(i) Nearly-Identical		(ii) Similar group		(iii) Diff.SyllStrc group	
REAL	NOVL	REAL	NOVL	REAL	NOVL
cígú	cagu	kkíni	keni	súgap	suga
cup^{h}á	cop^{h}a	ssɨ́lgé	tamge	cáguk	cagu
tubú	kubu	pindé	cipde	cóp^{h}án	cop^{h}a
madí	nadi	kjésɨ́ŋ	kasɨŋ	kúbun	kubu
kúksá	kukda	tédáp	padap	kámpáŋ	kamba
néŋgí	nemgi	kɨ́nóm	kɨnɨm	hə́tge	hətgaŋ
kɨríl	kɨriŋ	pə́sət	kusət	pə́sət	pəpsət
hobán	hobat	seŋgáŋ	hətgaŋ		
		tangún	tangoŋ		
		pánccók	pancup		

References

Allopenna, P., Magnuson, J., & Tanehaus, M. 1998. Tracking the time course of spoken word recognition using eye movements: evidence for continuous mapping models. *Journal of Memory and Language* 38: 419-439.

Baker, R. & Smith, P. 1976. A psycholinguistic study of English stress assignment rules. *Language and Speech* 19: 9-27.

Bybee, J. 1985. *Morphology: a Study of the Relation between Meaning and Form.* Amsterdam: John Benjamins.

Bybee, J. 2000. Lexicalization of sound change and alternating environments. In M. Broe and J. Pierrehumbert (eds.), *Laboratory Phonology V: Acquisition and the Lexicon*, 250-268. Cambridge: Cambridge University Press.

Bybee, J. 2001. *Phonology and Language Use*. Cambridge, U.K.: Cambridge University Press.

Bybee, J. 2006. From usage to grammar: The mind's response to repetition. *Language* 82: 711-733.

Daelemans, W., Gillis, S., & Durieux, G. 1994. The acquisition of stress: A data-oriented approach. *Computational Linguistics* 20: 421-451.

Eddington, D. 2000. Spanish stress assignment within the analogical modeling of language. *Language* 76: 92-109.

Face, T. 2004. Perceiving what isn't there: non-acoustic cues for perceiving Spanish stress. In Timothy L. Face (eds.), *Laboratory Approaches to Spanish Phonology*, 117-141. Mouton de Gruyter, Berlin.

Guion, S. Clark, J. Harada, T. and Wayland, R. 2003. Factors affecting stress placement for English nonwords include syllabic structure, lexical class, and stress patterns of phonologically similar words. *Language and Speech* 46: 403-427.

Hayes, B. & Londe, Z. 2006. Stochastic phonological knowledge: the case of Hungarian vowel harmony. *Phonology* 23: 59-104. Cambridge University Press.

Kenstowicz, M. & Sohn, H. 2001. Accentual adaptation in North Kyungsang Korean. In M. Kenstowicz (eds.), *Ken Hale: a Life in Language*, 239-270. Cambridge, MA: MIT Press.

Kim, H-J. In press. Emergent hidden grammar: Stochastic patterning in Korean accentuation of novel words. *The Proceedings of the 36th Annual Meeting of the Berkely Linguistics Society*. eLanguage.

Kim, N. 1997. *Tone, Segments, and Their interaction in North Kyungsang Korean: A Correspondence Theoretic Account*. PhD dissertation, Ohio State University.

Skousen, R. 1989. *Analogical Modeling of Language*. Dordrecht: Kluwer Academic Publishers.

Marslen-Wilson,W. 1987. Functional parallelism in spoken word recognition. *Cognition* 25: 71-102.

Zuraw, K. 2000. *Patterned Exceptions in Phonology*. PhD dissertation, UCLA.

A Component-by-Component Analysis of the Japanese Rendition of Korean Names

MIRA OH*
Chonnam National University

1. Introduction

This paper investigates Korean names loaned into Japanese. To fully explain the adaptation of Korean names into Japanese, we need to answer the following three questions: First, what is the unit of analysis for the adaptation of complex loanwords? Second, how are complex loanwords different from simplex loanwords in terms of vowel epenthesis and sound mappings? Third, to what extent can morphological and phonetic information in complex words from a source language influence the adaptation of complex words?

Most of the previous studies of the adaptation of Korean segments into Japanese focus on the adaptation of simplex words (Ito et al., 2006; Kim, 2008). However, names are complex in that they consist of family and given names. Korean names typically consist of a monosyllabic family

*This study was financially supported by Chonnam National University, 2011.

Japanese/Korean Linguistics 21.
Edited by Seungho Nam, Heejeong Ko and Jongho Jun.

name, followed by a disyllabic given name, e.g., Oh Mira. Korean names have been adapted into Japanese since the 1970s based on Korean pronunciation as opposed to the Japanese reading of Chinese characters in Korean names (Shinohara, 2008). In the present study, we analyze a total of 591 Korean names loaned into Japanese from the following three Japanese websites: http://www.weblio.jp/ontology/ 日本で活躍する韓国の芸能人_1, http://www.yahoo.co.jp/, and http://tv.nilenile.net/list/korea.html.

We demonstrate the asymmetrical behavior of family or given name-edge and name-internal consonants with respect to vowel epenthesis and sound mappings in loan adaptation. We show that the family name-final consonant patterns with the simplex word-final consonant in vowel epenthesis and segmental mappings. This suggests that each part of a name is subject to loan adaptation independently of other parts of the name.

Loanword phonology reveals how foreign forms are repaired and thus has been proven to be an especially revealing source of information on native-language phonology. However, there is an ongoing debate over the effect of input information on loanword adaptation between the phonological view (LaCharité & Paradis, 2005) and the perceptual view (Silverman, 1992; Peperkamp & Dupoux, 2003). According to the phonological view, L2 signals are mapped to L1 phonemes via L2 phonemes (LaCharité & Paradis, 2005), whereas according to the perceptual view, L2 signals are directly mapped to L1 phonemes (Silverman, 1992; Peperkamp & Dupoux, 2003; Kang, 2003). In the present study, we show that the adaptation of Korean stops into Japanese varies according to their position. That is, the word-initial lenis stop in Korean is loaned as a voiceless stop in Japanese, but the intervocalic lenis stop in Korean, which is realized as voiced, is adapted as a voiced stop in Japanese. Then the adaptation of Korean names into Japanese favors the perceptual view because the allophonic realization is reflected in loan adaptation.

By investigating the adaptation of Korean names into Japanese, we make the following three claims:

(1) a. Each part of a full name is a unit for loan adaptation in determining vowel epenthesis and in calculating sound mappings.
b. The adaptation of Korean full names into Japanese favors the percep-tual view because the allophones realized in a full name determine the loanword sound.
c. The integrated model of loan adaptation (Kenstowicz & Suchato, 2006) is supported because the morphology of source words plays a crucial role in loanword adaptation and because the phonetic output of complex words as a whole in the source language still influences sound mappings in the adaptation of complex loanwords.

The rest of this paper is organized as follows: Section 2 provides a review of previous research on the adaptation of Korean stops into Japanese, and Section 3 presents a component-by-component analysis of the adaptation of Korean names into Japanese based on vowel epenthesis and segmental mappings. Section 4 provides an explicit formalization for the analysis of complex loanwords based on optimality theory (McCarthy & Prince, 1995). Section 5 discusses the results of the component-by-component analysis of the adaptation of Korean names into Japanese in light of general theories of loanword adaptation and concludes.

2. Adaptation of Korean stops into Japanese

Korean exhibits a three-way laryngeal contrast for stops, e.g., /pul/ (lenis) "fire"~/p'ul/ (tense) "horn"~/p^{h}ul/ (aspirated) "grass." By contrast, Japanese has a two-way laryngeal contrast for stops, e.g., /kiN/ (voiceless) "gold"~/giN/ (voiced) "silver." Korean syllables are maximally CVC, whereas Japanese syllables consist of CV, allowing geminate obstruents and homorganic nasal-obstruent sequences across syllable boundaries. Thus, Korean syllables ending with a stop are adapted with an epenthetic vowel to satisfy the syllable structure in Japanese, e.g., K. [čuk] → J. [tsu.ku] "rice porridge" (Kim, 2008). In the rest of this paper, K and J refer to Korean and Japanese, respectively.

The examples in (2) illustrate how Korean stops are loaned into Japanese:

(2) Adaptation of Korean stops in simplex words into Japanese (Kim, 2008)

Korean	Japanese	
	Word-initial	Between sonorants
Lenis /p/	[p]: K. /**p**æ/ [**p**æ]→ J. [**p**e] "pear"	[b]: K. /apəči/ [abəǯi]→ J. [a.**b**o.zi] "father"
Aspirated /p^h/	[p]: K. /**p**^{h}a/ [**p**^{h}a]→ J. [**p**a]"green onion"	[p] K. /ap^{h}ajo/ [a**p**^{h}ajo]→ J. [a.**p**a.jo] "(I) am sick"
Tense /p'/	[p] K. /**p'**alli/ [**p'**al.li]→ J. [**p**a.ru.ri] "quickly"	[pp] or [p]: K./op'a/ [o**p'**a]→ J. [o**p.p**a] "older brother"

Word-initial lenis, aspirated, and tense stops in Korean are all adapted as voiceless in Japanese, as shown in (2) (Kim, 2008). However, in the word-medial position, Korean lenis stops between vowels are borrowed into Japanese as voiced. In Korean, voiceless lenis stops are realized asvoiced between sonorants. Such differences in the adaptation of Korean lenis stops depending on their position within a word clearly suggest that the adaptation of Korean stops favors the perceptual approach, not the phonological approach, to loan adaptation because the same phonemes can be loaned differently depending on their phonetic output in the source language.

Previous studies of the adaptation of Korean consonants into Japanese focus mainly on the adaptation of simplex words (Ito et al., 2006; Kim, 2008). In the next section, we investigate the adaptation of complex loanwords by examining the rendition of Korean names in Japanese.

3. A component-by-component analysis of the adaptation of Korean names into Japanese

In this section, we argue that the domain of Korean-name adaptation is each part of a full name. If a full name in Korean is borrowed as a single unit into Japanese, i.e., the singleton hypothesis, then the full name behaves like a single word. By contrast, if each part of a full name is adapted independently of other parts of the full name, i.e., the component-by-component hypothesis, then it is subject to loan adaptation independently of the other parts.

We provide two arguments for the component-by-component analysis. The first argument derives from the asymmetry between family name-final and name-internal consonants with respect to vowel epenthesis. The second one comes from different sound mappings of consonants between in the morpheme-internal position and the morpheme boundary.

3.1 Asymmetry between morpheme-final and morpheme-internal consonants in vowel epenthesis

The examples in (3) illustrate that the family name-final consonants trigger vowel epenthesis even when the given name begins with a vowel, although such epenthesis can never occur word-internally, as shown in (2).

(3) Asymmetry in vowel epenthesis: Word-internal vs. family name-final consonants ("-" indicates the boundary between the family and given names, and "." indicates a syllable boundary. Segments of interest are in bold type.)

Simplex word		Full name
Word-internal consonant (Kim, 2008)	Word-final consonant	
K. /ka**k**e/ [ka**g**e] → J.[ka.**g**e] "store"	K. /ču**k**/ [ču**k**] → J. [tsu.**ku**] "rice porridge"	K. 박인기<pak-inki> [pagiŋgi] → J. [pa.**ku**.iN.gi] *[pa.giN.gi]

K./č^h**im**a/[č^h**im**a] → J.[ʧi.**ma**] skirts"	K. /kim/ [kim] → J. [ki.**mu**] "Korean family name"	K. 김아중 <kim-ačuŋ> [ki.ma. ǰuŋ] → J. [ki.**mu**.a.zuN] *[ki.ma.zuN]

Family name-final consonants pattern with simplex word-final consonants with respect to vowel epenthesis. This suggests that the family name constitutes the domain for loan adaptation on its own.

3.2 Asymmetry in segmental mappings: The morpheme-internal position vs. the morpheme boundary

The examples in (4) provide support for the component-by-component analysis by showing that family name-final and given name-initial consonants behave differently from word-medial consonants in sound mappings.

(4) a. Adaptation of Korean nasals derived from nasal assimilation into Japanese

Name-internal	Family name-final
K. 복남 <poknam> [po**ŋ**.nam]→ J. [po**N**.na.mu] ~[po.ku.na.mu]	K.박노식<pak-nosik> [pa**ŋ**.no.sik] → J.[pa.**ku**.no.si.ku] *[pa**N**.no.si.ku]

b. Adaptation of Korean /h/ into Japanese

Name-internal	Family name-initial
K. 국희<ku**kh**i> [ku.k^{h}i]→ J. [ku**k.k**i] K. 이덕화 <i-tə**kh**wa> [idək^{h}wa]→ J. [i.do**k.ku**.a]	K.박희태<pa**k-h**ɨyt^{h}e> [pa.k^{h}ɨyt^{h}e]→ J. [pa.**ku**.**h**i.te] *[pak.ki.te]
K. 신혜 <si**nh**e> [sine] → J. [si**n**e]	K.손호영<so**n-h**ojəŋ> [son.ho.jəŋ]→ J. [so**N**.**h**o.joN] *[so.no.joN]

c. Adaptation of geminate stops in Korean into Japanese

Name-internal	Family name-initial (Component straddling)
K. 석규<sə**kk**ju>[sək.k'ju]→ J. [so**k.k**ju] "given name"	K.박근혜<pa**k-k**ɨnhye> [pakk' ɨnhye]→ J. [pa.**ku.k**u.ne] *[**pak.k**u.ne]
K.독고 <to**kk**o> [tok.k'o]→ J. [to**k.k**o] "family name"	K.박길수<pa**k-k**ilsu> [pakk'ilsu]→ J. [pa.**ku.k**i.ru.su] *[pa**k.k**i.ru.su]

d. Adaptation of Korean /ny/ into Japanese

Name-internal	Family name-initial (Component straddling)
K. 긍영<kɨ**nj**əŋ>[kɨnjəŋ]→ J. [ku.**nj**oN] "given name"	K.신영균 <si**n-j**əŋkjun> [sinjəŋgjun]→ J. [siN.**j**oN.gjuN] *[si.**nj**oN.gjuN]

Korean stops take on the nasal property of the following nasals. For example, a sequence of obstruents and nasals is realized as a nasal sequence via nasal assimilation in Korean, e.g., /pek-man/ [peŋman] "one million." /poknam/ "a given name" is realized as [po**ŋ**.nam] in Korean, and it is adapted as either [poN.na.mu] or [po.ku.na.mu] into Japanese, as shown in (4a). However, such nasal assimilation is not reflected in the adaptation of full names in Korean. Specifically, <pak-nosik> [paŋnosik] "a movie star's name" is adapted as [pa.ku.no.si.ku], not as *[paN.no.si.ku], into Japanese. Such a rendition can be explained by the component-by-component analysis. For example, /pak/ and /nosik/ are independently loaned as /paku/ and /nosiku/, respectively, and they are combined as [pa.ku.no.si.ku].

In Korean, a sequence of a stop and /h/ yields an aspirated stop. However, the aspiration is loaned differently depending on the position of /h/, as shown in (4b). Only the given name-initial consonant /h/ is mapped to [h] in Japanese. This can also be explained by the component-by-component analysis: For example, /pak/ and /hɨyt^{h}e/ are independently loaned as /paku/ and /**h**ite/, respectively, and they are combined as [pa.ku.**h**i.te].

The examples in (4c) illustrate that a sequence of identical stops within some part of a name is loaned as a geminate into Japanese: K. <to**kk**o> [tok.k'o] "a family name"→J. [to**k.k**o]. By contrast, family name-final and given name-initial stops are separated by an epenthetic vowel when they are identical: K. <pa**k-k**ɨnhye> [pakk'ɨnhye]→ J. [pa.**ku.ku**.ne] *[pa**k.ku**.ne]. This can also be explained by the component-by-component analysis: K. /pa**k**/ + /**k**ɨnhye/ → J. [pa.**ku**] + [**ku**.ne] → [pa.ku.ku.ne].

Finally, the examples in (4d) show that the sequence of /n/ and /j/ is loaned differently depending on its position in the full name. When it is located within some part of the name, then /n/ is loaned as part of the onset. By contrast, when /n/ is the end of the last name and /j/ belongs to the given name, then /n/ is adapted as a moraic nasal. This can also be explained by the component-by-component analysis: K. /sin/ + /**j**əŋkjun / → J. [sin] + [**j**oN.gjuN] → [siN.**j**oN.gjuN].

Similarly, the sequence of the same sounds can be adapted differently depending on whether it is name-internal or component-straddling. Such differences in sound mappings based on the position within a constituent word provide strong support for the component-by-component analysis.

3.3 Adaptation of the given-name initial lenis stop

In previous subsections, we have shown that each component, either the family name or the given name, constitutes the domain for loan adaptation. This raises the question of whether the output of the full name as a whole from a source language ever influences sound mappings in the adapting language.

Obstruents are voiced between sonorants in Korean. The intervocalic voiced stop in the given name is rendered as a voiced stop in Japanese, whereas the family name-initial lenis stop is adapted as voiceless in Japanese, as shown in (5a). The family name-final lenis stop triggers vowel epenthesis before the vowel-initial given name, as shown in (5b):

(5) (F: family name; G: given name)
   a. K. 대근 $_G$/**tekɨn**/ [**tegɨn**] → J. [te.**gu**N]
   b. K. 박일 $_F$/pak/ -$_G$/il/ [pagil] → J. [pa.**ku**] [i.ru] → [pa.**ku**.i.ru]
   c. K. 김대중 $_F$/kim/-$_G$ /**teč**uŋ/ [kim**de**ǰuŋ] → J. [ki.mu.**de**.ǰuN]
      "full name of a former president"

In contrast to the example in (5a), the given name-initial consonant /t/ in (5c) is loaned as voiced when it comes along with a family name and the family name ends in a sonorant. Then the full name [ki.mu.**de**.ǰuN] may appear to be problematic for the compound-by-compound analysis because the initial consonant of the first name, /t/, is rendered as [d] in the full name in (5c).

We now summarize the predictions by the component-by-component analysis for the adaptation of complex words.

(6) Comparison between the component-by-component analysis and the singleton analysis

Analysis / K->J. Loan pattern	Singleton analysis	Component-by-component analysis
[Cons]$_F$-$_G$[Vowel]: resyllabification	Incorrect prediction; K. 박일 $_F$/pak/-$_G$/il/ [pa.gil] → J. *[pa.**gi**.ru]	Correct prediction; K. 박일 $_F$/pak/ -$_G$/il/ J.[pa.ku][i.ru]→ [pa.**ku**.i.ru]
[Obst]$_F$ -$_G$[Nasal]: nasal assimilation	Incorrect prediction; K.박노식 $_F$/pak/-$_G$/nosik/ [pa**ŋ**.no.sik]→ J. *[paN.no.si.ku]	Correct prediction; K.박노식 $_F$/pak/- $_G$/nosik/ J.[pa.ku][no.si.ku]→ [pa.**ku**.no.si.ku]

[Obst]$_F$-$_G$[h]: Aspiration	Incorrect prediction; K.박희태 $_F$/pak/-$_G$/**h**ɨjt^{h}e/ [pa.k^{h}ɨjt^{h}e]→ J. *[pak.ki.te]	Correct prediction: K.박희태 $_F$/pak/-$_G$/**h**ɨjt^{h}e/ J. [pa.**k**u] [hi.te]→ [pa.**k**u.hi.te]
[Son]$_F$-$_G$[Stop]: stop voicing	Correct prediction; K. 김대중 $_F$/kim/-$_G$/**t**ečuŋ/ [kim.**d**e.ǰuŋ]→ J. [ki.mu.**d**e.ǰuN]	Incorrect prediction; K. 김대중 $_F$/kim/-$_G$/**t**ečuŋ/ J. [ki.mu] [**t**e.ǰuŋ]→ *[ki.mu.**t**e.ǰuN]

In each case, vowel epenthesis applies at the morpheme boundary, and the Japanese rendition is faithful to the underlying voicing of the final consonant of the family name, although the surface Korean form is not.

However, the adaptation of K. <kim-**t**ečuŋ> as J. [ki.mu.**d**e.ǰuN] raises the question of why the voiceless stop mapping of the voiceless stop of the source form is possible for family name-initial and family name-final lenis stops but not for given name-initial lenis stops.

Shinohara (2008) accounts for the voiced stop adaptation of the first name-initial lenis stop in the full name, as in (5c), in terms of the [Øvoice] specification. She contends that Korean lenis stops are specified for [Øvoice] and that Japanese speakers apply a post-sonorant voicing process in Korean to Korean lenis stops. However, her analysis has three drawbacks. First, it is questionable whether Japanese speakers apply the Korean phonological rule to loanword adaptation. Second, it does not explain why the family name-final stop, although it is phonetically voiced in Korean, does not undergo voicing before the vowel-initial given name, as shown in (5b). Third, it does not account for why only the voicing alternation in Korean is treated in such a special manner.

Another possible analysis for this voiced stop adaptation of the given name-initial lenis stop in the full name can be found in Rendaku in Japanese, where N_2-initial obstruents get voiced in Japanese compound words consisting of N_1 and N_2. However, the voiced stop adaptation of the given name-initial lenis stop in a full name cannot be attributed to Redanku in Japanese for the following three reasons: First, Rendaku rarely occurs in loanwords (Takayama, 2000). Second, Rendaku cannot be applied when N_2 contains voiced obstruents, e.g., /ama-sake/ [ama**z**ake] "sweet sake" vs. /yamato-kotoba/ [yamato**k**oto**b**a] "native words." However, K. <kim-tečuŋ> [kim**d**eǰuŋ] is adapted as J. [ki.mu.**d**e.ǰuN], even though the second part, the given name, already contains a voiced obstruent.

We contend that the output of the whole complex word also determines the sound mapping in loanword adaptation. The output of the full name in Korean is [kim**d**eǰuN]. Then the occurrence of [d] in the output of the source language influences Japanese speakers to render it as a voiced stop in the full name. Figure 1 provides evidence that the rate at which Korean lenis stops are rendered into voiced stops in Japanese is determined by their allophonic output. That is, the voiceless stop in Korean is mapped to the voiceless stop in Japanese, whereas the voiced stop in Korean is mapped to the voiced stop in Japanese.

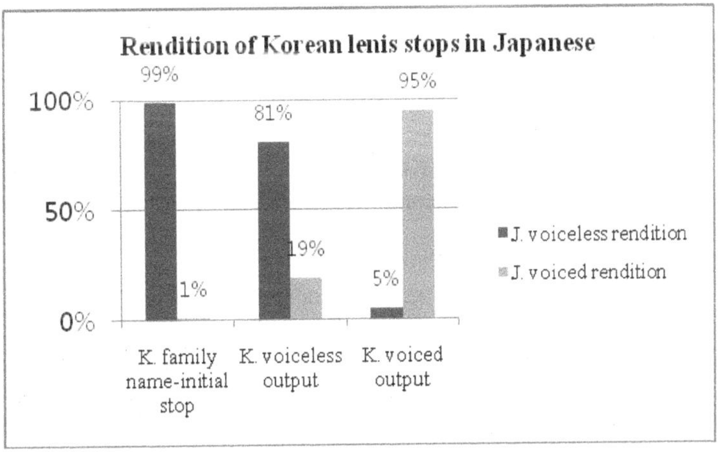

Figure 1: Asymmetry between the family name-initial lenis stop and the given name-initial lenis stop with respect to sound mappings depending on their phonetic output

The family name-initial lenis stop in Korean is always voiceless and is almost always mapped to the voiceless stop in Japanese. On the other hand, the given name-initial lenis stop in Korean can be realized as either voiced or voiceless depending on the phonetic context. Figure 1 clearly shows that when it surfaces as voiced between sonorants, it is rendered as voiced in Japanese 95% of the time. By contrast, when it is realized as voiceless, it is mapped to the voiceless stop in Japanese 81% of the time. Thus, we claim that the output of the whole complex word also determines the sound mapping in loanword adaptation. In the next section, we explore how the component-by-component analysis of the adaptation of complex loans can be formalized within the OT framework.

4. An OT analysis of the rendition of Korean names in Japanese

In this section, we provide an explicit formalization for the analysis of the adaptation of Korean names into Japanese couched within the OT framework

(McCarthy & Prince, 1995). Following Oh (2012), we contend that each component, the family name or the given name, is loaned as an independent base in the lexicon and combined with other components in the adaptation of complex loanwords.

First, constraints for the OT analysis are given in (7):

(7) a. JJ-Ident [voice]/V__V: The voicing specification of the output must be faithful to that of the base in the intervocalic position.
b. JJ-Ident [voice]: The voicing specification of the output must be faithful to that of the base.
c. KJ-Ident [voice]: The voicing specification of the output must be faithful to that of the Korean input.
d. JJ-Max Seg: Every segment in the base has a correspondent in the output.

The discussion thus far reveals that the given name-initial lenis stop is faithful to the output in Korean to satisfy KJ-Ident [voice]: K. $_F$/kim/-$_G$/**t**ečuŋ/ [kim**d**ejuŋ] → [kimu**d**ejuN]. This means that KJ-Ident [voice] outranks JJ-ID(voice). However, the family name-final stop does not satisfy KJ-Ident [voice]. JJ-Ident [voice]/V__V protects the voicing of the family name-final stop because it is rescued by an epenthetic vowel according to the component-by-component analysis. This indicates that JJ-Ident [voice]/V__V outranks KJ-Ident [voice]. Then the constraint ranking is given as (8):

(8) Constraint ranking for the adaptation of Korean names into Japanese:
JJ-ID (voice)/ V__V, JJ-Max Seg >>KJ-ID(voice) >> JJ-ID(voice).

Given the constraint ranking in (8), the tableaux (9)-(11) illustrate how the constraints in (7) interact to yield the optimal output.

(9) Korean input: 박일 $_F$/pak/ -$_G$/il/ [pa.gil]

Japanese base: [pa.ku], [i.ru]	JJ-Ident [voice]/ V__V	JJ-Max Seg	KJ-Ident [voice]	JJ-Ident [voice]
a. [pa.gi.ru]	*!			*
☞ b. [pa.ku.i.ru]			*	
c. [pa.ki.ru]		*!		

Candidate (9a) violates JJ-Ident [voice]/V__V, which protects the voicing value of the Japanese base in the intervocalic position. Candidate (9c) violates JJ-Max Seg because the epenthetic vowel in the J. base is deleted. Then candidate (9b) is optimal because it does not violate higher-ranked constraints.

The sound mapping discussed in (4a) can also be analyzed, as shown in (10).

(10) Korean input: 박노식 $_F$/pak/- $_G$/nosik/ [paŋ.no.sik]

Japanese base: [pa.**ku**], [no.si.ku]	JJ-Ident [voice]/ V__V	JJ-Max Seg	KJ-Ident [voice]	JJ-Ident [voice]
a. [paN.no.si.ku]	*!	*		*
☞ b. [pa.**ku**.no.si.ku]			*	

The Korean family name /pak/ is first adapted as [paku] and constitutes the Japanese base for the adaptation of the full name. Candidate (10a) is suboptimal because it violates the higher-ranked constraint JJ-Ident [voice]/V__V. Candidate (10b) is optimal because it satisfies JJ-Ident [voice]/V__V, although it violates the lower-ranked constraint KJ-Ident [voice], which requires a voicing match between the Korean input and the Japanese output.

Finally, we examine how the constraints interact to produce the optimal output for the adaptation of given name-initial lenis stops as voiced in Japanese in (11).

(11) Korean input: 김대중 $_F$/kim/- $_G$/**t**ečuŋ/ [kim**d**eǰuŋ]

Japanese base: [kimu], [**t**eǰuN]	JJ-Ident [voice]/ V__V	JJ-Max Seg	KJ-Ident [voice]	JJ-Ident [voice]
a. [kimu**t**eǰuN]			*!	
☞ b. [kimu**d**eǰuN]				*

Although candidate (11b) violates JJ-Ident [voice], which requires a voicing match between the Japanese base and the loanword, it is chosen as the optimal output because it satisfies the higher ranked constraint KJ-Ident [voice].

5. Discussion and conclusions

In this paper, we propose a model for the adaptation of complex loanwords. In contrast to most of the previous studies of loanword adaptation, we argue that complex loanwords behave differently from simplex loanwords in terms of vowel epenthesis and segmental mappings. The analysis of the adaptation of Korean names into Japanese reveals that a consonant terminating the family name before the vowel-initial given name patterns with word-final consonants, e.g., K. /pak-inki/ → [pa.**ku**.iN.gi] and K. /čuk/ [čuk] → J. [tsu.**ku**] "rice porridge," but not with word-medial consonants in terms of vowel epenthesis, e.g., K. /ka**k**e/ [ka**g**e] → J. [ka.**ge**] "store." Vowel epenthesis applies at the morpheme boundary to give a licit Japanese syllabification. Further, we provide evidence that some part of a name-edge consonant is mapped to sounds differently from that of a name-internal consonant from several cases, e.g., word-final lenis obstruents (K <pak-il> → J. [pa.ku.i.ru] *[pa.gi.ru]), manner assimilation (K. <pak-nosik> →J. [pa.ku.no.si.ku] *[paN.no.si.ku]), and laryngeal coalescence (K <pa**k**-**h**ɨyt^{h}e> → J. [pa.ku.hi.te] *[pak.ku.hi.te]). Based on such asymmetry between component-internal and component-straddling segments with respect to vowel epenthesis and sound mappings, we argue for a component-by-component analysis of the adaptation of Korean names into Japanese.

The component-by-component analysis of the adaptation of Korean names into Japanese sheds some light on three issues surrounding loanword adaptation. First, in terms of the input in loan adaptation, the morphological structure of source words determines sound mappings. Second, in terms of the domain of loan adaptation, each component is loaned as an independent base in the lexicon and combined with other components. Third, the rendition of a Korean voiced stop in a full name as a voiced stop in Japanese has some bearing on the debate over the perceptual vs. the phonological view of loanword adaptation. It provides support for the perceptual approach to loanword adaptation. Voiced stops in Korean are allophones, but they play a crucial role in determining the phonetic match. In other words, a given phoneme of the source language is not uniformly adapted as expected by the phonological approach but as predicted by the perceptual approach.

The investigation of complex English loanwords in Korean (e.g., "cut off") indicates that the surface form of the whole complex word from the source language influences sound mappings (Oh, 2012). Specifically, the intervocalic /t/ is flapped in "cut off" in English, and the voiced allophone is mapped to [d] in [k^{h}ədop^{h}ɨ] to the exclusion of *[k^{h}ət^{h}op^{h}ɨ] in Korean. This output-to-output correspondence between the whole complex word from the source language and the complex loanword provides support for the perceptual view, not the phonological view, of loanword adaptation, because allophones of the source language (e.g., voiced flaps in English) can determine loanword sounds in the adapting language.

In sum, sound mappings in loan adaptation are conditioned by the morphological structure of source words and two types of the output-output correspondence: each component in the source language to the base in the adapting language and the whole complex word in the source language to the loanword in the adapting language. This provides support for Kenstowicz and Suchato's (2006) integrated model of loan adaptation because sound mappings take into account various factors to achieve the best match for the source word.

References

Ito, C., Kenstowicz, M., & Kang, Y. 2006. The adaptation of Japanese loanwords into Korean. *MIT Working Papers in Linguistics* 52: 65-104.

Kang, Y. 2003. Perceptual similarity in loanword adaptation: English postvocalic word-final stops in Korean. *Phonology* 20: 219-273.

Kenstowicz, M., & Suchato, A. 2006. Issues in loanword adaptation: A case study from Thai. *Lingua* 116: 921-949.

Kim, H. 2008. Loanword adaptation between Japanese and Korean: Evidence for L1 feature-driven perception. *Journal of East Asian Linguistics* 17: 331-346.

Lacharité, D., & Paradis, C. 2005. Category preservation and proximity versus phonetic approximation in loanword adaptation. *Linguistic Inquiry* 36: 223-258.

McCarty, J., & Prince, A. 1995. Faithfulness and reduplicative identity. *University of Massachusetts Occasional Papers in Linguistics* 18: *Papers in Optimality Theory*, ed. J. Beckman, 249-384. Massachusetts: Graduate Linguistic Student Association.

Oh, M. 2012. Adaptation of English Complex Words into Korean. *Journal of East Asian Linguistics* 21: 267-304.

Peperkamp, S., & Dupoux, E. 2003. Reinterpreting loanword adaptations: The role of perception. Proceedings of the 15th International Congress of Phonetic Sciences, 367-370.

Prince, A., & Smolensky, P. 1993. *Optimality Theory: Constraint interaction in generative grammar.* Ms., Rutgers University and University of Colorado.

Shinohara, S. 2008. Are L2 contrasts reached by L1 grammar?: Japanese adaptation of Korean obstruents. Presented at CIL, Korea.

Silverman, D. 1992. Multiple scansions in Loanword Phonology: Evidence from Cantonese. *Phonology* 9: 289-328. Cambridge University Press.

Takayama, T. 2000. Rendaku in loanwords, MS.

Rendaku in Japanese Dialects that Retain Prenasalization

TIMOTHY J. VANCE*
National Institute for Japanese Language and Linguistics

MIZUKI MIYASHITA
University of Montana

MARK IRWIN
Yamagata University

1. Rendaku

The Japanese morphophonemic phenomenon known as *rendaku* 連濁 occurs mainly in compounds. In the Tōkyō dialect, a morpheme that shows *rendaku* has one allomorph beginning with a voiceless obstruent and another allomorph beginning with a voiced obstruent, and the latter can appear only when it is a non-initial morph in a word. For example:

(1) a. /tori/ 鳥 'bird'
    b. /tori+kago/ 鳥籠 'birdcage'
    c. /ahoH+dori/ あほう鳥 'goony bird' [='albatross']

The /d/ in /ahoH+dori/ (1c) is an instance of *rendaku*. However, *rendaku* is highly irregular. First, many morphemes do not alternate in this way, although in some cases there are known factors that systematically inhibit *rendaku*. Second, many morphemes that do alternate behave unpredictably,

* The research reported here was supported by project funds from the National Institute for Japanese Language and Linguistics and from the Research Institute for Humanity and Nature, and also by grants-in-aid from the Japan Society for the Promotion of Science to the first author (no. 22820085) and the third author (no. 23520546).

Japanese/Korean Linguistics 21.
Edited by Seungho Nam, Heejeong Ko and Jongho Jun.

appearing with voicing in some words and without voicing in others, for no apparent reason.

Because of well-known historical changes, some of the alternations in the modern Tōkyō dialect involve more than just a difference in voicing (Vance 2005: 28). As a result, *rendaku* in the Tōkyō dialect is rather opaque phonetically. For example, /b/ alternates with /h/ or /f/ (realized as [ɸ]), not with /p/:

(2) a. /hone/ 骨 'bone' /se+bone/ 背骨 'backbone'
 b. /fukuro/ 袋 'bag' /gomi+bukuro/ ゴミ袋 'trash bag'

In *kana* spelling, however, *rendaku* is transparent: the difference between the voiced alternant and the voiceless alternant of a morpheme is always just the presence versus absence of the *dakuten* 濁点 diacritic on the first letter:

(3)					
	a.	/fune/ 'boat'	/kawa+bune/ 'river boat'	ふね	かわぶね
	b.	/hako/ 'box'	/haši+bako/ 'chopstick box'	はこ	はしばこ
	c.	/tama/ 'ball'	/me+dama/ 'eyeball'	たま	めだま
	d.	/kami/ 'paper'	/kabe+gami/ 'wallpaper'	かみ	かべがみ
	e.	/cuka/ 'mound'	/ari+zuka/ 'anthill'	つか	ありづか
	f.	/sora/ 'sky'	/hoši+zora/ 'starry sky'	そら	ほしぞら
	g.	/či/ 'blood'	/hana+ǰi/ 'nosebleed'	ち	はなぢ
	h.	/šika/ 'deer'	/ko+ǰika/ 'baby deer (fawn)'	しか	こじか

There is little doubt that Tōkyō speakers see all the *rendaku* alternations as instances of the same general phenomenon.

2. Tōhoku Dialects

In some other dialects, notably those of the Tōhoku (northeastern Honshū) region, *rendaku* is even more phonetically opaque.[1] Also, since non-Tōkyō dialects are not usually written, there is no orthographic support for treating the *rendaku* alternations in such a dialect as a unitary phenomenon.

Many Tōhoku dialects preserve the word-medial prenasalized voiced obstruents that historical linguists typically infer for eighth-century Old Japanese (OJ) (Asayama 1943; Hamada 1952; Martin 1987: 20–26; Frellesvig and Whitman 2008: 3). That is, these dialects have word-medial [ᵐb], [ⁿd], [ⁿdz], and [ᵑg] (or [ŋ]) corresponding to Tōkyō word-medial [b d z g] (ignoring more traditional Tōkyō varieties that have medial [ŋ] in many

[1] Sasaki (2008) shows how opaque *rendaku* has become in a dialect that shares some phonological characteristics with Tōhoku dialects (although it does not have prenasalization).

words).[2] In fact, the standard diachronic account of the origin of *rendaku* depends crucially on the presence of such prenasalization in prehistoric Japanese (Unger 1975: 8–9; Vance 1982: 335–338; Frellesvig 2010: 40–43). There is solid evidence that the Kyōto dialect preserved some prenasalization as late as the early seventeenth century (Hashimoto 1932; Irwin and Narrog 2012: 250).

3. Yamagata

This paper will focus on one of the traditional dialects of Yamagata 山形 Prefecture. One of the authors (Miyashita) grew up in Kahoku-chō 河北町, which is in the Murayama 村山 region of the prefecture (see the maps in Figure 1 below), and we therefore use the Kahoku-chō dialect as a representative Yamagata dialect.

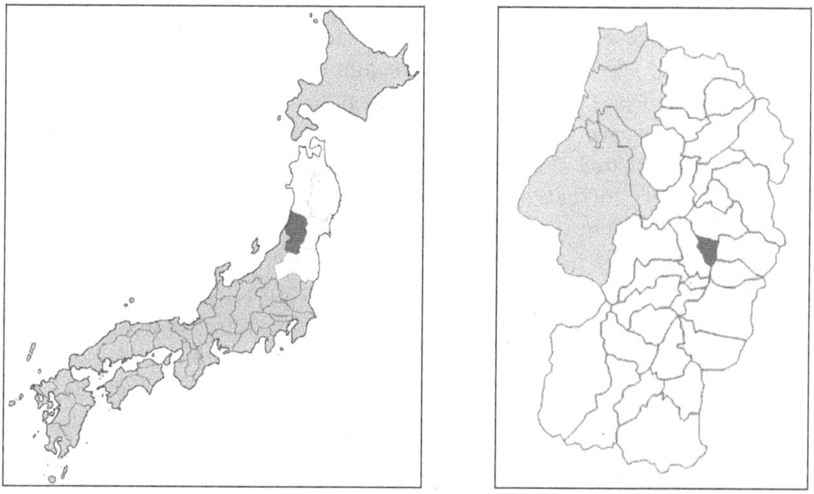

Yamagata Prefecture (dark gray) and the other Tōhoku prefectures (white)

Kahoku-chō (dark gray) and the Shōnai region (light gray)

Figure 1. Maps showing the Tōhoku region, Yamagata Prefecture, and Kahoku-chō

There is considerable diversity in the prefecture, and there are differences from village to village even within Kahoku-chō, but Yamagata dialects generally have prenasalized voiced obstruents corresponding to word-medial plain voiced obstruents in the Tōkyō dialect.[3] Kahoku-chō [mã^{n}do] 'win-

[2] Inoue (1961) and Hibiya (1999), among many others, provide details on syllable-initial [ŋ] in Tōkyō.

[3] Gotō, Saitō, and Watanabe (1970) provide an account of the diversity within the prefecture. Miyashita finds the dialect spoken in the Shōnai 庄内 region near the Sea of Japan quite

dow', with a prenasalized medial stop, corresponds to Tokyo [mɑdo] (/mado/). In addition, word-medial plain voiced stops in Yamagata dialects correspond to voiceless stops in Tōkyō. For example, Kahoku-chō [mɑdo] 'target' corresponds to Tōkyō [mɑto] (/mato/).

4. Kahoku-chō *Rendaku*

We would expect instances of *rendaku* in Yamagata to be realized as prenasalized voiced obstruents, and this is what we find in many semantically opaque, fossilized compounds. For example, Tōkyō /hamaguri/ 'clam' is etymologically a compound of /hama/ 'beach' and /kuri/ 'chestnut', and the corresponding word in Kahoku-chō has prenasalization: [hɑmɑ̃ᵑgɨɾi]. However, a compound newly coined within a Yamagata dialect apparently will lack *rendaku*, as will a transparent compound borrowed from the Tōkyō dialect. An example of what is probably a borrowing is the word corresponding to Tōkyō /te+gami/ 'letter' (cf. /te/ 'hand' and /kami/ 'paper'). The Kahoku-chō word is pronounced [tegɑmi], not [tẽᵑgɑmi].

Needless to say, the situation in Yamagata Prefecture is complicated by the strong influence of the Tōkyō dialect (so-called "standardization"), which has intensified since the mid-twentieth century. This influence may well be indirect, of course, with "standard" forms diffusing not straight from Tōkyō itself but via other urban centers (especially Yamagata City, the prefectural capital). In any case, many vocabulary items allow alternative pronunciations. For example, the Kahoku-chō word corresponding to Tokyo /mi+goto/ 'wonderful' (lit. 'something to see'; cf. /mi/ 'seeing' and /koto/ 'thing') can be either [mĩᵑgodo] (which in this case feels old-fashioned to native Kahoku-chō speakers) or [migodo] (without prenasalization). The name of the prefecture shows the same kind of variation: old-fashioned [jɑmɑ̃ᵑgɑdɑ] versus [jɑmɑgɑdɑ].

5. [ᵐb b p h]

Kahoku-chō examples corresponding to Tōkyō words with /b/ are of particular interest. As noted in (2) above, *rendaku* in the Tōkyō dialect pairs /h/ (< OJ [p]) with /b/. For example:

(4) /hana/ 花 'flower' /beni+bana/ 紅花 'safflower'

---

difficult to understand. Incidentally, the first attestation for the technical term *rendaku* is in an early nineteenth-century description of the Shōnai dialect by one Ujie Ryūkei 氏家竜渓 (Suzuki 2004). One town in the Shōnai region, Tsuruoka 鶴岡, has been the site of longitudinal sociolinguistic research carried out by the National Institute for Japanese Language and Linguistics. The four Tsuruoka surveys were conducted in 1950, 1971, 1991, and 2011 (http://www2.ninjal.ac.jp/keinen/turuoka/).

Safflowers, used to make rouge (/beni/), are not native to Japan, but they were an important product in the pre-modern Yamagata economy. The corresponding Kahoku-chō forms are:

(5) [hɑnɑ] 花 'flower' [beɲibɑnɑ] 紅花 'safflower'

Note the absence of prenasalization in the compound in (5): [beɲibɑnɑ]. It is possible that this Kahoku-chō word for 'safflower' used to have prenasalization and lost it, as seems to have happened in the case of [migodo] 'wonderful' (see Section 4 above). But even if it was borrowed recently, the explanation for [b] is essentially the same: assimilation to the "standard". The medial [b] in Kahoku-chō [beɲibɑnɑ] cannot be the result of "undoing" *rendaku* in a transparent compound. Undoing *rendaku* would give us [h], not [b].

There is a three-way [h]≠[p]≠[b] contrast in word-intial position in Kahoku-chō, just as there is in Tōkyō. But Kahoku-chō has a four-way [h]≠[p] ≠[b]≠[^{m}b] contrast word-medially. For example:

(6) a. [hɑsɨ] 'chopsticks' cf. Tōkyō /haši/
b. [pɑpɑ] 'daddy' cf. Tōkyō /papa/
c. [bɑgɑ] 'fool' cf. Tōkyō /baka/
d. [sɨohɑ̃mˑɑ] 'salt flat' cf. Tōkyō /šio+hama/
e. [piɾipiɾi] 'spicy' cf. Tōkyō /piri+piri/
f. [jɑmɑbigo] 'echo' cf. Tōkyō /yama+biko/
g. [dẽ^{m}beso] 'protruding navel' cf. Tōkyō /de+beso/

Typical descriptions of Tōhoku dialects imply that a word-initial voiceless stop and the corresponding word-medial voiced stop are realizations of the same phoneme:

(7) [toɾi] 'bird' [mɑdo] 'target'
/tori/ /mato/

Such descriptions also imply that a word-initial voiced stop and the corresponding word-medial prenasalized stop are realizations of the same phoneme:

(8) [doɾo] 'mud' [mɑ̃^{n}do] 'window'
/doro/ /mado/

However, our native-speaking author has the intuition that initial [b] and medial [b] are the same phoneme:

(9) [beɲibɑnɑ] 'safflower'
/benibana/

Needless to say, this intuition about [b] casts doubt on the usual assumption that initial [t k] are realizations of the same phonemes as medial [d g]. Consider the Kahoku-chō pronunciations of some typical Sino-Japanese binoms:

(10) a. [do:ro] 道路 'road' c. [gagɨbɨ] 学部 'academic department'
b. [kaido:] 街道 'highway' d. [daigagɨ] 大学 'university'

The Sino-Japanese morphemes meaning 'path' and 'learning' are realized as [do:] (10a) and [gagɨ] both word initially, in (10a) and (10c), and word-medially, in (10b) and (10d). Surely examples like these encourage speakers to analyze all instances of [d] as /d/ and all instances of [g] as /g/.

The point, of course, is that we need a synchronic analysis of the phonological system of the Kahoku-chō dialect before we can decide what counts as *rendaku*. The analysis of this dialect, and any other dialect for that matter, needs to abandon the presupposition that the "underlying" system is just like Tōkyō Japanese. It is also necessary to resist the temptation to think that all Tōhoku dialects are pretty much the same. As mentioned above in Section 3, there is significant diversity even within Yamagata Prefecture.[4]

6. Some Remaining Issues

First of all, there are phonetic details in the Kahoku-chō dialect that require careful consideration. One is that prenasalization seems to have developed into a moraic nasal in some (but not all) words:

(11) a. [bãm:ba] 婆 'grandma' cf. Tōkyō /baba/
b. [kamã^{m}bogo] 蒲鉾 'fish paste' cf. Tōkyō /kamaboko/

In fact, we know of one case in which the same etymological source has developed into two separate words:

(12) a. [kãŋ:ge] 陰 'shade; behind'[5]
b. [kã^{ŋ}ge] 影 'shadow'
cf. Tōkyō /kage/ for both

---

[4] A dialect dictionary such as the one produced by the Yamagata-ken Hōgen Kenkyū-kai (1970) can be a useful resource for a synchronic phonological analysis of a non-standard variety, but it does little more than provide hints. Like other traditional dialect dictionaries in Japan, it focuses on lexical items that either diverge semantically from a Tōkyō cognate or lack a Tōkyō cognate entirely. Furthermore, it follows the standard practice of taking a modern prefecture as the geographical entity of interest, despite the fact that prefectural boundaries do not ordinarily coincide with dialect boundaries based on linguistic criteria.

[5] The initial [k] both in (12a) and (12b) is strongly aspirated. We have not marked aspiration here or on other voiceless stops because we have not yet determined the conditions under which it appears. This is another phonetic detail that remains to be investigated.

Another problematic detail is that some nasals corresponding to Tōkyō syllable-initial nasals are longer than others, and these longer nasals make the preceding vowel nasal:[6]

(13) a. [odoçɨme] 乙姫 'maiden' cf. Tōkyō /oto+hime/
b. [kɨdzɨçɨ̃m·o] 靴紐 'shoestring' cf. Tōkyō /kucu+himo/

It could be that the Kahoku-chō dialect has developed a phonemic distinction between nasal and oral vowels:

(14) a. [çɨme] 姫 'princess' ?/hɨme/
b. [çɨ̃m·o] 紐 'string' ?/hɨ̃mo/
c. [tɑmɑdebɑgo] 玉手箱 'treasure chest' ?/tamadebago/
d. [tẽᵐbɨgɨro] 手袋 'glove' ?/tẽbɨgɨro/

A second source of difficulty is the problem of how to model the phonological system of a bi-dialectal speaker. It is well known that the languages of bilingual speakers influence each other to some degree even when the two languages are not related or typologically similar. Surely this kind of mutual influence is even more profound in the case of two dialects, especially when one is a "standard" variety of a national language. Notions such as "coexistent phonemic systems" (Fries and Pike 1949) and "cophonologies" (Kager 1999: 405–407) have been around for more than half a century. In fact, many phonologists have argued that vocabulary stratification is an essential notion even in a phonological treatment of "standard" Tōkyō Japanese (McCawley 1968: 62–75; Itô and Mester 1999). Furthermore, a bi-dialectal speaker does not have just two discrete varieties. Instead, he or she controls a continuum that ranges from near-"standard" to something much closer to a "pure" traditional variety. The situation is no different in principle from notion of a "postcreole continuum" (DeCamp 1971).

When an un-prenasalized, word-medial voiced stop in Yamagata corresponds to a voiced stop in Tokyo, it is tempting to handle it as a kind of unassimilated or only partially assimilated loanword. This temptation is strengthened by the fact that some more transparent compounds have prenasalization, while some less transparent compounds lack it. For example:

[6] John Whitman has suggested to us that such length differences in nasals might be the residue of accent distinctions that have been lost. Kahoku-chō is within the large area in the northern Kantō and southern Tōhoku where there are no lexical accent distinctions, but this area is surrounded (aside from the Pacific coast) by dialects with so-called Tōkyō-type accent systems, so it would be possible to look for correspondences between nasal length in Kahoku-chō and accent location in nearby dialects.

(15) a. native

[te] 手 'hand'
[ɸɨgɨɾo] 袋 'bag'
[tẽᵐbɨgɨɾo] 手袋 'glove'

b. Tōkyō-influenced

[me] 目 'eye'
[ɸɨdɑ] 蓋 'lid'
[mɑbɨdɑ] 瞼 'eyelid'

Of course, as we have already seen, the influence of Tōkyō is not confined to straightforward cases of borrowing (i.e., the replacement of a Yamagata word with a Tōkyō word). A Tōkyō word can influence the pronunciation of a Kahoku-chō cognate, as in the case of innovative [jɑmɑgɑdɑ] pushing out old-fashioned [jɑmɑ̃ᵑgɑdɑ]. Although our native-speaking author pronounces the word meaning 'eyelid' as [mɑbɨdɑ], without prenasalization, she remembers her grandfather saying [mɑ̃ᵐbɨdɑ], so this is presumably not a case of simple borrowing.

One of example that does appear to be simple borrowing is [mɑjɨge] for 'eyebrow'. The Tōkyō cognate /mayu+ge/ has *rendaku* (cf. /mayu/ 'eyebrow'; /ke/ 'hair'), but the Kahoku-chō word lacks prenasalization. The word it replaced was [konoge], which appears to derive from a phrase, with the genitive particle [no] as the second element and the noun meaning 'hair' as the third element. The first element [ko] is probably cognate with the last syllable of Tokyo /manako/ 眼 'eye', which is etymologically /ma/(~/me/) 'eye' followed by an alternative genitive form /na/ followed by /ko/ 'child'. The cognate of this longer word for 'eye' is [mɑnɑgɨ] in our native-speaking author's version of Kahoku-chō dialect, with the innovative final vowel obscuring the etymological connection to [ko] in [konoge]. She herself does not use this word, but she remembers hearing it. Her word for 'hair' is [ke]. The [g] in [konoge] shows that it is phonologically a word rather than a three-word phrase. The absence of prenasalization is expected, since *rendaku* following genitive [no] would be anomalous.[7]

7. Conclusion

It has often been suggested that the overall frequency of *rendaku* differs from dialect to dialect, but we know of no solid evidence to support this claim. When it comes to *rendaku* in Tōhoku dialects, obviously we cannot investigate how frequent *rendaku* is until we determine what (if anything) counts as *rendaku*. This problem promises to keep us busy for some time to come.

---

[7] Since Miyashita does not have this item in her active vocabulary, she is less than completely confident that she remembers its pronunciation correctly, but Yamagata-ken Hōgen Kenkyūkai (1970) lists it as we have transcribed it.

References

Asayama, Shin'ya. 1943. Kokugo no tō-onsetsu ni okeru dakuon ni tsuite. *Kokugo to Kokubungaku* 20:422–432.

DeCamp, David. 1971. Toward a Generative Analysis of a Post-Creole Speech Community. *The pidginization and creolization of languages*, ed. by Dell Hymes, 349–370. Cambridge: Cambridge University Press.

Fries, Charles C., and Kenneth L. Pike. 1949. Coexistent Phonemic Systems. *Language* 25:29–50.

Hamada, Atsushi. 1952. Hatsuon to dakuon to no sōkan-sei no mondai. *Kokugo Kokubun* 21(4):18–32.

Frellesvig, Bjarke. 2010. *A History of the Japanese Language.* Cambridge: Cambridge University Press.

Frellesvig, Bjarke, and John Whitman. 2008. Introduction. *Proto-Japanese: Issues and Prospects*, ed. by Bjarke Frellesvig and John Whitman, 1–9. Amsterdam: John Benjamins.

Gotō, Toshio, Gishichirō Saitō, and Tomojirō Watanabe. 1970. Yamagata-ken hōgen gaisetsu. *Yamagata-ken hōgen jiten*, ed. by Yamagata-ken Hōgen Kenkyū-kai, 667–768. Yamagata: Yamagata-ken Hōgen Jiten Kankō-kai.

Hashimoto, Shinkichi. 1932. Kokugo ni okeru bi-boin. *Hōgen* 2(1). [References are to the version reprinted in Hashimoto 1950: *Kokugo on'in no kenkyu*, 1–9. Tōkyō: Iwanami.]

Hibiya, Junko. 1999. Variationist Sociolinguistics. *The Handbook of Japanese Linguistics*, ed. by Natsuko Tsujimura, 101–120. Oxford: Blackwell.

Inoue, Fumio. 1961. Ga-gyō shiin no bunpu to rekishi. *Kokugogaku* 86:26–41

Irwin, Mark, and Heiko Narrog. 2012. Late Middle Japanese. *The Languages of Japan and Korea*, ed. by Nicolas Tranter, 246–267. London: Routledge.

Itô, Junko, and Armin Mester. 1999. The Phonological Lexicon. *The Handbook of Japanese Linguistics*, ed. by Natsuko Tsujimura, 62–100. Oxford: Blackwell.

Kager, René. 1999. *Optimality Theory.* Cambridge: Cambridge University Press.

Martin, Samuel E. 1987. *The Japanese Language through Time.* New Haven: Yale University Press.

McCawley, James D. 1968. *The Phonological Component of a Grammar of Japanese.* The Hague: Mouton.

Sasaki, Kan. 2008. Hardening Alternation in the Mitsukaido Dialect of Japanese. *Gengo Kenkyū* 134:85–118.

Suzuki, Yutaka. 2004. 'Rendaku' no koshō ga kakuritsu suru made. *Koku-bungaku Kenkyū* 142:11–21.

Unger, J. Marshall. 1975. Studies in Early Japanese Morphophonemics. Doctoral dissertation, Yale University.

Vance, Timothy J. 1982. On the Origin of Voicing Alteration in Japanese Consonants. *Journal of the American Oriental Society* 102:333–341.

Vance, Timothy J. 2005. Sequential Voicing and Lyman's Law in Old Japanese. *Polymorphous Linguistics: Jim McCawley's Legacy*, ed. by Salikoko S. Mufwene, Elaine J. Francis, and Rebecca S. Wheeler, 27–43. Cambridge: MIT Press.

Yamagata-ken Hōgen Kenkyū-kai, ed. 1970. *Yamagata-ken hōgen jiten.* Yamagata: Yamagata-ken Hōgen Jiten Kankō-kai.

Part II

Syntax

Non-subject Antecedent Potential of *Caki* in Korean

CHUNG-HYE HAN
Simon Fraser University

DENNIS RYAN STOROSHENKO
Yale University

1. Introduction

Traditionally, *caki* has been described as subject-oriented, always taking a clausal subject as its antecedent (Lee 1973, Chang 1977). This view predicts that in (1), only the matrix subject *Yuli* can be the antecedent of *caki* in the embedded clause.*

(1) *Yuli-nun* *Swuni-lopwuthe* *[caki-ka* *iki-lke-lako]*
Yuli-Top Swuni-from self-Nom win-Fut-Comp
tul-ess-ta.
hear-Past-Decl
'Yuli heard from Swuni that self would win the race.'

However, the view that *caki* has the potential for non-subject antecedents has steadily been gaining ground (Yoon 1989, Cho 1994, Kim 2000, Sohng 2004, Madigan 2006). Yoon (1989), for instance, describes *caki* as logophoric, be-

* We thank Jennifer Hinnell and Samantha Kim for their help with data collection, and Ilkyu Kim for assistance in the piloting stage of the scale experiment. This research is partially funded by SSHRC grant #410-2007-2169 to Han.

Japanese/Korean Linguistics 21.
Edited by Bjarke Frellesvig and Peter Sells.

ing sensitive to a logophoric centre (Sells 1987), described in Büring (2005) as the "source of information." So, according to Yoon, in (1), as the matrix indirect object *swuni* is the source of information, it can be the antecedent of *caki*. Sohng (2004), on the other hand, without making any reference to logophoricity, observes that though the subject is preferred to be the antecedent of *caki*, the object can also be an antecedent, and takes examples such as (1) to be ambiguous. A moderated view can be found in Kim (2000), proposing that 'potential antecedents for *caki*' are ranked according to a thematic prominence hierarchy, where 'potential antecedents' are defined as third person nominals that are higher in the thematic hierarchy than *caki*, and that any given instance of *caki* will prefer an antecedent highest on that hierarchy. While subjects are highly-ranked in this system, it leaves open the possibility for non-subject antecedents, and leaves *caki* free to corefer with any nominal when no potential antecedent is present.

In an experiment that combined a forced-choice task and eye-tracking, Han et al. (2011) found that speakers predominately choose the matrix subject over the matrix indirect object as the antecedent for embedded *caki*, even when the discourse context makes the object reference salient. This result re-opens the question of whether a non-subject is a grammatically possible antecedent of *caki* at all. But, what Han et al. found might be a function of a verb effect and/or a task effect arising from the experimental design rather than from any properties of *caki* itself. In their experiment, all test sentences contained *malha-* (say) as the matrix verb, as in (2). So, their findings could be restricted to *say*-sentences, and may not be representative of the behaviour of *caki* in general.

(2) *Jongwu-ka* *Yuli-eykey* *chilphan* *yeph-eyse* *caki-ka*
Jongwu-Nom Yuli-Dat blackboard beside-at self-Nom
sihem-ul *cal* *chi-ess-tako* *malha-n-ta.*
test-Acc well take-Past-Comp say-Pres-Decl

'Jongwu says to Yuli beside the blackboard that self did well on the test.'

Furthermore, in Han et al.'s experiment, participants had to choose between the subject and the object as the antecedent of *caki*. So, even if the object antecedent interpretation was possible, speakers could have chosen the subject because that is what they prefer; a forced-choice task may not necessarily reveal ambiguity or even the presence of a second potential antecedent.

In this paper, we present two experiments on the antecedent potential of *caki*, a Likert scale experiment and a Truth Value Judgment task (TVJT) experiment, controlling for the potential verb and task effects. In the Likert scale experiment, we found that an object is indeed a grammatically possible antecedent for *caki*, though speakers showed preference for the subject antecedent. In the follow-up TVJT experiment, we found that the preference for the subject interacts with the preference for a logophoric centre, the source of information. Speakers are more likely to accept an object antecedent interpretation of *caki* if the object is the source of information. But a subject antecedent interpretation of *caki* is available regardless of the logophoric status of the subject.

This paper is organized as follows. In Section 2, we describe the Likert scale experiment, and present the findings. The TVJT experiment and its findings are described in Section 3. We conclude in Section 4 with implications of our findings and a brief discussion of future work.

2. Likert scale experiment

It is generally assumed that *caki* is third person, and as such, it can only take a third person nominal as its antecedent (Sohng 2004, Kim and Madigan 2011).[1] This means that if a bi-clausal sentence contains *caki* in the embedded subject with two nominal arguments in the matrix clause, one third person and the other first person, then the third person nominal is the only possible antecedent of *caki*. Exploiting this fact, we designed a scale experiment to address the following research question.

(3) Research question in the Likert scale experiment
How readily do speakers allow a third person object to be the antecedent of *caki* when the subject is first person?

2.1. Task

Participants were presented with a short text followed by a test sentence describing the text on a computer screen. They were then asked to rate the appropriateness/naturalness of the test sentence using a seven point scale, where one is not appropriate/natural and seven is appropriate/natural, by pressing a button on the keyboard.

A screen shot of an example trial is given in Figure 1. In the short text, participants read that Swuni and I were talking in the kitchen, about to make ramyen, and I said that Swuni always made ramyen well. They then read the test sentence (shown in the middle of Figure 1 in a smaller, lighter text), glossed and translated in (4). The last line at the bottom of the display presents the scale.

[1] *caki* also acts as a term of intimate address, with a second person reading. As this most often occurs as a vocative in spoken discourse with no sentential antecedent, we do not consider this usage to interfere with the judgments of *caki* in argument positions requiring an antecedent.

순이와 나는 부엌에서 이야기하고 있었다. 순이와 나는 라면을 끓이려고 하였다. 나는 순이가 라면을 항상 잘 끓인다고 말하였다.

나는 순이에게 자기가 라면을 항상 잘 끓인다고 말하였다.

(부자연스러움) 1-2-3-4-5-6-7 (자연스러움)

FIGURE 1 Screen shot of an example trial in the scale experiment

(4) *Na-nun Swuni-eykey caki-ka lamyen-ul hangsang cal*
I-Top Swuni-to self-Nom ramyen-Acc always well
kkulhi-n-tako malha-yess-ta.
make-Pres-Comp say-Past-Decl
'I told Swuni that self always made ramyen well.'

If the participants allow the object interpretation of *caki* in sentences such as (4), they will judge such sentences to be appropriate/natural.

2.2. Design, participants and procedure

The experiment had two within-subjects factors with two levels each: Person (the matrix arguments of test sentences are both third person, or one of them is first person) and Antecedent (the text is compatible with the subject or the object antecedent interpretation). Crossing the factors thus gives rise to four different conditions, summarized in Table 1. The example trial described in subsection 2.1 belonged to the First person/Object condition where the matrix subject argument of the test sentence is first person, and the text is compatible with the object antecedent interpretation.

Twenty native speakers of Korean residing in Vancouver, Canada were tested. All had been educated in Korea until at least the age of fourteen and all had lived at most a total of twelve months outside of Korea at the time of testing. Participants were first introduced to the task with four practice trials. They were then given sixteen test trials (four trials per condition) along with

TABLE 1 Likert scale experimental design

First person/Subject	Test sentences containing matrix third person subjects and first person objects are presented in contexts compatible with the subject antecedent interpretation of embedded *caki*.
First person/Object	Test sentences containing matrix first person subjects and third person objects are presented in contexts compatible with the object antecedent interpretation of embedded *caki*.
Third person/Subject	Test sentences containing matrix third person subjects and third person objects are presented in contexts compatible with the subject antecedent interpretation of embedded *caki*.
Third person/Object	Test sentences containing matrix third person subjects and third person objects are presented in contexts compatible with the object antecedent interpretation of embedded *caki*.

sixteen filler trials. Experimental trial ordering was fully randomized, with a unique order generated for each participant.

2.3. Test sentences

We constructed four test sentences for each of the four conditions. In each condition, two test sentences contained *malha-* (say) as the matrix verb, and the other two contained *tut-* (hear). Examples from the four conditions are given in (5)-(8) ((6) repeated below from (4)).

(5) First person/Subject condition

Swuni-nun na-eykey caki-ka iki-lke-lako malha-yess-ta.
Swuni-Top I-to self-Nom win-Fut-Comp say-Past-Decl

'Swuni told me that self would win the race.'

(6) First person/Object condition

Na-nun Swuni-eykey caki-ka lamyen-ul hangsang cal
I-Top Swuni-to self-Nom ramyen-Acc always well
kkulhi-n-tako malha-yess-ta.
make-Pres-Comp say-Past-Decl

'I told Swuni that self always made ramyen well.'

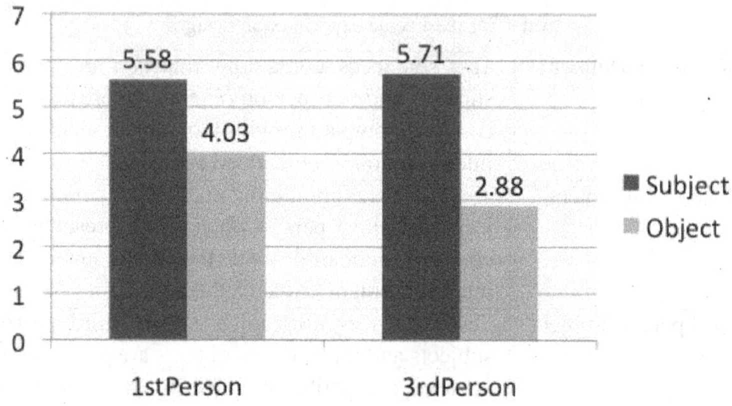

FIGURE 2 Mean Rating

(7) Third person/Subject condition

Swuni-nun	*Yuli-eykey*	*caki-ka*	*hwacangsil-ul*
Swuni-Top	Yuli-to	self-Nom	bathroom-Acc

chengsoha-keyss-tako	*malha-yess-ta.*
clean-Fut-Comp	say-Past-Decl

'Swuni told Yuli that self would clean the bathroom.'

(8) Third person/Object condition

Swuni-nun	*Yuli-eykey*	*caki-ka*	*nemeci-ci*	*anh-ulke-lako*
Swuni-Top	Yuli-to	self-Nom	fall-Conn	Neg-Fut-Comp

malha-yess-ta.
say-Past-Decl

'Swuni told Yuli that self was not going to fall.'

2.4. Findings and discussion

Mean ratings from all participants on each of the Person/Antecedent combinations are shown in Figure 2. A repeated-measures ANOVA revealed a main effect of Antecedent ($F(1,19) = 56.461$, $p < .001$) and an interaction between Person and Antecedent ($F(1,19) = 5.865$, $p = .026$). This means that speakers are significantly more likely to rate sentences with a subject antecedent higher than those with an object antecedent, but speakers' preference for the subject antecedent over the object antecedent is significantly greater in sentences with third person arguments than those that contained a first person argument in the matrix clause.

Furthermore, pairwise comparisons of means across conditions with Bonferroni adjustment revealed that while the rating in the First person/Object condition is significantly lower than the rating in the First person/Subject condition ($t(1,19) = 5.294$, $p < .001$), it is significantly higher than the rating in the Third person/Object condition ($t(1,19) = 3.363$, $p = .003$).

In sum, when a test sentence contains a first person subject and a third person object, speakers readily allow the object antecedent interpretation, as evidenced by the higher rating in the First person/Object condition than in the Third person/Object condition (4.03 vs. 2.88). But given a choice between the subject and the object antecedent interpretation, when both the matrix subject and the matrix object are third person, the object antecedent interpretation is dispreferred (5.71 vs. 2.88). This result supports that an object argument is a grammatically possible antecedent of *caki*, although there is a preference for the subject antecedent.

It should be noted that the First Person/Object condition of this experiment constructs the exceptional scenario in which, according to Kim's (2000) definition, *caki* actually has no potential antecedent: the matrix subject is not third person, and the matrix indirect object is thematically less prominent than the embedded subject. That *caki*'s interpretation as having a non-subject antecedent is significantly better when there is no other possible antecedent can be interpreted as an expected outcome of this exceptional circumstance. Kim's approach is not entirely predictive of the results here though, as her system of preferential ranking of potential antecedents predicts a categorical distinction between the two third person conditions. While we do find a significant difference between these two conditions, a rating of 2.88 may be seen as unexpectedly high for a structure which ought to be completely ruled out.

We have not yet provided any discussion or analysis of the sub-cases within each condition which made use of the matrix verb *malha-* (say) versus those with *tut-* (hear). With only two tokens of each per condition, there is insufficient data to make any strong statistical claims, but we do note anecdotally that higher ratings for the object antecedent conditions tended to be more frequent with *hear* than with *say*. This ties back to Yoon's (1989) proposal that *caki* interpretation may be sensitive to logophoricity. We thus move on to the TVJT experiment which directly tests whether or not *caki* is sensitive to a logophoric bias.

3. Truth Value Judgment task (TVJT) Experiment

The purpose of the TVJT experiment is to test whether the subject preference observed in the Likert scale experiment interacts with another factor, the preference for the source of information, or logophoric centre. For this purpose, we manipulated the type of the matrix verb, *malha-* (say) vs. *tut-* (hear), as an independent variable. In *say*-sentences, as in (9), the matrix subject is the source of information, while in *hear*-sentences, as in (10) (repeated below from (1)), the matrix indirect object is the source of information.

(9) *Yuli-nun Swuni-eykey [caki-ka iki-lke-lako] malha-yess-ta.*
Yuli-Top Swuni-to self-Nom win-Fut-Comp say-Past-Decl
'Yuli said to Swuni that self would win the race.'

(10) *Yuli-nun Swuni-lopwuthe [caki-ka iki-lke-lako]*
Yuli-Top Swuni-from self-Nom win-Fut-Comp
tul-ess-ta.
hear-Past-Decl
'Yuli heard from Swuni that self would win the race.'

Using this fact, we designed a TVJT experiment that addresses the research question in (11).

(11) Research question for the TVJT experiment
Can the subject preference observed in the scale experiment be attributed to the preference for the source of information?

3.1. Task

Participants were presented with a combination of visual and aural stimuli. While watching a screen with two characters (one male and one female) on a computer screen, they heard a scene setting statement by a narrator. They then heard a brief conversation by the two characters, and then a test sentence presented by the narrator. For instance, while watching the picture in Figure 3, participants heard a narrator state that Chelswu (a typical male name) and Swuni (a typical female name) are at a swimming pool and they are going to race. They then heard a male voice stating "You belong to the school swimming team," a female voice stating "So I practice swimming for an hour every day," and then the male voice stating "You will win the race." A test sentence, as in (12), is then presented by the narrator. The participants' task was to answer whether the test sentence is True or False in the context of the conversation between characters.

(12) *Swuni-ka Chelswu-lopwuthe taiping tay yep-eyse*
Swuni-Nom Chelswu-from diving board beside-at
caki-ka iki-lke-lako tul-ess-ta.
self-Nom win-Fut-Comp hear-Past-Decl
'Swuni heard from Chelswu beside the diving board that self would win.'

If the participants allow the subject antecedent interpretation of *caki* in *hear*-sentences, then they will say 'True' in this trial. But if they only allow the object antecedent interpretation of *caki* in *hear*-sentences, then they will say 'False' in this trial.

FIGURE 3 Screen shot of an example trial in the TVJT experiment

3.2. Design, participants and procedure

The experiment had two within-subjects factors: Verb (the matrix verb of the test sentence is *malha-* (say) or *tut-* (hear)) and Antecedent (the dialogue is compatible with the subject or the object antecedent interpretation of *caki*). Crossing the factors again gives rise to four different conditions, as summarized in Table 2. The example trial described in Subsection 3.1 was presented in the condition in which the matrix verb of the test sentence is *tut-* (hear) and the dialogue is compatible with the subject antecedent interpretation.

Twenty native speakers of Korean, different from the Likert scale experiment, were tested. Each participant received 64 test trials (16 trials in each condition) and 64 fillers, counterbalanced for order of presentation.

3.3. Test sentences

We constructed sixteen *say*-sentences, as in (13), and sixteen *hear*-sentences, as in (14) (repeated below from (12)).

(13) *Chelswu-ka* *Swuni-eykey* *taiping* *tay* *yep-eyse* *caki-ka*
Chelswu-Nom Swuni-Dat diving board beside-at self-Nom
iki-lke-lako *malha-n-ta.*
win-Fut-Comp tell-Pres-Decl
'Chelswu tells Swuni beside the diving board that self will win.'

TABLE 2 Likert scale experimental design

Say/Subject	*Say*-sentences are presented with a dialogue compatible with the subject antecedent interpretation of *caki*.
Say/Object	*Say*-sentences are presented with a dialogue compatible with the object antecedent interpretation of *caki*.
Hear/Subject	*Hear*-sentences are presented with a dialogue compatible with the subject antecedent interpretation of *caki*.
Hear/Object	*Hear*-sentences are presented with a dialogue compatible with the subject antecedent interpretation of *caki*.

(14) *Swuni-ka* *Chelswu-lopwuthe* *taiping* *tay* *yep-eyse*
Swuni-Nom Chelswu-from diving board beside-at
caki-ka *iki-lke-lako* *tul-ess-ta.*
self-Nom win-Fut-Comp hear-Past-Decl
'Swuni heard from Chelswu beside the diving board that self would win.'

Each sentence was presented twice: once with a dialogue compatible with the subject antecedent interpretation, and once with a dialogue compatible with the object antecedent interpretation. The test sentences were balanced with equal number of male and female subjects.

3.4. Findings and discussion

Mean percent acceptance from all participants on each of the Verb/Antecedent combination are shown in Figure 4. A repeated-measures ANOVA revealed a main effect of Antecedent ($F(1,19) = 40.862$, $p < .001$) and an interaction between Verb and Antecedent ($F(1,19) = 25.415$, $p < .001$). That is, speakers are significantly more likely to accept sentences with a subject antecedent than those with an object antecedent, but speakers' preference for the subject antecedent is significantly higher in *say*-sentences than in *hear*-sentences. Pairwise comparisons of means across conditions with Bonferroni adjustment revealed that the acceptance rate in Say/Subject condition is significantly higher than the acceptance rate in Say/Object condition ($t(1,19) = 12.107$, $p < .001$), but the difference between the Hear/Subject condition and Hear/Object condition is not significant.

These findings suggest that the subject preference observed in the scale experiment cannot be attributed to the preference for the source of informa-

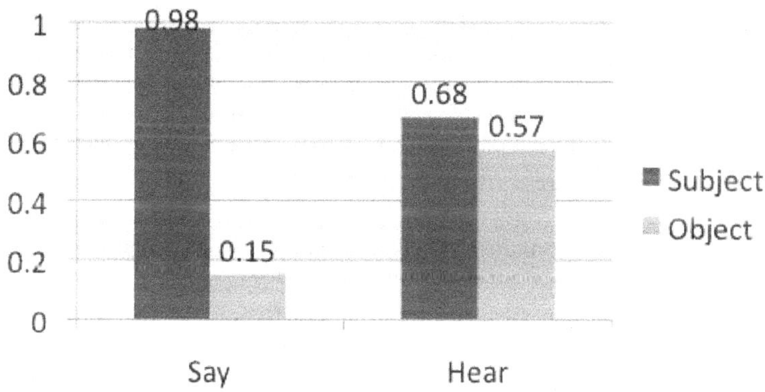

FIGURE 4 Mean Percent Acceptance

tion, and that both the preference for the subject and the preference for the source of information are at work in the speakers' choice of the antecedent of *caki*. In *say*-sentences, both the source and the subject preference converge on the subject antecedent accounting for the high 98% acceptance rate in Say/Subject condition and the low 15% acceptance rate in Say/Object condition. But in *hear*-sentences, the two preferences diverge: the subject preference points to the matrix subject, and the source preference points to the matrix object antecedent. The fact that the acceptance rates in both Hear/Subject and Hear/Object conditions hover around 60% strongly suggests that the two preferences are in competition, interacting with each other.

This result is contrary to both the view that *caki* is subject-oriented, as in Lee (1973) and Chang (1977), and the view that *caki* is simply logophoric, as in Yoon (1989). It also provides a more robust counterexample to Kim's (2000) prominence hierarchy, as she would predict there to be no difference between the *say* and *hear* cases. In all conditions, the only potential antecedent for *caki* under her definition should be the matrix subject, as the matrix indirect object is less prominent than the embedded subject. However, the results in the *hear* condition show that this is not the case, and that a manipulation based on logophoricity can make a thematically less-prominent antecedent more acceptable. The non-categorical result in the *hear* condition points to a more complex system of competing factors rather than a system with an overarching preferential antecedent ranking according to a single factor such as a thematic prominence hierarchy.

4. Conclusion

Echoing the results in Han et al., and hearkening back to the earliest literature on *caki*, both the Likert scale and TVJT experiments demonstrate a preference for *caki* to have a subject antecedent. However, our experiments also demonstrate that this preference is in competition with other factors, leading speakers to accept instances of *caki* with non-subject antecedents. As a result, we are left with a more nuanced view of how *caki* must be treated. Any formal analysis of *caki* must be flexible enough to admit subject and non-subject antecedents; where there is the potential for ambiguity, other factors such as agreement and logophoricity militate against certain readings, though the dispreferred option must remain available in principle. Rather than aligning with single-factor preferential antecedent ranking treatments of *caki*, our overall findings are compatible with the multiple-constraints approach to anaphor resolution in that interpretation of anaphors is determined by multiple interacting constraints (Kaiser et al. 2009, and references therein). Future work in this area will seek to identify further factors influencing the interpretation of *caki*, using on-line methodology such as eye-tracking. Using experimental methods which allow us to identify the effects of biases as the sentence unfolds, we can find further evidence that multiple such effects exist.

References

Büring, D. 2005. *Binding theory*. Cambridge University Press.

Chang, S. 1977. Korean reflexive pronoun *caki* and its referent NP's point of view. *Language Research* 13:35–48.

Cho, M-H. 1994. On the orientation problem in Korean 'caki' binding and the typology of X reflexive binding. In *Kansas Working Papers in Linguistics*, volume 19, 165–183.

Han, C-H, D. R. Storoshenko, and R. Calen Walshe. 2011. An experimental study of the grammatical status of *caki* in Korean. In *Japanese/Korean linguistics 19*, ed. Ho min Sohn, Haruko Cook, William O'Grady, Leon A. Serafim, and Sang Yee Cheon, 81–94. Stanford: CSLI Publications.

Kaiser, E., J. T. Runner, R. S. Sussman, and M. K. Tanenhaus. 2009. Structural and semantic constraints on the resolution of pronouns and reflexives. *Cognition* 112:55–80.

Kim, S-Y. 2000. Acceptability and preference in the interpretation of anaphors. *Linguistics* 38:315–353.

Kim, K, and S. Madigan. 2011. The nature of associative plurality in Korean: Accounting for *ney* and *tul*. In *Proceedings of the 19th Japanese/Korean Linguistics Conference*, ed. Ho min Sohn, Haruko Cook, William O'Grady, Leon A. Serafim, and Sang Yee Cheon, 283–296. University of Hawaii at Manoa, Stanford: CSLI Publications.

Lee, C. 1973. Abstract syntax and Korean with reference to English. Doctoral Dissertation, University of Indiana.

Madigan, S. 2006. Exhaustive and partial control in Korean: Long-distance *caki* as an overt form of PRO. In *Havard studies in Korean Linguistics XI*, 642–655. Cambridge, Ma: Department of Linguistics, Harvard University.

Sells, P. 1987. Aspects of logophoricity. *Linguistic Inquiry* 18:445–479.

Sohng, H-K. 2004. A minimalist analysis of X^0 reflexivization in Chinese and Korean. *Studies in Generative Grammar* 14:375–396.

Yoon, J-M. 1989. Long-distance anaphors in Korean and their cross-linguistic implications. In *Papers from the 25th Annual Meeting of the Chicago Linguistic Society*, ed. Caroline Wiltshire, Randolph Graczyk, and Music Bradley, 479–495. Chicago Linguistic Society.

The Japanese Auxiliary *-Noda* and Its Comparable Linguistic Forms in Korean and Ainu: A Force-Dynamic Account

KATSUNOBU IZUTSU*
Hokkaido University of Education

1. Introduction

The Japanese *-noda*, instantiated in (1), is a notoriously versatile auxiliary. Noda (1997), its first extensive study, cites Yoshida's (1988) comprehensive description that classifies its usages into eleven: 'rephrasing,' 'confession,' 'instruction,' 'emphasis,' 'decision,' 'order,' 'discovery,' 'rediscovery,' 'reconfirmation,' 'rearrangement,' and 'objectification.' An abundant literature has attempted to explain the meaning and function of the auxiliary only to end up as partial treatments of some major usages (Mikami 1953; Kindaichi 1955; Hayashi 1964, Kuno 1973; Teramura 1984 *inter alia*).

* I am very grateful to Rumiko Shinzato, Takeshi Koguma, and Shoichi Yamada for helpful comments on a draft of this article, and to Yuki-Shige Tamura, Mika Fukazawa, Yuki Nagata, Yohei Oseki, Yusuke Sugaya, Kyohei Nakata, Hiromi Kurashige, Aya Miura, Airi Ueno, and Mitsuko Narita Izutsu for their stimulating discussions during the preparatory stages of the article. However, any shortcomings of the article are solely my responsibility.

Japanese/Korean Linguistics 21.
Edited by Seungho Nam, Heejeong Ko and Jongho Jun.

(1) a. *(Igirisu-ni iku-nzyanai(-yo).) Amerika-ni iku-nda(-yo).*
UK-to go-*noda*:NEG(-FP) US-to go-*noda*(-FP)[1]
'(Not going to the UK.) Going to the US.'

b. *Amerika-ni iku-nda.*
US-to go-*noda*
'Going to the US.'

Grounded on those partial but insightful earlier works, Noda has succeeded in presenting a total account of the meaning and function by dividing the relevant usages into two major categories: "scope" specification and "mood" marking. She subdivides the modal usage into "event-oriented" and "addressee-oriented" *-noda*, which are respectively characterized as denoting that the speaker "grasps" the clausal content and that he "presents" the content to the addressee. Examples like (1a) instantiate the scope specifying usage, where *Amerika-ni* (*iku*) is emphasized, its alternative *Igirisu-ni* (*iku*) being put in the scope of negation and rephrased. In contrast, examples like (1b) illustrate the modal usage that covers interpretations like (i) the speaker's informing or reminding the addressee of his decision or plan (e.g., 'I am going to the US.'), (ii) his sudden recollection or rediscovery of the schedule (e.g., 'I forgot that I am going to the US.'), (iii) his discovering the addressee's or someone else's plan (e.g., 'Oh, you are [she is] going to the US!'), and (iv) his urging the addressee to follow his order (e.g., 'Go to the US.'). The interpretations of (ii) and (iii) are ascribed to the event-oriented *-noda* while those of (i) and (iv) are to the addressee-oriented *-noda*.

Noda has thus managed to capture a whole picture of the relevant usages. But her descriptions do not go far enough to give a unified account of the two major usages, let alone two subtypes of the modal usage. Scope specification would appear to be something distinct from the modal usage. The commonality between the subtypes of modal usage remains unclear. Split or sporadic explanations would be inconsistent with the following observations. Examples like (1a) can have interpretations like (i) through (iv) along with scope specification. The interpretation of (iii) can be ambiguous between the event-oriented and addressee-oriented *-noda*, depending on whether the subject refers to the addressee or not.

The present article argues that a "force-dynamic" (Talmy 1988; Sweetser 1990) model of speech event conception helps to provide a unified account of the relevant usages of *-noda*. The model, diagramed as in Figure 1, encompasses the speaker's conception of a speech event in which he and his

[1] The following abbreviations are used in the gloss of examples sentences: ACC (accusative), ADN (adnominal), COMP (complementizer), FP (final particle), NEG (negation), NOM (nominative), NR (nominalizer), PROG (progressive), Q (question), PRS (present), and TOP (topic).

addressee (the two circles) assess a conceived event (the bold square) as being in either realis or irrealis (cf. Akatsuka's (1985) "realis" and "counterfactual"; Langacker's (1991) "reality" and "irreality"). The bold square corresponds to the conceived event 'going to the US' in (1b).

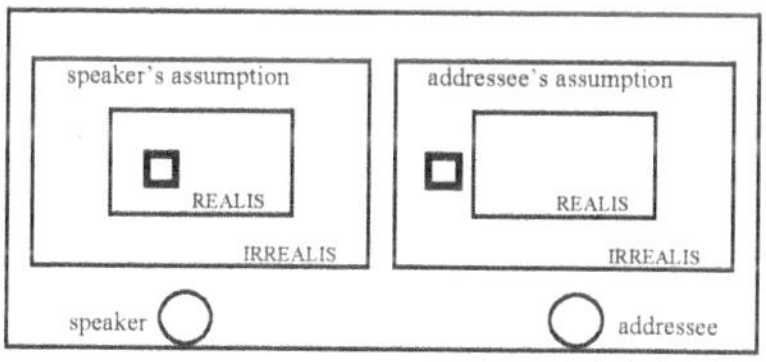

Figure 1: Force-dynamic model of speech event conception

The overall structure of the model is relevant to the (i) and (iv) interpretations above. The speaker exerts force on the square in the addressee's assumption, bringing it into the realis as is the case in the speaker's assumption. This change in assumption makes the addressee recognize the conceived event as something (to be) true. In contrast, the (ii) and (iii) interpretations only involve the speaker's assumption (the left half of Figure 1). The bold square lies outside the realis before the time of speech, probably outside the irrealis because its presence is not yet assessed. It is brought into the realis by the speaker's perception or reasoning in the discourse context that informs or reminds him of the plan to go to the US. The change in assumption alerts the speaker to the presence of the conceived event.

The model also provides a straightforward account of the negative form of *-noda* as exemplified in the parenthesized sentence in (1a). The bold square in Figure 1 corresponds to the conceived event 'going to the UK,' which is taken out of the realis in the speaker's or addressee's assumption; the sentence means '(Now I remember or I will tell you that) the subject entity is not going to the UK.' The second sentence in (1a) serves to put another conceived event 'going to the US' anew in the realis, hence '(Now I remember or I will tell you that) the subject entity is going to the US.'

The negative form amounts to "metalinguistic negation" (Horn 1985) or negation at the "speech-act domain" (Sweetser 1990). Then the corresponding affirmative *-noda* will naturally be viewed as, so to speak, metalinguistic affirmation. The model proposed here is eligible to analyze such negative and affirmative auxiliaries because the metalinguistic or speech-act-oriented meaning and function are cross-linguistically apt to involve force-dynamic notions like the speech-event participants' interactions and their mental manipulations of some conceived entities (Izutsu 2001; Izutsu and Izutsu 2008). The auxiliary *-noda* is describable as conveying that the conceived event is brought into or out of the realis of the participants' assumption. The present article further demonstrates that comparable expressions in Korean and Ainu (an indigenous language in Japan) can also be appropriately dealt with by the force-dynamic model.

2. Previous Accounts

To the best of my knowledge, Noda (1997) is the first comprehensive study of *-noda*. Based on an extensive literature and data, she proposes to make a clear distinction between 'scope-specifying' *noda* and 'mood-marking' *noda*. She further divides the mood-marking *noda* into four on the basis of the distinction between event-oriented (*taijiteki*) and addressee-oriented (*taijinteki*) and between relational and nonrelational.[2] In Noda's (1997) account, (2a-b) instantiate the scope specifying usage. Here *Tomoko-ni* (*itta*) in (2a) and *Kanasiku-te* (*nai-teru*) in (2b) are put in the scope of negation and rephrased, and their alternatives, *Satiko-ni* (*itta*) and *Uresiku-te* (*nai-teru*), are emphasized. In contrast, (3) illustrates the modal usage. (3a-d) are, respectively, an example of the relational use of event-oriented *-noda*, the non-relational use of event-oriented *-noda*, the relational use of addressee-oriented *-noda*, and the non-relational use of addressee-oriented *-noda*.

(2) a. *Tomoko-ni itta-nzyanai. Satiko-ni itta-nda.*
Tomoko-to said-*noda*:NEG Sachiko-to said-*noda*
'I didn't tell Tomoko. I told Sachiko.'

b. *Kanasiku-te nai-teru-nzyanai. Uresiku-te nai-teru-nda.*
be:sad-ing cry-PROG:PRS-*noda*:NEG be:glad-ing cry-PROG:PRS-*noda*
'I'm not crying because I'm sad. I'm crying because I'm glad.'
(Noda 1997: 35)[3]

(3) a. *Yamada-san-ga ko-nai-naa. Kitto yoozi-ga aru-nda.*
Yamada-Mr-NOM come-NEG:PRS-FP probably business-NOM is-*noda*
'Yamada hasn't come. He probably has something to do.'

b. *Soo-ka, kono-suitti-o osu-nda.*
be:so-Q this-switch-ACC push-*noda*
'Ah, I'm supposed to press this switch.'

c. *Boku asita-wa ko-nai-yo. Yoozi-ga aru-nda.*
I tomorrow-TOP come-NEG:PRS-FP business-NOM is-*noda*
'I'm not coming tomorrow. I have something to do.'

d. *Kono-suitti-o osu-nda!*
this-switch-ACC push-*noda*
'Press this switch!' (Noda 1997: 67)

---

[2] I follow Shinzato's (2006: 21) translation of Noda's (1997) terms *taijiteki* and *taijinteki*.

[3] The English gloss and translation in (2) and (3) are my addition.

Noda describes the relational and non-relational uses as follows. The relational use of event-oriented *-noda* as illustrated in (3a) "indicates that the speaker grasps P, a situation or forgoing context, as more meaningful and understandable Q," which is either the background or meaning of P (*ibid*.: 84). The non-relational use of event oriented *-noda* as illustrated in (3b) "is used when the speaker grasps Q as an unrecognized predetermined event" (*ibid*.: 89). The relational use of addressee-oriented *-noda* as illustrated in (3c) "refers to the speaker's mental attitude in which he presents Q, the event he has recognized though the addressee has not, as the background or meaning of P, a situation or foregoing context, so that the addressee will recognize it" (*ibid*. 94). The non-relational use of addressee-oriented *-noda* as illustrated in (3d) "refers to the speaker's mental attitude in which he presents Q, what he has recognized though the addressee has not, as a predetermined event so that the addressee will recognize it" (*ibid*. 98).

Noda (1997: 69) diagrams *-noda*'s function as in Figure 2. With the event-oriented *-noda* "the event that the speaker has not recognized" comes into the speaker. With the addressee-oriented *-noda* "the event that the addressee has not recognized" goes out of the speaker into the addressee.

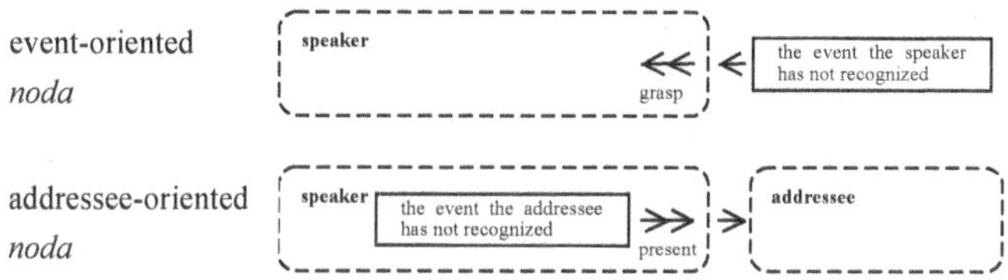

Figure 2: Noda's diagram of event- and addressee-oriented *-noda*

Noda (1997) is basically on the right track, managing to capture a whole picture of *-noda*. But the characterizations do not go far enough to give a unified account of the two major usages and two subtypes of the modal usage. This article shows that a "force-dynamic" analysis can provide a unified account of all the usages. Affirmative *-noda* is described as indicating that some force moves an event conception in or into the speaker's or addressee's assumption. Negative *-nodewanai* is described as indicating that some force moves an event conception out of the assumption.[4]

3. Force-Dynamic Account

Talmy (1988: 49) argues that force dynamics is a generalization over the traditional linguistic notion of causative and includes such concepts as the exertion of force, resistance to such exertion and the overcoming of such

[4] Hereafter, I will refer to *-noda* and *-nodewanai* by their colloquial forms *-nda* and *-nzyanai*, respectively, because our discussion is centered around colloquial examples.

resistance, blockage of a force and the removal of such blockage, and so forth. Sweetser (1990) points out that causation or causality is applicable to three different domains as exemplified in the uses of the causal conjunction *because* in (4). In her account (*ibid*.: 77), (4a) means "his love was the real-world cause of his coming back"; with epistemic causation like (4b), "the speaker's knowledge of John's return (as a premise) causes the conclusion that John loved her"; with conversational causation like (4c), "the *because*-clause gives the cause of the *speech act* embodied by the main clause."

(4) a. John came back because he loved her.
b. John loved her, because he came back.
c. What are you doing tonight, because there's a good movie on.
(Sweetser 1991: 77)

Noda's (1997) scope-specifying and mood-marking uses of *-nda*, can both be described in terms of force dynamics. Examples like (5a-b) instantiate the two uses simultaneously. They can be analyzed as conveying that some perceptual or linguistic evidence brings the event conception of raining into the speaker's (and the addressee's) assumption.

(5) a. *Yuki-ga hut-teru-nzyanai(-na/ne). Ame-ga hut-teru*
snow-NOM fall-PROG:PRS-*noda*:NEG(-FP) rain-NOM fall-PROG:PRS
-nda(-na/ne).
-noda(-FP)
'It's not SNOWING. It's RAINING.'
b. *Ame(?-ga) hut-teru-nda(-na/ne). Hut-tenai(-nda)-to*
rain-NOM fall-PROG:PRS-*noda*(-FP) fall-PROG:NEG:PRS(-*noda*)-COMP
omotteta(-na/ne).
thought(-FP)
'It IS raining! I [We] thought it ISN'T.'

The speaker and his assumption can be diagramed as in Figure 3. The circle stands for the speaker. The assumption consists of realis (what the speaker assumes to be true) and irrealis (what he assumes to be false) (cf. Akatsuka 1985; Langacker 1991). The two sentences in (5a) designate a change from Figure 3(a) to 3(b). The first sentence conveys that the perceptual or linguistic evidence (the flat ellipse in the diagram) exerts force (double arrows) to take the conception of snowing (the bold triangle) out of the assumption. The second sentence indicates that similar force brings the conception of raining (the bold square) into the assumption.

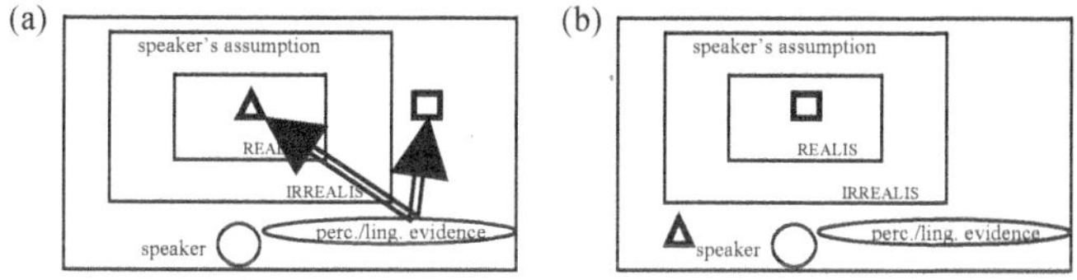

Figure 3: conceptual structure of (5a)

In (5b), by contrast, the second sentence conveys that the conception of raining was first located in irrealis as diagramed in Figure 4(a). The conception of 'raining' in irrealis amounts to 'not raining.' The first sentence indicates that the inference from some perceptual or linguistic evidence (the double arrow) moves the conception into realis as depicted in Figure 4(b).

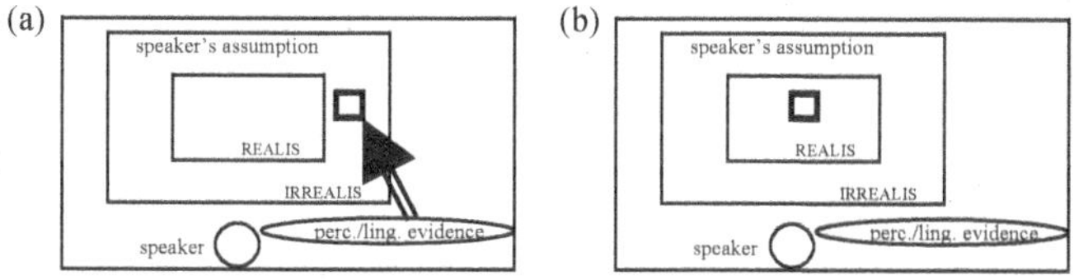

Figure 4: conceptual structure of (5b)

The force that moves an event conception into or out of the assumption does not necessarily come from perceptual or linguistic evidence. The speaker himself can exert such force when he tries to inform the addressee of what he has in his assumption. When the sentences are accompanied by the final particle *-yo* as in (6a), the speaker has the conception of raining (the lightface square) in his assumption as diagramed in Figure 5. He removes the conception of snowing (the triangle) from the addressee's assumption and moves the conception of raining (the bold square) into it as depicted in Figure 5(b). Likewise, when the first sentence is accompanied by *-yo* and the second one by *-(da)ro* or *-desyo* as in (6b), the speaker moves the conception of raining from irrealis to realis as represented in the transition from Figure 6(a) to 6(b). In sentences (6a-b), the speaker intends to reproduce the configuration of his assumption in the addressee's assumption.

(6) a. *Yuki-ga* *hut-teru-nzyanai-yo.* *Ame-ga* *hut-teru*
snow-NOM fall-PROG:PRS-*noda*:NEG-FP rain-NOM fall-PROG:PRS
-nda-yo.
-noda-FP
'It's not SNOWING. It's RAINING.'

b. *Ame(*$^{?}$*-ga) hut-teru-nda-yo. Hut-tenai(-nda)-to*
rain(-NOM) fall-PROG:PRS-*noda*-FP fall-PROG:NEG:PRS-(*noda*)-COMP
omotteta-(da)ro/desyo.
thought-FP
'It IS raining! You thought it ISN'T, right?'

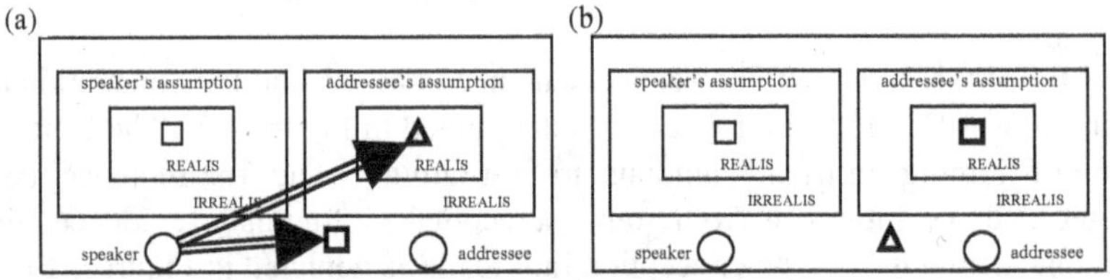

Figure 5: conceptual structure of (6a)

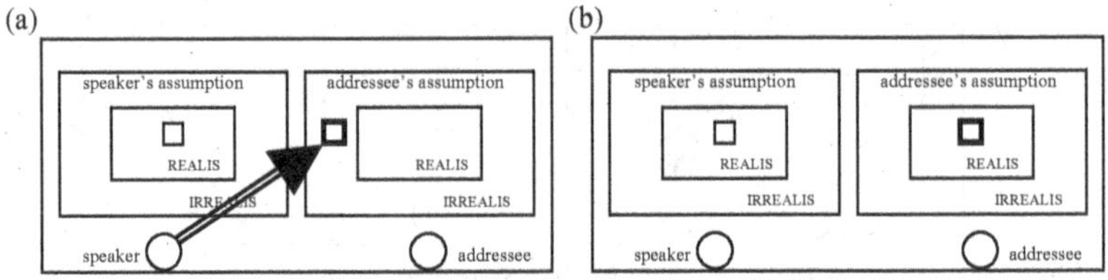

Figure 6: conceptual structure of (6b)

One advantage of our force-dynamic account is that it can explain Noda's event- and addressee-orientation as well as her scope specification function at the same time. In force-dynamic terms, the event-oriented use is concerned with the conceptualization of 'some force's moving the relevant event conception in(to) or out of the speaker's assumption.' Contrastively, the addressee-oriented use pertains to a similar conceptualization, in which the addressee's assumption is more relevant. It also covers the fact that event-oriented examples like (5) can easily be used as addressee-oriented ones if the final particle *-na/ne* is replaced by *-yo* as in (6). The speaker's assumption in (5) is reinterpreted as the addressee's in (6).

In the force-dynamic account, examples of the event-oriented use like (3a-b) quoted in section 2 can be described as denoting that some perceptual or linguistic evidence moves the relevant event conception into the speaker's assumption. This conceptualization is essentially the same as that in the second sentence in (5a) above. Thus, the meaning of *-nda* in (3a-b) can be diagramed as in Figure 7, which coincides with Figure 3 except that it lacks the bold triangle and the arrow pointing to it.

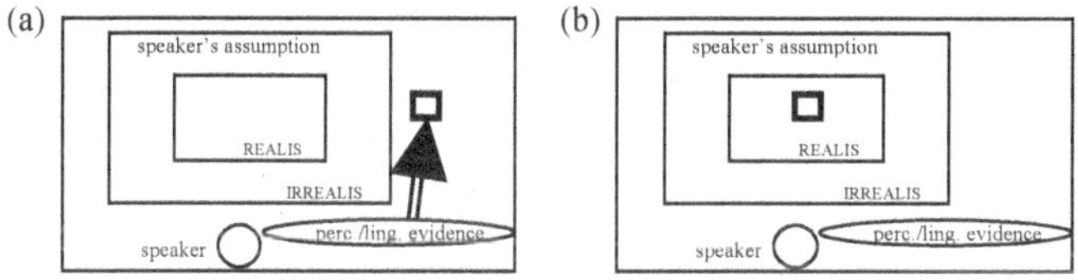

Figure 7: conceptual structure of (3a-b)

On the other hand, examples of the addressee-oriented use like (3c-d) quoted in section 2 can be described as meaning that the speaker moves the relevant event conception into the addressee's assumption. Their conceptualizations are almost the same as that of the second sentence in (6a) and the first sentence in (6b), respectively. Thus, the meaning of *-nda* amounts to Figure 8 in (3c) and coincides with Figure 6 in (3d).

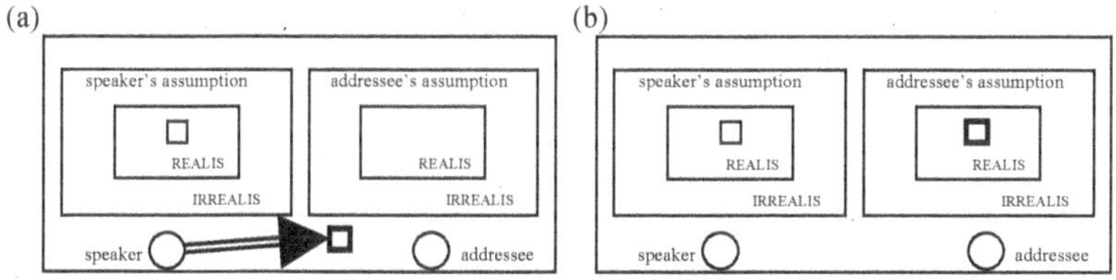

Figure 8: conceptual structure of (3c)

Another advantage of our force-dynamic account is that it can also give a plausible explanation for the difference between Noda's (1997) relational and non-relational uses. The relational use illustrated in (3a) and (3c) corresponds to cases in which some linguistic evidence previously expressed exerts force to move the relevant event conception. The difference between (3a) and (3c) is analyzable as that between Sweetser's "epistemic" causation and "conversational" causation mentioned above. In (3a), the content of the first sentence moves the event conception in Figure 7, while in (3c) the speaker's utterance of the first sentence moves it in Figure 8. With the non-relational use, in contrast, some non-linguistic evidence as in (3b) or the speaker himself as in (3d) exerts force to move the event conception.

4. More Advantages of Force-Dynamic Account

There are at least two more advantages of our force-dynamic account of *-nda*. First, it can account for so-called metalinguistic negation. Negative sentences like (2), (5a), and (6a) largely correspond to the "marked" use of negation, termed "metalinguistic negation" (Horn 1985), "contrastive negation" (McCawley 1991), or "form denial" (Geurts 1998). Horn (1985: 121) argues that the marked use is "a device for objecting to a previous utterance on any grounds whatever—including its conventional or conversational implicata, its morphology, its style or register, or its phonetic realization."

In fact, English examples of the marked negation must be translated into Japanese using *-nda* as in (7). Here the speaker does not deny the existence of the event designated. As Horn (1985: 134) notes in his explanation for a similar English example, the speaker of (7a) "does not intend to suggest that his wife is not a lady." Likewise, the speaker does not deny the occurrence of the relevant events in (7b-c). In force-dynamic terms, the speaker removes the unsuitable expression along with its implicature, style or register, or phonetic realization, replacing it with another expression with appropriate connotations (Izutsu 2001).

(7) a. *Boku-wa zyosei-to issyoni ita-nzyanai. Tuma-to ita-nda.*
I-TOP lady-with together was-*noda*:NEG wife-with was-*noda*
'I wasn't with a lady. I was with my wife.'
b. *Watasitati-wa aisiatta-nzyanai. Yatta-nda.*
we-TOP loved:each:other-*noda*:NEG did-*noda*
'We didn't make love. We fucked.'
c. *Kare-wa tomeitoo-o marugoto tabeta-nzyanai-yo. tomato-o*
he-TOP tomato-ACC whole ate-*noda*:NEG-FP tomato-ACC
marugoto tabeta-nda-yo.
whole ate-*noda*-FP
'He didn't eat a whole "to-may-toh." He ate a whole "to-ma-to."'

One more advantage is that the force-dynamic model can account for the sequence of two *-nda*'s. As Noda (1997: 201) points out, scope-specifying *-nda* in its negative form (*-nzyanai*) and mood-marking *-nda* can occur in sequence as in (8a), but two *-nda*'s both in their affirmative forms cannot as in (8b). In (8a), the speaker does not only remove the conception of 'his asking the addressee' from the assumption but also brings in another conception like 'his speaking to himself' or 'his asking someone else.' Hence, two *-nda*'s are used to express the two movements or transfers. In (8b), however, the speaker does nothing but move the event conception into the assumption. Thus one *-nda* is appropriate, not two.

(8) a. "*Watasi-ni kii-teru-no?*" "*Iya, omae-ni kii-teru-nzyanai-nda.*"
I-to ask-PROG-FP no you-to ask-PROG-*noda*:NEG-*noda*
'Are you asking me?' 'No, I am not asking you.'
b. "*Watasi-ni kii-teru-no?*" *"*Aa, omae-ni kii-teru-nona-nda.*"
I-to ask-PROG-FP yes you-to ask-PROG-*noda-noda*
'Are you asking me?' 'Yeah, I am asking you.' (Noda 1997: 201)

5. Cross-Linguistic Perspective on -*Noda*

As discussed so far, Japanese *-nda* can be adequately captured in force-dynamic terms. Affirmative *-nda* designates 'some force's moving an event conception in or into the speaker's or addressee's assumption.' Negative *-nzyanai* designates 'such force's moving the conception out of the assumption.' In both cases, *-nda* refers to a conceptualization in which an agent/causer exerts force to transfer an event conception in, into, or out of the speaker's or addressee's assumption that consists of realis and irreals. It denotes a "subjective/intersubjective" interaction with, or manipulation of, a relevant event conception in Shinzato's (2006) sense of the terms.

The possible combinations of constituents in *-nda*'s conceptualization can be summarized as in Table 1. The ellipse, double arrow, and two rectangles represent the agent/causer, force, and the source and goal of transfer, respectively. The bold square and the single arrow starting from it stand for the event conception and its transfer.

Table 1: Possible constituent combinations in *-nda*'s conceptualization

AGENT/CAUSER	FORCE	SOURCE	GOAL	example
perceptual/linguistic evidence	inferential	outside S/A's assumption	S/A's assumption	(9a) (9b)
perceptual/linguistic evidence	inferential	S/A's assumption	outside S/A's assumption	(9c) (9d)
perceptual/linguistic evidence	inferential	S/A's irrealis	S/A's realis	(9e)
perceptual/linguistic evidence	inferential	S/A's realis	S/A's irrealis	(9f)
S	illocutionary	S's assumption	A's assumption	(9g)
S	illocutionary	A's irrealis	A's realis	(9h)
S	illocutionary	A's realis	A's irrealis	(9i)
S's utterance	inferential	outside A's assumption	A's assumption	(9j)

The sentences in (9) exemplify eight major combinations of the constituents in *-nda's* conceptualization and two combinations in *-nzynai*'s conceptualization. (3a-b) are the same type as (9a-b), (3c) as (9j), and (3d) as (9h).

(9) a. (I can see people walking under umbrellas) [*Ame-ga hut-teru*]*-nda(-na/ne)*.
b. (It is not SNOWING.) [*Ame-ga hut-teru*]*-nda(-na/ne)*.
c. (I can see people walking without umbrellas) [*Ame-ga hut-teru*]*-nzyanai(-na/ne)*.
d. [*Ame-ga hut-teru*]*-nzyanai(-na/ne)*. (It is SNOWING.)
e. (I thought it wasn't raining but) [*Ame(?-ga) hut-teru*]*-nda(-na/ne)*.
f. (I thought it was raining but) [*Ame(?-ga) hut-tenai*]*-nda(-na/ne)*.
g. [*Ame-ga hut-teru*]*-nda(-yo)*.
h. [*Ame(-wa/?ga) hut-teru*]*-nda(-yo)* (though you say it isn't raining).
i. [*Ame(-wa/?ga) hut-tenai*]*-nda(-yo)* (though you say it's raining).
j. You need an umbrella. [*Ame-ga hut-teru*]*-nda(-yo)*.

A similar force-dynamic account is applicable to Korean examples like (10), translations of Japanese sentences (1a-b) in section 1. Whereas -*(neu)n geosida* is a fuller form, *-(neu)n geoya* is a most frequently used counterpart of Japanese *-nda*. The scope-specifying meaning as in (1a) is expressed in Korean with *-(neu)n geoya* and its negative form *-(neu)n geoaniya* as in (10a). On the other hand, the addressee-oriented meaning of (1b) is denoted by *-(neu)n geoya* as in (10b), while its event-oriented meaning is designated by*-(neu)n geoguna* as in (10c).

(10)a. *Yeonggug-euro ga-neun-geoaniya. Migug-euro ga-neun-geoya.*
UK-to go-ADN-*noda*:NEG:PRS US-to go-ADN-*noda*
'Not going to the UK. Going to the US.'
b. *Migug-euro ga-neun-geoya.*
US-to go-ADN-*noda*
'Going to the US.'
c. *Migug-euro ga-neun-geoguna.*
US-to go-ADN-*noda*
'Going to the US.'

In force-dynamic terms, *-(neu)n geoya* expresses that the speaker's illocutionary force moves the relevant event conception into the addressee's assumption, whereas *-(neu)n geoguna* conveys that the inferential force from some evidence moves the event conception into the speaker's assumption. Negative *-(neu)n geoaniya* and *-(neu)n geoaniguna* convey that such force moves the event conception out of the addressee's or speaker's assumption.

The force-dynamic account also seems applicable to Ainu, an indigenous language in Japan. *Ru(we) ne* is used in declarative sentences as exemplified in (11a), whereas *ru(we) un* is used in exclamatory sentences like (11b) or in affirmative answers to questions. Neither is used in interrogative sentences. Contrastively, *ru(we) an* is used in *wh*-questions or exclamatory sentences as illustrated in (11c-d). In a force-dynamic account, (11a) and the answer with *ru(we) un* are describable as expressing that the speaker has the relevant event conception in his assumption and moves its copy into the addressee's assumption. (11b) and (11d) are analyzable as conveying that the speaker's inference from some evidence moves the event conception into his assumption. Thus *ru(we) un* appears to be Janus-faced.

(11)a. *pirka cihoki ottena kor ek ruwe ne.*[5]
good fur senior have come *noda*
'There came a senior with a good fur.' (Nakagawa 1995: 418)

[5] The English gloss and translation in (11) and (12) are my addition.

b. *pirka ikarkar pe patek ne ruwe un.*
good embroider NR only be *noda*
'Wow, everything is a beautiful piece of embroidery!' (*ibid.*)

c. *"totto ney ne oman ruwe an?"*
mom where to go *noda*
'Where's your mom gone?' (Ueno 2008: 108)

d. *"nep ta kusu kamuy sasuysir askay ru_an."*
what indeed for god descendant be:skillful *noda*
'What a skillful you are, a descendant of gods. (*ibid.*: 116)

Further, *ru(we) un* and *ru(we) an* are not used in Noda's scope specification use, while *ru(we) ne* alone can be used as illustrated in (12). (12a) can be characterized as conveying that the speaker's illocutionary force removes the conception of 'his survival' from the addressee's assumption, replacing it by another conception of 'his death' and 'his body reaching the addressee.' Similarly in (12b) as well, the speaker's illocutionary force removes the conception of 'his being a stranger' from the assumption, moving in another conception of 'his being a cousin of the addressee's.'

(12)a. *tane tan koraci an=an yakka siknu=an ruwe ka somo ne. ray=an*
now this like be=I though survive=I *noda*:NEG die=I
wa ouse a=kewehe a=ewak usike ta sirepa ruwe ne na.
and only I=body:of I=inhabit house at arrive *noda* FP
'Although I am here like this, it is not that I survived. It is that I died but the body alone remained and arrived home.' (Izutsu 2005: 218)

b. *tan an=akihi, itak=an ciki e=inu katu ene*
this I=younger:brother speak=I if you=listen behavior this:way
an ihi, anokay anakne nep oyapihi an=ne ru ka somo ne wa
be NR I TOP what stranger I=be *noda*:NEG and
e=onaha irwaki or wa siko p an=ne ruwe ne.
you=father sibling place from be:born NR I=be *noda*
'My brother, what I will say and you will hear is that I am no stranger but a child born from your father's sister.' (Izutsu 2004: 9)

In the force-dynamic account, *ru(we) ne* is describable as indicating that the speaker's illocutionary force moves the relevant event conception into the addressee's assumption, while *ru(we) an* is as denoting that the inferential force of some evidence moves the event conception into the speaker's assumption; *ru(we) un* appears to share both types of conceptualizations. Negative *ru(we) ka somo ne* is analyzable as denoting that the illocutionary force moves the event conception out of the addressee's assumption.

6. Conclusion

This article demonstrated that a force-dynamic model of speech event conception allows us to describe affirmative *-nda* as indicating that some force moves an event conception in or into the speaker's or addressee's assumption. Negative *-nzyanai* is described as indicating that some force moves an event conception out of the assumption. In either case, *-noda* serves to designate a "subjective/intersubjective" interaction with, or manipulation of, a relevant event conception in the speaker's speech event conception.

The article further showed that the speech-event conception designated consists of such constituents as agent/causer, its force, the source and goal of an event conception's transfer. A notional taxonomy such as Table 1 in section 5 seems viable for further examinations of Korean and Ainu counterparts of Japanese *-nda* and *-nzyanai*. Different combinations of those constituents may account for the distinction between more than one counterpart of *-nda* in those languages as well as different dialects of Japanese.[6] I hope many more students and researchers will be engaged in further studies in the same vein, which I believe will help promote a further comparison, analysis, and understanding of Japanese, Korean, and Ainu.

Assuming that *noda* and "Kakari Musubi" (KM) are comparable in function, Shinzato (1998) claims that they are in complementary distribution. In Japanese, *noda* has taken over the function from Old Japanese KM. In Okinawan, by contrast, KM has been retained, and *siyan* (nominalizer+copula) has not developed into a *noda*-like expression. Shinzato (2011) argues that Japanese *noda* and Okinawan KM are intertranslatable. I believe that a force-dynamic account as proposed in this article can be applied to KM in Old Japanese and Okinawan as well.

References

Akatsuka, Noriko. 1985. Conditionals and the Epistemic Scale. *Language* 61: 625-639.

Geurts, Bart. 1998. The Mechanisms of Denial. *Language* 74: 274-307.

Hayashi, Oki. 1964. Da to Nanoda. *Kooza Gendaigo 6: Koogo Bunpoo no Mondaiten*. Tokyo: Meijishoin.

Horn, Laurence R. 1985. Metalinguistic Negation and Pragmatic Ambiguity. *Language* 61: 121-174.

Izutsu, Katsunobu. 2001. Conceptual Structures of Negation. *Proceedings of the First Seoul International Conference on Discourse and Cognitive Linguistics*, 847-860. Seoul: Hankuk Munhwasa.

---

[6] Such Japanese dialectal counterparts include *-noya*, *-neya*, *-n'ya*, and *-nen* in the Osaka dialect, *-gan'ya* and *-gen* in the Ishikawa dialect, *-nosa* in the Hokkaido dialect, and so on.

Izutsu, Katsunobu (ed.). 2004. *Ainugo Asahikawa Hoogen Shiryoo Shuusei 1*. Hokkaido University of Education.

Izutsu, Katsunobu (ed.). 2005. *Ainugo Asahikawa Hoogen Shiryoo Shuusei 2*. Hokkaido University of Education.

Izutsu, Katsunobu, and Mitsuko Narita Izutsu. 2008. A Cognitive Mechanism of "Mirative" Connectives. *Lingua Posnaniensis* 50: 127-142.

Kindaichi, Haruhiko. 1955. Nihongo III. Bunpoo. Sanki Ichikawa and Shiro Hattori (eds.), *Sekai Gengo Gaisetsu Gekan*, 160-200. Tokyo: Kenkyusha.

Kuno, Susumu. 1973. *Nihon Bunpoo Kenkyuu*. Tokyo: Taishukan.

Langacker, Ronald W. 1991. *Foundations of Cognitive Grammar II: Descriptive Application*. Stanford: Stanford University Press.

McCawley, James D. 1991. Contrastive Negation and Metalinguistic Negation. *Papers from the Chicago Linguistic Society 27, Part Two*, 189-206.

Mikami, Akira. 1953. *Gendai Gohoo Josetsu: Shintakusu no Kokoromi*. Tokyo: Kuroshio.

Nakagawa, Hiroshi. 1995. *Ainugo Chitose Hoogen Jiten*. Tokyo: Sofukan.

Noda, Harumi. 1997. *"No(da)" no Kinoo*. Tokyo: Kuroshio.

Shinzato, Rumiko. 1998. *Kakari Musubi* Revisited: Its Functions and Development. *Japanese/Korean Linguistics* 8: 203-216.

Shinzato, Rumiko. 2006. Subjectivity, Intersubjectivity, and Grammaticalization. In Satoko Suzuki (ed.), *Emotive Communication in Japanese*, 15-33. Amsterdam/Philadelphia: John Benjamins.

Shinzato, Rumiko. 2011. Nominalization in Okinawan: From a Diachronic and Comparative Perspective. In Yap Foong Ha, Karen Grunow-Hårsta, and Janick Wrona (eds.), *Nominalization in Asian Languages: Diachronic and Typological Perspectives*, 445-472. Amsterdam/Philadelphia: John Benjamins.

Sweetser, Eve. E. 1990. *From Etymology to Pragmatics: Metaphorical and Cultural Aspects of Semantic Structure*. Cambridge: Cambridge University Press.

Talmy, Leonard. 1988. Force Dynamics in Language and Cognition. *Cognitive Science* 12: 49-100.

Tamura, Suzuko. 1996. *Ainugo Saru Hoogen Jiten*. Tokyo: Sofukan.

Teramura, Hideo. 1984. *Nihongo no Shintakusu II*. Tokyo: Kuroshio.

Ueno, Airi. 2008. Ainugo Asahikawa Hoogen no *Ru(we)* o Mochiita Gimonbun, Kantanbun. Katsunobu Izutsu (ed.), *Ainugogaku to Gendai no Gengo Riron*, 99-124. Hokkaido University of Education.

Yoshida, Shigeaki. 1988. Noda Keishiki no Koozoo to Hyoogen Kooka. *Kokubun Ronsoo* 15: 46-55. Kobe University.

Gradient Acceptability of Case Ellipsis on Subtypes of Subject: A Probabilistic Account

HANJUNG LEE AND HAEJEONG CHOI
Sungkyunkwan University

Particle ellipsis is the phenomenon whereby speakers omit NP-final particles. One common type of particle ellipsis in Korean is case ellipsis, whereby case markers like *-i/-ka* and *-(l)ul* are omitted. An example of ellipsis of case markers is given in (1):

(1) a. Ecey Myengswu-ka maykcwu-lul manhi masyesse.
yesterday Myoungsoo-Nom beer-Acc a lot drink-Past
'Myoungsoo drank a lot of beer yesterday.'
b. Ecey Myengswu maykcwu manhi masyesse.
yesterday Myoungsoo(-Nom) beer(-Acc) a lot drink-Past
'Myoungsoo drank a lot of beer yesterday.'

Acceptability of case ellipsis on focused subject NPs of differing argument roles exhibits clear asymmetry which so far has not received a plausible explanation. This study explores the gradient acceptability of case ellipsis on the focused subject NPs of three subtypes of one-place predicates

Japanese/Korean Linguistics 21.
Edited by Seungho Nam, Heejeong Ko and Jongho

in Korean. Through a rating experiment which tested the acceptability of case marking and case ellipsis for the subject of unergative verbs and two types of unaccusative verbs that are contrastively focused, we demonstrate that the graded acceptability of case ellipsis for subtypes of focus subject is correlated with the frequency with which the subject accommodates new information. This finding provides strong support to the view that native speakers' knowledge of grammar includes not only some degree of knowledge of probabilistic information, as suggested by prior work, but even access to fine-grained probabilities.

1. Focus and the Graded Acceptability of Case Ellipsis

The notion of contrastive focus has been claimed to be one of the most important factors affecting case ellipsis in Japanese and Korean. A number of previous studies have suggested that case markers in Korean and Japanese cannot be dropped when the argument they mark is contrastively focused (Tsutsui 1984; Masunaga 1988; Yatabe 1999; Ko 2000; D. Lee 2002, among others). The claims about the unacceptability of particle ellipsis on contrastively focused arguments, however, were not based on a careful comparison between the subject and the object. Consider the following example in (2), which illustrates case ellipsis for a contrastively focused transitive subject:

(2) A: i computer cikum-un toy. Ney-ka kochi-ess-e?
this computer now-Top work you-Nom fixed
'This computer is working now. Did you fix (it)?'
B: ani, i chinkwu-ka/???i chinkwu kochi-ess-e.
No, this friend-Nom/ this friend(-Nom) fixed
'No, this guy fixed (it).'

In this context, the version of (2B) with a case-ellipsed subject is much less natural than that with the case-marked counterpart and judged to be nearly unacceptable by native speakers. By contrast, case ellipsis on contrastively focused objects generally does not result in unacceptability. (3B) below is an example that contains a contrastively focused object. All native speakers we have consulted agree that both versions of (3B) are acceptable.

(3) A: Cinmi-ka computer(-lul) sa-ss-e.
Jinmi-Nom computer(-Acc) bought
'Jinmi bought a computer.'
B: aniya, hywutayphon(-ul) sa-ss-e.
No, cell phone(-Acc) bought
'No, (she) bought a cell phone.'

It appears that the ellipsis of case markers marking a focused transitive subject is unnatural whether the focused subject is contrastive or not. However, with few exceptions, hardly any linguistic treatments of case ellipsis in Korean have neither recognized nor provided a persuasive account of such differences between subject case ellipsis and object case ellipsis.

Another issue that has received little attention in previous discussions of particle ellipsis is particle ellipsis on the subject of intransitive verbs. Here we can observe some interesting difference between the subject of unergative verbs and that of unaccusative verbs with respect to the naturalness of case ellipsis: while explicit case marking seems to be the preferred option for encoding the focused subject of both classes of intransitive verbs, case ellipsis is more acceptable for the focused subject of some subclasses of unaccusative verbs such as *issta* 'exist' and *ota* 'come' than for that of unergative verbs. This is illustrated by the contrast between the examples in (4) and (5).

(4) A: ecey swuep-eyse Yengmi-ka col-ass-ci?
yesterday class-in Youngmi-Nom fall asleep-Pst-Int
'Is it Youngmi who fell asleep in class yesterday?'
B: ani, Minswu-ka/??Minswu col-ass-e.
no, Minsoo-Nom/Minsoo(-Nom) fall asleep-Pst-Ind
'No, it was Minsoo who fell asleep.'

(5) A: cikum konghang-ey Yenghi-ka tochak hay-ss-ci?
now airport-at Younghi-Nom arrive-Pst-Int
'Is it Younghi who just arrived at the airport?'
B: ani, Cinmi-ka/?Cinmi pangkum tochak hay-ss-e.
no, Jinmi-Nom/Jinmi(-Nom) just arrive-Pst-Ind
'No, it was Jinmi who just arrived.'

In sum, acceptability of case ellipsis on contrastively focused NPs of differing roles exhibits systematic variation. Case ellipsis on contrastively focused direct objects occurs naturally, whereas case ellipsis on contrastively focused transitive subjects is unnatural whether the subject is contrastively focused or not. A comparison of the acceptability of sentences with contrastively focused unergative subjects and sentences with contrastive focus subjects of some subclasses of unaccusative verbs further shows that case ellipsis occurs more naturally on unaccusative subjects than on unergative subjects.

2. Usage Probability and the Graded Acceptability of Argument Case Ellipsis

In H. Lee (2010a), we investigated the question of how focus affects case ellipsis for subjects and objects through an elicitation experiment that tested speakers' judgments on the acceptability of sentences containing case-marked or unmarked forms of focused arguments. A total of 56 students from a university in Seoul participated in this experiment. Each participant was asked to read short conversations between speakers and indicate to what degree the two object forms were suitable in the given context. To do this, they had to rate the acceptability of sentences containing case-marked or unmarked arguments by assigning them a grade from 1-5 on a five-point rating scale (The questionnaire was given to the participants in Korean orthography.).

As Table 1 shows, focus (transitive) subjects showed a strong preference for explicit case marking over case ellipsis, whereas focus objects did not show such a preference: while there was no significant difference in average ratings between sentences with a case-marked focus object versus sentences with a case-ellipsed focus object (3.15 vs. 3.47), sentences with a case-ellipsed focus subject were judged as significantly less acceptable than sentences with a case-marked focus subject (1.27 vs. 4.05).

(6) Table 1. Average ratings

	Transitive Subject	Direct Object
Case-marked	4.05	3.15
Case-ellipsed	1.27	3.47

In H. Lee (2010a) we have suggested that this difference is likely due to asymmetry in the probabilistic properties of transitive subjects and direct objects. Crosslinguistically and also in Korean, focus is more frequently associated with objects than subjects in transitive clauses. Because focus is a rare and unexpected property for subjects, they are expected to show a strong overall preference for explicit case marking over case ellipsis. The rarity of new information subjects in Korean is supported by empirical data from H. Lee (2010b), in which we examined the encoding and the information status of referents in three grammatical roles (the subject of transitive predicates (A), the subject of one-place predicates (S), and the object of transitive predicates (O)) in conversational Korean. The study found a clear asymmetry between the subject (A and S) and the object (O) in their accommodation of new information. New mentions tend to go into the O role (54.8%). The A slot shows the smallest proportion of new mentions (8.7%), whereas the S slot shows a higher proportion (36.5%) (see also T. Kim (2008)).

Overall, S seems to pattern with A in its accommodation of given/inferable information and with O in its accommodation of new information. However, there were some interesting observations regarding the information structural properties of S when the subtypes of S are analyzed separately. Table 2 shows the proportions of new referents in the subtypes of S.

(7) Table 2. Distribution of new information for subtypes of S

Subtypes of S	Given/Inferable		New		Total	
	No.	%	No.	%	No.	%
Subject of verbs of existence/ continuous state	160	4.7	146	16.3	306	7.2
Subject of verbs of change of location	355	10.5	194	21.7	549	12.9
Subject of non-verbal predicates	550	16.3	206	23	756	17.7
Subject of other unaccusative verbs (state change verbs)	586	17.4	102	11.4	688	16.1
Subject of passives	662	19.6	96	10.7	758	17.8
Subject of unergative verbs	1056	31.5	151	16.9	1207	28.3
Total	3369	100	895	100	4264	100

As shown in Table 2, S shows considerable variation in its accommodation of new information. The two subclasses of unaccusative verbs, namely verbs of existence/continuous state and verbs of change of location, show the highest relative proportion of new mentions (146/306 = 47.7% and 194/549 = 35.3%, respectively). The subject of non-verbal predicates shows a slightly lower proportion (206/756 = 27.2%). The subject of unergative verbs show the lowest relative proportion of new mentions (151/1056 = 12.5%). In addition, a large proportion of all new Ss occur with verbs of existence/continuous state and verbs of change of location, which are often used to introduce or present a referent into the discourse (38%), and with non-verbal predicates, which encompass nominal predicates and adjectival predicates (23%). In terms of semantics, these verbs are informationally light in that they do not contribute much information about properties of their argument's referent (Ono et al. 2000). Verbs of existence/continuous state and verbs of change of location are semantically rather empty, and non-verbal predicates, unlike verbal predicates whose semantics typically specify something about the nature of the participants involved, only name a class or a property without necessarily invoking any participants.

Looking at where argument focus goes in our data, Table 3 shows the distribution of all tokens of argument focus over the various grammatical roles in the data.

(8) Table 3. Distribution of argument focus among grammatical role

O	S						A	Total
	S-1	S-2	S-3	S-4	S-5	S-6		
78 (35%)	45 (20.2%)	32 (14.4%)	36 (16.1%)	13 (5.8%)	9 (4%)	6 (2.7%)	4 (1.8%)	223 (100%)

(S-1: subject of verbs of existence/continuous state; S-2: subject of change of location; S-3: subject of non-verbal predicates; S-4: subject of other unaccusative verbs; S-5: subject of passives; S-6: subject of unergative verbs)

Of the total 223 tokens of argument focus, the great majority (85.7%) goes into the O role(35%) and the subject of the same three classes of one-place predicates (50.7%) that accommodate new information as their subject at a rate greater than the average rate of S (21%). Hence, it seems possible to regard these four argument types as the main locus for argument focus. But argument focus tends to avoid the other subtypes of S in the data, and as expected, smaller proportions of argument focus appear in the A role (1.8%).

On the basis of our conversation data, we proposed a newness hierarchy of argument NPs in (11) ('S_{light}'indicates the subject of the three classes of one-place predicates that are informationally light (verbs of existence/continuous state, verbs of change of location and non-verbal predicates; '$S_{other\ unacc}$' indicates the subject of unaccusative verbs other than verbs of existence/continuous state and verbs of change of location (e.g. verbs of change of state and passives); 'S_{unerg}' indicates the subject of unergative verbs):

(9) Argument Newness Hierarchy (ANH): O > S_{light} > $S_{other\ unacc}$ > S_{unerg} > A

The more to the left a referent is in this hierarchy, the more likely it is to be new information. As we have seen, the O role shows the highest percentage of new information, and the A role, the lowest percentage. Furthermore, although they do not differ morphologically, the subtypes of S show very different discourse profiles in their accommodation of new information, with S_{light} being closer to O than A, and $S_{other\ unacc}$ and S_{unerg} patterning more similarly with A than O.

The ANH makes it possible to capture variation in the degree of acceptability of particle ellipsis for focused NPs of differing argument types. The generalization seems to be that there is a steady increase in the degree of acceptability of particle ellipsis for a focused argument according to the salience of the argument's referent in the hierarchy. As discussed in section 2, the ellipsis of case markers marking a focused A argument is judged to be nearly unacceptable whether the focused subject is contrastive or not, whereas both the case-ellipsed and case-marked form of a focused O argument are acceptable. Interestingly, case ellipsis on a focused S argument shows variation in the degree of acceptability: while case marking seems to be slightly preferred over case ellipsis for encoding the focused S_{light} argument, both forms are generally acceptable. By contrast, case ellipsis on S_{unacc} and S_{unerg} that are in focus is not completely acceptable, and explicit case marking is more strongly preferred. On the basis of these observations, we will hypothesize that the degree of acceptability of case ellipsis on focused NPs of differing argument types correlates with the frequency with which the NPs accommodate new information.

3. Usage Probability and Case Ellipsis for Focus Subject: An Experiment

In this study, we elicited judgments for sentences which contain the case-marked or case-ellipsed form of the focused subject of three subtypes of intransitive verbs: unergative verbs, change of state unaccusative verbs and informationally light unaccusative verbs (verbs of existence/continuous state and verbs of change of location). We used an elicitation method similar to that used in H. Lee (2009, 2010a). The aim was to further test the hypothesis that the degree of acceptability of case ellipsis on the focused argument increases according to the argument's salience on the ANH. This hypothesis predicts that case ellipsis is most acceptable for the subject of informationally light unaccusative verbs and least acceptable for that of unergative verbs.

The present experiment compared the acceptability of case marking and case ellipsis on the contrastively focused subject of three subclasses of one-place predicates: unergative verbs, change of state unaccusative verbs and informationally light unaccusative verbs. Following Keller and Sorace (2003), 'unergative verbs' are defined here in semantic terms as intransitive verbs denoting a process-event and 'unaccusative verbs' as verbs denoting a non-process event (state or change). Although they do not differ each other morphologically in Korean, these two subtypes of intransitive verbs show very different discourse profiles in their accommodation of given and new information (see section 2) as well as different syntactic behaviors (Y. Kim 1990).

The two subclasses of unergative verbs were used in the experiment: verbs of uncontrolled process and verbs of controlled process. Verbs of uncontrolled process refer to involuntary reaction or non-volitional processes, i.e., processes not controlled by the subject (e.g., *ttelta* 'shiver' and *colta* 'fall asleep'), whereas verbs of controlled process denote volitional processes either not involving motion (e.g. *cata* 'sleep' and *ttetulta* 'make noise') , or involving motion (e.g., *talita* 'run' and *ttwyta* 'jump').

The unaccusative verbs used in this experiment are verbs denoting a change of state other than a change of location. Change of state verbs can be inherently telic, such as *cwukta* 'die' and *saracita* 'disappear' or they can denote an indefinite change of state with no explicit end point, e.g., *carata* 'grow' or *nulkta* 'become old'. This experiment also used the following three subclasses of informationally light unaccusative verbs: verbs of change of location, verbs of existence (of state) and verbs of continuation of state. Verbs denoting a change of location are inherently telic, and class members include verbs such as *ota* 'come', *kata* 'go', and *toraota* 'come back; return'. Verbs of existence of state include verbs denoting a concrete physical state (e.g. *issta* 'exist' and *epsta* 'not exist') and (complex) verbs denoting the maintenance of a position like *su-e issta* 'stand up' and *anc-a issta* 'lie down'. Verbs of continuation of state denote the continuation of a pre-existing state like *salta* 'live' and *namta* 'remain'. A sample stimulus is shown in (10):

(10) Example stimuli (unergative subject)

Instruction: Please read through the following conversations, then make a judgment on underlined sentences in each conversation by assigning them grades from 1-5. Use the following scale to make your judgments:

1 = Completely Unacceptable
2 = Unacceptable
3 = Just Barely Acceptable
4 = Acceptable
5 = Completely Acceptable

1) [Context: A and B are working on a joint class project with their friends, Youngmi and Minsoo. As soon as Youngmi and Minsoo went out for lunch, A and B start talking about them.]

A: ecey swuep-eyse Yengmi-ka col-ass-ci?
yesterday class-in Youngmi-Nom fall asleep-Pst-Int
'Is it Youngmi who fell asleep in class yesterday?'

B-1: ani, Minswu-ka col-ass-e.
no, Minsoo-Nom fall asleep-Pst-Ind
'No, it was Minsoo who fell asleep.' Your score: ______

B-2: ani, Minswu col-ass-e. no, Minsoo(-Nom) fall asleep-Pst-Ind 'No, it was Minsoo who fell asleep.' Your score: ______

60 students from a university in Seoul, ages 20-26, participated in the study. The procedure was the same as in the previous experiment. Each participant was asked to read short conversations between speakers and indicate to what degree the two argument forms were suitable in the given context. To do this, their task was to rate the acceptability of sentences containing a case-marked or case-ellipsed argument by assigning them grades from 1-5 on a five-point rating scale with 1 indicating completely unacceptable and 5 perfectly acceptable.

There were 15 items per each condition, and there were two versions of the target sentences of each item: one version contained a case-marked subject and the other version an unmarked subject. These 90 items were combined with 80 fillers belonging to another experiment. The stimuli and fillers were combined in three different orders for each list, to avoid ordering effect. Thus, the experiment followed 3 × 2 design, where the factors were 1) subject type (unergative subject vs. unaccusative subject (change of state verb) vs. subject of informationally light unaccusative verbs) and 2) subject form (case-marked vs. unmarked). The two versions of the target sentences (e.g., B-1 and B-2 in (10)) were presented in a factorial design so that half the participants saw 45 stimuli with a case-marked subject, and half saw 45 stimuli with an unmarked subject. Time of participation was approximately 30-35 minutes.

The mean judgments for the two forms of each argument role compared in this study are shown in Table 4 (The mean judgments for transitive subjects and direct objects are from H. Lee (2010a).). As expected from its intermediate status on the ANH, the S argument showed intermediate acceptability values for both forms (case marking: 3.85; case ellipsis: 2.47). For this argument type, we found a significant main effect of subject form ($F1(1, 177) = 170.21$, $p = .000$; $F2(1, 42) = 39.85$, $p = .000$). This indicates that the mean judgments for case-marked intransitive subjects are significantly higher than those for case-ellipsed intransitive subjects. The higher acceptability of case marking compared to case ellipsis is likely due to the (contrastive) focus status of the subjects.

(11) Table 4. Average ratings

	A	S	O
Case-marked	4.05	3.85	3.15
Case-ellipsed	1.27	2.47	3.47

The ANOVA also indicates a significant main effect of subject type in the subject analysis ($F1(2, 177) = 7.03, p = .001$ $F2(1, 42) = 1.09, p = .347$). As Table 5 shows, the mean judgments for the case-marked form are higher for the subject of unergative verbs (3.98) than for the subject of unaccusative verbs (change of state verbs: 3.88; informationally light unaccusative verbs: 3.60), whereas the mean judgments for the case-ellipsed form show the reverse pattern. This confirms our major prediction that case marking is most acceptable for the subject of unergative verbs, while case ellipsis is most acceptable for the subject of informationally light unaccusative verbs. We can observe that the three subtypes of intransitive subjects all prefer the case-marked form over the case-ellipsed form, but the subject of unergative verbs does so to a greater extent than that of unaccusative verbs.

(12) Table 5. Average ratings

	S_{unerg}	$S_{state\ change}$	S_{light}
Case-marked	3.98	3.88	3.60
Case-ellipsed	1.91	2.48	3.04

In summary, overall the data indicate that the degree of acceptability of case ellipsis on the focus subject of intransitive verbs correlates with the position of the argument on the ANH. As predicted, case ellipsis is most acceptable for the subject of informationally light unaccusative verbs and least acceptable for that of unergative verbs.

The correlation between newness and the higher acceptability of case ellipsis raises the question why case ellipsis is more acceptable for the argument roles that are more frequently associated with new information. We argue that this correlation is motivated by considerations of efficiency in language production and can be explained in terms of frequency asymmetry. It has long been noted that frequent words generally have shorter linguistic forms (Zipf 1935). More recent evidence suggests that word length (in phonemes or syllables) correlates even strongly with words' average predictability in context (Manin 2006; Piantadosi, Tily and Gibson 2009). This inverse link between probability and phonological form is expected given the nature of language as an efficient sign system in which costs correlate with signal length. The more probable (expected) a word is in its context, the more redundant it is. Hence, it is intuitively efficient to produce more probable instances of words with shorter duration, thereby trading off redundancy and reduction.

If language is organized to be efficient in that speakers prefer to avoid the articulation of complex material when its properties are readily inferable contextually, it is expected that the inverse link between probability/

predictability and linguistic form would be found in syntactic reduction as well, i.e., the form with more linguistic material should be less likely for more probable syntactic elements or for more predictable meanings or referents (Haiman 1983; Hawkins 2004). A growing body of research supports this idea, suggesting that potentially all levels of language could be organized to be efficient (see Jaeger (2006) for detailed discussion) and follow the following economy principles (Hawkins 2004; Haspelmath 2008):

(13) a. The more predictable a sign is, the shorter it is.
b. The more frequent a sign is, the shorter it is.

Evidence from syntactic reduction provides support for the pervasive effect of the principles in (13). In a study using a database of spontaneous English, Wasow et al. (in press) found that speakers are less likely to mention the relativizer *that* in non-subject-extracted relative clauses (e.g., *I like the way (that) it vibrates*) when the relative clause is predictable (see also Jaeger 2006). Further evidence comes from the optional *that*-mentioning in English complement clauses. Jaeger (2006) analyzed the same spontaneous database that was employed for the study by Wasow et al. (2011) and found that speakers are less likely to mention the complementizer *that* when the complement clause is predictable.

The data from Korean case ellipsis discussed in this study provides additional new support to the view that syntactic reduction follows the pattern of the inverse link between probability/frequency and linguistic form: case ellipsis for a focused NP is more acceptable for the argument type that has a high probability of accommodating new information, whereas case marking is more acceptable for the argument type that has a low probability of accommodating new information. Using case markers to mark less probable phrases has been argued to have a processing advantage (Jaeger 2010): when speakers use case markers to mark less probable phrase, they can buy more time to produce syntactic elements that are difficult to process and spread information on the phrase's grammatical (and discourse) function over a longer time, thereby leading to more uniform information density compared to leaving it unmarked. Thus, from the perspective of usage probability, the presence of case markers can be interpreted as a signal to expect the unexpected, a rational exchange of time for reduced information density or a meaningful delay.

4. Conclusion

The central hypothesis of this study was that the degree of acceptability of particle ellipsis on a focused argument NP correlates with the position of the argument on the ANH. On the basis of this hypothesis, this study addressed the questions whether the degree of acceptability of case ellipsis on a focused argument NP steadily increases according to the position of the argument on the ANH.

The results, on the whole, provide an affirmative answer to this question. In H. Lee (2009, 2010a), we compared speakers' judgments for sentences which contain the case-marked or case-ellipsed form of an A argument and sentences with a case-marked or a case-ellipsed form of an O argument. The results provide clear support for the view that the degree of acceptability of particle ellipsis on the focused argument NP correlates with its position on the ANH. Case ellipsis is more acceptable for the focused O argument whereas case marking is more acceptable for the focused A argument.

The experiment reported in section 4 provides additional evidence for the correlation of the degree of acceptability of case ellipsis on the focused argument NP with its position on the ANH. We found that the S arguments exhibit intermediate acceptability of both case marking and case ellipsis. It was also found that as predicted, case ellipsis is most acceptable for the subject of informationally light unaccusative verbs and least acceptable for that of unergative verbs. These findings lend support to the view that language users' intuitions of acceptability in context are probability-sensitive in that their preferences are affected by the usage probability of properties of argument NPs and that native speakers' knowledge of grammar includes access to fine-grained probability (Bresnan 2007; Bresnan and Ford 2010).

References

Bresnan, J. 2007. Is Knowledge of Syntax Probabilistic? Experiments with the English Dative Alternation. *Roots: Linguistics in Search of Its Evidential Base* (Studies in Generative Grammar), eds. S. Featherston and W. Sternefeld, 75-96. Berlin: Mouton de Gruyter.

Bresnan, J. and M. Ford 2010. Predicting Syntax: Processing Dative Constructions in American and Australian Varieties of English. *Language* 86:168-213.

Haiman, J. 1983. The Iconicity of Grammar. *Language* 56:515-540.

Haspelmath, M. 2008. Frequency vs. Iconicity in Explaining Grammatical Asymmetries. *Cognitive Linguistics* 19:1-33.

Hawkins, J. 2004. *Efficiency and Complexity in Grammar.* Oxford: Oxford University Press.

Jaeger, F. T. 2006. Redundancy and Syntactic Reduction in Spontaneous Speech. Doctoral dissertation, Stanford University.

Jaeger, F. T. 2010. Redundancy and Reduction: Speakers Manage Syntactic Information Density. *Cognitive Psychology* 61:23-61.

Keller, F. and A. Sorace. 2003. Gradient Auxiliary Selection and Impersonal Passivization in German: An Experimental Investigation. *Journal of Linguistics* 39:57-108.

Kim, T. 2008. Subject and Object Markings in Conversational Korean. Doctoral dissertation, State University of New York at Buffalo.

Kim, Y. 1990. The Syntax and Semantics of Korean Case: The Interaction between Lexical and Syntactic Levels of Representation. Doctoral dissertation, Harvard University.

Ko, E.-S. 2000. A Discourse Analysis of the Realization of Objects in Korean. *Japanese/Korean Linguistics* 9:195-208. Stanford: CSLI Publications.

Lee, D.-Y. 2002. The Function of the Zero Particle with Special Reference to Spoken Japanese. *Journal of Pragmatics* 34:645-682.

Lee, H. 2009. Contrastive Focus and Variable Case Marking: A Comparison between Subjects and Objects. *Language and Information* 13:1-27.

Lee, H. 2010a. Explaining Variation in Korean Case Ellipsis: Economy versus Iconicity. *Journal of East Asian Linguistics* 19:291-318.

Lee, H. 2010b. Usage Probability and Gradients in Korean Case Ellipsis: An Experimental Investigation. Manuscript under review.

Manin, D. 2006. Experiments on Predictability of Word in Context and Information Rate in Natural Language. *Journal of Information Processes* 6:229-236.

Masunaga, K. 1988. Case Deletion and Discourse Context. *Papers from International Workshop on Japanese Syntax*, ed. W. Poser, 145-156. Stanford: CSLI Publications.

Ono, T., S. A. Thompson, and R. Suzuki. 2000. The Pragmatic Nature of the So-called Subject Marker *ga* in Japanese: Evidence from Conversation. *Discourse Studies* 2:55-84.

Piantadosi, S., H. Tily and E. Gibson. 2009. The Communicative Lexicon Hypothesis. Paper presented at 22nd Annual CUNY Conference on Human Sentence Processing, UC Davis.

Tsutsui, M. 1984. Particle Ellipsis in Japanese. Doctoral dissertation, University of Illinois at Urbana-Champaign.

Wasow, T., F. T. Jager, and D. Orr. 2011. Lexical Variation in Relativizer Frequency. *Expecting the Unexpected: Exceptions in Grammar*, eds. H. Wiese and H. Simon, 175-196. Berlin and New York: Mouton de Gruyter.

Yatabe, S. 1999. Particle Ellipsis and Focus Projection in Japanese. *Language, Information, Text*, vol. 6:79-104. Department of Language and Information Sciences, University of Tokyo.

Zipf, G. 1935. *The Psycho-Biology of Language. An Introduction to Dynamic Philology*. Cambridge: The Riverside Press.

A Decompositional Approach to Japanese Passive

TAKASHI NAKAJIMA*
Toyama Prefectural University

There is a long held assumption that passives in Japanese are derived with a single morpheme *(r)are* that is taken either as a suffix or a verb. This paper argues that analyses that are based upon this assumption cannot adequately explain the true nature of the constructions. It argues instead that *(r)are* must be decomposed into constituting parts, *a, e* and *r* in which *a* and *e* are the grammaticalized verbal roots of the copula *a-ru* 'be' and *e-ru* 'get' (Nakajima, to appear). *r* is the 'elsewhere' consonant (Kuginuki 1985, Labrune 2005). They appear in the designated head positions in Root Domain (RD), a syntactic structure in which a root appears. These heads compositionally derive various types of passive. This is schematized in (1) below.[1]

---

* I am indebted to a number of people for informative and stimulating discussions that brought substantial improvements to this paper. They include Hiroshi Aoyagi, Yukinori Takubo, John Whitman, Shin Fukuda, Masahiro Yamada, Ji Young Shim, Nozomi Tanaka, Hideaki Yamashita, Chai-song Hong as well as anonymous reviewers. All errors and shortcomings are of course mine.

[1] I exclude TP and CP domains since they do not play an immediate role in the syntax and the semantics of the passives.

Japanese/Korean Linguistics 21.
Edited by Seungho Nam, Heejeong Ko and Jongho Jun.

(1)

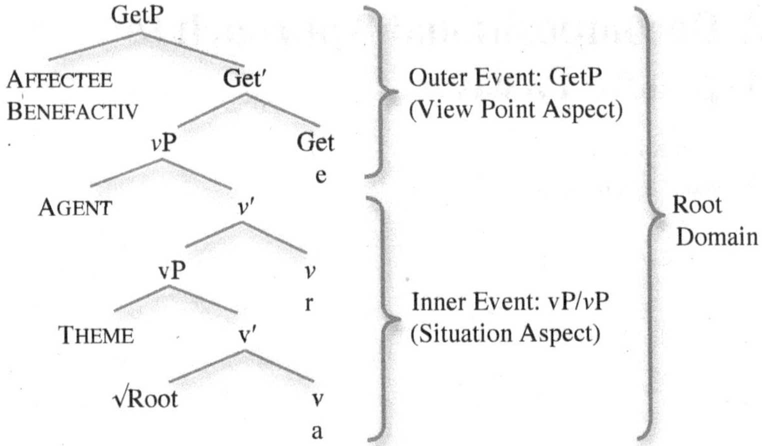

Starting from the bottom, v is 'little' v (Maranz 1997) that types the category neutral root as verb. A THEME argument appears in the spec of this head if the root is either transitive or unaccusative. If the root is unergative, the spec vP position does not appear. *v* is the 'small' v (or v*, Chomsky 2001) that determines the basic predicate type that the root creates. It licenses an AGENT in its spec position if the root is either transitive or unergative. If the root is unaccusative, the spec *v*P position is not licensed. vP and *v*P together constitute the Inner Event where basic semantics of the event including Aktionsart is established (Kratzer 2006, Ramchand 2008). It is thus equivalent to Situation Aspect (Smith 1997). In passive, *v* has the phonetic exponent *r*, and this is the heart of passive: it generates a conventional implicature that relates the event in *v*P onto GetP above it (Bosse et al. to appear). This is the source of the affectedness interpretation.

GetP is a projection that has *e*, the root of the verb *e-ru* 'get' [2]. It licenses an NP that is interpreted as AFFECTEE or BENEFACTIVE depending on the implicature *v*P makes. This projection constitutes the Outer Event, which is roughly equivalent to View Point Aspect (Smith, ibid.). 'Little' v, 'small' *v* and Get compositionally syntacticize the arguments of the root in the form of passive and derive relevant semantics in RD. [3] In what follows,

---

[2] This *e* could be taken as the adverbial form of another (archaic) verb *u* 'get'. I do not discuss this issue here since nothing hinges upon this point.

[3] See Chomsky (2007: 21) for the possibility that v and *v* (v*) heads are affixal. The √Root position (as well as the spec positions) in (1) is radically empty (de Belder 2011) in narrow syntax. Relevant lexical itemss are inserted post-syntactically at PF following the 'Y' model proposed by Distributed Morphology. I further assume that each spec agrees with its sister at the point of merger by adjacency (Bobaljik & Thráinsson 1998) for argument licensing.

I will show how the structure in (1) explains various types of passive in Japanese. Let us begin with examining two different types of passive first.

1. Two Types of Passive

Passives in Japanese have been under heavy scrutiny for decades, and basically three different approaches have been proposed in the literature: they are uniform, non-uniform and mixed approaches. They are so named according to how they treat what is called the 'direct' and the 'indirect' passives in (2a) and (2b), respectively, below.

(2) a. Direct Passive
Taro ga Hanako ni ø ker- are- ta.
NOM by kick-PASS-PST
'Taro was kicked by Hanako.'
b. Indirect Passive
Taro ga Hanako ni kai-inu o ker- are- ta
NOM by care-dog ACC kick-PASS-PST
'Taro got his dog kicked by Hanako.'

The direct passive is similar to the 'be' passive in English where the direct object becomes the passive subject, and the original object position is left as a gap ('ø'). Furthermore, the subject in the active counterpart becomes oblique in passive. In Japanese the oblique subject is marked with *ni*, the Japanese equivalent of the English 'by' phrase.

The indirect passive has puzzled grammarians. First, the promotion of the THEME argument does not occur as in (2b) where the THEME *kai-inu* 'dog' bears the syntactic ACC case marker *o*. Second, as a consequence, there is no gap that is observed in the direct passive. Third, there is a new argument AFFECTEE that is often adversely affected by the event. In other words, the valence of the predicate increases rather than decreases (Shibatani 1990).

The focus of researchers on the Japanese passives is concentrated on the function of *(r)are*, the morpheme presumably introduces this complex state of affairs. The uniform theorists (Hasegawa 1964, Kuroda 1979, 1985, Kuno 1983, Kitagawa & Kuroda 1992 and others) maintain that *(r)are* is a verb, and both the indirect and the direct passives take the form of sentential complementation. According to this view, the direct passive is a special kind of indirect passive in that it contains an empty category in the object position. This empty category (*pro*) is coindexed with the passive subject.

The non-uniform theorists (Kuno 1973, Harada 1973, Inoue 1976, Shibatani 1990 and others) contest this claim and argue that *(r)are* actually is homonymous between a verb and the passive suffix. *(r)are* as a verb derives the indirect passive in much the same way as the uniform theory does. *(r)are* as a passive suffix, however, behaves more like English *-ed* in that it absorbs ACC case, assigns no θ-role to subject and triggers NP movement.

The mixed approach theorists (Hoshi 1991, Goro 2006 and others) argue that both the uniform and the non-uniform analyses are partially right in analyzing the direct passive. The subject status of the *-ni* phrase in the uniform theory cannot explain the *zibun* binding facts. Similarly, the adjunct status of the *-ni* phrase in the embedded clause in the non-uniform theory fails to explain why *-ni yotte* 'owning to' instead of *-ni* is required when the passive subject is immutable.[4] Thus, they propose a mixed approach that treats *(r)are* as V in line with the uniform theory, but also claim that the empty category in the object position of the embedded clause is PRO, which moves subsequently to the subject position within the same clause. It is then coindexed with the passive subject that *(r)are* licenses.

The basic strategy of the previous analyses is that they take *(r)are* as a *single* passive morpheme, and employ various syntactic apparatuses to account for the complex state of affairs. The analysis that will be developed here takes a completely different approach: *(r)are* consists of a series of independent argument licensing heads. One of the reasons for this move is that as soon as one assumes that *(r)are* is a single morpheme, be as it may verb or suffix, it makes other related agglutinative predicate formations opaque. For instance, *a, e,* and *r* independently appear in the paradigm of 'lexical' inchoative–transitive alternations (Jacobsen 1992, e.g., *tat-u* 'stand up$^{\text{intr.}}$' vs. *tat-**e** ru* 'stand$^{\text{tr.}}$'). If one treats *(r)are* as a single morpheme, it would simply be another morpheme that is independently listed in the lexicon, and as a result, this blocks a meaningfully incisive analysis on agglutination. The RD analysis proposed here makes it possible to treat them as grammatical continuum. Note also that RD derives a single predicate with a unique root that is isomorphic between syntax and morphology. That is, on the one hand the root and the heads *a, r* and *e* are analyzed as a passive predicate in syntax, they are interpreted as a prosodic 'word' at PF on the other. This means that the question whether *(r)are* is a suffix or verb disappears. This is another important advantage of the current analysis.

A good example to see how the analysis works at the morphological level would be the root √*tukam-* 'grab'. Examine the following paradigm, which exhaustively shows the agglutinative patterns that involves *a, e* and *r*.

[4] We will come back to the *zibun* binding and *-ni*/*-ni yotte* distinction in Sections 3 and 4 below, respectively.

(3) Table 1

Root	V	*v*	Get	Tense	Semantics
a. √tukam-				u	grab
b. √tukam-	a			ru	hold onto
c. *√tukam-		r			----
d. √tukam-	a	r		u	get caught
e. √tukam-			e	ru	be able to grab
f. √tukam-	a		e	ru	catch
g. *√tukam-		r	e		----
h. √tukam-	a	r	e	ru	get grabbed, be able to grab

Since there are three heads, and each head could either be null or overt, the theory predicts that there are eight (2^3) combinatory possibilities altogether. Of the predicted eight forms, however, only six are actually attested while the remaining two, namely (3c) and (3g), are not.

The reason for the exclusion of (3c) and (3g) is phonetic: Japanese does not allow CC hiatus. In these examples, the root final consonant /*m*/ and the phonetic exponent /*r*/ in *v* make /*mr*/ sequence, which is not possible in this language. The six attested ones are given interpretations.

When none of the heads appears, it is a simple transitive (3a), and this is the default case. An interesting contrast is seen between (3b) and (3d) where *r* appears either as a part of the present tense *-ru* or the head of *v*. In the case of the former, the root shares its accentuation pattern with the default (3a) in that the pitch rises at the second mora as in *tukám-u*. In the case of the latter, however, the root loses the pitch contour, and the derived word *tukam-a-r-ø u* is pitch-less. The positions where *r* appears presumably trigger the distinction. In fact, (3h) that has *r* in *v* is also pitch-less. Note, importantly, that (3d) and (3h) in which *r* appears as *v* head are exactly the cases in which the passive meaning arises. This is consistent with the long held assumption among the traditional and the generative grammarians alike that *r* induces passivity/inchoativity. (3h) is interesting in its own right: it is ambiguous between passive and potential interpretations, but this is precisely what we expect due to the presence of both passive *r* and the potential *e* 'get' (cf. 3e).[5]

Importantly, the analysis in (3) cuts across lexicon and syntax. In addition to the default (3a), (3b) *tukam-a-ø-ø ru* 'hold onto' and (3d) *√tukam-a-r-ø u* 'get caught' (3f) *√tukam-a-ø-e ru* 'catch' are all considered

[5] The theory makes a strong prediction in that there are at most eight agglutinative patterns per root. Not all the possibilities are utilized; however, due to independent constraints as in (3). Whether this prediction is correct or not needs to be tested with thorough research.

lexical while the potential (3e) √*tukam-ø-ø-e ru* 'be able to grab' and the passive/potential (3h) √*tukam-a-r-e ru* 'get grabbed, be able to grab' are derived. It is not clear what makes this distinction in intuition; however, the late insertion model under DM makes this unified account possible.

Another crucial point that needs to be addressed here is that *r* could alternate with *s* in (3d) and (3h) and derive causative predicates. (See (6) below.) The complementarity of *r* and *s* suggests that they compete for the same position, namely *v*. This analysis supports the idea that *(r)are* and *(s)ase* are ultimately related morpho-syntactically (Nishiyama 1998). As shown, the current approach brings a new insight into the phenomenon of agglutination that has never been possible before.[6]

2. Direct and Indirect Passive

Let us turn our attention now to how the theory explains each type of passive syntactically. The direct and the indirect passives in (2a) and (2b) have the structures (4a) and (4b), respectively.

(4)

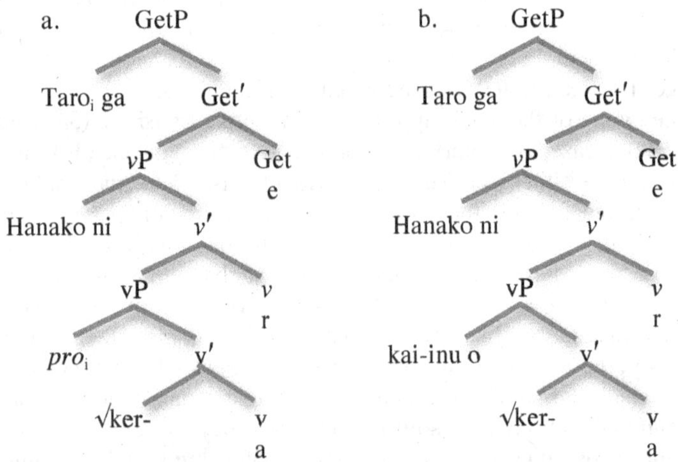

In (4a), the direct object is a base generated *pro* (Kitagawa & Kuroda 1992) that is coindexed with the subject in GetP. This is called the direct passive

[6] The analysis in (3) has diachronic consequences as well. For example, the root √*tukam-* could further be decomposed into √*tuk-*$^{tr.}$ 'attach, supply', *a* and *m*. The reason for this analysis is the existence of derivations of the following type with *m*, which is presumably a part of the pre-OJ causative morpheme *sim-u*.

(i) a. √*har-* 'bloated' → √*har-a-m u* 'impregnated'
b. √*kar-* 'wear' (Eastern dialect in OJ) → √*kar-a-m u* 'entangle'

The derived words are now conceived as listed. This suggests that a derived RD could be reanalyzed as a single root. Similar cases of reanalysis can be seen in causative pairs such as √*ki-ru* 'ware' → √*ki-s-e ru* 'put on' or √*mi-ru* 'see' → √*mi-s-e ru* 'show' (Frellesvig 2010: 63).

because the passive subject *Taro* is the same as the THEME in *v*P. Thus, *Taro* is directly affected by the action *Hanako* takes. The structure dictates that Taro got into a situation in which *Hanako* was an agent who kicked him. He has no control over this event, and this is exactly what (4a) (=2a) means. Note that although this is similar to the English type passive in terms of its interpretation, the grammar is very different. First, there is no ACC case absorption. Second, as a result, no movement takes place. Third, the agent θ-role is assigned to the external argument *Hanako* as in ordinary transitive sentences.

(4b) is the syntactic representation of the indirect passive (2b). Note that there is no gap and ACC case is available to the THEME. Consequently, NP movement does not take place since there is no motivation for it. In terms of semantics, the sentence means something like *Taro* had a situation in which *Hanako* was the agent, and she kicked his dog. Again, *Taro* has no control over the event. If these analyses are correct, the direct and the indirect passives differ minimally with the overtness and the coindexiation of the THEME argument. This is basically what Kitagawa & Kuroda (1992) argue. They postulate the following schematic bi-eventive representation for both types of passive (Kitagawa & Kuroda (ibid: 37).

(5) *rare*: [EXPERIENCER/AGENT [EVENTUALITY ____]]

The current RD based approach can be seen as a Minimalist reinterpretation of their insight.

With respect to the affectedness interpretation, it arises due to the bilateral relations between the Inner Event in *v*P and the Outer Event of GetP. On this point, Bosse et al (to appear: 19) proposes an insightful analysis in which the affectedness interpretation on passive subject arises because of the function of a conventional implicature. More specifically, the head Aff(ected), which is their equivalent of our Get, "takes the event property denoted by its sister constituent to be the source of the affected experiencer's experience via a conventional implicature."[7] Here, the sister constituent is to be taken as the [EVENTUALITY ____] in (5) or the Inner Event *v*P in RD.

I further add, however, that the head Aff or Get alone is not sufficient to bring the affectedness interpretation in the passives. This can be seen in the Causative–Passive "minimal pair" in (6).

[7] The affectedness relation is analyzed as follows (Bosse et al. to appear: 20).

(i) a. $[\![\text{Aff}]\!] = \lambda P_{vt}.\ \lambda x.\ \lambda e.\ P(e)\ \&\ \exists e'\ (\text{exper}(e')\ \&\ \text{Exp}(x)(e') : \forall e''(P(e'') \rightarrow \text{Source}(e'')(e')) \in D_{<vt,\, evt>}$

b. $\text{Source} \rightarrow \lambda e.\ \lambda e'.$ e is the source of e′

Conventional implicature is represented after the colon ':' in (ia).

(6) a. Taro ga Hanako ni musuko o sikar- a -***r***- e- ta.
NOM by his son ACC scole- v-*v*-GET PAST
'Taro got his son scold by Hanako'

b. Taro ga Hanako ni musuko o sikar- a -***s***- e- ta.
NOM by his son ACC scole- v-*v*-GET PAST
'Taro made Hanako scold his son.'

(6a) and (6b) differ only with the single consonant *r* in the former and *s* in the latter, yet the interpretations differ completely in that the former is passive while the latter is causative. Since both the passive and the causative morphemes *(r)are* and *(s)ase* contain the head of GetP *e*, the emergence of the conventional implicature in passive must partially be attributed to *r* in *v*P. This fact strongly supports our decompositional approach to complex predicates.[8]

Finally, I would like to add another piece of evidence that supports our decompositional approach to the passives in Japanese. The evidence comes from a commonly observed colloquial speech style called '*ra*-dropping'. Consider (7), which has a potential reading.

(7) Kono ringo, bukakkoo da kedo, tabe-re ru yo.
this apple funny shaped COP but eat-POT. IMPF. PCL
'This apple looks funny but is edible, I assure you.'

The predicate in (7) is considered phonetically reduced from *tabe-**ra**re-ru* in that the *-ra-* part in the suffix is elided. '*ra*-dropping' makes perfect sense since, first, the form disambiguates it from the homophonous passive sibling, and second, *e* in Get is sufficient enough to convey the potential interpretation with the BENEFACTIVE argument in its spec. '*ra*' in v is thus superfluous and affects neither the grammaticality nor the interpretation. Recall that *v* could be null in potential as in (3e) $\surd$*tukam-ø-ø-e ru* 'being able to grab'. This means that *r* appears as the elsewhere consonant in *v* to break the VV hiatus *ee* in (7) at PF. Without the internal decomposition, it would be difficult to give '*ra*-dropping' an insightful and satisfactory explanation.

To sum up, I have shown that the two types of passive in Japanese are extremely compositional, and the morpho-syntactic and morpho-semantic coherency is brought in by the isomorphism between syntax and morphology and the conventional implicature that *v*P creates. In the next two sections, I will take up other long-standing problems in Japanese passives, namely, *zibun* binding and *-ni/ni yotte* distinctions in the *by*-phrase.

---

[8] See Nakajima (to appear) for an early adaptation of the decompositional approach to the lexical inchoative–transitive alternations and causative in Japanese.

3. *Zibun* Binding

It is well known that the Japanese reflexive pronoun *zibun* is generally bound with a subject. This property, however, is relativized in the passives. See (8a) and (8b) for the direct and indirect passive, respectively.

(8) a. Taro$_i$ ga Hanako$_j$ ni ø$_i$ [zibun$_{i/*j}$ no heya de] koros are ta.
NOM by self GEN room LOC kill-PASS PAST
'Taro was killed by Hanako in his room.'

b. Taro$_i$ ga Hanako$_j$ ni [zibun$_{i/j}$ no heya de] sin- are ta.
NOM by self GEN room LOC die-CAUSE PAST
'Hanako died in his room, and Taro was adversely affected by it.'

The reflexive *zibun* in the locative vP adjunct [*zibun no heya de*] "in self's room" is bound only with the passive subject *Taro* in the direct passive (8a) but, it is bound either with the passive subject *Taro* or the oblique agent *Hanako* in the indirect passive (8b). This fact has been used to support the non-uniform analysis (Shibatani 1990). The uniform analysis has difficulty especially with (8a) since it cannot explain why *zibun* is insensitive to *Hanako* even though it is the agent in the active counterpart.

The key to understanding the situation, I believe, is the bi-eventuality of the passives. Note in (8a), the passive subject in GetP *Taro* is also the THEME whose position is indicated by 'ø'. This makes GetP and *v*P one coherent unit of eventuality. In fact, the GetP event of the affectedness of *Taro* and the *v*P event of *Hanako*'s killing of him must be simultaneous. This cohesiveness of events makes *Taro* the "grammatical" subject, the subject a predicate requires. Assuming that there is only one subject per eventuality, *zibun* is insensitive to the *ni*-marked oblique *v*P subject *Hanako*. As a result, only the grammatical subject *Taro* binds it.

In the indirect passive in (8b), there is no gap and the Outer Event (GetP) and the Inner Event (*v*P) remain independent. This separation can easily be verified by the semantics; it is not difficult to imagine a situation in which *Taro* did not know that *Hanako* died for, say, ten years let alone where it happened. Under these circumstances, there are two subjects: *Taro*, which is the "major" subject in the sense of Kuroda (1986), and *Hanako,* which is the grammatical subject in *v*P. The former is predicated by *v*P as a syntactic effect of the conventional implicature as we have seen above. These two subjects could equally bind *zibun*, and this is the source of the ambiguity that is observed only in the indirect passive.

3.1 Unaccusative Roots

The *zibun* binding shows that the eventuality of *v*P plays a crucial role in the passives. This makes a prediction that if *v* is inactive and the Inner

Event is not established, passive is impossible. The prediction is borne out since unaccusative verbs that lack active *v* are not able to be made passive in general. See the following examples.

(9) Table 2

a. √oti-	'fall'	*oti-rare ru
b. √kusar-	'rot'	*kusar-are-ru
c. √toke-	'melt [intr.]'	*toke-rare-ru
d. √uk-	'float'	*uk-are-ru

The root √*uk*- 'float', for example, would make the following direct and indirect passive sentences, but they are all ungrammatical.

(10) a. Direct Passive
   *Fune ga uk-are-ta.
   boat NOM float-PASS-PST
   *'The boat was floated.'
  b. Indirect Passive
   *Taro ga fune ni uk-are-ta.
   NOM boat by float-PASS-PST
   *'Taro got a boat floated on.'

Their structures would look like the following.

(11)

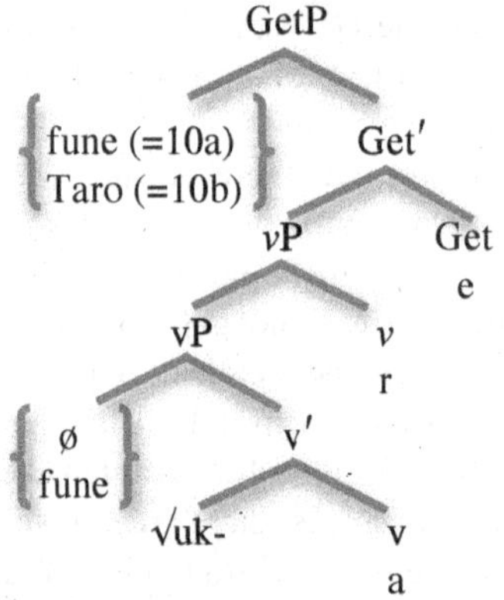

The unaccusative root √*uk*- has only THEME argument in spec, vP. In addition, the lack of active *v* makes the *v*P eventuality defective or incomplete. These conditions cause the following consequences. In the direct passive of a transitive root, a THEME becomes an AFFECTEE through affectedness that the subject in spec *v*P brings about as external force. With unaccusative roots, however, THEME goes under a change of state by itself and appears as AFFECTEE on the surface. Thus, the lack of involvement of external force in unaccusative roots does not satisfy the conditions for the direct passive formation. In addition, an incomplete and defective *v*P cannot predicate a Major subject in GetP since such predication requires an agent. That means that an indirect passive cannot be formed.[9]

As we can see here, the proposed analysis gives a convincing argument for the impossibility of unaccusative roots to be passivized, which gives further support to the decompositional approach. In the next section, I would like to analyze another long-standing problem of *-ni/-ni yotte* distinction.

4. *-ni/-ni yotte* Distinction

Kuroda (1979) points out that when the passive subject is immutable, the *by*-phrase in Japanese passive must be the *-ni yotte* 'owning to' variant rather than the simple *-ni* variant.

(12) a. Kaikai$_i$ ga gichyo ni *(yotte) ø$_i$ sengens are ta.
opening NOM chair person by declare PASS PAST
'The opening (of the event) was declared by the chairperson.'

b. Sensei$_i$ ga gakusei ni (yotte) ø$_i$ hinans are ta.
teacher NOM students by criticize PASS PAST
'The teacher was criticized by the students.'

In (12a) in which the subject *kaikai* 'opening' is immutable, the agent introducing by-phrase must be *-ni yotte*. This is not the case in (12b) where the passive subject is not immutable. Kuroda (ibid.) argues that (12a) is a different type of passive that is neither the direct nor the indirect passive since the uniform theory is not capable of explaining the fact.

Under the current analysis, the postulation of another type of passive is not necessary. To see this, let us first see the nature of the particle *-ni* that attaches to the agent in *v*P. It is well known that *-ni* alternates with NOM marker *-ga* in stative predicates. See the following sentence with Multiple Nominative Construction (MNC).

(13) Taro ga/ni Furaunsugo ga wakar- u (koto).
NOM/DAT French NOM understand PRS. fact
'the fact that Taro understands French.'

The appearance of this particle on the *v*P subject in passive is natural since passive is generally a stative predicate. In other words, passive changes an

[9] The analysis here gives a reliable diagnostic test for unaccusativity. Namely, an intransitive root is unaccusative if indirect passive cannot be formed from it. If this is correct, the root √*sin-* 'die' in (8b) is unergative. See Kageyama (1996), Kishimoto (2000), Kuno & Takami (2004) and others sited there for detailed analysis of unaccusativity in Japanese.

otherwise active *v*P into a stative one, and this is presumably why the agent is marked with *-ni*. If the anticipated change of state or affectedness occurs on the THEME, passive is well formed. This is why (12b) with the animate passive subject *sensei* 'teacher' is grammatical.

(12a) is, however, different. The passive subject *kaikai* 'opening' is abstract and is neither affected nor goes under any change of state. That is, the agent is ineffective and cannot bring about the expected affectedness or a change of state on the passive subject. As a result, the conventional implicature of *v*P cannot be generated. This is the source of the oddity with the ungrammatical *-ni* marking.

This being said, however, the syntax of passive forces such interpretation due to the fact that *kaikai* 'opening' is both the passive subject and the THEME in *v*P. (12a) after all consists of one unified eventuality. To solve the discrepancy, grammar makes the *v*P subject a SOURCE argument with *-ni yotte* 'owning to'. See the following sentence that shows a typical use of this item.

(14) Kono ziken wa Yamada kisya **ni yotte** saishyo ni tutae-rare-ta.
this case TOP reporter by first at report-PASS-PST
'This case was first reported by Yamada.'
(Kuno 1983: 199, slightly modified)

Here, *-ni yotte* phrase introduces the source of the report *Yamada*. Thus, I claim that the *-ni*/*-ni yotte* distinctioin is largely semantic in nature in line with Inoue (1976) and Kuno (1983).

A piece of supporting evidence for this analysis comes from the passivization of ditransitive verbs. Ditransitve verbs bring two possibilities for the passive subject; one is the direct object (DO) and the other the indirect object (IO). Interestingly, *-ni yotte* is obligatory for either case.

(15) a. Medaru$_i$ ga zaidan ni *(yotte) $\emptyset_i$ Taro ni atae- rare- ta.
medal NOM foundation by DAT award-PASS-PST.
'A medal was awarded to Taro by the foundation.'

b. Taro$_i$ ga zaidan ni $^{?}$*(yotte) $\emptyset_i$ medaru o atae- rare- ta.
NOM foundation by medal ACC award-PASS-PST.
'Taro was awarded a medal by the foundation.'

This is puzzling since the expected affectedness or change of state did take place: in (15a) the DO *medaru* 'medal' changed possession, and in (15b) *Tanaka* was affected (rather favorably) by the action of the foundation.

I believe that the reason of this restriction is disambiguation. The particle *ni* is extremely homophonous and is used for introducing AGENT, GOAL, or LOCATION. Therefore, when DO is passivized as in (15a), the two remaining NPs, AGENT and GOAL, could both bear *ni* with the *v* head licensing the former while the Appl(icative) head doing the latter. See (16a).

(16)

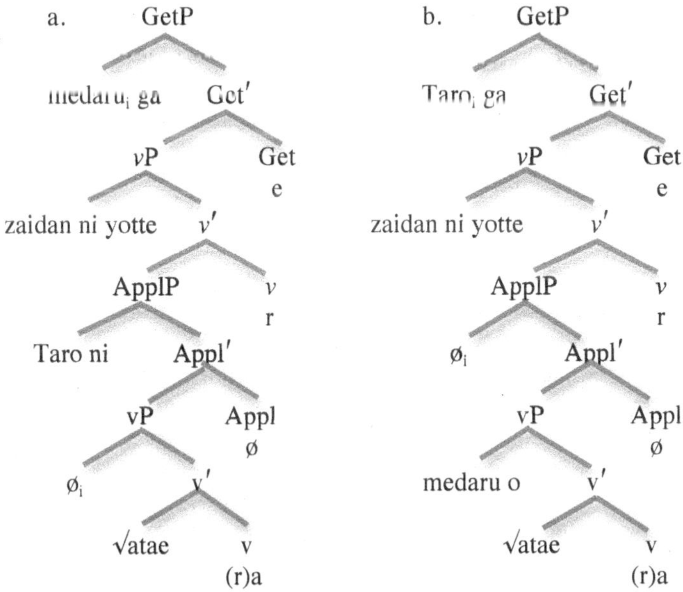

The Appl head does not have phonetic exponents, but it is nonetheless capable of licensing an argument with *-ni* since it is the designated particle used. Having two *ni*-attached NPs, however, is not allowed.

(17) *NP-ni NP-ni

As a result, the *v*P subject is marked with *-ni yotte* for agency/source. I assume that the same mechanism is responsible for (15b) and (16b). Interestingly, a similar situation occurs in Korean as well. Sohn (1999: 370–371) shows that when *hanthey*, the regular agentive particle in passive, could be interpreted as locative or goal, "the idiomatic phrase *ey uyha.ye(se)* or *ey uyhay(se)* 'by, owning to, in accordance with' is used."

(18) ce kenmul un cwuin **ey uyhayse** hak.kyo ey phal-ly-see-ta.
that building TC owner by school to sell-PASS-PST-DC.
'The building over there was sold to the school by the owner.'

The replacement of *ey uyhayse* with regular *hanthey* could either result in ungrammaticality or change in meaning. The parallelism between Japanese and Korean is not surprising given the fact that these two languages share so many characteristics of agglutination in morpho-syntax.

5. Conclusion and Further Topics

In this paper, I gave an analysis of Japanese passive under a decompositional view of the morpheme *(r)are*. The analysis gives us a very natural account for the two types of passive as well as other related issues as we have seen above. I also showed that grammaticalization plays an important role in agglutination morpho-syntactically. These results give us very incisive and comprehensive theory of predicate formation both diachronically and synchronically.

Although I believe that the approach I took in this work is correct, there are some remaining issues. For example, it asks a fundamental question about the relations between forms and meaning. I.e., is there a limited number of hard-wired structures that languages use (Borer 2005), or are structures secondary to possible feature compositions? Another issue concerns diachronic point of view. The analysis developed here could shed a new light on the development of lexical items in the language (See fn. 7 above.). If that is on the right track, it strongly suggests that the same mechanism for predicate formation has been used continuously throughout its history. Although there is a limitation as to how far back we could go in terms of the origin of language, it could provide an interesting piece of information about how it evolved. (Chomsky 2007). Another question has to do with cross-linguistic variations. I proposed that there are three independent heads in RD in Japanese. Other languages may differ as to how these features to be morpho-syntactically materialized under the view that UG could assemble a head with different features (Bobaljik & Thréinsson 1998). I leave these and other related issues for future research.

References

Bobaljik J.D. & H. Thréinsson. 1998. Two Heads Aren't Always Better than One. *Syntax*. Vol. 1–1. 37–71. Oxford: Blackwell.

Borer, Hasit. 2005. *Structuring Sense, Vol. I & II*. Oxford: Oxford University Press.

Bosse, Solveig, B. Bruening & M. Yamada. To appear. Affected Experiencers. *NLLT*. Berlin: Springer.

Chomsky, Norm. 2001. Derivation by Phase. *Ken Hale: A Life in Language*. ed. Kenstowicz, 1–52. M. Cambridge, MA: MIT Press.

Chomsky, Norm. 2007. Approaching UG from Below. *Interface + Recursion = Language?* eds. Sauerland, Uli & H-M Gärtner. 1–29. Berlin: de Gruyter.

de Belder, Borijke. 2011. *Roots and Affixes: Eliminating Lexical Categories from Syntax*. Ph.D. Dissertation. Amsterdam: LOT.

Frellesvig, Bjarke. 2010. *A History of the Japanese Language*. Cambridge, UK: Cambridge University Press.

Inoue, Kazuko. 1976. *Henkeibunpo to Nihongo*. Tokyo: Taishukan.

Kageyama, Taro. 1996. *Doushi Imiron*. Tokyo: Kroshio Syuppan.

Kishimoto, Hideki. 2000. Hitaikakusei Saiko. *Nitieigo no Zita no Kootai*. eds. Maruyama, T. & K. Suga. 71–110. Tokyo: Hitsuji Shyobo.

Kitagawa, Yoshihisa & Kuroda, S.Y. 1992. *Passive in Japanese*. (ms. Version 5.2.). University of Rochester and UCSD.

Krazter, Angelika. 1996. Serving external argument from the verb. *Phrase Structure and the Lexicon*. eds. Rooryck, J. & L. Zaring. 109–137. Dordrecht: Kluwer.

Kuginuki, Toru. 1982. Zyodai Nihongo 'Ra'-gyo Onko. *Toyama University Kiyo 6*: 37-51. Toyama: Toyama University.

Kuno, Susumu. 1983. *The Structure of Japanese Language*. Cambridge, MA: MIT Press.

Kuno, S. & K. Takami. 2004. *Functional Constraints in Grammar*. Amsterdam: John Benjamins.

Kuroda, S-Y. (1979). On Japanese Passives. *Exploration in Linguistics: Papers in honor of Kazuko Inoue*. eds. Bedell, G., E. Kobayashi & M. Muraki. 305–347. Tokyo: Kaitakusya.

Kuroda, S.Y. 1988. Whether We Agree or Not. *Japanese Syntax*. ed. Poser, William J. 103–143. Stanford: CSLI Publications.

Labrune, Laurence. 2005. *The Phonology of Japanese /r/: a panchronic account*. (ms.). Université Bordeaux 3 & CNRS.

Maranz, Alec. 1997. No Escape from Syntax: Don't Try Morphological Analysis in the Privacy of Your Own Lexicon. *University of Pennsylvania Working Papers in Linguistics Vol. 4.2*. 201–225. Philadelphia: UPenn Department of Linguistics

Nakajima, Takashi. to appear. Morpho-Syntactic Transparency of *(S)ase* and GetP. *Proceedings of the 19th Japanese/Korean Linguistics Conference*. Stanford: CSLI Publications.

Nishiyama, Kunio. 1998. *The Morphosyntax and Morphophonology of Japanese Predicates*. Doctoral dissertation. Cornell University.

Park, Sang Doh & John Whitman. 2003. Direct Movement Passive in Korean and Japanese. *Proceedings of the 12th Japanese/Korean Linguistics Conference*. ed. McClure, William. 307–321. Stanford: CSLI Publications.

Ramchand, Gillian C. 2008. *Verb Meaning and the Lexicon: A First Phase Syntax*. Cambridge: Cambridge University Press.

Shibatani, Yoshio. 2001. *The Languages of Japan*. Cambridge: University Press.

Sohn, Ho-Min. 1999. *The Korean Language*. Cambridge, UK: Cambridge University Press.

External Possession by Derivation

JISUNG SUN
Stony Brook University

A nominal phrase in a certain case form usually reminds people of a particular grammatical relation, such as subject or object. On the other hand, a grammatical relation is expected to be in a particular case form. In the nominative-accusative paradigm, for example, subjects are usually in nominative form, while objects are most likely accusative. This simple mapping, however, does not always hold in languages. Well-known quirky subjects in Icelandic, for example, would be a challenge to such simple correspondence. Many languages, such as Korean, Japanese, Greek, etc. that are not genetically related to each other, have nominative objects. If we consider subject and object grammatical primitives, it would be difficult to approach to such constructions, since we would have to either 'look into' the primitives or deal with massive exceptions.

This paper concentrates mostly on subject, more precisely on nominative case. The primary language of interest is Korean, in which nominative case usually marks the subject, and accusative case marks the direct object, as in other nominative-accusative languages. In Korean, however, an extracted possessor is identically case-marked with its host DP, which is often called possessor raising (PR) or possessor ascension. This study investigates the nature of the extracted possessor and its relation to its host.

Japanese/Korean Linguistics 21.
Edited by Seungho Nam, Heejeong Ko and Jongho Jun.

1. Introduction

External Possession is among the most notable and widely studied phenomena in Korean and Japanese linguistics. There are two major types of external possession constructions in Korean: the *Double Nominative Construction* (DNC), as shown in (1a) and the *Double Accusative Construction* (DAC), as shown in (2a), whose corresponding genitive constructions are given in (1b) and (2b) respectively.[1]

(1) a. *Mary-**ka** nwun-**i** yeyppu-ta*[2]
Mary-NOM eye-NOM pretty-DECL
b. *Mary-uy nwun-i yeyppu-ta*
Mary-GEN eye-NOM pretty-DECL
'Mary's eyes are pretty.'

(2) a. *John-i Mary-**lul** son-**ul** cap-ass-ta*
John-NOM Mary-ACC eye-ACC grab-PST-DECL
b. *John-i Mary-uy son-ul cap-ass-ta*
John-NOM Mary-GEN eye-ACC grab-PST-DECL
'John grabbed Mary's hand.'

Most researchers, as far as I understand, agree that the possessor, *Mary*, is outside of the phrase that contains the possessee, whether they analyze it as raising or as initial merge. This study aims to decide which approach is better supported empirically, as well as theoretically. This paper concentrates on the double nominative construction, such as (1a). Due to its apparent resemblance with the double accusative construction, however, I will consult with the DAC, where necessary.

2. Derivational and Nonderivational Approaches

There are two major lines of approaches to the external possession. The derivational approach analyzes (1a) as a derived structure from (1b) via possessor raising (PR). In the non-derivational approach, on the other hand, the two constructions are not derivationally related, and the external possessor, Mary, in (1a) initially merges to a position outside of the possessee. This study is in favor of the derivational approach. This section will point out major problems of the non-derivational approach from an empirical, as

---

[1] Japanese lacks DAC due to so-called Double-*o* Constraint, which prohibits multiple occurrences of accusative nominal phrases under certain conditions. See Harada (1973) for details.

[2] *Ka* and *i* are allomorphs in the sense that choice between them depends on the phonological environment. When the noun ends with an open syllable, *ka* is used. When the final syllable of the noun has a coda consonant, *i* is used. The question of how the two suffixes with no resemblance have the same function would be beyond the range of the current study.

well as theoretical point of view; and defend the position of the derivational approach by counter-arguing claims against PR.

2.1 Subjacency

Yoon (2009) refuses the derivational approach, in which the DNC is derived via possessor raising. His biggest concern is that possessor raising would violate the *Subjacency Condition*, moving the possessor out of a *Subject Island* (Ross 1967) that typically restricts extraction.

(3) *Subjacency Condition*
: Extraction cannot cross more than one bounding node (S or NP).[3]

His reasoning is like this: If the DNC involves possessor raising, the sentence would be ungrammatical, because the movement violates the subjacency condition. But it is grammatical as opposed to the expectation. Therefore, it cannot be a result of possessor raising. It is of course a legitimate way to argue against something, except for violability of the subjacency condition in reality, which Yoon (2009) either overlooked or failed to notice. His claim only holds on the assumption that subjacency can absolutely not be violated, which is objected by the following examples.

(4) a. **Which cars**$_i$ were $[_S [_{NP}$ the hoods of $\mathbf{t}_i$] damaged]?
b. These were **the Iranian dignitaries**$_i$ that $[_S [_{NP}$ my talking to $\mathbf{t}_i$] was considered unacceptable].

(5) a. *siitaa-ne socaa ki* $[_S [_{NP}$ *mohan ke saare bacce*] *kal*
Sita-ERG thought that Mohan POSS all children tomorrow
vah phal khaaege]
that fruit eat-FUT-PL
b. ***mohan ke***$_i$ *siitaa-ne socaa ki* $[_S [_{NP}$ $\mathbf{t}_i$ *saare bacce*]
Mohan POSS Sita-ERG thought that all children
kal vah phal khaaege]
tomorrow that fruit eat-FUT-PL
'Sita thought that all of Mohan's children will eat that fruit tomorrow.' (Hindi, Mahajan 2003: 37-38)

Apparently, there are cases reported crosslinguistically, where possessor extraction has been postulated with significant empirical support. In (4a–b), although they are not instances of possessor raising, extraction out the sub-

[3]Here I use S and NP, instead of TP and DP, following the original definition of subjacency. Besides the notations, it is a big theoretical question how subjacency condition can be implemented in the current minimalist framework. For the discussional purpose, however, I leave aside this issue and stick with the condition as it is. Examples in (4-5) are more like a fundamental challenge to the old framework than Yoon's (2009) analysis itself.

ject does not cause ungrammaticality. The Hindi example in (5b) illustrates a clear case of possessor raising. It is hard to deny possessor raising in this case, because the possessor of the embedded subject merges onto the matrix clause, whose predicate does not seem to be entitled to an extra argument. In both (4) and (5), the bold-faced elements move across two bounding nodes, which are indicated by square bracket, and it is a subjacency violation by definition. Even though subjacency has been considered a strong condition, it cannot be an absolute criterion, as long as there are such cases as (4) and (5). This makes Yoon's (2009) argument against the derivational approach look not as strong as he believes.

Moreover, it is not clear how Yoon's (2009) subjacency argument accommodates *double accusative constructions* (DAC) in Korean, in which extraction applies to the possessor of an object NP, as shown below.

(6) a. [$_S$ *John-i* [$_{VP}$ *Mary$_i$-lul* [$_{NP}$ t$_i$ *son-ul*] *cap-ass-ta*]][4]
John-NOM Mary-ACC hand-ACC grab-PST-DECL
'John grabbed Mary by the hand.'

b. [$_S$ *Bill-i* [$_{VP}$ *John$_i$-ul* [$_{NP}$ t$_i$ *meli-lul*] *ttayli-ess-ta*]]
Bill-NOM John-ACC head-ACC hit-PST-DECL
'Bill hit John on the head.'

In (6), the possessor neither moves out of the subject, nor crosses more than one bounding node. In other words, there is no island constraint violation or subjacency violation. If Yoon (2009) wants to refuse the derivational approach to the DAC too, which I believe he does, he should be able to justify his argument with independent evidence. The subjacency condition obviously cannot prevent extraction out of an object NP. Even if there was some constraint in the theory that prevents possessor raising out of an object NP, it would be offended by such cases as (6).

The subjacency argument motivates Yoon (2009) to analyze DNC's with the concepts of *Major Subject* (MS) and *Grammatical Subject* (GS),[5]

---

[4] I assume the extracted possessor stays within the VP for the moment. Tomioka and Sim (2005), in their discussion of double accusative constructions in Korean, suggest that a higher head is present in the DAC and the accusative case-marked possessor moves to its spec position. As far as I understand, this head is similar to the (low) applicative head proposed by Pylkkänen (2008) except for the relation introduced by this extra head is 'affect', rather than simple possession, in Tomioka and Sim (2005).

[5] These two concepts are similar to *broad subject* and *narrow subject* respectively, which are proposed by Heycock and Doron (2003) and Doron and Heycock (2010) (henceforth collectively, HD) to analyze double nominative constructions in Hebrew and Japanese. Their analysis is is extensively attacked by Landau (2009, 2011) who argues that unlike Japanese DNC's in Hebrew are instances of Left-Dislocation. If the current proposal succeeded, it could be another challenge to HD's analysis. On the assumption that DNC's in Japanese and Korean

the former being the first occurrence of nominative phrase and the latter being the second, as illustrated below.

(7) [$_{\text{MS}}$ *Mary-ka*] [$_{\text{SENT-PRED}}$ [$_{\text{GS}}$ *nwun-i*] *yeyppu-ta*]]
Mary-NOM eye-NOM pretty-DECL
'Mary's eyes are pretty.'

According to Yoon (2009), the grammatical subject and the predicate form a new predicative unit, namely a *Sentential Predicate*, and the major subject is introduced to the construction as what is predicated of the sentential predicate.

In spite of a broad empirical coverage and no potential complication with the subjacency condition, such an analysis has potential problems. First of all, posing a sentential predicate creates a type mismatching in terms of the strict compositionality.

(8)

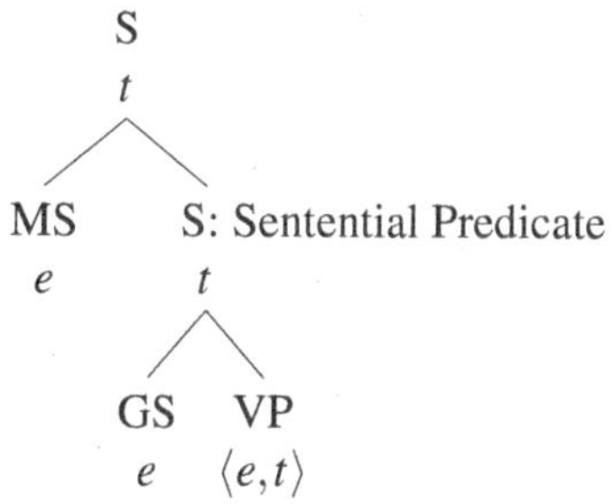

By the usual definition in the type theory, the sentential predicate is of type t, since its value is truth or falsity, and both MS and GS are supposed to be of type e, because they are separate argument NP's, as claimed by Yoon (2009). There arises a mismatching, when the MS is introduced, since we would want the sentential predicate of type t to take an argument of type e and create an expression of the same type t. This requires type shifting of the sentential predicate into $<e,t>$, but there seems to be no legitimate way to do it, because the sentential predicate does not include any variable in it.

2.2 Nonconstituency

Tomioka and Sim (2005), dealing with the double accusative construction in Korean, claim that non-constituency between the possessor and the possessee provides evidence against the PR analysis. In (9) below, intervention of the locative adjunct and the frequency adverb does not cause ungrammaticality. They state that this fact shows non-constituency between the posses-

behave in the same way, which I believe they do, even Japanese DNC cannot be analyzed in terms of broad subject and narrow subject.

sor and the possessee: If they formed a constituent, intervention of other elements would be ruled out.

(9) *Chelswu-ka Sunhee-lul* ***cha-eyse nul*** *son-ul cap-ass-ta*
Chelswu-NOM Sunhee-ACC car-in always hand-ACC hold-PST-DECL
'Chelswu always held Sunhee's hand in the car.'

According to Szabolcsi (1994), however, once the possessor leaves the host DP, it behaves as an independent, though anaphorically related, argument from the host. Based on this observation, underlying constituency would not jeopardize the PR analysis, which also allows intervention between the possessor and the possessee after the movement.

(10)

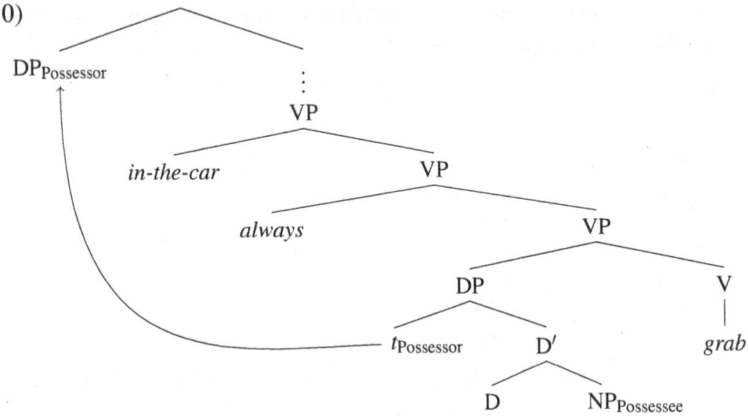

2.3 Semantic Differences

Yeon (2010) favors the non-derivational approach, due to semantic differences between DNC's and their corresponding genitive constructions, which are often used as counter-examples for the derivational approach.

(11) a. *Yenghuy-ka son-i khu-ta*
Yenghuy-NOM hand-NOM big-DECL
(i) Literal: 'Yenghuy's hands are big.'
(ii) Idiomatic: 'Yenghuy is generous.'

b. *Yenghuy-uy son-i khu-ta*
Yenghuy-GEN hand-NOM big-DECL
(i) Literal: 'Yenghuy's hands are big.'
(ii) *Idiomatic: 'Yenghuy is generous.'

In (11a) has idiomatic reading, while (11b) can only be interpreted literally. Meaning change is usually considered an A′-property, whereas licensing an external possessor is probably an A-operation, since (nominative) case checking is involved. Due to this seemingly mixed nature of PR, Heycock and Doron (2003) claim that the external possessor is a separate argument which merges to an A-position. However, I find the unavailability of idiomatic reading in the DNC lexical, rather than syntactic.

(12) a. *Yenghuy-ka son-i acwu khu-ta*
Yenghuy-NOM hand-NOM very big-DECL
(i) Literal: 'Yenghuy's hands are very big.'
(ii) Idiomatic: 'Yenghuy is very generous.'

b. *Yenghuy-ka acwu son-i khu-ta*
Yenghuy-NOM very hand-NOM big-DECL
(i) ??Literal: 'Yenghuy's hands are very big.'
(ii) Idiomatic: 'Yenghuy is very generous.'

The degree adverb *acwu* 'very' in Korean usually comes right before adjectives. If it is separated from the adjective it modifies, the sentence would be significantly degraded, as in (13). However, (12b) with the idiomatic reading is perfectly fine, even though the degree adverb is distant from the adjective.

(13) a. *Mary-ka ttal-i acwu yeyppu-ta*
Mary-NOM daughter-NOM very pretty-DECL
'Mary's daughter is very pretty.'

b. ??*Mary-ka acwu ttal-i yeyppu-ta*
Mary-NOM very daughter-NOM pretty-DECL

Idioms pass a few *wordhood* tests, which supports the idea that they are more like lexical a unit. If an element is a word, a part of it may not be conjoined with another element. The potential idiomatic interpretation is not available in (14).

(14) *Yenghuy-ka son-i khu-ko ttattusha-ta*
Yenghuy-NOM hand-NOM big-and warm-DECL
'Yenghuy's hands are big and warm.'

Idioms may correspond to some sort of complex predicates, although I am not dedicated to such a claim. Whether they are complex predicates or not, it is obvious that (11a) is distinct from the DNC of interest in this paper. The argument inspired by the idiomatic usage of the DNC is not strong enough to jeopardize the derivational analysis.

2.4 Ordering Restriction

Word order restriction between the possessor and possessee supports the possessor raising analysis. No formal theoretical machinery can capture this restriction without movement. If the possessor and possessee are both independent arguments, as claimed by nonderivationalists, nothing would prevent the possessee from scrambling over the possessor. It should be able to precede the possessor. The expectation is not borne out, as confirmed by (15).

(15) a. *Mary-ka nwun-i yeyppu-ta*
Mary-NOM eye-NOM pretty-DECL
'Mary's eyes are pretty.'

b.**Nwun-i Mary-ka yeyppu-ta*
eye-NOM Mary-NOM pretty-DECL
Intended Reading: 'Mary's eyes are pretty.'

In the nonderivational approach, there seems to be no systematic way to rule out (15b). Among various researchers on the nonderivational side, only Tomioka and Sim (2005) explicitly mention this issue.[6] In order to account for the ordering restriction, they posit a semantic condition that prevents the possessee from preceding the possessor. Such a claim has obvious problems besides the general problems of the nonderivational approach that I mentioned in the previous sections. In order to claim that reversed order as in (15b) is blocked by semantics, we have to assume that it does not cause any problem in terms of syntax, which, in turn, means (15b) is not actually ungrammatical but just semantically unacceptable. Tomioka and Sim (2005) are not entirely clear on this issue. They put '*' on instances of reversed order between the possessor and the possessee, instead of '#'. If it really means that such cases are ungrammatical, the constraint they suggest would be some sort of representational condition, but it is not clear how semantics restricts certain syntactic representations. There are a num-

---

[6] Tomioka and Sim (2005) only deal with the *double accusative construction* (DAC), as shown below.

a. *Bill-i Mary-lul oscalak-ul cap-ass-ta*
Bill-NOM Mary-ACC sleeve-ACC grab-PST-DECL
'Bill grabbed Mary by her sleeve.'

b.* *Bill-i oscalak-ul Mary-lul cap-ass-ta*
Bill-NOM sleeve-ACC Mary-ACC grab-PST-DECL
Intended Reading: 'Bill grabbed Mary by her sleeve.'

As example *b* indicates, the same kind of ordering restriction is observed in the DAC. I assume that the relative order between the possessor and the possessee is constrained by a single mechanism in both DNC and DAC.

ber of well-known representational conditions. Besides this theory-internal concern, Tomioka and Sim (2005) cannot account for the grammaticality of the following sentences.

(16) a. *Mary-nun nwun-i yeyppu-ta*
Mary-TOP eye-NOM pretty-DECL
'As for Mary, her eyes are pretty.'

b. *Nwun-un Mary-ka yeyppu-ta*
eye-TOP Mary-NOM pretty-DECL
'As for eyes, Mary's are pretty.'

(16a-b) are examples of topicalization. Even though we are not sure whether their derivation include possessor raising or not, Tomioka and Sim's (2005) condition should be valid in either case. When we look at (16b), however, the condition is violated by scrambling the possessee over the possessor, but the sentence is fine.

Approached derivationally, (15b), repeated with bracketed structure in (17), is an instance that shows the alleged PBC effect. Following the original definition of the *Proper Binding Condition*[7], (15b) is ruled out because the trace of the extracted possessor fails to be *properly bound*.

(17) a.*[$_{CP}$ [$_{DPi}$ **t_j** *nwun-i*] [$_{TP}$ **[$_{DPj}$ *Mary-ka*]** t_i [$_{vP}$ t_i *yeyppu-ta*]]]
eye-NOM Mary-NOM pretty-DECL
Intended Reading: 'Mary's eyes are pretty.'

Although there are many cases reported crosslinguistically, where apparent PBC violations do not cause ungrammaticality, we can at least expect there to be some sort of formal account for such instances as (15b) in the derivational approach. If the possessor and possessee are both full-fledged arguments that are not derivationally related, syntax could not filter out (15b) without speculations. Many studies attempt to reduce the PBC effect to something relevant in more recent theories. I am not going to get into the detail of the PBC effect, since it is beyond the range of this paper. However, I believe that this issue should be revisited in order for further support for the derivational approach. If successful, it could be extended to PBC effects in general, which have been investigated by many but still remain unresolved.

[7] *Proper Binding Condition* (PBC; Fiengo 1977): A trace must be c-commanded by its antecedent.

3. Licensing Condition

As observed by many researchers (Ura 1996, Yoon 2007 among others), possessor raising is not always possible to form a double nominative construction. This section is intended to find out what property makes a possessor able to raise.

3.1 Previous Accounts

Double nominative and double accusative constructions have been traditionally characterized as *inalienable possession*. Many recent studies, such as Ura 1996, keep describing the pattern with this concept. Contrast between alienable and inalienable possession appears to filter out some instances of external possession. When you see the examples in (18), however, both relations are inalienable, according to the strong definition, but (18a) is grammatical and (18b) is not.

(18) a. *Mary-ka ttal-i yeyppu-ta*
Mary-NOM daughter-NOM pretty-DECL
'Mary's daughter is pretty.'

b.**Mary-ka sinpal-i yeyppu-ta*
Mary-NOM shoe-NOM pretty-DECL
Intended Reading: 'Mary's shoes are pretty.'

There are ill-formed examples, even though the possessor and the possessee are in inalienable relationship. Although (18a) and (19b) below include the same relationship, the latter is out for some reason, which is obviously not the inalienability restriction.[8]

(19) a. *John-uy ttal-i sophwung-ul ka-ss-ta*
John-GEN daughter-NOM picnic-ACC go-PST-DECL
'John's daughter went on a picnic.'

b. **John-i ttal-i sophwung-ul ka-ss-ta*
John-NOM daughter-NOM picnic-ACC go-PST-DECL

There are also cases, where PR is licensed in spite of apparently alienable relationships, as shown (20–21).

(20) a. *Mary-uy chalimsay-ka swuswuha-ta*
Mary-GEN outfit-NOM unpretentious-DECL
(lit.) 'Mary is dressed unpretentiously.'

[8] Even if we include kinship relations in the inalienable possession (the weak definition), the asymmetry between (18a) and (19b) would remain questionable.

b. *Mary-ka chalimsay-ka swuswuha-ta* (DNC)
Mary-NOM outfit-NOM unpretentious-DECL
(lit.) 'Mary is dressed unpretentiously.'

(21) a. *John-i Mary-uy oscalak-ul cap-ass-ta*
John-NOM Mary-GEN sleeve-ACC grab-PST-DECL
'John grabbed Mary's sleeve.'

b. *John-i Mary-lul oscalak-ul cap-ass-ta* (DAC)
John-NOM Mary-ACC sleeve-ACC grab-PST-DECL
'John grabbed Mary's sleeve.'

Examples in (19–21) clearly show that inalienable possession is not the correct condition that licenses double nominative constructions, as well as double accuasative constructions.

3.2 Predicate Type

Looking at the contrast between (22a) and (22b), one might think it is different types of predicates that make the contrast.

(22) a. *John-i ttal-i kwiyep-ta*
John-NOM daughter-NOM cute-DECL
'John's daughter is cute.'

b.**John-i ttal-i sophwung-ul ka-ss-ta*
John-NOM daughter-NOM picnic-ACC go-PST-DECL
Intended Reading: 'John's daughter went on a picnic.'

(22a) includes an Individual-level predicate, while (22b) has a Stage-level predicate (Kratzer 1995). This hypothesis, however, is easily nullified by the asymmetry between (18a–b). These examples include the same predicate 'pretty', but only (18a) is grammatical.

3.3 Gnomicity

If it is neither the possessor-possessee relationship nor selection of predicate, what else could be the true licensing condition for DNC? The following examples provide an interesting clue.

(23) a. *Mary-uy ttal-i kongbwu-lul ha-n-ta*
Mary-GEN daughter-NOM study-ACC do-PRS-DECL
(i) 'Mary's daughter is studying (now).'
(ii) (lit.) 'She is a graduate student.'

b. *Mary-ka ttal-i kongbwu-lul ha-n-ta*
Mary-NOM daughter-NOM study-ACC do-PRS-DECL
(i) *'Mary's daughter is studying (now).'
(ii) (lit.) 'She is a graduate student.'

(24) a. *Mary-uy atul-i chwukku-lul ha-n-ta*
Mary-GEN son-NOM soccer-ACC do-PRS-DECL
(i) 'Mary's son is playing soccer (now).'
(ii) (lit.) 'She is a (professional) soccer player.'

b. *Mary-ka atul-i chwukku-lul ha-n-ta*
Mary-NOM son-NOM soccer-ACC do-PRS-DECL
(i) *'Mary's son is playing soccer (now).'
(ii) (lit.) 'She is a (professional) soccer player.'

(25) a. *Mary-uy atul-i (chinkwu-tul-eykey) mac-nun-ta*
Mary-GEN son-NOM friend-PL-DAT be.beaten-PRS-DECL
(i) 'Mary's son is getting beaten by his friends (now).'
(ii) (lit.) 'Mary's son is beaten by his friends.'

b. *Mary-ka atul-i (chinkwu-tul-eykey) mac-nun-ta*
Mary-NOM son-NOM friend-PL-DAT be.beaten-PRS-DECL
(i) *'Mary's son is getting beaten by his friends (now).'
(ii) (lit.) 'Mary's son is beaten by his friends.'

In (23–25), *a* examples can be interpreted either (i) episodically or (ii) generically, whereas *b* examples only have the generic readings. We can now go back to the previous examples and check with them. In (1a), 'pretty' refers to Mary's personal property, which, according to Chierchia (1995), gives rise to inherent generics. The same applies to 'cute' in (24a), while we can hardly imagine 'going on a picnic' in (22b) become a characteristic of a person.

Based on the pattern stated above, I argue that *gnomic* aspect of the clause licenses double nominative constructions. Carlson (1982) treats habitual sentences equivalently to generic sentences under the notion of gnomicity. According to Carlson (1982), our conceptual world consists of the world of space-time and the organization of the world. Based on this definition, *episodics* is about the space-time world, *gnomics* is about the organization of it, and *individuals* are viewed as integral parts of the organization. The DNC is licensed for facts about this integral entity.

4. Case Checking

Now we need to figure out how two nominative cases are checked within a single clause. Double nominative constructions are often analyzed as a multiclausal structure, but I refuse such claims for a similar reason I refused the sentential predicate analysis in Section 2.1, and restrict the discussion to monoclausal analyses. There are two hypothetical ways to check double nomiantives: We could have one case assigner, most likely T, checks more than one case, or we could posit two case assigners, one per each.

4.1 Multiple Case Checking

Ura (1996) proposes a multiple feature checking analysis for licensing double nominative constructions in Japanese. He extends Chomsky's (1995) general idea that nominative case is checked by finite T, and claims that both nominative cases in DNC are checked by finite T. Presumably, the whole DP (possessor-possessee) receives nominative case from the finite T in the inner spec of T position in the usual manner, and the raised possessor DP gets its nominative case in the outer spec of T, also from the finite T. Nominative case checking on the possessor is an optional operation, which violates *Procrastinate*. In order to avoid ruling out this optional operation, he suggests the following condition.

(26) Violability of Procrastinate (Ura 1996)
: When a head H tolerates an unforced violation of Procrastinate, H has a formal feature such that it is not required, but allowed to be checked off before SPELL-OUT.

According to Ura (1996), when a language has parameter setting such that a head H tolerates a single unforced violation of Procrastinate, another element E 'may' be attracted to an outer spec of H, after H's innermost spec is filled with the element that entered into the first checking relation with H.

I have one theoretical and one empirical questions. First of all, what licenses multiple specs? Does T have two separate EPP features or some kind of multi-valued EPP feature? As far as I understand his analysis, T in Japanese simply 'tolerates' multiple nominative feature checking. It does not have to enter into multiple checking relations. The bottom line is that T in the DNC and T in the corresponding genitive construction do not have different feature specifications, which means that PR is obviously not motivated.

Second, the empirical issue is related to the fact that the raised possessor and the possessee can be separated by another phrase, as in (27).

(27) *Mary-ka* **cengmal** *nwun-i* *yeyppu-ta*
Mary-NOM actually eye-NOM pretty-DECL
'Mary's eyes are actually pretty.'

There are two options for advervial placement in this structure: to adjoin it to a maximal projection or to locate it in the spec of a functional projection. However, neither option is possible here, if we assume that the two nominative cases are multiply checked by a single head, where both are in the spec of the same projection. Therefore, I argue that we need two separate projections to check two nominative cases in the DNC.

4.2 Another Nominative Case Assigner

In modern generative syntactic theory, it is widely assumed that finite T head is the nominative case-assigner. In the external possession construction, however, two nominal phrases are assigned nominative case. Alexiadou (2003) suggests another potential nominative case assigner, introducing instances of nominative object in Greek. In normal cases, T with [+finite] feature, assigns nominative case to the moved NP to its specifier position. When a certain feature [αF][9] is introduced on Asp, however, it becomes the nominative case assigner. This gives rise to so-called *Quirky Subject Constructions* in many languages (Icelandic, Lithuanian, etc.). The question is, what kind of feature enables Asp to check nominative case in the DNC?

(28)

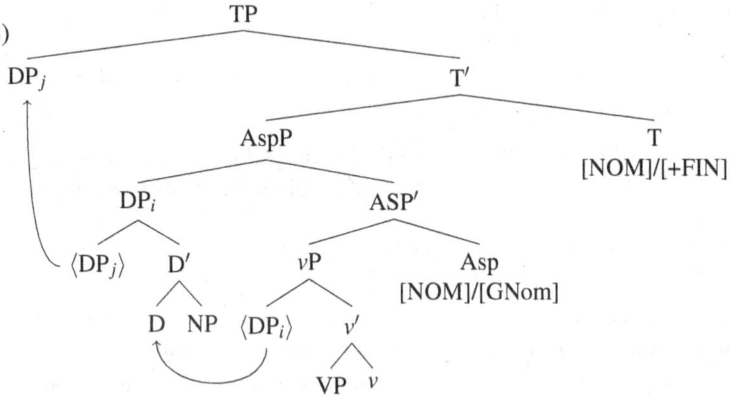

In the previous section, we observed that DNC is only possible in gnomic contexts. I propose an aspectual feature [GNOM] on Asp. Its presence licenses the DNC, enabling Asp to be an extra nominative case assigner in Korean, as in (31).

5. Concluding Remarks

This paper investigated *Double Nominative Constructions* in Korean, focusing on instances that include external possession. The current analysis is in

[9] Alexiadou (2003) proposes [-person] feature, since only third person nominals are allowed for nominative objects in Greek.

favor of the derivational approach, in which the possessor and the possessee in the DNC are originally a constituent, and the DNC is formed via possessor raising. In Section 2, I provided evidence that shows that the derivational approach is more reasonable way to analyze DNC's. The suggested analysis does not induce complications in terms of compositionality, and provides a better account for word order restriction in the DNC. Due to the fact that possessor raising is only valid in gnomic environments, I suggested that an aspectual feature [GNOMIC] is the true licensor of the double nominative construction.

I did not give a complete explanation for external possession in double accusative constructions and other types of double nominative constructions with no possessor raising included. I will leave these issues for my future investigation.

References

Alexiadou, Artemis. 2003. On Nominative Case Features and Split Agreement. In *New Perspectives on Case Theory*, eds. E. Blander and H. Zinsmeister, 23–52. CSLI Publications.

Carlson, Greg N. 1982. Generic Terms and Generic Sentences. *Journal of Philosophical Logic* 11:145–181.

Chierchia, Genaro. 1995. Individual-Level Predicates as Inherent Generics. . In *The Generic Book*, eds. G.N. Carlson and F.J. Pelletier, 176–223. The University of Chicago Press.

Fiengo, Robert. 1977. On Trace Theory. *Linguistic Inquiry* 8: 35–61.

Harada, Sin-iti. 1973. Counter Equi-NP Deletion. *Annual Bulletin* 7:113–148. Research Institute of Loopaedics and Phoniatrics, Tokyo University.

Heycock, Caroline and Edit Doron. 2003 Categorical Subject, Gengo Kenkyu 123: 95–135.

Kratzer, Angelika. 1995. Stage-Level and Individual-Level Predicates. In *The Generic Book*, eds. G.N. Carlson and F.J. Pelletier, 224–237. The University of Chicago Press.

Mahajan, Anoop. 2003. Word Order and (Remnant) VP Movement. In *Word Order and Scrambling*, ed. S. Karimi. Blackwell Publishers.

Ross, John. 1967. Constraints on Variables in Syntax. Doctoral Dissertation, Massachusetts Institute of Technology.

Szabolcsi, Anna. 1983. The Possessor Ran Away from Home. *The Linguistic Review* 3: 89–102.

Szabolcsi, Anna. 1994. The Noun Phrase. In *Syntax and Semantics 27: The Syntactic Structure of Hungarian*, eds. F. Kiefer and K. Kiss, 179–274. Academic Press.

Ura, Hiroyuki. 1996. Multiple Feature Checking: A Theory of Grammatical Function Spliting. Doctoral Dissertation, Massachusetts Institute of Technology.

Yeon, Jaehoon. 2010. Constraints on Double Accusative External Possession Constructions in Korean: A Cognitive Approach. In Selected Papers from the 2nd European Conference on Korean Linguistics, eds. J.H. Yeon and J. Kaier, 188–201.

Yoon, James H.S. 2009. The Distribution of Subject Properties in Multiple Subject Constructions. *Japanese-Korean Linguistics* 16. CSLI Publications.

A Korean Grammatical Borrowing in Early Middle Japanese *Kunten* Texts and its Relation to the Syntactic Alignment of Earlier Korean and Japanese

JOHN WHITMAN AND YUKO YANAGIDA
NINJAL/Cornell University and the University of Tsukuba

1. Introduction

Modern Korean and Japanese are textbook examples of accusative alignment. However there have been persistent suggestions over the last 25 years that earlier stages of both languages had ergative or active alignment. In this paper we focus on the postnominal particle *–i*, which has been analyzed as the reflex of an original ergative marker in Korean (King 1988), in Japanese (Vovin 1997, Takeuchi 2008), and as a loan from Korean to Japanese (Kobayashi 2009, Vovin 2010). Our conclusions are (i) there is little evidence that *–i* in earlier Korean was an ergative marker (ii) Old Japanese (OJ) was indeed a split active system (Yanagida 2005, 2007, Yanagida & Whitman 2007), but the agent marker was not *–i*, (iii) *–i* in one genre of OJ prose and in 9th century glossed texts has the subject marking and bound pronominal functions of earlier Korean *–i*, suggesting that it did originate as a loan, but in the former function it serves to mark broad focus subjects.

Japanese/Korean Linguistics 21.
Edited by Seungho Nam, Heejeong Ko and Jongho Jun.

2. Alignment in earlier Korean

2.1 The ergative hypothesis for earlier Korean

King (1988) suggests that prior to late middle Korean (LMK; 15th c.) earlier Korean had ergative or perhaps active alignment. This is based on differences in case marking between Late Middle Korean (LMK; 15th century) and modern standard written Korean. King observes that "[c]ase marking in MK seems to have been more semantically-based than in modern Korean, and zero marking more frequent: non-referential objects tend to have zero marking, and 'nominative' nouns tend to get zero marking in two types of configurations" (1988: 2). The first of these ("Configuration A") involves non-referential and/or indefinite DPs adjacent to non-transitive verbs:

(1)

CENG un	pal Ø	is-no-n	TUNG	ila.
Ceng TOP	foot	exist-PROC-PADN	lamp	is

'A Ceng is a lamp with feet.'

Wŏrin sŏkpo 1.8b (1459), King 1988: 2

"Configuration B" involves subjects of intransitive verbs in adjunct clauses:

(2)

PWUTHYE Ø	NYELQPPAN	ho-sya-n	HHWUW	ey
Buddha	nirvana	do- HON-PADN	after	at

'after the Buddha achieved nirvana'

Sŏkpo sangjŏl 23.6.verso (1447)

King presents the following hypothesis for the diachronic development of alignment in Korean.

(3) Stage 1: Ergative (Pre-Middle Korean)

	Subject	Object
Intransitive	Ø	
Transitive	-i	Ø

Stage 2: Extension of Ergative

	Subject	Object
Intransitive	i ~ Ø	
Transitive	-i	Ø/-γɨ l

Stage 3: Accusative (15th century LMK)

	Subject	Object
Intransitive	Ø /-i	
Transitive	Ø /-i	Ø /-l

The basic idea is that at Stage 1, the language realized ergative case as *–i* and absolutive case as zero on objects and intransitive subjects. At Stage 2, ergative marking is extended to some intransitive verbs, perhaps to unergatives in an active alignment pattern. By the 15th century, the alternation between overt case and zero no longer marks grammatical relations. We examine this hypothesis in the next two sections

2.2 Configurations A and B

King's Configuration A is not necessarily an indicator of earlier ergativity. For example, Fry (2002) shows that adjacency to the predicate and nonspecificity/indefiniteness are predictors for so-called case drop in contemporary spoken Japanese, but this language is not ergative, nor was the Late Middle Japanese system which is its diachronic source.[1]

Furthermore, "absolutive" patterns grouping together nonspecific/indefinite objects and unaccusative subjects are common across languages, irrespective of alignment. A well-known example is the Russian genitive of negation (Pesetsky 1982), which applies to nonspecific/indefinite objects and unaccusative subjects in negative sentences. Again, the pattern has nothing to do with a prior diachronic stage of ergativity. Instead, it has been argued that it reflects the shared VP-internal status of both nonspecific/indefinite objects and unaccusative subjects. Similarly, Takezawa (1987) argues that case drop on subjects and objects in Japanese is conditioned by their VP-internal status.

The final problem with Configuration A is that it is unclear how it is related to Configuration B. While configuration A is sensitive to the specificity/definiteness of the subject or object, configuration B is not.

Configuration B, however, seems more significant. Kim 1972 (246-249) makes the related observation that zero marked subjects are highly frequent in complex NPs.[2] All of Kim's (1972: 247-248) 22 examples from the *Sŏkpo sangjŏl* (1447) involve the adnominal endings *–(o/u)l* or *–(o/u)n*, which originally marked a high or clausal nominalization. In fact, Kim and King's observations intersect: all but 2 of Kim's 22 examples involve complex NPs

[1] The ancestor of the contemporary Japanese case marking pattern was a system in Middle Japanese where the subject of certain embedded clauses was marked with genitive *no* and the object with accusative *wo*. In Late Middle Japanese, *ga* replaced *no*, and the pattern was generalized to main clauses. See Yanagida & Whitman (2009) for details.

[2] Complex NPs correlate also show a high incidence of zero marked objects. Sugai (2004) presents a detailed study of object marking in the *Sŏkpo sangjŏl* (1447) and *Samgang haengsil to* (1481). He finds a low proportion of zero-marked objects (11.6% of 276 tokens) in main clauses, but a higher proportion in nominalized clauses (62.6% of 123 tokens) and a very high proportion in complex NPs (82.5% of 160).

which are also adjuncts, like (2). In argument complex NPs, there is a strong tendency for the subject to be marked genitive (Whitman 2004).

(4) na-y (L) ciz-wu-n CCWOY
I-GEN commit-MOD-PADN sin
'the sin that I committed *Sŏkpo sangjŏl* 24.17.verso

The pattern whereby subjects in argument complex NPs are marked genitive, and subjects in adjunct complex NPs are zero (nominative) marked, resembles the same pattern in modern Turkish, as described by Kornfilt (2003). However in Turkish the non-genitive marked pattern is an innovation, not a retention.

Summarizing the results of this section, the distribution of zero marked subjects and objects in 15th century does not provide a strong indication of earlier ergativity in Korean. A tendency toward zero marking of nonspecific/indefinite subjects and objects can be found in modern Japanese. Zero marking of the subject in adjunct complex NPs occurs in modern Turkish. Neither of these patterns results from an immediately prior stage of ergative alignment.

2.3 What was going on before the 15th century: Data from kugyŏl texts

To clarify what might have been going on before the 15th century, we investigated kugyŏl texts from the 13th century and earlier. Kugyŏl are a graphic system for glossing Chinese texts to be read in Korean (we discuss a similar textual source for earlier Japanese in 4). Kugyŏl materials provide our earliest substantial pre-LMK source, dating from perhaps as early as the 10th century. Since kugyŏl texts contain instances of ancestor of the LMK subject marker *–i*, they provide an opportunity for checking whether –i functioned as an ergative marker at an earlier stage of the language.

The answer is negative. Consider for example one of the first kugyŏl texts to have been discovered, several leafs of the *Kuyŏk Inwang-gyŏng* (舊譯仁王經 *Humane King Sutra*), glossed in the 13th century. Character glosses for *–i* in this text do not show a clear correlation with transitivity. Subjects marked with *–i* appear with both transitive and intransitive verbs.
A count of the examples of the particle *–i* in the *Kuyŏk Inwang-gyŏng* fragment shows 9 transitive subjects and 30 intransitive subjects. Although some examples of nonspecific/indefinite subjects occur with zero marking, as in (5a), other instances of nonspecific/indefinite subjects directly adjacent to an unaccusative verb occur with *–i* marking (5b).

(5) a. ...CHYWUNG Ø is-kye-mye
sentient [beings] Ø be-PAST-and
'and there were (countless) sentient beings'
(*Kuyŏk Inwang-gyŏng* 2:3)

b. ...KWUKTHWO-**i** is-wo-n toy
land-NOM be-MOD-PADN place
'and there were (countless) lands' (*Kuyŏk Inwang-gyŏng* 2:3)

This is not an ergative pattern.

To investigate the distribution of DP-*i* in the oldest kugyŏl texts, we surveyed the drypoint glosses in fascicle 20 of the Chin-bon *Hwaŏm-gyŏng* (*Avataṃsaka Sūtra*), based on the analysis of Lee et al 2009.[3] Clear glosses for –*i* as a subject marker in this text are relatively rare. We counted 19 unambiguous examples. There are 4 examples of transitive and/or agentive subjects with –*i*. We have followed Lee et al's (2009) notation for kugyŏl glosses. The gloss marked as diagonal line in position 35 [35(/)] indicates –*i*.

(6) a. 一切如來[35(/)]成最正覺([41(· -) 35 (· .) 51(·)]
b. all Tathāgata-**i** achieve highest enlightenment-l
c. all Tathāgata-**NOM** highest enlightenment-ADN achieve- ADN
'(that) all the Tathāgatas achieved highest enlightenment' (based on Lee et al 2009: 144)

There are 15 examples of intransitive subjects marked with –*i*, 5 in adnominal clauses,10 in other contexts. (7) shows –*i* in a comparative clause.

(7) 法界[35(/)]皆如虛空([24(·) 12 (:) ...]
Dharma world-**i** all similar emptiness-ADV do-ADN
Dharma world-NOM all emptinessØ resembl-ing do-ADN
'that the Dharma worlds all are similar to emptiness' (based on Lee et al 2009: 196)

In sum, the distribution of –*i* in fascicle 20 of the Chin-bon *Hwaŏm-gyŏng* is no more ergative than the distribution of this particle in the 13th century *Kuyŏk Inwang-gyŏng*, or 15th century hangŭl texts. It appears on animate and inanimate subjects of all kinds, with transitive and intransitive verbs, including unaccusatives. Prior to Koryŏ period kugyŏl texts, our information about –*i* is scanty, but attestations in *hyangga* and early *idu* texts also do not support an ergative analysis. A famous example is the fourth line of the hyangga *Ch'ŏyong-ga* 'Song of Ch'ŏyong' (9th century).

[3]This text may be as old as the 10th century. It is a xylograph with stylus-inscribed drypoint glosses, in the collection of the Seong'am Museum, Seoul.

(8) 脚烏伊四是良羅
katol-**i** neyh il-el-a
leg-NOM 4 COP-RET-ASSERT
'It's four legs!' (Transliteration following Lee & Ramsey 2011)

Here the indefinite, inanimate *-i*-marked DP "legs" is the subject of an intransitive predicate, the copula.

2.4 The etymology of *-i*

We conclude this section with a brief discussion of the etymology of the nominative particle *–i*. King (1988) suggests that the postnominal particle originates from the adverbial suffix *–i*. However adjunct markers that develop into ergative markers are typically instrumental or genitive, but adverbial *–i* has neither of these functions. Furthermore, adverbial *-i* in earlier Korean was a suffix that attached to bound forms, the bare stem of verbs and adjectives. Throughout the history of Korean, suffixes and particles appear to have been distinct, with particles following only non-bound forms.

A likelier etymology for nominative particle *–i* relates it to the bound pronominal *i* "(the one) that...", or the proximal demonstrative *i* 'this', which are at least etymologically most likely the same morpheme. The bound pronominal usage is found in LMK, kukyŏl materials, and Koryŏ period hyangga. (9) is an LMK example from the *Yongbi ŏch'ŏn ka* (1447):

(9) Ka-l-ila ho-l **i** isi-na.
go-FADN-COP-INDIC do-FADN BOUNDPRO be-ADVERS
'There are ones who want to go, but...' *Yongbi ŏch'ŏn ka* (1447) 45

Nam (2012: 27) suggests that in Koryŏ period hyángga, *i* functioned specifically as a [human] bound pronominal. The same combination of functions is exemplified by literary Burmese *thii*, which functions as a demonstrative pronoun, a nominative marker, and a clausal nominalizer (Simpson 2008). Simpson argues that the pronominal function was original, and that this was generalized to nominative marker and clausal nominalizer.

3. Alignment in earlier Japanese

3.1 Two theories of active alignment in Old Japanese

On the basis of examples like (10-11), Vovin 1997, followed by Takeuchi 2008, suggest that *i* functioned as an active marker in Old Japanese (OJ; 8th century), and *wo*, the ancestor of the modern Japanese accusative particle, as an absolutive marker.

(10) Nakamaro Kwomaro-ra i sakasima ni aru tomogara wo
Nakamaro Komaro-PL I revolt be exist gang WO
izanap-i pikiwite
luring leading
'Nakamaro Komaro et al. leading his gang in revolt'
(*Senmyō* 19, 757, Emperor Tenmu)

(11) Asuka-gapa yuk-u se wo paya-mi
Asuka river go-ADN shallows WO fast-mi
'as the shallows flowing in Asuka River are fast'
(*Man'yōshū* 11/2713, 8th century)

There are numerous problems with this hypothesis. First, outside of the *Shoku Nihongi senmyō* imperial edicts as in (10), the active marker *i* is a chimera. Kobayashi (2009: 6) counts 7 examples in the *Man'yōshū* poetic anthology, and 5 examples in other OJ verse texts. Of these, four actually appear to function as an object marker, and another as a dative marker. In light of these difficulties, Kobayashi (2009) and Vovin (2010) independently propose that subject marking *i* is a loan from Korean.

The problems with *wo* as an absolutive marker are similar. *Wo* occurs on the subject of intransitive predicates in ECM contexts (where it is in fact an argument of the higher verb; cf. Yanagida 2006), or in the adjective-*mi* pattern in (11). The latter pattern is limited to embedded adjunct contexts, and has been analyzed as an experiencer control construction (Aoki 2004), with *–mi* possibly derived from the stem of the verb *mi-* 'see'. (For a recent update of this idea, see Tsuta 2007.) Crucially, *wo* never marks the subject of a matrix intransitive predicate.

Wo also has a number of characteristics that are unexpected of an absolutive marker. As pointed out by Yanagida (2006, 2007) it marks non-themes, including PPs. Finally, DPs marked by *wo* are specific (Yanagida 2006, 2007, Yanagida & Whitman 2009). We know of no other language where an absolutive marker is restricted to [specific] DPs.

3.2 Active *ga*, absolutive ∅ (Yanagida 2005, 2007a, b)

A different split active system is posited for OJ by Yanagida (2005, 2007a, b). On this analysis, active alignment is restricted to nominalized clauses (adnominal, nominalized, realis and irrealis conditional). In such clauses the genitive marker *ga* functions as the active marker (12), while absolutive is zero marked (13). Absolutive objects adjacent to the verb are incorporated (Yanagida 2007a). Matrix non-nominalized clauses have accusative alignment, with zero-marked subject and object.

(12) Saywopimye no kwo **ga** pire ∅ puri-si yama
Sayohime GEN kid AGT scarf wave-PST.ADN mountain
'the mountain where the kid Sayohime waved her scarf'
(*Man'yōshū* 5/868)

(13) pisakwi ∅ opu-ru kiywoki kapara ni
hisagi grow-ADN clear riverbank on
'on the clear river banks where the hisagi grows'
(*Man'yōshū* 6 /925)

This system shows a number of typical features of non-accusative alignment, such as genitive/active syncretism, and an alignment split where the non-accusative pattern appears in embedded clauses. As is typical of active languages, *ga*-marked subjects are DPs higher on the nominal hierarchy (Silverstein 1976). In contrast to the hypothesis described in 3.1, *ga*-marking on active subjects is categorical; that is, active marking with *ga* is the norm, and obligatory with DPs high on the nominal hierarchy, such as personal pronouns.

We therefore conclude that the system where *ga* functions as the active marker in a split active system is the more accurate analysis of OJ alignment. But the question remains: what is the source of subject marking *i* in early Japanese data where it appears?

4. The particle –*i* in earlier Japanese

4.1 9th century kunten texts; the explosion in the frequency of *i*

Kobayashi (2009) points out that compared to its highly limited distribution in 8th century texts, there is an explosion in the frequency of *i* in 9th century kunten material. Kunten are the counterpart of Korean kugyŏl, a system for glossing Chinese texts and reading them in the vernacular (Yoshida et al 2001). Like kukyŏl, kunten materials are an important source of information about earlier Japanese. Particularly during the beginning of the Early Middle Japanese period in the 9th century, when other vernacular sources are almost completely absent, the quantity of kunten texts (all glossed versions of sutras and sutra commentaries in Middle Chinese) greatly increases. Kobayashi observes that virtually all 9th century Buddhistic kunten texts employ *i*. He also points out that the frequency of *i* increases by factor of 10 or more: compared to the 17 examples of *i* in the 62 *Shoku Nihongi senmyō*, there are approximately 290 examples in a single kunten text, the Saidaiji-bon *Konkōmyō saishō ōkyō* (ca. 830).[4] This particle is not found in other

[4]The count is due to Ōtsubo (1981: 442).

texts of any genre in the EMJ period, with the exception of two examples from a *senmyō* imperial edict of 842 (Kobayashi 2009: 7).

Kobayashi points out that in the Saidaiji-bon *Konkōmyō saishō ōkyō* both *i*-marked subjects and zero-marked subjects occur, with zero marking more common. The same DP can occur as subject with either type of marking:

(14) Toki ni moromoro no bissyu oyobi **daisyu Ø** kotogotoku mina
time at all GEN monk and crowd completely all
kokoro wo itasi… to tansu
mind ACC extend COMP intone
'At this time the monks and the crowd all focused their minds, and intoned…' (Saidaiji-bon *Konkōmyō saishō ōkyō* fascicle 10, 26 l. 30)

(15) … toki ni muryau asokiya no nin.ten **daisyu i** mina
time at countless infinite GEN humans.celestials crowd I all
opi ni kanasibi yorokobi-te… to tansi-te
greatly despair rejoicing-GER COMP intone-GER
'at … time a crowd of countless innumerable humans and celestials greatly despaired and rejoiced, and intoned…' (ibid fasc.10, 26 l. 256)

(16) Sanzen sekai no naka ni syupens-eru ten **daisyu i**
3,000 world GEN middle in spread-STAT heaven crowd I
kotogotoku kankisi-ki.
completely rejoiced-PAST
'A crowd of celestials spread across 3,000 worlds all rejoiced.'
(Saidaiji-bon *Konkōmyō saishō ōkyō* fasc. 9, 21 l. 28)

All three of the preceding examples involve the same DP subject head, the expression *daisyu* (大衆) 'crowd, great multitude'. (14) and (15) involve the same transitive predicate, *tansu* (歎す), 'intone, recite', but in (14) the subject is zero-marked, while in (15) it is marked with *i*. In (16) *daisyu* is again marked with *i*, but this time it is the subject of the intransitive predicate *kankisu* (歓喜す) 'rejoice, exult'.

Kobayashi's (2009) explanation of this variation is that the glossators of the Saidaiji-bon *Konkōmyō saishō ōkyō* transferred the glosses for *i*-marking from manuscripts originally glossed in Korea (Silla), or perhaps copies of such Sillan manuscripts. He points to other evidence suggesting that Sillan glossing (the ancestor of surviving Korean kugyŏl materials) influenced glossing practice in Japan in the late 8th and early 9th century. He suggests that *i* was marked when the original Chinese text was complex, or the subject difficult to discern.

If this is correct, however, it is not clear why *i* is marked in (16), a simplex clause. In other instances where we know EMJ glossators to have borrowed or adapted Korean glosses, they fit them to the norms of Japanese syntax (Lee 2006, Whitman 2009). For example, Lee (2006) points out that in an early EMJ manuscript of the Avataṃsaka sūtra held by the Kyoto National Museum, a phonogram gloss used to mark locative case in Korean kugyŏl is borrowed to mark dative case in Japanese. EMJ uses the same particle (*ni*) to mark dative/locative, but in Korean locative and dative are distinct. It thus seems reasonable to suppose that *i* was used to mark a significant grammatical distinction in Japanese.

Looking back at (14-16), we notice that there is an information structural difference in the three examples of *daisyu* 'crowd'. The existence of the zero-marked 'crowd' in (14) can be inferred from prior discourse (it is the crowd that the Buddha has been addressing in the text). The crowds in (15) and (16), in contrast, are newly invoked; their existence cannot be inferred from prior discourse. In a Korean original glossed version of this text, it is very likely that 'crowd' in (14) was marked with the topic marker *–(o/u)n*. But EMJ glossators did not borrow or adapt this gloss. We know that EMJ had both *pa*-marked and bare topics (Yanagida, Watanabe 2007); either would have been an appropriate choice for marking the subject in (14). 'Crowd' in (15-16), in contrast, has an interpretation corresponding to broad focus *ga* in Modern Japanese (Heycock 2008). EMJ had particles (so-called kakari particles) for marking narrow focus, but no specific segmental marker for marking broad focus. We suggest that *i* was adapted by EMJ glossators to mark broad focus subjects.

4.2 Bound pronominal *i* in 9th century kunten texts

As noted by previous researchers (Ōtsubo1981: 438, Kobayashi 2009: 7) *i* also functions as a bound pronominal, preceded by the adnominal form of the predicate:

(17) Bodai no papu wo gyapusuru **i** byaudou no
Bodhi GEN dharma acc practice BOUNDPRO equality GEN
gyapu wo syusuru wo ipu.
practice=Acc following-do=acc say
'Practicing the dharma of the Bodhi, we call it following the practice of nondiscrimination.'
(Saidaiji-bon *Konkōmyō saishō ōkyō* fasc. 5, 10 l. 19)

Although the bound pronominal function of *i* and the subject marking function of *i* (which we have hypothesized to mark broad focus) are sometimes difficult to distinguish, (17) is clearly a case of the former, because the adnominal clause marked by *i* is the topic, not the subject of the main clause. Bound pronominal *i* may also be followed by the topic marker *pa* and the narrow focus particle *si*. As we saw in 2.4, Korean *i* also functions as a bound pronominal. This usage also is attested in kugyŏl texts, so it would have been known to any Japanese glossator consulting Korean glossed texts. The co occurrence of these two exact same functions in kugyŏl and EMJ kunten texts makes it extremely probable that the EMJ pattern was borrowed. However we have suggested that it was borrowed and adapted to a specific discourse structural function.

4.3 *I* in the *Senmyō* imperial edicts

The 17 examples of *i* in the *Shoku Nihongi* senmyō (imperial edicts) are the main basis for Yamada's (1954) claim that this particle was a subject marker. As in early EMJ kunten texts, *i* in the *Shoku Nihongi* senmyō is used both as a subject marker and a bound pronoun preceded by the adnominal form of the embedded predicate.

(18) Nakamaro Kwomaro-ra **i** sakasima ni aru tomogara wo
Nakamaro Komaro-PL SUBJ revolt be exist gang OBJ
izanap-i pikiwite...
lure leading
'Nakamaro, Komaro et al leading their gang in revolt'
(*Senmyō* 19, 757, Emperor Kōken)

(19) Kwo pa oya no kokoro nasu **i** si kwo ni pa aru besi.
kid TOP parent GEN mind do BNDPRO FOC kid be TOP exist should
'As for kids, doing their parents' minds should be (the property of) kids.'
(*Senmyō* 13, 747)

As was the case with 9th century kunten texts, the subject marking and the bound pronominal functions of *i* can be clearly distinguished by syntax and discourse structural status. In (18), as in the kunten examples (15) and (16), *i* marks a broad focus subject. The rebels Nakamaro and Komaro are being introduced for the first time in this edict, and the entire clause presents new information. In (19), the adnominal clause headed by *i* receives narrow focus, marked by the focus particle *si*. The sequence DP *i si* never occurs; that is, *si* never follows *i* when the latter marks a simple DP.

In fact, these discourse structural properties of *i* have been hinted at by previous researchers. Ishida (1937) argues that *i* is an exclamatory particle that gives special emphasis to the preceding phrase. Kobayashi (1953) argues that it is secondary or semantic particle with a similar function. Iwai (1981: 222-223) argues that the bound pronominal function of *i* is primary, and the DP marking function derived from it. He interprets DP *i* as DP *sono mono* 'DP itself'. All of these researchers have detected the focus marking function of *i*.

The main thrust of the argument that *i* was an emphatic or focus marker has been to argue against the previous claim that *i* was a case marker. But the fact remains that in the senmyō and early EMJ kunten texts where *i* seems well established, DP *i* invariably marks subjects. Takeuchi (2008) makes a more specific claim: following Vovin (1997), he argues specifically that *i* is an active case marker, picking out only transitive and intransitive agentive (unergative) subjects. Takeuchi's argument is obscured by the fact that he groups all OJ texts where *i* occurs together, so that he must dismiss non-subject marking examples of *i* in OJ verse texts as "exclamatory". He also fails to distinguish the bound pronominal and subject marking functions of *i*; if one were to include (19) as an example of subject marking *i*, it could not be considered agentive. However when we confine our attention to the 17 examples of *i* in the *Shoku Nihongi* senmyō, Takeuchi's observation is verified.

(20) **Particle *i* in the *Shoku Nihongi* senmyō**

(a) Agentive intransitive	0 examples
(b)Transitive	12 examples
(c) Topic	1 example
(c) Bound pronominal	4

Despite this correlation, the hypothesis that *i* is a subject (or active) marker faces serious problems. The most obvious is why the particle is not used to mark all agentive subjects. In particular, it is unclear why *i* is never used in the senmyō to mark first or second person subjects, despite the fact that these referents are the highest on the nominal hierarchy. A possible response to this is that *i*-marking was somehow "vestigial" or "archaic". But there is nothing archaic or formulaic about (18), which describes a moment of immediate crisis at the court. Likewise, we might expect *i* to mark the emperor, the first person "speaker" of the senmyō texts. DPs designating the emperor are by far and away the most frequent agentive subjects in the senmyō, but they are never marked by *i*.

This distribution is explained by the hypothesis that *i* marked broad focus subjects. Since personal pronouns, and in this text, the emperor, are discourse-presupposed, they are never marked with *i*. Existential subjects (King's Configuration A) were unmarked, so *i*-marked nonagentive intransitive subjects are less frequent, but in a more extensive text such as the Saidaiji-bon *Konkōmyō saishō ōkyō*, we find them in examples such as (15).

To clarify the difference between *i*-marked subjects and zero-marked subjects in the Shoku Nihongi senmyō, let us look at an example where both occur.

(21) ...Pudino no Mapito Kiyomaro **Ø** si ga ane Popukun to ...
Fujino no Mahito Kiyomaro he GEN sister Hōkun with

ituparigoto wo tukuri-te Popukun **i** mono mawos-eri.
slander ACC make- GER Hōkun SUBJ thing say-STAT
'Fujino no Mahito Kiyomaro with his sister Hōkun made up a slander (about me),and Hōkun has said the thing.' (*Senmyō* 44, 769)

In (21) Kiyomaro and Hōkun are both agentive subjects of transitive verbs. If *i*-marking were determined by grammatical relation or thematic role alone, there is no reason why both should not be marked with *i*. The difference between the two subjects is their information structural status. The clause whose subject is Kiyomaru (whose name is preceded by a long list of his rank and titles) is the background information for this sentence. The main assertion of the sentence, whose subject receives broad focus, is the clause 'Hōkun has said the thing.'

5. Conclusion

This paper has supported the claim of Kobayashi (2009) and Vovin (2010) that –*i* in EMJ kunten texts and the 8th century *Shoku Nihongi* senmyō, is a borrowing from Korean. The identity of form and function, in particular the fact that the Japanese texts have both the subject marking and bound pronominal functions also found in Korean, are too complete to be coincidental, or for the forms to be inherited from a remote protolanguage.

At the same time we have argued that –*i* in the 8th and 9th century Japanese texts has a more specific function than its Korean counterpart: it marks broad focus subjects. This fact also supports the borrowing hypothesis. While matrix subjects were zero-marked in OJ and EMJ, they are identified by many components of the syntactic system, including word order and honorific agreement. Broad focus subjects, on the other hand, were not dis tinctively marked, at least in written texts. It is quite possible that they were prosodically distinguishable, as in the modern language; at any rate, the notion of broad focus subject was provided by universal grammar, not the donor language.

For EMJ kunten texts, the loan status of –*i* fits within a general picture of a heavy continental, and in particular Sillan, component in the establishment of kunten glossing practice in Japan. The nearly identical usage of –*i* in the *Shoku Nihongi* senmyō suggests a similar component in the development of senmyō textual practice, a possibility which has heretofore escaped Japanese scholarship.

References

Aoki, Hiroshi. 2004. *–Mi* gohō no kōbunteki seikaku – kotengo ni okeru reigakiteki keishiki [The grammatical characteristics of the *–mi* pattern: an exceptional form in classical Japanese]. *Nihongobunpō* 4.2, 38-49.

Babyonyshev, Maria. 1996. *Structural Connections in Syntax and Processing: Studies in Russian and Japanese*. Ph.D. dissertation, Massachusetts Institute of Technology.

Fry, John. 2002. Ellipsis and *wa*-marking in Japanese conversation. Ph.D. dissertation, Stanford University.

Heycock, Caroline. 2008. Japanese *-wa*, *-ga*, and information structure. In Miyagawa, Shigeru and Saito, Mamoru (eds.) *The Oxford. Handbook of Japanese Linguistics*, 54-83. Oxford: Oxford University Press.

Ishida, Haruaki. 1937. *I* wa kaku joshi ni arazu [*I* is not a case particle]. *Kokugo kokubun* S 12.11.

Kim, Twuchan. 1997. *Kuyŏk Inwang-gyŏng* kugyŏl haedok siko [An attempt at an exegesis of the *Kuyŏk Inwang-gyŏng*]. *Kugyŏl yŏngu* 2, 161-241.

Kim, Yŏng-bae. 1972. *Sŏkpo sangjŏ che 23, 24 chuhae*. Seoul: Iljogak.

Kasuga, Masaji. 1969. *Konkōmyō Saishō Ōkyō Koten no Kokugogakuteki Kenkyū*. Benseisha, Tokyo.

King, Ross. 1988. Towards a history of Transitivity in Korean. Paper given at the 24th Meeting of the Chicago Linguistic Society.

Kobayashi, Yoshinori. 1953. Iwayuru shukaku joshi 'i' wa fuku joshi to kangau beki de aru [The so-called nominative particle 'i' should be considered a semantic particle]. *Kokugo* S 28.9

Kobayashi, Yoshinori. 2009. Nihon no kyōten kundoku no ichi genryū – joshi *–i* o tegakari ni. *Kyūko* 55, 1-9.

Kornfilt, Jaklin. 2003. Subject case in Turkish nominalized clauses. In Junghanns, Uwe & Szucsich, Luka (eds.) Syntactic structures and morphological information, 129–215. Berlin: Mouton de Gruyter.

Lee, Ki-moon and Ramsey, Robert. 2011. *A history of Korean*. Cambridge and New York: Cambridge University Press.

Lee, Seung-jae et al. 2009. Kakphil kugyŏl ŭi haedok kwa ponyŏk 2 – Chubon 'Hwaŏm kyŏngkwan 36. Seoul: Th'aehaksa.

Lee, Seung-jae et al. 2009. *Kakphil kugyŏl ŭi haedok kwa ponyŏk 2 – Chubon Hwaŏm kyŏng kwan 36*. Seoul: Th'aehaksa.

Lee, Seung-jae. 2006. Kyōto Kokuritsu Hakubutsukan-zō no Kegon-kyō kan 17 no kunten. *Kuntengo to kunten siryō* 117, 1-17.

Nam, Pung-hyun. 2009. Kodae han'gugŏ yŏngu. Seoul: Sigan ui Mulley.

Nam, Pung-hyun. 2011. Chunggo Han'gugŏ ui munpŏp kaygwan. Kugyŏl yŏngu 27, 5-21.

Ōtsubo, Heiji. 1981. *Heian jidai ni okeru kuntengo no bunpō* [The grammar of kunten texts in the Heian period]. Tokyo: Kazama shobō.

Pesetsky, David. 1982. *Paths and categories*. Ph.D. dissertation, Massachusets Institute of Technology.

Silverstein, Michael. 1976. Silverstein, Michael (1976) "Hierarchy of Features and Ergativity," In R.M.W. Dixon (ed.) *Grammatical Categories in Australian Languages*, Australian Institute of Aborignal Studies, Canberra, pp. 112-171.

Simpson, Andrew. 2008. The grammaticalization of clausal nominalízers in Burmese. In Lopez-Couso, Mara. and Seouane, Elena (eds.) *Rethinking Grammaticalization*, 265-288. Amsterdam: John Benjamins.

Sugai, Yoshinori. 2004. Taykyek cosa uy yumu wa muncang uy kyeychung kwuco – *Sekpo Sangcel, Samgang hayngsilto* lul cwungsim ulo. *Kwukehak* 43.

Tsuta, Kiyoki. 2007 *Mi* no sekai [The world of *mi*]. *Kokugo kokubun* 75: 10-29.

Vovin, Alexander. 1997. On the Syntactic Typology of Old Japanese. *Journal of East Asian Linguistics* 6, 273-290.

Vovin, Alexander. 2010. *Koreo-Japonica: A re-evaluation of a common genetic origin* Hawai`i Studies on Korea. Honolulu: University of Hawai`i Press and Center for Korean Studies, University of Hawai`i.

Watanabe, Akira. 2007. Topic-Focus articulation in Old Japanese: *So/zo* and *koso*. *Proceedings of the Workshop on Altaic Formal Linguistics II*, MIT Working Papers in Linguistics52, 121-137.

Whitman, John. 2009. Kōketsu shiryō to kunten shiryō no setten – Satō-bon *Kegon mongi yōketsu* no okototen/toten o chūshin ni. 100th Meeting of the Kuntengo gakkai, Kyoto University, May 2009.

Yanagida, Yuko. 2005. Ergativity and Bare Nominals in Early Old Japanese. Paper presented at the Workshop on Theoretical East Asian Linguistics, Harvard University, Cambridge, MA.

Yanagida, Yuko. 2006. Word Order and Clause Structure in Early Old Japanese. *Journal of East Asian Linguistics* 15, 37-68.

Yanagida, Yuko (2007a) Miyagawa's (1989) Exceptions: An Ergative Analysis. *MIT Working Papers in Linguistics* 55, 265-276.

Yanagida, Yuko. 2007b. Jôdaigo no Nôkakusei ni tuite [On Ergativity in Old Japanese], In Hasegawa, Nobuko (ed.) *Nihongo no Shubun Genshō* [Main Clause Phenomena in Japanese] Hituzi Shobo, Tokyo, pp. 147-188.

Yanagida, Yuko, and John Whitman. 2009. Alignment and word order in Old Japanese. *Journal of East Asian Linguistics* 18, 101-144.

Yoshida, Kanehiko, Tsukishima, Hiroshi and Ishiduka, Harumiti. 2001. *Kuntengo jiten*. Tokyo: Tōkyō-dō shuppan.

Part III

Semantics

Reference Resolution in Discourse with Multiple Knowledge Representations: A View from *NP-no-koto* in Japanese

YOUNGJU KIM[*] AND HIROMU SAKAI
Hiroshima University

1. Introduction

In the dynamic process of discourse, the speaker and the hearer keep track of how much knowledge about the discourse topic is shared between them and actively update their shared knowledge representations to maintain the discourse coherence (Stalnaker, 1978; Kamp, 1981; Heim, 1982; Fauconnier, 1985). In this paper, we inquire into the role of Japanese expression *NP-no-koto* from the viewpoint of maintenance of knowledge representations in discourse.[1] Previous semantic analyses of the morpheme *-no-koto*

[*] This research was supported by the grant-in-aid for scientific research (A) from the Japanese Society for Promotion of Science ('Typological variation and plasticity of neurocognitive mechanism for language processing: A Vie from comparative studies on East Asian

[1] Earlier versions of this inquiry are found in Kim and Sakai (2010) and Kim (2011). We adopted the framework of mental space theory by Fauconnier (1985) in these articles.

Japanese/Korean Linguistics 21.
Edited by Seungho Nam, Heejeong Ko and Jongho Jun.

assume that use of this morpheme is optional if it is attached to definite or quantificational NPs (Kurafuji, 1998; Takubo, 2007). We first challenge this assumption by presenting a novel set of data showing that the morpheme *-no-koto* is not totally optional even if it is attached to definite or quantificational NPs. We point out that this morpheme is frequently found in a copula sentence used as an answer to a question about referential content of certain linguistic expressions.[2] To answer this type of question, the speaker often uses the sentence frame such as 'what A means is B'. The morpheme *-no-koto* is typically used to mark the expression B in the above sentence frame. Based on this observation, we argue that this morpheme has a discourse function for resolving reference uncertainty by linking the reference of a linguistic expression that does not have a value in one of the discourse participant's knowledge representation to the existing file entity in the shared knowledge representation. The overall results support the view that the Japanese language is sensitive to the knowledge state of discourse participants and employs overt morphological markers designed for maintenance of knowledge representations (Takubo, 1989; Takubo and Kinsui, 1996).

2. How do Speakers and Hearers Resolve Reference Uncertainty in Discourse?

In Heim's theory (1982), the dynamic process of semantic interpretation in discourse contexts is assimilated to file keeping operation. Indefinite NPs create a new 'file entry' whereas definite NPs update the content of existing file entry within the knowledge representation shared by discourse participants ('common ground' in the sense of Stalnaker, 1978). Consider the following example from Heim (1982).

(1) A woman was bitten by a dog. She hit him with a puddle. It broke in half. The dog ran away.

In this context, the newly introduced NPs such as *a woman* or *a dog* create a new file entry. Definite NPs in the subsequent part of discourse, *she, him, or the dog*, update the discourse knowledge by adding new information, such as *bitten by a dog, hit with a puddle*, etc., to the existing entry.

Applying Heim's theory to actual discourse, we often find that the matter is not as simple as shown in the example above. It is particularly problematic when there is some asymmetry between the speakers' and the hearers' knowledge representations. That is, in the process of actual discourse,

[2] Previous research mostly focused on *NP-no-koto* that appears in the object position of transitive sntences. See Sasaguri (1999), Sasaguri, Kinjo, and Takubo (1999) for overview.

the speakers and the hearers do not always share their knowledge representations, and make effort to fill their knowledge gaps to maintain discourse coherence.[3] Let us consider the following discourse in Japanese as an illustration of this point.

(2) Speaker A: Kaminarioyaji-ni shikarare-ta-yo.
Thunderbolt father-DAT be scolded-PAST
'I was scolded by the thunderbolt father.'
Speaker B: Kaminarioyaji-***tte*** dare?
Thunderbolt father-to say who
'Who is "the thunderbolt father"?'
Speaker A: Kaminarioyaji-tte iu-no-wa
Thunderbolt father-to say-TOP
uchi-no otoosan ***#(-no-koto)*** da-yo.
my father (-GEN-KOTO) is
'The "thunderbolt father" refers to my father.'

Speaker A's utterance is intended to add new information related to the speaker himself and the NP *kaminarioyaji* 'the thunderbolt father'. He assumes that the file entry corresponding to *kaminarioyaji* has already been created in their knowledge representations. This is shown by the fact that he does not include any information about the identity of this person in his utterance. Speaker B's response indicates that this assumption is actually incorrect. He does not now the identity of the person called *kaminarioyaji*, and therefore asks Speaker A to provide him sufficient information for identification.

The Japanese language sometimes employs overt linguistic markers to facilitate this kind of discourse knowledge maintenance. Notice that, in Speaker A's response, the NP *kaminarioyaji* is followed by a morpheme -*tte*. According to Takubo (1989), this morpheme signals that the NP cannot pick up its referent within Speaker B's knowledge representation.[4] To be more precise, the morpheme *-tte* overtly indicates that Speaker B uses this

---

[3] See Gunlogson (2003) for an example of elaboration of Stalnaker's (1978) original idea by incorporating disagreement concerning common belief among discourse participants.

[4] Takubo (1989: 255) presents an example like (i).

(i) A: Tanaka-san-ni att-ta-yo.
-Mr.-DAT meet-PAST
'I met Mr. Tanaka.'
B: Tanaka-san-tte dare?
-Mr.-to say who
'Who is Mr. Tanaka?'

The morpheme *-tte* indicates that Speaker B does not know the referent of the NP *Tanaka-san* 'Mr. Tanaka'.

NP as a kind of meta-linguistic expression without any value. Based on such observation, we argue that the Japanese language is sensitive to discourse knowledge of speakers and hearers.

Now, notice further that there is another morpheme *-no-koto* associated with the definite NP *uchi-no otoosan* 'my father' in Speaker B's utterance. This morpheme *-no-koto* is often assumed as 'semantically vacuous (Takubo, 2007)' or 'has no semantic contribution (Kurafuji, 1998)' when it is added to definite or quantificational NPs. We then predict that this morpheme should be optional in this context. Contrary to this prediction, Speaker A's response sounds quite odd if we remove the morpheme *-no-koto*.

The question thus arises as to the role of this morpheme in discourse. Before examining the function of this morpheme from the viewpoint of discourse knowledge maintenance, let us review the semantic or pragmatic properties of this morpheme discussed in previous literature.

3. Previous Approaches to *NP-no-koto*

The Japanese morpheme *koto* 'fact' has been well known for its syntactic property that introduces a sentential complement (Kuno, 1973; Josephs, 1976). In such case, its meaning and function is similar to the corresponding English expression *the fact (that)*. Surprisingly, the Japanese *koto* has another syntactic property that is not observed in its English counterpart *the fact (that)*. That is, it can be associated with noun phrases along with a genitive case particle *-no*. A series of recent research (Kurafuji, 1998; Sasaguri, Kinjo, and Takubo, 1999; Sasaguri, 1999; Takubo 2007) focuses on this unique property and discusses its semantic or pragmatic function. Consider the example shown in (3) below.

(3) a. Takashi-wa sensei-o sagashite-iru.
-TOP teacher-ACC is searching for
'Takashi is looking for a teacher.'

b. Takashi-wa sensei-no-koto-o sagashite-iru.
-TOP teacher-GEN-KOTO-ACC is searching for
'Takashi is looking for the teacher.'

c. Takashi-wa Mayumi/dareka (-no-koto)-o sagashite-iru.
-TOP teacher (-GEN-KOTO)-ACC is searching for
'Takashi is looking for Mayumi/someone.'

In the example (3b) and (3c), the object NP is followed by the particle *-no* and the morpheme *-koto*.

The bare NP object *sensei* 'teacher' in (3a) can be interpreted either as definite/specific or indefinite/non-specific, whereas the object *sensei-no-koto* in (3b) only has a definite/specific interpretation. Kurafuji (1998) points out this distinction and argues that *-no-koto* introduces an iota-operator as the English definite article *the*.[5] In his analysis, *-koto* takes a common noun as its argument and its semantic function is mostly identical to that of the English definite article.[6]

Sasaguri, Kinjo, and Takubo (1999) present a more comprehensive study on the distribution and function of this morpheme. They argue that the expression *NP-no-koto* denotes a set of properties of NP. Takubo (2007) formalizes this idea by assuming that *-no-koto* is an overt marker of semantic operation of sublimation in the sense of Dowty et al. (1981). That is, this morpheme takes a particular individual as its argument and yields a set of properties attributed to the individual. In Takubo's view, the host NP must be specific because the speakers must know the properties attributed to the NP in order to execute the sublimation operation. Regardless of the difference in semantic mechanisms, Kurafuji's and Takubo's analyses share an important point that the semantic effect of *-no-koto* is almost vacuous when it is attached to a definite NP or a quantificational NP.[7] These previous analyses thus predict that addition of *-no-koto* to a definite or quantificational NP should be optional. As we have shown in the previous section, this prediction does not bear out. The morpheme is strongly preferred in one context whereas in other context it is nearly unacceptable. These purely semantic approaches do not explain such contrast.

Another type of approach is found in Sasaguri (1999) or Kageyama (2010). Sasaguri points out that this morpheme is used to express the speakers' emotional attitude and should be classified into modality expressions.[8] This type of view can be supported by the observation that the morpheme should not be added to an unknown person as shown in the following example.

---

[5] The iota-operator takes a set of individuals denoted by NP and picks up the individuals uniquely determined by the contest.

[6] See Hara, Kim, Sakai and Tamura (2011) for this line of approach. They argue that the morpheme *-no-koto* introduces a maximality operator in the sense of Schwarzschild (1991, 1992).

[7] The important difference is that Kurafuji assumes the NP in *NP-no-koto* as indefinite whereas Takubo assumes that it must be either definite or specific indefinite.

[8] To be more precise, Sasaguri argues that modality is expressed by the sentence-final morpheme expressing modality. The morpheme *-koto* overtly represent that the speaker recognize the NP according to the modality.

(4) a. Ijimekko-ga boku-no-koto-o but-ta.
Bully-NOM me-GEN-KOTO-ACC hit
'The bully hit me.'
b. Ijimekko-ga shiranai-hito (?-no-koto)-o but-ta.
Bully-NOM unknown person (-GEN-KOTO)-ACC hit
'The bully hit an unknown person.'

Although the contrast between (4a) and (4b) is very subtle, it corroborates the view that the morpheme expresses a certain kind of emotional attitude. Kageyama also discusses similar cases along with other interesting observations, and argues that one of the functions of this morpheme is to express empathy or affectedness.

Neither of these approach covers all the cases where the morpheme *-no-koto* is used. In particular, when this morpheme is attached to exactly the same NP as we shall see shortly, it seems very difficult to explain its function. Another limitation of the previous approach is that they do not examine the use of this morpheme within broader discourse contexts. Most of the examples they have cited are sentences isolated from their discourse contexts. In section 4, we present examples along with preceding contexts or actual situations. After that, we return to the points addressed by the previous literature and discuss similarities and differences in section 5.

4. Discourse Function of *NP-no-koto*

In this section, we examine three sets of contexts in which the use of *-no-koto* is preferred or dispreferred depending on the contexts. We first present the most typical case in which the morpheme *-no-koto* is found, i.e. the case in which the speaker gives explanation or definition about linguistic expressions unknown to the hearer. In this case, the host NP for *-no-koto* is usually indefinite. We then present an example in which the use of *-no-koto* is preferred even when it is associated with definite or quantificational NPs. The third example, which is crucial to our proposal, indicates that certain 'gap' of knowledge representations among discourse participants motivates the use of *-no-koto*. Examination of these examples leads us to conclude that the use of *-no-koto* is constrained by knowledge representations of the discourse participants.

4.1 Japanese Restaurant Context

Suppose that the Speaker A and the Speaker B are looking at the menu in a Japanese restaurant in Seoul. Speaker A has little knowledge about Japanese cuisine and asks Speaker B for assistance about the selection from the menu.

(5) Speaker A is looking through the menu and pointing at one of the pictures:

Speaker A: Kore-wa nan-desu-ka.
this-TOP what-is
'What is this?'

Speaker B: (Sore-wa) Sushi (#-no-koto) desu.
(that-TOP) sushi (-GEN-KOTO) is
'That is sushi.'

In this context, Speaker B should use a bare NP *sushi* in his answer. The use of morpheme *-no-koto* makes the speaker B's response very awkward or almost unacceptable. In a minimally contrasting context shown below, the use of *-no-koto* is perfectly legitimate and even preferred.

(6) Speaker A is looking through the menu and pointing at the Hangul character indicating the Korean word 'chobap':

Speaker A: Chobap-to-iu-no-wa nan-desu-ka.
-to say-GEN-TOP what is
'What does the expression "chobap" mean?'

Speaker B: (Chobap-to-iu-no-wa) Sushi # (-no-koto) desu.
-to say-GEN-TOP sushi (-GEN-KOTO) is
'(The expression "chobap") is sushi.'

The difference between the context in (5) and the context (6) can be attributed to the difference in the knowledge state of Speaker A. In (5), Speaker A asked for information needed for identification of the pictured object. Using file-keeping analogy, there is an existing file-entry corresponding to 'this' and he requires information for updating the file page. Since Speaker B answered that it is sushi, the new information *is sushi* is added to the file page. In (6), Speaker A expresses that there is no entry corresponding the expression *chobap* in his file. He thus asks for information to create a new file-entry. Speaker B helps in this process by pointing out that even though the expression *chobap* is unfamiliar to Speaker A, its referent actually exists in Speaker A's file. Namely, the denotation of *chobap* is identical to that of the expression *sushi*.

One can assimilate the process described above to giving a word definition in foreign language dictionaries. In a foreign language dictionary, the referent of the target language expression is usually unknown to the dictionary users. So the dictionary gives the information necessary for reference resolution by giving the corresponding expression in the source language whose referent is established in the knowledge representations by the users. In this sense, providing word definition is to introduce a link between two distinct knowledge representations, the knowledge representations of the target language and those of the source language.

We can thus hypothesize that the primary discourse function of the morpheme *-no-koto* is to provide such link among multiple knowledge representations. By overtly indicating the existence of multiple knowledge representations, the morpheme *-no-koto* helps discourse participants to resolve reference uncertainty. The morpheme *-no-koto* indicates that the referent of unknown linguistic expressions can be found within the shared knowledge representations as the referent of its host NP.

4.2 Lost Cell-Phone Context

In the previous subsection, we presented a context that involves a question about the content of unknown words. In the example we have presented, the morpheme *-no-koto* is attached to an indefinite NP. It might be argued that it functions as a kind of definiteness marker as proposed by Kurafuji (1998) or a marker for 'sublimation' as argued by Takubo (2007). According to these views, the primary function of this morpheme is semantic. The pragmatic/discourse function might be derived from its semantic function as secondary effect.

In this subsection, we make sure that the primary function of *-no-koto* is discourse pragmatic by presenting another with definite NPs. Suppose that you are a high school teacher who just finished a class. You found a cell-phone lost under a desk in the classroom. A student came back into the classroom.

(7) The student is anxiously searching for something under the desk:

Teacher: (Sagashite-iru-no-wa) kore (#-no-koto)-desu-ka.
what is being looked for-TOP this (-GEN-KOTO) is
'Is this the thing you are looking for?'

In this context if the teacher used the morpheme *-no-koto* with the definite NP *kore* 'this', his utterance would sound very strange. Actually, his utterance sounds as if he is a mind reader. Now, please consider a slightly different context as shown below.

(8) The student is anxiously searching for something under the desk but found nothing. Then she/he asked the teacher:

Student: Keitai-o mikake-masen-deshita-ka.
Cell phone-ACC find-NOT-Q
'Didn't you find any cell phone lost in this room?'
Teacher: (Keitai-toiu-no-wa) kore *(no-koto)-desu-ka.
what is called cell phone-TOP this (-GEN-KOTO) is

'Is this the cell phone you are looking for?'

The use of *-no-koto* is strongly preferred in this context. Since previous analyses assume that the semantic function of *-no-koto* is vacuous if they are attached to definite NPs, this clear contrast is quite unexpected.

We argue that the morpheme *-no-koto* plays the same role in the previous example from the discourse pragmatic point of view. In the former context, there is no reference uncertainty of linguistic expressions. The teacher is just talking about the objects directly observable within the visual context. In the latter context, the student introduces the linguistic expression *keitai* 'cell phone' whose referent is unknown to the teacher. The teacher therefore wants to link its referent to the referent within the shared knowledge representations. The teacher thus asks the student: I am not sure about the referent of your expression *keitai*. Can we identify its referent to the referent of *this*, which is well established between us?

In our analysis, a unified analysis is possible for the *-no-koto* attached to either indefinite NPs or definite NPs. In either of the cases, the morpheme indicates that the referent of the expression exists within the domain of knowledge representations shared among the discourse participants.

4.3 Three Bad Students Context

The examples presented in the last two subsections indicate that the morpheme *-no-koto* has a unique discourse pragmatic function even if it has no obvious semantic function. We argued that it plays a role in resolving reference uncertainty within discourse with multiple knowledge representations. At the same time, since we have examined relatively simple discourse contexts so far, one might still argue that the function of this morpheme can be captured without introducing the concept of 'multiple knowledge representations'. In this subsection, we will present a more complex discourse context that is crucial to our argument. That is, we will show that context in which the 'gap' of knowledge representations among discourse participants crucially motivates the use of *-no-koto*.

Let us imagine that there are a group of bad students in a high school. They are talking about one of the group members who has recently been kicked out from the school because of misbehavior.

(9) Student A, a member of the student group, is talking to Student B, another member of the group:

Student A: Tsugi-wa futari taigaku-ni naru-mitaida-ze.
Next time two kick out find-NOT-Q
'It seems that two more will be kicked out from the school next time.'

Student B: (Taigaku-ni-naru-no-wa) oretachi (#-no-koto) ka-na.
going to be kicked out we (-GEN-KOTO) are
'Are we going to be kicked out?'

In this context, a bare NP is preferred over *NP-no-koto*. The use of *-no-koto* is not preferred and makes the sentence very awkward. In contrast, the use of *-no-koto* is legitimate and *NP-no-koto* is preferred over a bare NP in the following context.

(10) Student C, not a member of the student group, approached them and made the following remark and went away:

Student C: Tsugi-wa futari taigaku-ni naru-mitaida-ze.
Next time two kick out find-NOT-Q
'It seems that two more will be kicked out from the school next time.'

Student A and B (talking to each other):
(Taigaku-ni-naru-tteiu-no-wa) oretachi #(-no-koto) ka-na.
going to be kicked out-to say-TOP we (-GEN-KOTO) are
'Are we going to be kicked out?'

What distinguishes these two contexts? It is the knowledge representations among discourse participants. In the first context, all the discourse participants have the same information about the students who are going to be kicked out. There is only one single knowledge representation shared by all the discourse participants. Therefore, it is not necessary to link across knowledge representations. In the second context, Student C, who is not a member of the group, seems to have the information that is not shared with Student A and Student B's group. The referent of expression *taigaku-ni-naru-gakusei* 'the students who are kicked out' might have specific referents in Student C's knowledge representation, but it is not the case in Student A and Student B's knowledge representation. It is therefore necessary to ask whether the referents of *taigaku-ni-naru-gakusei* 'the students who are kicked out' might be the referents of *oretachi* 'us' within their shared knowledge representation. In short, contexts (9) and (10) are distinguishable only with respect to knowledge representations of discourse participants. Our proposal makes correct prediction about whether the morpheme *-no-koto* can be used or not depending on the contexts.

5. NP-*no-koto* with or without discourse context

Let us return to the previous semantic or pragmatic analyses of *-no-koto*. The aim of this paper is somewhat limited to examining discourse function of the morpheme *-no-koto* from the viewpoint of theory of knowledge maintenance in discourse. The result thus does not argue for or against existing analyses. For instance, Kurafuji (1998) or Takubo (2007) argued that *-no-koto* has a semantic function introducing definite or specific NPs. Since definite or specific NPs in principle refer to existing file-entries within discourse, it naturally marks referents within shared knowledge representations. The crucial difference lies in the case when the morpheme *-no-koto* is attached to the definite NP. In such cases, its function is vacuous according to the semantic analysis. Our discourse pragmatic analysis still assumes that it fulfills a non-trivial discourse function to resolve reference uncertainty.

As for its function for expressing emotional modality or empathy of speakers, as pointed out by Sasaguri (1999) or Kageyama (2010), the contrast reported in previous literature is often very subtle. It might be possible to find some relationship between these functions and the discourse pragmatic function because the entity located within the shared knowledge representation might attract more emotional content or speakers' empathy. We should wait for more detailed descriptive study on these functions before presenting theoretical analysis.

6. Concluding Remarks

In this paper, we examined the role of Japanese expression *NP-no-koto* from the viewpoint of maintenance of knowledge representations by speakers and hearers. We presented a novel set of data showing that the use of morpheme *-no-koto* is constrained by discourse contexts, and argued that its discourse function is to indicate that the referent of the host NP already exists within the shared knowledge representations. In active discourse, speakers and hearers do not always share their discourse knowledge. In such cases, one of the discourse participants sometimes ask the other for information about identification of unknown linguistic expressions. In such cases, the morpheme *-no-koto* explicitly marks the NP whose referent has already been in the shared knowledge representations. Using this morpheme, the speaker thus helps the hearer to resolve reference ambiguity within discourse with multiple knowledge representations.

The results of this study make two significant contributions to research on natural language discourse. First, they revealed a unique property of Japanese with respect to knowledge maintenance in discourse. That is, the Japanese language has overt morphological markers for linguistic expressions wherein the referent has already been established in discourse. It thus provides another piece of empirical support for the claim that the Japanese language is sensitive to knowledge representations in discourse (Takubo, 1989; Takubo and Kinsui, 1996). Second, they provide an empirical support for the view that the discourse participants' knowledge representations are divided into multiple sub-domains. The discourse participants actively maintain discourse coherence by filling the 'gap' among knowledge representations. Theories of natural language discourse should therefore incorporate such dynamic process of knowledge maintenance.

At the same time, the present study is limited in its scope because we have discussed only a sub-case of cases in which the morpheme *-no-koto* is used. A more comprehensive study on the role of this morpheme in discourse is left for future research.

References

Dowty, D., W. Robert and S. Peters. 1981. *Introduction to Montague semantics.* Dordrecht: Reidel.

Fauconnier, G. 1985. *Mental Spaces.* Cambridge, MA: MIT Press.

Gunlogson, C. 2003. True to Form: Raising and Falling Declaratives as Questions in English, New York: Routledge.

Hara,Y. Y. Kim, H. Sakai, and S. Tamura. 2012. Semantic realization of the layered TP: Evidence from the ambiguity of the sentential *koto*-nominal, *Japanese/Korean Linguistics,* vol. 20.

Heim, I. 1982. The Semantics of Definite and Indefinite Noun Phrases, Doctoral dissertation, University of Massachusetts, Amherst.

Josephs, L. S. 1976. Complementation, In M. Shibatani, ed. *Syntax and Semantics 5: Japanese Generative Grammar*, New York: Academic Press.

Kageyama, T. 2010. Gengogaku-to Kikai Honyaku-wo Tsunagu Goi Imiron [Lexical Semantics Connecting Linguistics to Machine Transration]. A Talk Presented at the First Meeting of Studies on Industrial Japanese, Tokyo University.

Kamp 1981. A theory of truth and semantic representation. In J. Groenendijk, T. Janssen, and M. Stokhof (eds.), *Formal Methods in the Study of Language.* Amsterdam: Mathematisch Centrum.

Kim, Y. and H. Sakai. 2010. Keishikimeishi koto-no modariti: Danwa-ni-okeru chishikikanri-no kanten-kara. [Modality of formal noun *koto*: A view from knowledge management in discourse.] *Proceedings of the* 140th Meeting of *Linguistic Society of Japan:* 92-97.

Kim, Y. 2011. *Gendai Nihongo-ni-okeru 'Meishi-no koto'-no Imi-to Kinou.* [Meaning and Function of *NP-no-koto* in Modern Japanese.] Ph.D. Dissertation, Hiroshima University.

Kuno, S. 1973. *The Structure of the Japanese Language.* Cambridge: MIT Press.

Kurafuji, T. 1998. Definiteness of koto in Japanese and its nullification. In *RuLing Papers*, 169–184, Rutgers University.

Sasaguri, J. 1999. Meishiku-no modaliti-toshite-no *koto*: 'N-no koto'-to jyutsugo-no soukan-kara. [Koto as modality of noun phrases: A view from relationship between *N-no-koto* and predicates.] *Gengogaku-to Nihongo Kyouiku [Linguistics and Japanese Langauge Education]*, 161-173. Tokyo: Kurosio Shuppan.

Sasaguri, J., Y. Kinjou, and Y. Takubo. 1999. Shinteki koui-ni okeru ninshiki shutai-to Taishou-tono kankei. [Relationship between cognitive agent and theme in psychological performance.] *Proceedings of the 16th Annual Meeting of Japanese Cognitive Science Society* (http://www.jcss.gr.jp/iccs99OLP/p3-8/p3-08.htm).

Schwarzschild, R. 1991. *On the Meaning of Definite Plural Noun Phrases*. Ph. D. Dissertation, University of Massachusetts at Amherst.

Schwarzschild, R. 1992. Types of plural individuals. *Linguistics and Philosophy* 15(6): 641–675.

Stalnaker 1978. Assertion. In P. Cole ed., *Syntax and Semantics 9: Pragmatics*, New York: Academic Press.

Takubo, Y. 1989. Meishiku-no modariti [The modality of noun phrase]. *Nihongo-no Modality [Modality in Japanese]*, 211-233. Tokyo: Kurosio Shuppan.

Takubo, Y. 2007. An overt marker for individual sublimation in Japanese. In M. S. B. Frellesvig and J. C. Smith (eds.), *The History and the Structure of Japanese*, 135–151. Tokyo: Kurosio Shuppan.

Takubo, Y and S. Kinsui. 1996. Hukusuu-no shinteki ryouiki-niyoru danwakanririron. [Discourse management in terms of multiple mental spaces.] *Japanese Cognitive Science Society 3*: 57-74.

Semantic Functions of *Always* and *Only* in Korean: Evidence from Prosody

YONG-CHEOL LEE* AND SATOSHI NAMBU
University of Pennsylvania

1. Introduction

Well known as focus-sensitive operators, focus particles (henceforth FPs), such as *only*, are sensitive to the placement of focus as in (1).

(1) a. Jan only gave Bill $[\text{money}]_F$.
  b. Jan only gave $[\text{Bill}]_F$ money.
  (Beaver et al. 2007:249)

In (1), a subscripted F marks the focused elements accompanied by prosodic salience, and two interpretations are available depending on which element is focused. For example, when *money* is focused (1a), the sentence means: *Everything Jan gave Bill was money*. When *Bill* is focused (1b), the

*This paper is an extended version of Lee and Nambu (2012) with new sets of stimuli. For the comments on this work, our sincere thanks go to Aviad Eilam, Florian Schwarz, Satoshi Tomioka, Jiahong Yuan, Marielle Lerner, and Catherine Lai. Additionally, we would like to thank the audiences at the 21st Japanese/Korean Linguistics held in Seoul National University in 2011. Last but not least, we express our deep gratitude to Jiahong Yuan for providing subject fees.

Japanese/Korean Linguistics 21.
Edited by Seungho Nam, Heejeong Ko and Jongho Jun.

sentence means: *Everyone Jan gave money to was Bill*. Thus, the examples in (1) demonstrate that differentiating a placement of focus realized by prosody affects the truth conditions of the sentence. In this sense, FPs associate with focus (Jackendoff 1972, Rooth 1985).

Beaver and Clark (2002, 2003, 2008) investigate the properties of two FPs, *always* and *only*, in terms of how they associate with focus. They argue that both of the FPs can be analyzed as universal quantifiers, as shown in (2).

(2) a. Sandy always feeds $[\text{Fido}]_F$ Nutrapup.
b. Sandy only feeds $[\text{Fido}]_F$ Nutrapup.
c. $\forall x\ \text{feed}(\text{sandy}, x, \text{nutrapup}) \rightarrow x = \text{fido}$
(Beaver and Clark 2003:325)

(2a) and (2b) demonstrate the same interpretation: *Everything Sandy feeds Nutrapup to is Fido*. However, Beaver and Clark (2002:15) argue that elements quantified over by *always* and *only* are determined in a different way. Elements associated with *always* are 'determined entirely pragmatically,' whereas elements associated with *only* are 'constrained compositionally.' To ascertain the different properties of the two FPs, Beaver and Clark (2003, 2008) conduct three tests: reduced pronoun test, extraction test, and ellipsis test. Based on the results, they conclude that elements associated with *only* require prosodic prominence, whereas *always* is able to make an association without prosodic prominence in its domain. To explain the difference between *always* and *only*, Beaver and Clark (2008) propose the Quasi/Free/Conventional (QFC) Theory, which is a hybrid theory of semantics and pragmatics. They claim that associations of *always* and *only* with focus are formed differently, which contrasts with previous studies that make no difference in treatment of FPs (Büring 2008, Rooth 1992, 2010). In the QFC Theory, the function of *always* is categorized as a free association, which constructs an association with contextually salient sets of events or situations. *Only*, on the other hand, functions as a conventional association, which constructs an association based on a lexically encoded dependency on focus.

In this study, we investigate Korean FPs *hangsang* 'always' and *ocik* 'only' and their relationship with associated elements from the perspective of prosody. In the following sections, we provide data, which shows that the Korean FPs *hangsang* and *ocik* behave similarly to the English FPs in terms of how they associate with focus. Then we consider the prosodic realizations of focus and givenness in Korean. Finally, Section 1.3 presents our research question.

1.1 Hangsang and ocik

In this section, we provide examples of *hangsang* and *ocik* with respect to *association with focus*, using two tests (i.e. reduced pronoun test, ellipsis test) based on the studies of Beaver and Clark (2003, 2008). Using the reduced pronoun test, Beaver and Clark (2003) find that *always* can associate with a phonetically reduced pronoun, whereas *only* cannot. This evidence demonstrates that *always* does not need prosodic prominence to create an association in its domain. In contrast, the element associated with *only* must be prosodically prominent or, in a lax manner, must not be prosodically deaccented. Since reduced pronouns are not allowed in Korean, we substitute pro to investigate the phenomenon. The context below is designed to assign focus on the FPs in (3).

> Context: You had many discussions with Sandy, but what I want to know is the extent to which you talked about Fred. Of all the times you talked with Sandy, how often was Fred the person you talked about? (Beaver and Clark 2003:21)

(3) a. Na-nun [hangsang]$_F$ Sandy-wa pro tholon-ha-yess-ta.
I-Top always Sandy-with discuss-do-Pst-Decl
'I always discussed'im with Sandy.'

b. #Na-nun [ocik]$_F$ Sandy-wa pro tholon-ha-yess-ta.
I-Top only Sandy-with discuss-do-Pst-Decl
'I only discussed'im with Sandy.'

These examples demonstrate that *hangsang* can associate with pro, but *ocik* cannot. Given the evidence in (3), we claim that the element associated with *hangsang* does not have to be spelled out at PF, whereas the element associated with *ocik* must be pronounced at PF.

The second test (i.e. ellipsis) also clarifies the difference between *hangsang* and *ocik*. Beaver and Clark (2008) show that English *always* can associate with an elided element, which is opposed to *only*. (4) also proves that *hangsang* can associate with the elided element based on the context below. On the contrary, *ocik* cannot create such an association under the ellipsis condition. In this case, the Korean FPs behave the same as their English counterparts.

> Context: At the meeting, some people prepare their presentation and others clean up the table. Some do both. What about Yenghuy and Chelswu? (Modified from Beaver and Clark 2008)

(4) a. Yenghuy-ka hangsang palphyo-lul cwunpi-ha-ki
Yenghuy-Nom always presentation-Acc prepare-do-Nominal
ttaymwuney Chelswu-to hangsang kulehkey hap-ni-ta.
because Chelswu-too always so do-Hon-Decl
'Because Yenghuy always prepares presentations, Chelswu always does so, too.'

b. #Yenghuy-ka ocik palphyo-lul cwunpi-ha-ki
Yenghuy-Nomonly presentation-Acc prepare-do-Nominal
ttaymwuney Chelswu-to ocik kulehkey hap-ni-ta.
because Chelswu-too only so do-Hon-Decl
'Because Yenghuy only prepares presentations, Chelswu only does so, too.'

The two tests above demonstrate different behaviors of the Korean FPs *hangsang* and *ocik*. *Hangsang* can create an association freely, but *ocik* shows a more restricted association. In what follows, we consider the prosodic realization of focus and givenness in Korean.

1.2 Prosodic realizations of focus and givenness

It is well known that a focused element is generally characterized with prosodic prominence. However, the prosodic realization of focus is dependent on the intonational phonology of language (Jun 2011). For instance, languages are normally classified as 'head-prominence' and 'edge-prominence' languages (Jun 2006). In the edge-prominence languages (e.g. Korean and Japanese), focus is signaled by prosodic phrasing; that is, by the intonation at the edge of a phrase. In these languages, a strong phrase boundary is inserted in the focused area, where a focused element shows a larger pitch range than its unfocused counterpart. On the contrary, givenness is characterized with dephrasing, which is the absence of accentual phrase boundaries (Ladd 1996). Consider the following examples.

(5) a. {sachon-enni} {<u>ilum-i</u>} {mwue-ni}
cousin-old sister name-Nom what-Q
'What is sister-cousin's name?'

b. {sachon-enni <u>ilum-i</u>} swuni-ci}
cousin-old sister name-Nom Suni-Decl
'Sister-cousin's name is Suni.'
(Jun 1993:199)

In (5), curly brackets represent the accentual phrase. In (5a), the underlined NP *ilumi* is new information, thus forming a separate accentual phrase. However, in (5b), *ilumi* is given information. In this case, the accentual phrase of the NP *ilumi* is deleted, and then the NP is dephrased.[1] Jun (2011) argues that the dephrased phrase is realized with a substantially lowered pitch range.

As noted above, focus is marked with prosodic prominence and thus contrasts with givenness by prosody. Hence, the auditory perception of focus is assumed to be well perceived, since focus is generally signaled by prosodic prominence. Thus, although little is known about the auditory perception of focus and givenness in Korean (Jun p.c.), we expect Korean listeners to perceive the prosodic distinction between focus and givenness with high accuracy.

1.3 Research questions

We have examined the different properties of the Korean FPs *hangsang* and *ocik* based on the pro and ellipsis tests. We found that *hangsang* is able to associate with the pro and elided elements, whereas *ocik* is not able to associate with such elements. What is common between the pro and elided elements is that they are not spelled out at PF. In other words, the pro and the elided elements are phonetically empty. Therefore, these tests clearly demonstrate that *ocik* requires the element that must be phonetically present at PF, which is opposed to *hangsang*.

With this in mind, we assume that *ocik* disfavors the element that is phonetically reduced as the English *only*, but *hangsang* is able to associate with such a phonetically reduced element. To address the assumption, we manipulate pitch contours of *hangsang* and *ocik* and the elements associated with the FPs. The purpose of the manipulation is to find an answer to the following question: whether or not the element associated with the Korean FPs is prosodically prominent. According to the QFC theory, we assume that the element associated with *hangsang* does not have to show prosodic prominence, but the element associated with *ocik* must be prosodically prominent. The goal of this study is complete through a perception study.

2. Methodology

2.1 Stimuli

The stimuli were provided in three different environments: (i) the sentence in isolation (6a); (ii) the sentence preceded by a prompt question (6b); and (iii) the sentence given with a discourse context (6c). The last two environments were designed to elicit a focus effect on the elements *cenchelul* 'the

---

[1]Ladd (1996) argues that Korean dephrasing is corresponding to English deaccenting, saying they are just different surface realizations of the same underlying effects.

subway' and *phicalul* 'pizza'. In total, seventy-two sound files (2 FPs x 2 target sentences x 3 prosody models x 2 speakers x 3 environments) served as stimuli. In (6), the target sentences are in square brackets; the FPs are in boldface. Korean data is transliterated through the Yale Romanization system.

(6) a. The sentence in isolation
  i. [Cenun chwulkunhal ttay **hangsang/ocik** cenchelul thapnita.]
    'I always/only take the subway to work.'
  ii. [Cenun cemsimey **hangsang/ocik** phicalul meksupnita.]
    'I always/only have pizza for lunch.'
 b. The sentence preceded by a prompt question
  i. Q: Chwulkunhal ttay cwulo mwuesul thaseyyo?
    'Which transportation do you usually take to work?'
   A: [Cenun chwulkunhal ttay **hangsang/ocik** cenchelul thapnita.]
    'I always/only take the subway to work.'
  ii. Q: Cemsim-ey cwulo mwues-ul tusey-yo?
    'What do you usually have for lunch?'
   A: [Cenun cemsim-ey **hangsang/ocik** phicalul meksupnita.]
    'I always/only have pizza for lunch.'
 c. The sentence given with a discourse context
  i. Sewuleynun manhun kyothongswutani isssupnita. Haciman achimeynun kyothongcheycungi simhaki ttaymwuney cenun chwulkunhal ttay cisangkyothongul thaci anhsupnita. [Cenun chwulkunhal ttay **hangsang/ocik** cenchelul thapnita.]
    'There are many kinds of transportation in Seoul. Because the traffic jam is terrible in the morning, however, I don't take ground transportation to work. I always/only take the subway to work.'
  ii. Myechmyech chinkwutulun cemsimey ceeykey kokina laymenul mekcako hayessnuntey, cenun cemsimey kokiwa lamyenul meknun kesul cohahaci anhsupnita. [Cenun cemsimey **hangsang/ocik** phicalul meksupnita.]
    'Some friends of mine told me to have rice or noodles for lunch, but I don't like having them for lunch. I always/only have pizza for lunch.'

2.2 F0 Manipulation

As noted earlier, we manipulated the pitch contours of *hangsang* and *ocik* and the elements associated with the FPs. This manipulation was done using praat (Boersma and Weenik 1992-2012). Depending on the placement of a peak in a sentence, we have three different prosody models (i.e. *HangsangH/OcikH*, *FocusH*, *DoubleH*).

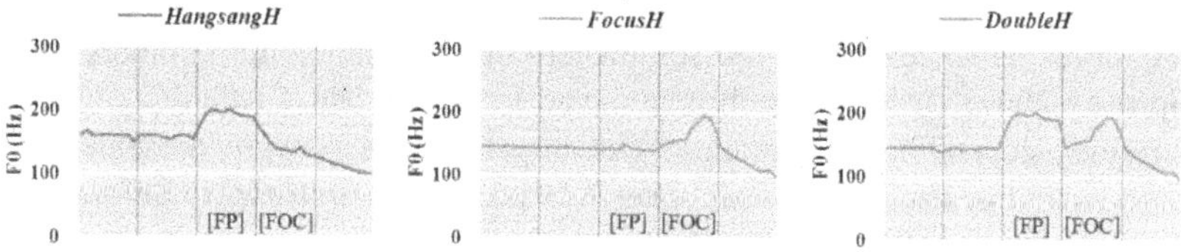

Figure 1. Three prosody models of the sentence, *Cenun cemsimey hangsang phicalul meksupnita* 'I always have pizza for lunch'. A vertical line delimits each word of the target sentence.

Figure 1 shows the sample F0 contours of the sentence *Cenun cemsimey hangsang phicalul meksupnita*. *HangsangH* is for the FP with prosodic prominence, and *FocusH* is for the focused element with prosodic prominence. *DoubleH* exhibits the prosody when the FP and the focused element simultaneously have prosodic prominence.

2.3 Procedure

In this study, we conducted a rating experiment using a five-point scale ("very natural" = 5; "natural" = 4; "okay" = 3; "unnatural" = 2; "very unnatural" = 1). The experiment was performed using PowerPoint slides. Figure 2 displays a screenshot of the sentence in isolation.[2] At the top of the screenshot, there is an instruction of the experiment procedure. In the middle is a sound icon; when clicked, the sound of the target sentence is played through a computer.

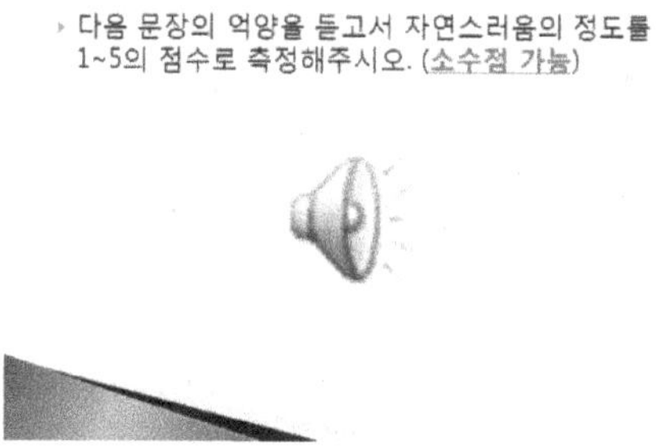

Figure 2. A screenshot of the perception experiment.[3]

The experiment was conducted in a quiet room at the University of Pennsylvania. Listeners were asked to rate whether the target sentences sounded natural based on a five-point scale. They were allowed to use a

[2]In the second and third environment, the middle of the screenshot features a prompt question and a discourse context, respectively; at the bottom is a sound icon.

[3]The top of the screenshot can be translated as follows: "After you listen to the following sound file, please rate the naturalness of the intonation of a sentence (decimal point possible)."

decimal point (i.e. 1.5, 2.5, 3.5, 4.5). This is because a significant number of the target sentences would fall somewhere in between natural numbers (see Sprouse 2007). This approach is assumed to offer a better technique to determine acceptability judgments. The target sentences were presented in randomized order. The answer sheet was presented on a paper. Before the experiment, the stimuli were shown to the listeners to help them become acquainted with the experiment procedure. They were allowed to repeat the same sound file up to three times until they felt confident.

2.4 Subjects

Twenty-two Korean listeners (mean = 28.36 years) participated in the experiment. They were recruited at the University of Pennsylvania and naïve to the purpose of the experiment. They were paid for their participation, and consent forms were obtained from each participant. No one had hearing problems.

2.5 Statistics

As stated before, we designed three different prosody models (i.e. *HangsangH/OcikH*, *FocusH*, *DoubleH*), which were embedded in the three different environments. Therefore, this study includes two independent variables (CONTOUR and ENVIRONMENT) and one dependent variable (FIVE-POINT SCALE). In order to investigate the prosodic correlation between the FPs and the elements associated with the FPs (i.e. *cenchelul* 'the subway', *phicalul* 'pizza') in the three different environments, we conducted two-way repeated measures ANOVAs on the mean responses from the rating experiment. Furthermore, we conducted multiple pairwise comparisons so as to reveal which prosody model is most favored under the ENVIRONMENT effect.

3. Results

This study includes two target sentences: one uses the eventive verb *thapnita* 'take'; the other uses the eventive verb *meksupnita* 'eat'. This study does not aim to compare the differences between the two eventive verbs. Therefore, we compressed the results of the two target sentences for further analyses. Figure 3 shows the mean values of the three prosody models depending on the environment. The standard error bars represented are based on the statistical variation of the results across all the prosody models and participants. We describe Figure 3(a) and 3(b) in turn.

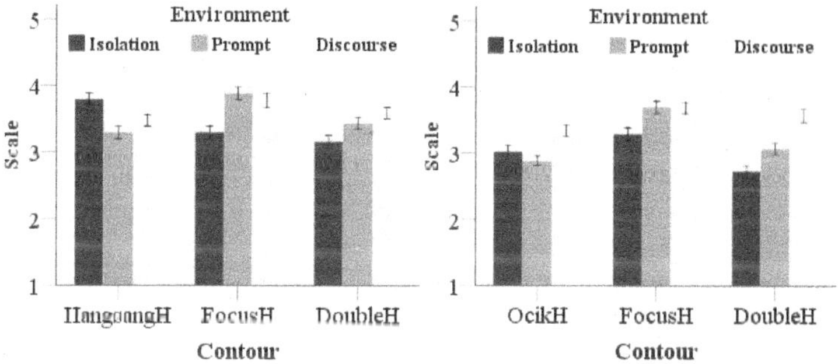

(a) (b)

Figure 3. Mean values and standard errors of the three different prosody models in the three different environments for *hangsang* (a) and *ocik* (b).

In Figure 3(a), the mean value of *HangsangH* is 3.52 (e.g. Isolation: 3.79, Prompt: 3.29, Discourse: 3.47). The mean value of *FocusH* is 3.65 (e.g. Isolation: 3.29, Prompt: 3.88, Discourse: 3.79). The mean value of *DoubleH* is 3.39 (e.g. Isolation: 3.15, Prompt: 3.43, Discourse: 3.59). The results of *hangsang* show that the values of *FocusH* are the greatest (mean: 3.65), followed by *HangsangH* (mean: 3.51) and *DoubleH* (mean: 3.39). Except when the sentence is in isolation, *FocusH* shows the greatest values.

In the case of *ocik*, the mean value of *OcikH* is 3.08 (e.g. Isolation: 3.02, Prompt: 2.88, Discourse: 3.34). The mean value of *FocusH* is 3.55 (e.g. Isolation: 3.28, Prompt: 3.69, Discourse: 3.69). The mean value of *DoubleH* is 3.12 (e.g. Isolation: 2.72, Prompt: 3.07, Discourse: 3.57). The results of *ocik* show that the values of *FocusH* are the greatest regardless of the environment. That is, Korean listeners evaluate *FocusH* as the most favored prosody model in any condition. In what follows, we consider the three prosody models under the ENVIRONMENT factor.

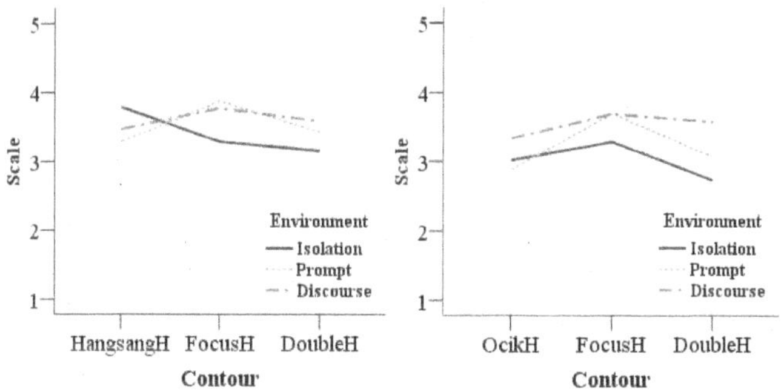

(a) (b)

Figure 4. ENVIRONMENT influence on the three prosody models for *hangsang* (a) and *ocik* (b).

In Figure 4(a), the three prosody models appear to behave differently depending on the environment. *HangsangH* is shown to be the most favored prosody model when the sentence is in isolation, whereas *FocusH* is shown to be most natural elsewhere. Conversely, the main effect of ENVIRONMENT appears to be insignificant for *ocik* despite the small variations across the prosody models. We find *FocusH* the most favored prosody model regardless of the environment. To verify the visual observations, we conducted two-way repeated measures ANOVAs on the mean responses. Table 1 below tabulates the results of the two-way repeated measures ANOVAs under the effects of CONTOUR and ENVIRONMENT.

In Table 1(a), the effect of CONTOUR is significant for *hangsang*, but the effect of ENVIRONMENT is not significant. However, there is a significant interaction effect between CONTOUR and ENVIRONMENT; that is, the ENVIRONMENT has a considerable effect on the three prosody models (i.e. *HangsangH*, *FocusH*, *DoubleH*). As for *ocik*, the effect of CONTOUR is discernable, and so is the effect of ENVIRONMENT. Furthermore, we find significant interactions between the effects of CONTOUR and ENVIRONMENT. The ENVIRONMENT also affects the prosody models of *ocik*.

Table 1. The panel (a) and (b) indicate *hangsang* and *ocik*, respectively (*ns* $= p > 0.05$, * $= p < 0.05$, *** $= p < 0.001$).

	Source	Sum of squares	df	Mean square	F	Sig.
(a)	CONTOUR (A)	2.19	2	1.10	4.52	*
	Subject error	10.18	42	0.24		
	ENVIRONMENT (B)	1.38	2	0.69	2.40	*ns*
	Subject error	12.04	42	0.29		
	A x B	7.99	4	1.20	8.68	***
	Subject error	19.33	84	0.23		
(b)	CONTOUR (A)	9.16	2	4.58	15.29	***
	Subject error	12.58	42	0.30		
	ENVIRONMENT (B)	9.16	2	4.58	18.69	***
	Subject error	10.29	42	0.25		
	A x B	3.67	4	0.91	5.14	***
	Subject error	14.86	84	0.18		

To analyze the prosodic patterns between the FPs and the elements associated with the FPs (i.e. *cenchelul* 'the subway', *phicalul* 'pizza') in more detail, multiple comparison tests were performed to examine which prosody model in a group is most favored under the ENVIRONMENT factor. Table 2 tabulates the results of multiple pairwise comparisons based on the three different environments when the sentences include *hangsang*.

Table 2. The differences of the three prosody models when the sentences include *hangsang* (** = $p < 0.01$, *** = $p < 0.001$).

		Isolation	Prompt	Discourse
(A) model	(B) model	$\Delta(\mu A\text{-}\mu B)$	$\Delta(\mu A\text{-}\mu B)$	$\Delta(\mu A\text{-}\mu B)$
FocusH	DoubleH	0.14	**0.45	0.19
FocusH	HangsangH	**−0.50	***0.59	0.31
HangsangH	DoubleH	***0.64	−0.14	−0.12

Before describing the results, note the structure of Table 2. If a value is positive between the prosody models, then the prosody model in Column (A) shows a greater value than that in Column (B). In contrast, if it is negative, then the prosody model in Column (B) shows a greater value.

In Table 2, *HangsangH* is shown to be most preferred when the sentence is in isolation. The value of *HangsangH* is significantly greater than those of *FocusH* and *DoubleH*. But, in this environment, there is no significant difference between *FocusH* and *DoubleH*. In the second environment, where the sentence is preceded by a prompt question, *FocusH* is shown to be the most natural prosody model. The value of *FocusH* is significantly greater than the other prosody models. We find, however, that there is no significant difference between *HangsangH* and *DoubleH*. In the third environment, where the sentence is embedded in discourse, any prosody model is not significantly greater than the others, although the value of *FocusH* is numerically the greatest. The results in Table 2 confirm that the prosody including *hangsang* is contingent on the environment. Next, Table 3 displays the results of multiple pairwise comparisons in the three different environments when the sentences include ocik.

Table 3. The differences of the three prosody models when the sentences include *ocik*. (* = $p < 0.05$, *** = $p < 0.001$).

		Isolation	Prompt	Discourse
(A) model	(B) model	$\Delta(\mu A\text{-}\mu B)$	$\Delta(\mu A\text{-}\mu B)$	$\Delta(\mu A\text{-}\mu B)$
FocusH	DoubleH	***0.56	***0.63	0.11
FocusH	OcikH	0.27	***0.82	*0.35
OcikH	DoubleH	0.29	-0.19	-0.24

In Table 3, *FocusH* is shown to be most preferred when the sentence is in isolation, but the difference between *FocusH* and *OcikH* is not significant, although *FocusH* shows a greater value. In the second environment, the value of *FocusH* is significantly greater than *OcikH* and *DoubleH*. The same is true of the third environment. In this environment, *FocusH* is significantly greater than *OcikH* but not significantly greater than *DoubleH*. While *FocusH* is not always significantly greater than *OcikH* and *DoubleH* in any condition, it is likely that the prosody including *ocik* prefers to have prosodic prominence on the element associated with *ocik*.

4. Discussion

We found that the results of *hangsang* differ in the three environments. First, *HangsangH* turns out to be most favored when the sentence is in isolation. We assume that the prosodic prominence on *hangsang* reflects contrast. It contrasts with an implicit generic operator since the sentence *Cenun cemsimey phicalul meksupnita* 'I have pizza for lunch' can be paraphrased as *Cenun cemsimey pothong phicalul meksupnita* 'I usually have pizza for lunch'. If *hangsang* replaces the implicit generic operator or *pothong* 'usually', the function of *hangsang* is to emphasize the fact that the predicate holds at all events under consideration. Therefore, it is understood that *hangsang* is marked with intonational prominence when the sentence is in isolation. Second, when the sentence is preceded by a prompt question and in discourse, *FocusH* (i.e. the element associated with the FP is prominent) turns out to be the most natural prosody model. This can be explained by the fact that the *wh*-question (2nd environment) and the discourse context (3rd environment) elicited contrastive focus on the elements *cenchelul* and *phicalul*. Therefore, such elements were characterized with prosodic prominence. Hence, based on the findings of *hangsang*, this study confirms Beaver and Clark's (2002, 2003, 2008) argument that elements associated with *always* are determined pragmatically.

On the other hand, the prosodic behaviors of *ocik* show little variance. The elements associated with *ocik* show prosodic prominence regardless of the environment; that is, *FocusH* (where the element associated with the FP has prosodic prominence) turns out to be the most favored prosody model in any condition. This result thus supports the QFC Theory, in which *ocik* constructs an association based on a lexically encoded dependency on focus (Beaver and Clark 2008). However, it is not certain whether the prosodic prominence was elicited by *ocik* or the contexts (e.g. a prompt question: 2nd experiment, a discourse: 3rd environment). It may be true that when the sentence is preceded by a prompt question or in discourse, the prosodic prominence on the elements *cenchel-ul* and *phicalul* were elicited by the *wh*-question and the discourse context. Nevertheless, it is obvious that the prosodic prominence was elicited by virtue of being associated with *ocik* in the first environment (i.e. when the sentence is in isolation). Therefore, the findings of this study, although more conclusive evidence is needed, support Beaver and Clark's claim (2002:15) that the element associated with *only* is 'constrained compositionally.'

Our research question asks whether or not the element associated with *hangsang* or *ocik* is prosodically prominent. We found that the most favored prosody model of *ocik* is *FocusH*, which shows rigid prosodic behavior as a conventional association. On the contrary, *hangsang* shows a free association, in which the prosodic behaviors depend on contextual conditions. On the basis of these findings, we conclude that the element associated with *ocik* must be prosodically prominent to create an association, whereas such prosodic prominence is not required for *hangsang* to make an association.

5. Conclusion

We have examined the issue of whether the element associated with the Korean FPs shows prosodic prominence. This question is addressed by a perceptual experiment in which the pitch contours of the target sentences were manipulated using Praat. Target sentences include examples such as *Cenun chwulkunhal ttay hangsang/ocik cenchelul thapnita* 'I always/only take the subway to work' and *Cenun cemsimey hangsang/ocik phicalul meksupnita* 'I always/only have pizza for lunch.' The manipulated prosody models were embedded in the three different environments. The results of this study demonstrate that *hangsang* shows a free association; that is, the prosody models of *hangsang* are dependent on the environment. In contrast, *ocik,* whose behavior in terms of a conventional association, prefers to have prosodic prominence on the element associated with *ocik* (i.e. *FocusH*). Based on these findings, we argue that the element associated with *hangsang* does not always have to be prosodically prominent, but instead there must be a prosodically prominent element when associated with *ocik*.

References

Beaver, D. and B. Clark. 2002. The Proper Treatments of Focus Sensitivity. *Proceedings of the 21st West Coast Conference on Formal Linguistics*, eds., L. Mikkelsen and C. Potts, 15-28. Somerville: Cascadilla Press.

Beaver, D. and B. Clark. 2003. Always and Only: Why Not All Focus-sensitive Operators are Alike. *Natural Language Semantics* 11: 323-362.

Beaver, D. and B. Clark. 2008. *Sense and Sensitivity: How Focus Determines Meaning*. Oxford: Wiley-Blackwell.

Beaver, D., B. Clark, E. Flemming, F. Jaeger, and M. Wolters. 2007. When Semantics Meets Phonetics: Acoustical Studies of Second-occurrence Focus. *Language* 83: 245-276.

Boersma, P. and D. Weenink. 1999-2012. Praat: Doing Phonetics by Computer. A software.

Büring, D. 2008. Been There, Marked That – A Theory of Second Occurrence Focus. Manuscript, UCLA.

Jackendoff, R. 1972. *Semantic Interpretation in Generative Grammar*. Cambridge: MIT Press.

Jun, S-A. 2006. Focus in English and Korean. Paper presented at the Annual Conference of Korean Society of Language and Information (KSLI), June 2006, Chuncheon.

Jun, S-A. 2011. Prosodic Markings of Complex NP Focus, Syntax, and the Pre-/Post-focus String. *Proceedings of the 28th West Coast Conference on Formal Linguistics*, eds., M. B. Washburn, K. McKinney-Bock, E. Varis, A. Sawyer, and B. Tomaszewicz, 214-230. Somerville: Cascadilla Press.

Jun, S-A. 1993. *The Phonetics and Phonology of Korean Prosody*. Doctoral dissertation, The Ohio State University.

Ladd, D. R. 1996. *Intonational Phonology*. Cambridge: Cambridge University Press.

Lee, Y-c. and S. Nambu. 2012. Prosody and Semantics of the Focus Particles *Always* and *Only* in Korean: Theoretical Implications from a Perception Experiment. *University of Pennsylvania Working Papers in Linguistics* 18(1): 151-159.

Rooth, M. 1985. *Association with Focus*. Doctoral dissertation, University of Massachusetts, Amherst.

Rooth, M. 1992. A Theory of Focus Interpretation. *Natural Language Semantics* 1: 75-116.

Rooth, M. 1996. Focus. *Handbook of Contemporary Semantic Theory*, ed., S Lappin, 271-297. Oxford: Blackwell.

Rooth, M. 2010. Second Occurrence Focus and Relativized Stress F. *Information Stucture: Theoretical, Typological, and Experimental Perspectives*, eds., C. Fery and Z. Malte, 15-35. New York: Oxford University Press.

Sprouse, J. 2007. *A Program for Experimental Syntax*. Doctoral dissertation, University of Maryland.

Korean Derived Inchoatives with Verbal Roots

DONGSIK LIM*
CCHS-CSIC

MARIA LUISA ZUBIZARRETA
University of Southern California

1. Introduction

In Korean, a deadjectival inchoative (translated as 'become+A') is derived by combining an adjectival root with the morpheme *(e)ci-*, as in (1):[1]

(1) a. Ku maktayki-ka kil-e ci-ess-ta.
That stick-NOM long-L *ci*-PAST-DECL
'That stick became longer.'

---

* This paper is a part of Lim and Zubizarreta (2011). We thank the audiences in J/K 21, Workshop on Verbal Elasticity (Universitat Autònoma de Barcelona, October 3-5, 2011), and Syntax/Semantics Colloquium (Seoul National University, October 25, 2011) for their comments and questions. All remaining errors are ours. This paper is partially supported by the project Estructura eventiva y 'construcción' léxico-sintáctica de las oraciones. Teoría y experimentación (FF-2009-07114, Project Leader: Professor Violeta Demonte, CCHS-CSIC), where the first author is participating.

[1] L in the gloss (*e* in *(e)ci-*) means a linking vowel, which we simply assume to be inserted for some phonological reason, but we will return to this question later. We will also discuss the comparative marker in (1a) below.

Japanese/Korean Linguistics 21.
Edited by Seungho Nam, Heejeong Ko and Jongho Jun.

b. Mary-ka yeyppu-e ci-ess-ta.
Mary-NOM pretty-L *ci*-PAST-DECL
'Mary became pretty.'

Note, however, that this morpheme *(e)ci-* can also combine with a class of verbal roots, and 'intransitivize' the root, as in (2):[2]

(2) a. Yulichang-i kkay-e ci-ess-ta.
window-NOM break-L *ci*-PAST-DECL
(lit.) 'The window became broken.'
b. Kumsok-i yalp-key twutulki-e ci-ess-ta.
Mary-NOM thin-*key* pound-L *ci*-PAST-DECL
(lit.) 'The metal became pounded thin.'

Traditionally *(e)ci-* with a verbal root is analyzed as a passivizer. However, this analysis misses several important characteristics of *(e)ci-*. For example, it does not explain why the apparent same morpheme *(e)ci-* can combine with adjectival roots as well as verbal roots, and why not all verbal roots are compatible with *(e)ci-*. Furthermore, as we will see later, among verbs compatible with *(e)ci-* we can find some syntactic/semantic differences, which we believe the traditional analysis of *(e)ci-* as a passivizer cannot capture.

In this paper we give a unified analysis of *(e)ci-* with verbs and *(e)ci-* with adjectives, by assuming that *(e)ci-* is the head of directed motion constructions (DMC), as proposed in Zubizarreta and Oh (2007: Z&O henceforth) and Lim and Zubizarreta (2012: L&Z henceforth), among others. In Section 2, we introduce the syntax of DMC proposed by Z&O (2007), which our analysis is based on. In Section 3 we show that verbs compatible with *(e)ci-* share the meaning of directed motion, which makes it plausible to analyze *(e)ci-* with verbs as the head of a DMC. In Section 4 we focus on verbs of change of state (COS verbs), and classify them into two different subclasses, based on their semantics and their different behaviors with respect to *(e)ci-*. In Section 5 we explain the differences shown in Section 4 by analyzing *(e)ci-* as a head of the DMC. In Section 6 we conclude the paper and briefly discuss further implications.

2. L-Syntax of Directed Motion

Z&O (2007) propose that the meaning of directed motion can be represented in the structure in (3), where the head V takes a path argument.

[2] For the ending *–key* with a secondary predicate, we simply glossed it as *–key*, following Son (2008) and Shim and Den Dikken (2008), among others.

(3)

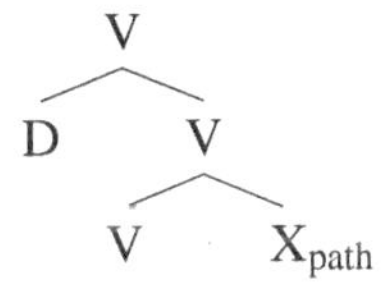

Here the term 'directed motion' is used in a broad sense, to refer to either physical movement (change of location) or abstract movement (change of state). Therefore, the structure in (3) can refer to either change of location or change of state, depending on the type of the path argument: if a path argument denotes a physical path, the structure denotes change of location, and if it denotes an abstract path (a scale associated with an adjective, for example), the structure denotes change of state.

Under this proposal, *ka-* 'go' and *o-* 'come' are treated as the head of the DMC, taking a path argument (for convenience hereafter we will only discuss *ka-*). Actually, *ka-* takes either a PP as its physical path argument, or an AP as its abstract path argument, as in (4a) and (4b), respectively:

(4) a. John-i kongwen-ey ka-ess-ta.
John-NOM park-LOC go-PAST-DECL
'John went to the park.'
b. John-uy sulphum-i kiph-e ka-ess-ta.
John-GEN sorrow-NOM deep-L go-PAST-DECL
'John's sorrow was getting deep.'

Under Z&O's (2007) proposal, the structure for (4a) and (4b) can be represented as (5), where *ka-* takes a PP with a physical path in (5a) and an AP with an abstract path in (5b), respectively:

(5) a.

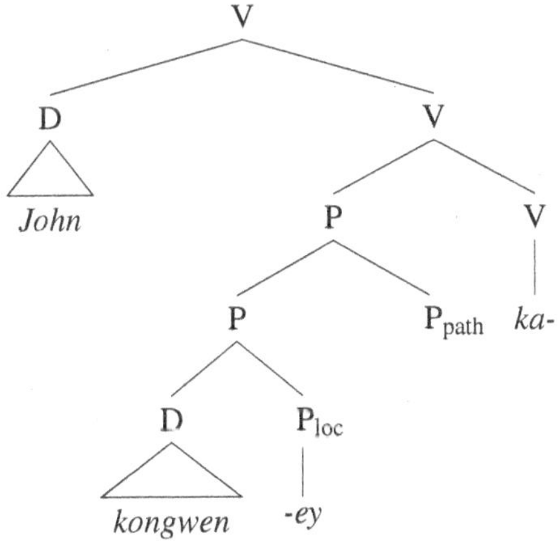

b.

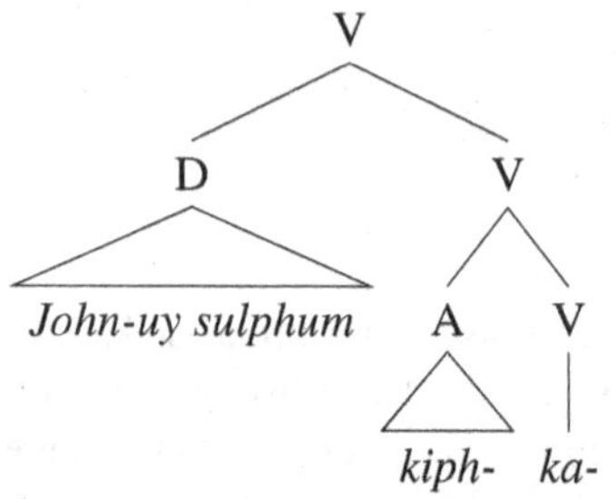

As shown in the introduction, putting verbs aside, *(e)ci-* can freely combine with an adjective and derive a deadjectival verb whose meaning is change of state. Given this, it is plausible to analyze *(e)ci-* as another head of directed motion. Adopting Z&O (2007), L&Z (2012) claim that the main difference between *ka-* and *(e)ci-* is that, unlike *ka-*, *(e)ci-* cannot combine with a PP argument, and the adjectival path of *(e)ci-* contains a comparative morpheme. This is supported by the fact that *(e)ci-* with an adjective can take a measure phrase (MeasP), which is only compatible with an adjective with comparative meaning.[3] In this analysis, the structure of (6a) is (6b):[4]

(6) a. Ku kang-i 3m kiph-e ci-ess-ta.
That river-NOM 3m deep-L *ci*-PAST-DECL
'That river became 3m deeper.'

b.

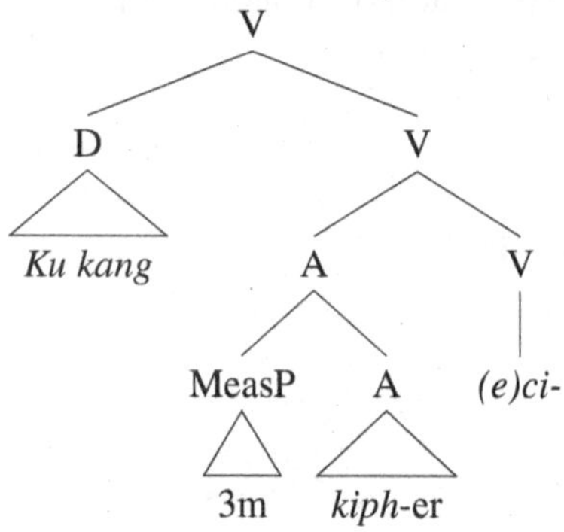

3. Verbal Roots Compatible with *(e)ci-*

Now let us return to *(e)ci-* with verbs. L&Z (2012) present a list of verbs compatible with *(e)ci-*, which is shown in (7):

---

3 Actually, Z&O (2007) claim that *ka-* takes a path with an *absolute* endpoint, whereas *(e)ci-* takes a *relative* endpoint (on behalf of a covert comparative morpheme). Since our main concern is *(e)ci-* with verbs, we will only discuss this issue briefly in the conclusion.

4 For simplicity we do not show the internal structure of A, but simply attach *-er* to the root.

(7) a. Verbs of transfer/change of location: *cwu-* 'give', *cenha-* 'report/convey', *wumciki-* 'move', *peli-* 'discard', *twicip-* 'reverse', *ketwu-* 'gather', *mou-* 'gather', *kyepchi-* 'lay over', *ssot-* 'spill', *eph* 'turn over/turn down', ...

b. Verbs of change of state (COS verbs): *twutulki-* 'pound/hammer', *takk-* 'wipe', *ssis-* 'wash', *ppal-* 'wash (laundries)', *coi-* 'tighten', *chilha-* 'paint', *kkay-* 'break', *pwuswu-* 'destroy', *kku-* 'turn off', *kkunh-* 'tear', *kochi-* 'fix/repair', *phye-* 'straighten', *calu-* 'cut', *meywu-* 'fill in', *ttwulh-* 'drill', *ciwu-* 'erase', *is-* 'connect', *cecilu-* 'commit', *ilwu-*'achieve/come true',...

c. Verbs of creation: *cis-* 'build', *mantul-* 'make', *kwup-* 'bake', *kuli-* 'paint/draw (a picture)', *ssu-* 'write', *sayki-* 'carve', *pic-* 'make porcelains (with clay) / make (event) happen', *kus-* 'draw (line)' ...

Here verbs are classified into three subclasses depending on their meaning. However, note that they have the meaning of directed motion in common. First, verbs of transfer/change of location obviously have the meaning of directed motion. Second, as we already saw in Section 2, the meaning of change of state can also be represented in terms of directed motion (along an abstract path). Finally, the meaning of creation can be regarded as a specific case of change of state (from non-existence to existence). This leads us to posit the following semantic condition for verbs compatible with *(e)ci-*:

(8) *(e)ci-* can combine with verbs whose meaning is related to directed motion.

Why do verbs satisfying (8) – and only these verbs – combine with *(e)ci-*? We believe this is because verbs with the meaning of directed motion specify the endpoint of the motion, or the result state, and therefore they can appear as a path argument of DMC. For example, verbs of transfer/change of location in (7a) entail that there is a goal of transfer/change of location, and verbs of creation in (7c) entail that there is a result of creation. However, it is to be noted that COS verbs in (7b) can be classified into two different subclasses. Below we discuss the difference between the two types of COS verbs, and argue that these two combine with *(e)ci-* in different ways.

4. Two Types of Verbs of Change of State

We classify COS verbs in (7b) into the following two subclasses:

(9) a. Verbs of *pound* type: *twutulki-* 'pound/hammer', *takk-* 'wipe', *ssis-* 'wash', *ppal-* 'wash (laundries)', *coi-* 'tighten', *chilha-* 'paint', ...

b. Verbs of *break* type: *kkay-* 'break', *pwuswu-* 'destroy', *kku-* 'turn off', *kkunh-* 'tear', *kochi-* 'fix/repair', *phye-* 'straighten', *calu-* 'cut', *meywu-* 'fill in', *ttwulh-* 'drill', *ciwu-* 'erase', *is-* 'connect', *cecilu-* 'commit', *ilwu-* 'achieve/come true',...

First, *pound* type-verbs are atelic, but *break*-type verbs are telic. Therefore the former are less acceptable with *in*-adverbials, whereas the latter are less acceptable with *for*-adverbials, as in (10):

(10) a. John-i kumsok-ul 3 pwun tongan/?maney twutulki-ess-ta.
John-NOM metal-ACC 3 min. for/in pound-PAST-DECL
'John pounded the metal for 3 minutes / ?in 3 minutes.'
b. John-i pyeng-ul 3 pwun maney/?tongan kkay-ess-ta.
John-NOM bottle-ACC 3 min. in/for break-PAST-DECL
'John broke the bottle in 3 minutes / ?for 3 minutes'

Second, *pound*-type verbs do not entail the change of state of the theme argument, whereas *break*-type verbs do. Therefore, (11a) can be felicitously followed by (11b), but (12a) cannot be felicitously followed by (12b):

(11) a. John-i ku kumsok-ul twutulki-ess-ta. Haciman...
John-NOM that metal-ACC pound-PAST-DECL but
'John pounded that metal. But...'
b. ...kukes-uy moyang-un pyenha-cianh-ass-ta.
...it-GEN shape-TOP change-NEG-PAST-DECL
'...its shape did not change.'

(12) a. John-i ku yulichang-ul kkay-ess-ta. Haciman...
John-NOM that window-ACC break-PAST-DECL but
'John broke that window. But...'
b. ...#kukes-uy moyang-un pyenha-cianh-ass-ta.
...it-GEN shape-TOP change-NEG-PAST-DECL
'...#its shape did not change.'

Finally, and most importantly, *pound*-type verbs require an adjectival resultative when combined with *(e)ci-*. Therefore, (13a) becomes less acceptable when the resultative *yalp-key* 'thin' is absent, but (13b) is fine regardless of whether the resultative *cal-key* 'tiny' is present or not.

(13) a. Ku kumsok-i ??(yalp-key) twutulki-e ci-ess-ta.
That metal-nom thin-*key* pound-l *ci*-past-decl
(lit.) 'That metal was pounded ?(thin).'
b. Ku yulichang-i (cal-key) kkay-e ci-ess-ta.
That window-nom tiny-*key* break-l *ci*-past-decl
(lit.) 'That window became broken (into tiny pieces).'

5. Proposal

We believe that the differences between the two types of COS verbs result in two different ways of how a COS verb interacts with the DMC. First, let us consider *pound*-type verbs. They are atelic (see 10a); they denote activities. Since they do not entail any result of change of state (see 11), they cannot directly appear as path complement of *(e)ci-* in the DMC. Then how do they combine with *(e)ci-*? Based on the data like (13a), where a resultative is required when a *pound*-type verbs combines with *(e)ci-*, we propose that in such structures, the resultative functions as path argument of *(e)ci-*. In this case, the lexical verb functions as a modifier of the DMC, and specifies the means by which the change of state comes about.

In contrast, as shown in (13b), *break*-type verbs do not require a resultative adjective when they combine with *(e)ci-* (see (13b)) because the verb itself denotes the result in such cases. In effect, *break*-type verbs are telic (see (10b)), and entail the result of change of state (see (12)). Given this fact, we propose that *break*-type verbs can function as path argument of *(e)ci-*, and a resultative with this type of predicates is just an adjunct, modifying the lexical verb that functions as path argument. In this sense, *break*-type verbs behave in the same way as verbs of transfer/change of location and verbs of creation: they can function as path argument in the DMC.

The above-mentioned differences between the two types of COS verbs lead us to posit two different ways of composing COS verbs with *(e)ci*. Specifically, *pound*-type verbs modify a DMC (which is headed by *(e)ci-* and already has an adjectival path) via a Generalized Transformation (GT, henceforth), namely the same type of syntactic mechanism that Z&O (2007) propose to account for the syntactic composition of a Simultaneous Serial Verb Construction (SSVC, henceforth). On the other hand, *break*-type verbs combine with *(e)ci-* via regular Merge.

Let us see how these two mechanisms actually work. First, we illustrate the case of *pound*- type verbs, with the example (14):

(14)	Kumsok-i	yalp-key	twutulki-e ci-ess-ta.
	Metal-NOM	thin-*key*	pound-L *ci*-PAST-DECL
	'The metal was pounded thin.'		

To derive (14), we assume two l-structures. The first one is a DMC in (15), where the head *(e)ci-* merges with the path *yalp-* 'thin', and the output in turn merges with the theme argument *kumsok* 'metal'. The structure denotes the change of state of the theme argument, that is, the metal's becoming thin (for convenience we ignore the comparative marker mentioned in (6)):

(15)

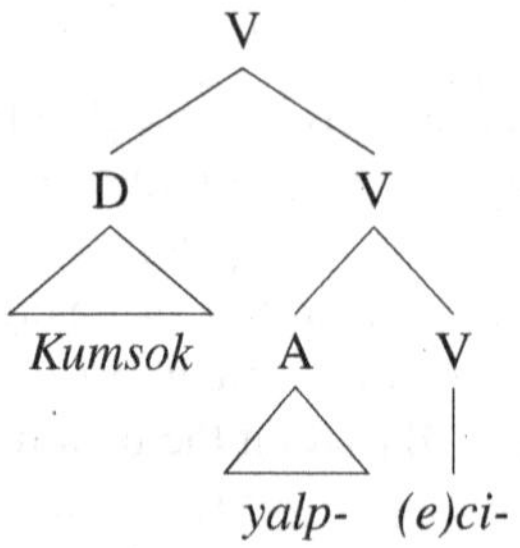

In the second l-structure, the lexical verb *twutulki-* 'pound' takes the theme argument *kumsok* 'metal':

(16)

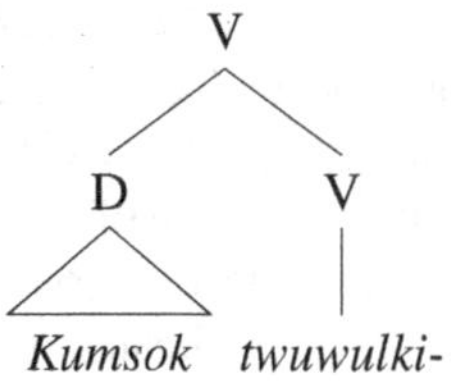

According to Z&O (2007), GT applies to two l-structures sharing the same argument, and adjoins one l-structure to the head of another. Since (15) and (16) share the argument, *kumsok*, (15) and (16) combine as in (17):

(17)

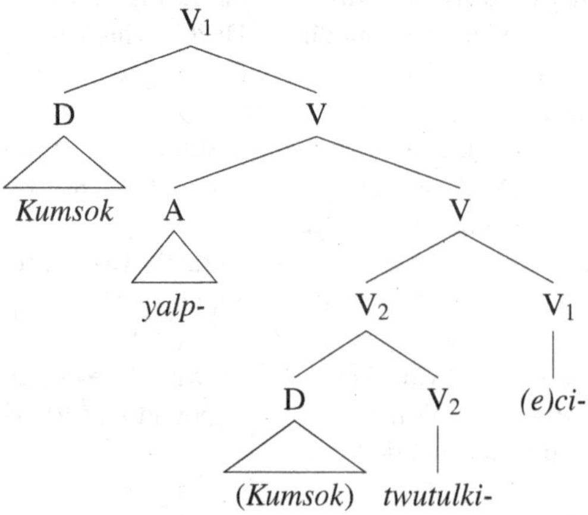

Note that, by positing such a structure, we interpret the Korean resultative construction in the DMC with *pound*-type verbs as a kind of SSVC. Specifically, we interpret this structure as denoting *two* separate eventualities which occur at the same time: the metal becoming thin and the metal being pounded, the latter modifying the former and specifying the manner in which the change of state denoted by the DMC occurs, just like the lexical verb denoting manner of motion in the SSVC, as in (18).[5]

(18) a. John-i kongwen-ey ka-ess-ta.
John-NOM park-LOC go-PAST-DECL
'John went to the park.'

b. John-i kongwen-ey ttwi-e/kel-e/ki-e... ka-ess-ta.
John-NOM park-LOC run-L/walk-L/crawl-L go-PAST-DECL
'John went to the park by running/walking/crawling...'

We illustrate the *break*-type case with the example in (19):

(19) Yulichang-i cal-key kkay-e ci-ess-ta.
Window-NOM tiny-*key* break-L *ci*-PAST-DECL
'The window was broken into tiny pieces.'

The syntactic composition proceeds as follows. The l-structure in (20) is obtained by merging the adjective *cal-* 'tiny' with the lexical verb *kkay-* 'break'. Thus, they compositionally denote the complex predicate *cal-key kkay-* 'break into tiny pieces'. In this complex predicate, the adjective *cal-* functions as the modifier of the lexical verb *kkay-*.

(20)

Then this complex predicate merges with the D *yulichang* 'window', as in (21), where *cal-key kkay-* is predicated of *yulichang*:

(21)

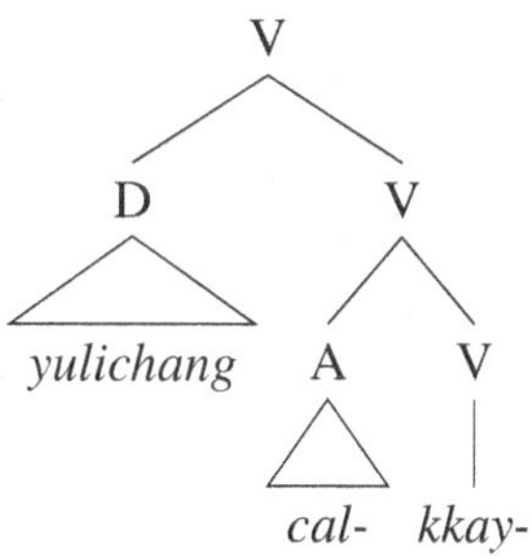

5 See Z&O (2007) and L&Z (2011) for further discussion.

Finally, the output in (20) merges with the head of the DMC *(e)ci-*, and functions as the path argument of the DMC. The output structure in turn merges with the copy of the D *yulichang*, as shown in (22):

(22)

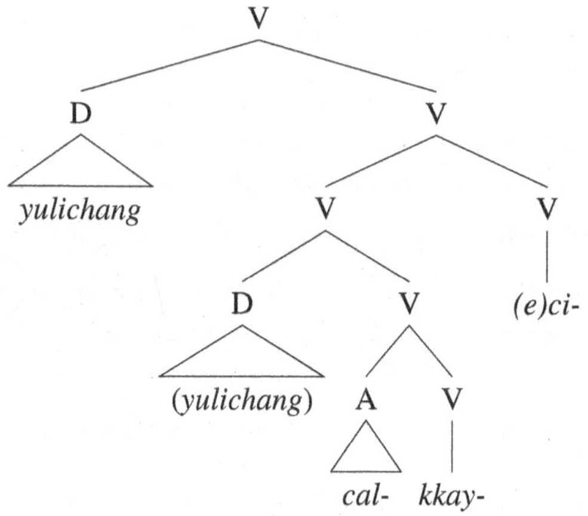

The construction in (22) denotes the directed motion of the window along the path of 'being broken' with the endpoint specified as 'broken into tiny pieces', or, in other words, the change of the window into the state 'broken into tiny pieces'. Note that, unlike (17), GT does not apply in the composition of (22), and therefore there is no interpretation corresponding to SSVC. This means that, whereas the structure in (17) denotes two eventualities occurring simultaneously, the construction in (22) denotes a single eventuality, that is the window's being broken into tiny pieces. Note also that our analysis leads to positing two different types of resultatives: the one formed by GT (see (17)), and the other formed by regular Merge (see (22)). Below we discuss the implication of this difference.

6. Conclusions and Further Discussion

In this paper, we propose to analyze the morpheme *(e)ci-* with a verbal root as the head of the DMC, just like *(e)ci-* with an adjectival root. By doing so, we obtain a unified analysis of *(e)ci-*, instead of two (separate) lexical entries for *(e)ci-* (one as a head of deadjectival inchoatives and the other as a passivizer). Furthermore, we identified what kind of verbs can combine with *(e)ci-*: only verbs whose meaning is related to the notion of directed motion. Finally, we classified verbs into two different types: the activity denoting verbs (*pound*-type verbs) and result-denoting verbs (the *break*-type verbs), and argue that, because of their different lexical semantics, they enter into the DMC via two different mechanisms. In the case of *pound*-type verbs, a verbal root combines with the DMC headed by *(e)ci-* via a Generalized Transformation or GT. GT adjoins the head of an l-structure with the head of another l-structure, and forms a SSVC, denoting two distinct eventualities occurring at the same time. In the case of *break*-type verbs, the head *(e)ci-* takes a verbal root directly as its path complement, via regular Merge, just like the cases of verbs of transfer/change of location and of verbs of creation.

Our proposal has several implications for the research of the lexicon-syntax interface as well as for the analysis of resultatives (in Korean). First, let us consider the implication of our proposal regarding the lexicon-syntax interface. There are two main lines of research as to how the lexical semantics of a predicate is related to the syntactic structure. One of them, pursued in Borer (2005a, b) among others, argues that the contribution of the lexicon is minimal: the lexicon only provides pairs of sound and concept, and most of the grammatical meaning comes from the structure and a set of functional heads. The other one, put forth by Levin and Rappaport Hovav (1995), argues that the contribution of syntax is minimal, and that grammatical meaning is mostly dictated by lexical-conceptual structure. Korean DMCs provide evidence against both (rather extreme) views, but in favor of what we call 'the mixed approach' (in particular, Hale and Keyser 2002 and Z&O 2007, a. o.): there is a set of l-structures expressing the general meaning such as directed motion, causation, and change of state, and substantive lexical items gravitate toward one or more l-syntactic structures due to their lexical meaning. Note that we assume an l-structure for the meaning of directed motion (the DMC in 3), and this structure interacts with the lexical verb in different ways depending on the lexical semantics of the verb.[6]

The second implication of our proposal concerns the syntactic composition of resultatives. Previous studies on resultatives (especially in Korean) diverge depending on whether they analyze Korean resultatives as complements (Kim 1999, among others) or as adjuncts (Shim and Den Dikken 2008, among others). Other studies argue that Korean has both types of resultatives, that is, resultatives as complements and resultatives as adjuncts (Son 2008, Yeo 2006, among others). Our analysis supports the view that there are two types of resultatives in Korean. However, we propose that a subset of the resultatives that have been analyzed as complements are actually not complements at all, but modifiers in a SSVC: they modify the directed motion construction taking an adjectival path argument, and specify the manner in which the change of state occurs. Note that, by positing these two different mechanisms, we can also account for various differences in interpretation between two types of resultatives, given that the resultative with *pound*-type verbs denotes two eventualities whereas the resultative

[6] See Ramchand (2008) for a different instantiation of the mixed approach.

with *break*-type verbs denotes a single eventuality. For example, L&Z (2011) point out that, when a resultative appears, only *break*-type verbs show ambiguity in scope between negation and a quantifier, as illustrated in (23), and explain this in terms of whether the construction denotes one or two eventualities (for a detailed explanation, see L&Z 2011).

(23) a. John-i kumsok myech cokak-ul napcakha-key
John-nom metal several CL-ACC flat-*key*
twutulki-cianh-ass-ta.
pound-NEG-PAST-DECL
i) ?? NEG > *several*: 'John pounded ALL pieces of metal flat.'
ii) *several* > NEG: 'There are several pieces of metal which John did not pound and therefore they did not become flat.'

b. John-i pyeng myech kay-lul cal-key
John-NOM bottle several CL-ACC tiny-*key*
kkay-cianh-ess-ta.
break-NEG-PAST-DECL
i) NEG > *several*: 'John broke ALL the bottles / NO bottle into tiny pieces.'
ii) *several* > NEG: 'There are several pieces of metal which John did not break into tiny pieces.'

There are several remaining issues in this paper. First of all, in this paper we do not discuss similarities and differences between the two heads of the directed motion construction, that is *(e)ci-* and *ka-*, and their division of labor. It is beyond the scope of this paper to deal with this issue in more detail, but let us briefly overview our proposal about this issue made in our previous studies (Z&O 2007, L&Z 2011, 2012, among others). Roughly speaking, *ka-* can combine with PPs denoting physical paths and (a limited class of) adjectives, whereas *(e)ci-* can combine with any type of adjectives (but not PPs). Crucially, L&Z (2012) point out that, adjectives with *ka-* do not contain any semantic component of comparatives, but adjectives with *(e)ci-* do. Given this, L&Z (2011) propose that *ka-* takes a path argument which has subintervals, whereas *(e)ci-* takes a path argument which does not have any subinterval. This explains why the adjectival complement of *(e)ci-* contains a covert comparative morpheme. When a gradable adjective combines with the comparative morpheme, what matters in the interpretation is whether the individual predicated of the adjective is beyond the standard of comparison or not, and therefore it can be regarded as having no subinterval in its associated scale (See L&Z 2011, 2012 for further discussion).

The other question is related to the nature of *-key*. In this paper we did not give a unified account for this morpheme: with *pound*-type verbs, we treat it as being inserted when two l-structures are adjoined to form an SSVC; with verbs of *break* type, it is assumed to be an adverbial morpheme. However, the status of *-key* remains to be more fully investigated.[7]

In addition, other questions still need to be addressed, including the internal structure of adjectival resultatives and other types of resultatives, and the nature of the linking vowel (glossed as L). We leave those as topics for future research.

References

Borer, H. 2005a. *In Name Only*. Oxford: Oxford University Press.

Borer, H. 2005b. *The Normal Course of Events*. Oxford: Oxford University Press.

Hale, K. and Keyser, S. J. 2002. *Prolegomenon to a Theory of Argument Structure*. Cambridge: MIT Press.

Kim, J.-B. 1999. Constraints on the formation of Korean and English resultatives, *Proceedings of the 29th North East Linguistics Society*, eds. M. Tamanji, M., Hirotani, and N. Hall, Amherst: GSLA Publications, 137-151.

Levin, B. and Rappaport Hovav, M. 1995. *Unaccusativity: At the Syntax-Lexical Semantics Interface*. Cambridge: MIT Press.

Lim, D. and Zubizarreta, M. L. 2011. On the syntactic composition of resultatives. Handout presented in 'Workshop on Verbal Elasticity', Universitat Autònoma de Barcelona, October 3-5, 2011.

Lim, D. and Zubizarreta, M. L. 2012. The syntax and semantics of inchoatives as directed motion: the case of Korean, *Telicity, Change, and State:A Cross-Categorial View of Event Structure,* eds. V. Demonte and L. McNally, Oxford: Oxford University Press, 212-251.

Ramchand, G. 2008. *Verb Meaning and Lexicon*. Cambridge: Cambridge University Press.

Shim, J. Y. and Den Dikken, M. 2008. Tense in resultatives. *Proceedings of North East Linguistics Society* 38, Amherst: GSLA Publications.

Son, M. 2008. Resultatives in Korean Revisited. *Nordlyd* 35: 89-113.

Son, M. and Svenonius, P. 2008. Microparameters of Cross-Linguistic Variation: Directed Motion and Resultatives, *Proceedings of West Coast Conference on Formal Linguistics* 27, eds. N. Abner and J. Bishop, Somerville: Cascadilla, 388-396.

Yeo, S. 2006. Some Notes on Resultatives in Korean. *Studies in Generative Grammar* 16(4): 687-706.

[7] See Son and Svenonius (2008) and Yeo (2011), among others, for the previous analysis of *-key*, although they do not discuss the cases where *-key* appears as an adverbial morpheme.

Yeo, S. 2011. The Morpheme *–key* in Resultatives and Periphrastic Causatives/Passives in Korean. *Studies in Generative Grammar* 21(1): 103-121.

Zubizarreta, M. L. and Oh, E. 2007. *On the Syntactic Composition of Manner and Motion*. Cambridge: MIT Press.

The Meaning of Modal Affective Demonstratives in Japanese

OSAMU SAWADA*
Mie University

JUN SAWADA
Kansai Gaidai University

1. Introduction

Observe the following example:

(1) Ano Federer-ga make-ta. (I can't believe it.)
That Federer-NOM lose-PAST
At-issue: Federer lost.
Implicature: Federer is highly unlikely to lose.

In (1) the speaker uses *ano* in order to express his/her surprise about the fact that 'Federer lost.' In (1) the speaker is not physically pointing to Federer (a professional tennis player); instead, he/she is mentally construing Federer as a highly unlikely person to lose. Note that if we replace *make-ta* 'lost' in (1) with *kat-ta* 'won', the sentence becomes odd, as shown in (2):

*We are grateful to Chris Davis, Anastasia Giannakidou, Heejeong Ko, Susumu Kubo, Yusuke Kubota, Chungmin Lee, Eric McCready, Bill McClure, Harumi Sawada, Yasutada Sudo, Kaori

Japanese/Korean Linguistics 21.
Edited by Seungho Nam, Heejeong Ko and Jongho Jun.

(2) ??Ano Federer-ga kat-ta. (I can't believe it.)
That Federer-NOM win-PAST
At-issue: Federer won.
Implicature: Federer is highly unlikely to win.

(2) is odd because, although Federer is a highly likely person to win (according to our world knowledge), the sentence implies that he is an unlikely person to win. In order to felicitously utter a sentence with a modal affective demonstrative, there must be a significant gap between the utterance situation and the speaker's expectations. In this sense, sentence (1) functions like a mirrative sentence (e.g. DeLancey 2001).[1] Since the demonstrative in (1) has both a modal (unlikelihood) meaning and an affective (speaker-oriented) meaning, we will call it a modal affective demonstrative.

The modal affective demonstrative has several seemingly puzzling properties that other kinds of demonstratives do not have. First, modal affective demonstratives naturally combine with a specific noun phrase, but they are difficult to use with a common noun:

(3) (The attached NP = common noun)
??Ano sensyu-ga kat-ta. (At-issue reading only)
Ano player-NOM win-PAST
'lit. That player won.'

This clearly contrasts with the spatial demonstratives. The spatial demonstratives can combine with a common noun (e.g. *ano/kono gakusei* 'that/this student'), but they cannot usually combine with a proper noun (e.g. ??*ano/kono Taro* 'that/this Taro').

The second puzzle is that although all three kinds of demonstrative (i.e. *kono* 'this', *sono* 'that', *ano* 'that') seem to have a modal affective use, it seems that each demonstrative has a different 'selectional restriction' regarding the choice of a target. For example, usually the modal affective *ano* combines with a third person specific noun:

(4) Ano {Taro /(?)watashi/(?)anata}-ga make-ta. (I can't believe it.)
That Taro / I / you -NOM lose-PAST
At-issue: {Taro/(?)I/(?)you} lost.
Implicature: {Taro/(?)I/(?)you} is/am/are highly unlikely to lose.

Note that the modal affective *ano* can select for the first person or the second person if they are interpreted like a 'third person.' On the other hand, *kono* usually combines with the first person:

---

[1] According to DeLancey (2001) the term refers to the linguistic marking of an utterance as conveying information that is new or unexpected to the speaker. Thanks to Anastasia Giannakidou for her valuable discussions of the connection with the notion of mirrativity.

(5) Kono {watashi/(?)Taro/(?)anata}-ga make-ta.
This I / Taro/ you -NOM lose-PAST
At-issue: {I/(?)Taro/(?)you} lost.
Implicature: {I/(?)Taro/(?)you} am/is/are highly unlikely to lose.

Finally, as for the modal affective *sono*, it is neutral about the selection of a target:

(6) a. {Taro/boku/anata}-wa totemo tsuyoi sensyu-da.
Taro/I /you -TOP very strong player-PRED
'{Taro/I/you} is/am/are a very strong player.'

b. Sono {Taro/boku/anata}-ga make-ta.
That Taro /I /you -NOM lose-PAST
At-issue: '{Taro/I/you} lost.' (I can't believe it.)
Implicature: '{Taro/I/you} is/am/are highly unlikely to lose.'

The above observations naturally induce the following questions. Why do the modal affective demonstratives combine with a specific noun? Where does the 'selectional restriction' of the modal affective demonstratives come from? How can we analyze the meaning of modal affective demonstratives in a theoretical way?

Although there have been a lot of studies on the meaning/use of Japanese demonstratives, to the best of our knowledge, no serious attention has been paid to the meaning/use of demonstratives like (1). The purpose of this paper is to investigate the meaning/use of modal affective demonstratives and to try to answer these questions.

Our argument/discussion proceeds as follows: First, we argue that the modal affective demonstrative is different from other kinds of demonstratives in that it conventionally implies that the at-issue proposition radical with respect to a specific individual target (i.e. a proposition without tense, modality, or speech act operators) is highly unlikely to be true. We will explain that the specificity requirement with respect to the target makes it difficult to combine the modal affective demonstratives with common nouns.

We will, however, also argue that there is a semantic parallelism between modal affective demonstratives and other kinds of demonstratives, as proven by the following facts:

(7) a. The modal affective *ano* 'that' is similar to the so-called 'episodic' *ano* 'that' (or the 'recognitional' use of demonstratives (e.g. Diessel 1999; Levinson 2004)) in that it refers to an entity in the speaker's memory.

b. The modal affective *kono* 'this' is similar to the spatial *kono* 'this' in that it specifies that the target is in the speaker's personal space.

c. The modal affective *sono* 'that' is similar to the 'anaphoric' use of *sono* 'that' in that it anaphorically refers to an entity that appears previously in the discourse.

We will claim that these properties affect the selection of the target of the modal affective demonstratives in terms of the person system.

Our approach to the meaning of modal affective demonstratives has a significant implication for the theory of conventional implicature as well. It is theoretically important that the modal affective demonstratives morphologically attach to nouns although semantically speaking they have to do with the probability of the at-issue proposition. This is because the phenomenon suggests that there is a mismatch between the at-issue meaning and the CI meaning in terms of the compositionality of meaning. The current theories of CI do not seem to be able to capture this mismatch phenomenon. In order to resolve this issue, we will propose that there is a new function application for the logic of conventional implicature (CI), a 'two-way' mixed application, and suggest that it can be a general compositional rule for various kinds of modal-like determiners or particles like *even* or (scalar) contrastive *wa*, which morphologically attach to a noun but semantically have to do with the probability of an at-issue proposition.

2. Japanese Demonstratives

Before looking at the modal affective use of demonstratives, let us briefly look at the basic uses (attested uses) of Japanese demonstratives. Japanese has three demonstrative prefixes—*ko-*, *so-*, and *a-*—as follows:

(8) a. Ko-no-hon-wa omoshiroi.
this-GEN-book-TOP interesting
'This book is interesting.'

b. So-no-hon-wa omoshiroi.
that-GEN-book-TOP interesting
'That book is interesting.'

c. A-no-hon-wa omoshiroi.
that-GEN-book-TOP interesting
'That book is interesting.'

In 'spatial use', where the referent is visible in speech location, *ko-* refers to something (somewhere) close to the speaker, *so-* refers to something (somewhere) close to the addressee (it can also refer to somewhere slightly removed from the speaker when it is part of the local pronoun), and *a-* refers to something (somewhere) far from the speaker (and the addressee). *Ko-*, *so-*, and *a-* also have a 'non-spatial use' (i.e. non-deictic), where the referent is not visible in the speech location. In this use, *ko-* refers to something functioning as a 'discourse topic', *so-* neutrally refers to something introduced in the discourse context, and *a-* refers to something located in the speaker's 'episodic memory.'[2]

The modal affective demonstratives are different from both the spatial demonstratives and the non-spatial demonstratives in that they have an expressive meaning of unlikelihood.

Note that the modal affective demonstratives are also different from the so-called affective demonstratives (Lakoff 1974). Naruoka (2003) claims that the Japanese adnominal demonstratives *konnna/sonnna/annna* (*-na* series) can behave as affective demonstratives and can express negative emotion (rejection) or surprise on the part of the speaker (See also Davis and Potts 2009; Potts and Schwarz 2010):

(9) Konna ryori-wa tabe-taku-nai.
This kind of food-TOP eat-want-NEG.
'lit. I do not want to eat this kind of food.'

Konnna in (9) triggers an implication that the speaker has a negative evaluation of the target NP (here, the food) but it does not have a modal meaning.

3. The Status of the Meaning of Modal Affective Demonstratives

Unlike the other uses of demonstratives, the modal affective demonstratives express the speaker's construal of the probability of the given proposition with respect to the target NP. We argue that this speaker-oriented modal meaning is a conventional implicature (CI). In the Gricean theory of meaning, CIs are considered to be part of the meanings of words but are independent of 'what is said' (e.g. Grice 1975; Potts 2005). Furthermore, it is mentioned that CIs have a semantic property of speaker-orientedness (at least by default) (Potts 2005, 2007).

There are several pieces of evidence that show that the meaning of the modal affective demonstratives is a CI (not part of what is said). First, we can determine the truth value of a given sentence. Second, the meaning of the modal affective demonstratives cannot be challenged. This is supported by the fact that if we deny (10) by saying *Sore-wa uso-da* 'That's false', the denial only targets the at-issue part of the sentence:

[2]See also Kuno (1973), Kuroda (1979), Yoshimoto (1986), Kinsui and Takubo (1992), Hoji et al. (2003), and Takubo (2010) among others.

(10) Ano Federer-ga make-ta. (I can't believe it.)
That Federer-NOM lose-PAST
At-issue: Federer lost.
Implicature: Federer is highly unlikely to lose.

Third, unlike other kinds of demonstratives, it is odd to question a sentence with a modal affective demonstrative using '*dono* NP?' (which NP?):

(11) A: Ano sensyu-ga make-ta. (spatial/recognitional use)
That player-NOM lose-PAST
'That player lost.'
B: Dono sensyu-ga?
Which player-NOM
'Which player?'

(12) A: Ano Roger Federer-ga make-ta. (modal affective use)
That Roger Federer-NOM lose-PAST
'lit. That Roger Federer lost.'
B: *Dono Roger Federer-ga?
Which Roger Federer-NOM
'lit. Which Roger Federer?'

In (10) the speaker cannot ask a question using *dono* NP 'which.' That is because in this sentence, *ano* and its host NP do not semantically interact, so we cannot form a question using *dono* NP.

One might think that the meaning of the modal affective demonstrative is a presupposition, rather than a CI. However, in this paper we will show that this is not so. One piece of evidence that shows that modal affective demonstratives are CIs is concerned with embeddability. It has been claimed that unlike presupposition, CI content can be anchored to the speaker even if it is embedded under an attitude predicate (i.e. a presupposition plug):

(13) Taro-wa ano Ziro-ga makeru-to omo-tteiru.
Taro-TOP that Ziro-NOM lost-that think-TEIRU
'lit. Taro thinks that that Ziro will lose.'

The meaning of *ano* is speaker-oriented and cannot be anchored to the subject Taro.[3] Although there has been an ongoing debate regarding the sta-

---

[3] However, the test of embeddability does not differentiate between the modal demonstrative and other kinds of demonstratives, because although the meaning of the latter contributes to the at-issue semantics, they are speaker-oriented (i.e. deictic):
(i) Taro-wa ano hon-ga omoshiroi-to omo-tteiru. (*ano* = spatial use)
Taro-TOP that book-NOM interesting-that think-TEIRU
'Taro thinks that that book is interesting.'
This suggests that the notion of speaker-orientedness is not a CI-specific characteristic.

tus/existence of the notion of conventional implicature, we would like to take the position based on the above discussion that the meanings of the modal affective demonstratives are CIs.

4. The Meaning of the Modal Affective Demonstratives

Based on the above background, let us now look at the meaning of modal affective demonstratives in more detail. We propose that unlike other kinds of demonstratives, the modal affective demonstratives have the following conventional implicature (CI):

(14) The modal affective demonstratives conventionally imply that the at-issue proposition radical (a proposition without tense, modality, question, or propositional attitude predicate) with a target individual is highly unlikely to be true.

The CI meaning in (14) creates a gap between the at-issue proposition (or utterance situation) and the speaker's expectations.[4]

The definition in (14) naturally explains why the modal affective demonstratives combine with a specific noun phrase but do not usually combine with a common noun:

(15) (The attached NP = common noun)

??Ano	sensyu-ga	kat-ta.	(At-issue reading only)
Ano	player-NOM	win-PAST	

'lit. That player won.'

(15) is odd because here the speaker is calculating the probability of the proposition without specifying/individualizing a target. Pragmatically, it is meaningless to calculate an unspecified person's probability of winning the game. This strongly contrasts with the deictic/non-deictic use of demonstratives, which combine with a common noun because their semantic function is to specify which entity the speaker is referring to.

Note that (15) becomes okay if *ano* is understood as an at-issue demonstrative (spatial/non-spatial). However, in that case we cannot get a modal meaning. This is corroborated by the fact that unlike the modal affective

---

[4] Note that the modal affective demonstratives can appear in non-factive environments. For example, they can be used in questions:

(i) Ano	Federer-ga	makeru-to	omou?	(No, you do not.)
That	Federer-NOM	lose-that	think	

At-issue: Do you think that Federer will lose?
CI: Federer is highly unlikely to lose.

The interesting point here is that (i) is interpreted as a rhetorical/biased question (not a simple Yes/No question) because of the presence of the modal affective demonstrative. Here the speaker in (i) strongly expects that the addressee's answer will be 'No.'

demonstratives, the at-issue demonstrative can co-occur with the speaker-oriented adverbs *yosoodoori* 'as expected' and *yosoo-ni hanhiste* 'contrary to my expectation':

(16) a. {Yosoodoori/ yosooni hansite} ano sensyu-ga kat-ta.
As expected/ contrary to expectation that player-NOM win-PAST
'{As expected/Contrary to my expectation}, that player won.'

b. {??Yosoodoori/yosooni hansite} ano Taro-ga kat-ta.
As expected/contrary to expectation that Taro-NOM win-PAST
'{??As expected/contrary to my expectation}, *that* Taro won.'
(CI: Taro is highly unlikely to win.)

The modal affective *ano* in (16b) cannot combine with the adverb *yosso-doori* 'as expected', because although the modal affective *ano* triggers the conventional implicature that the speaker thinks that Taro is highly unlikely to win, the speaker-oriented adverb *yossodoori* triggers an implication that the fact that Taro won is expected by the speaker. Thus there is a mismatch in the speaker's assumptions. On the other hand, the at-issue demonstrative *ano* (spatial/non spatial) can combine with the adverbs because it does not have a speaker-oriented likelihood meaning.

5. Analysis

5.1 The Meaning of Modal Affective Demonstratives

Let us consider the meaning of modal affective demonstratives more theoretically based on the following environment.

(17) [$\text{DEM}_{\text{MOD.AFF}}$ NP] PRED-past

We propose that the modal affective demonstratives have the following denotations for this environment:

(18) Denotations of modal affective demonstratives

a. $[[\text{ano}_{\text{MOD.AFF}}]] = \lambda x \lambda P.\ \textbf{unlikely}(P(x)) >!\ \text{STAND}$
(where x is in the speaker's memory)

b. $[[\text{kono}_{\text{MOD.AFF}}]] = \lambda x \lambda P.\ \textbf{unlikely}(P(x)) >!\ \text{STAND}$
(where x is in the speaker's personal space (utterance location))

c. $[[\text{sono}_{\text{MOD.AFF}}]] = \lambda x \lambda P.\ \textbf{unlikely}(P(x)) >!\ \text{STAND}$
(where x is in the previous utterance)

The modal affective demonstrative takes an individual and a predicate and conventionally implies that the degree of unlikelihood of P(x) is much greater than a contextually determined standard/norm. That is, P(x) is highly unlikely to be true. ('!>STAND' stands for 'greater than a contextual standard by a large amount'; cf. *much*, (Kennedy and McNally 2005)).[5]

The question is: Where does the selectional restriction on x come from? We argue that these selectional restrictions can be reduced to a semantic property of demonstratives (i.e. the semantic properties that other kinds of demonstratives have):

(19) a. The modal affective *ano* is similar to the 'episodic' *ano* (or the 'recognitional' use of demonstratives (e.g. Diessel 1999; Levinson 2004)) in that it refers to an entity in the speaker's memory.

b. The modal affective *kono* is similar to the spatial *kono* in that it specifies that the target is in the speaker's personal space.

c. The modal affective *sono* is similar to the 'anaphoric' use of *sono* 'that' in that it anaphorically refers to an entity that appears previously in the discourse.

These properties affect the choice of a target in terms of the person system. For example, as we observed in Section 1, usually the modal affective *ano* does not combine with a first or second person pronoun:

(20) Ano {Taro/$^{(?)}$watashi/$^{(?)}$anata}-ga make-ta. (I can't believe it.)
That Taro / I / you -NOM lose-PAST
At-issue: {Taro/$^{(?)}$I/$^{(?)}$you} lost.
Implicature: {Taro/$^{(?)}$I/$^{(?)}$you} is/am/are unlikely to lose.

We can say that this is because the first and second person are participants in the conversation, and we usually do not consider them to be in the speaker's memory. However, if we interpret the first person and second person in accordance with the speaker's memory, the modal affective *ano* can combine with them.
As for the modal affective *kono*, it naturally combines with the first person pronoun but not with the third person specific noun or the second person:

(21) Kono {watashi/$^{(?)}$Taro/$^{(?)}$anata}-ga make-ta.
This I / Taro / you -NOM lose-PAST
At-issue: {I/$^{(?)}$Taro/$^{(?)}$you} lost.
Implicature: {I/$^{(?)}$Taro/$^{(?)}$you} am/is/are unlikely to lose.

We can say that this is because we usually do not consider a third person/ a second person to be in the speaker's space. However, if we posit a context where the third person (here Taro) or the second person *is* in the speaker's space, then the sentence might sound natural.

---

[5] See, e.g. Lassiter (2011) for a detailed discussion of the scalar properties of modals such as *likely* and *possible*.

As for modal affective *sono*, it is neutral about the selection of a target, but it specifies that the target NP is already given:

(22) a. {Taro/boku/anata}-wa totemo {tsuyoi/??yowai} sensyu-da.
Taro/I /you -TOP very strong/ weak player-PRED
'{Taro/I/you} is/am/are a very {strong/weak} player.'

b. Sono {Taro/boku/anata}-ga make-ta.
That Taro /I /you -NOM lose-PAST
At-issue: *Sono* {Taro/I/you} lost.
Implicature: {Taro/I/you} is/am/are highly unlikely to lose.

We think that this discourse-given property of modal affective *sono* comes from the anaphoric use of *sono*. Note that (22a) with *yowai* 'weak' is odd because it does not fit with the CI meaning of (22b).

The above discussion strongly suggests that the selectional restriction of modal affective demonstratives is not arbitrary (nor syntactic). It is semantically motivated and it can be accounted for based on a semantic parallelism with other uses of demonstratives.

5.2 Compositionality of Modal Affective Demonstratives

The above analyses, however, pose a serious problem for the current theories of CIs (Potts 2005; McCready 2010). The current theories do not seem to be able to capture the relationship between the CI meaning and the at-issue meaning in sentences with modal affective demonstratives. Let us consider this step by step. Building on Kartunnen and Peters' (1979) two-dimensional theory of conventional implicature, Potts (2005) provides a novel multidimensional composition system:

(23) Potts's CI application

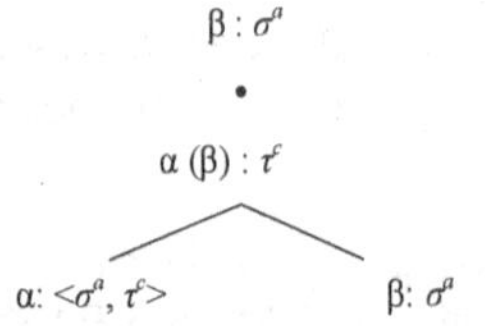

(Potts 2005: 64)

A α that is of type $<\sigma^a, \tau^c>$ takes a β of type σ^a and returns τ^c. The superscript *c* stands for a CI type and the superscript *a* stands for an at-issue type. Notice that β is resource insensitive, and is passed up to the level above the bullet. The bullet • is a metalogical device for separating independent lambda expressions.

McCready (2010) proposes several additional rules in order to explain the meaning of 'mixed content.' (See also Gutzmann 2011). This term describes elements that have both at-issue and CI meanings. For example, McCready analyzes the pejorative word for Germans *Kraut* as a mixed content trigger because it is predicative of at-issue content (i.e. the property of being a German), yet introduces a conventional implicature (i.e. the speaker's negative attitude toward German people). The following figures show simplified versions of the rules McCready proposes: [6]

(24) a. Mixed application A

$\alpha(\gamma): \tau^a$
$\bullet$
$\beta(\gamma): \upsilon^c$

$\alpha \blacklozenge \beta: \langle\sigma^a, \tau^a\rangle \times \langle\sigma^a, \upsilon^c\rangle \quad \gamma: \sigma^a$

b. Mixed application B

$\alpha(\gamma): \tau^a$
$\bullet$
$\beta(\gamma): \upsilon^c$

$\alpha: \langle\sigma^a, \tau^a\rangle \quad \gamma: \sigma^a$
$\bullet$
$\beta: \langle\sigma^a, \upsilon^c\rangle$

(Based on McCready 2010)

The mixed-type CI application A in (24) applies at the 'root' level, where $\alpha \blacklozenge \beta$ corresponds to a mixed-type CI trigger (word). On the other hand, the mixed-type CI application B in (24) is used in the middle of derivation.

However, these compositional rules are not adequate for capturing the relationship between the at-issue and CI meanings of sentences with the modal affective demonstrative. Let us consider this based on (25) and the proposed lexical item for the modal affective *ano*:

(25) Ano Federer-ga make-ta. (I can't believe it.)
That Federaa-NOM lose-PAST
At-issue: Federer lost.
Implicature: Federer is highly unlikely to lose.

(26) $[\![\text{ano}_{\text{MOD.AFF}}]\!] : \langle e^a, \langle\langle e^a, t^a\rangle, t^c\rangle\rangle = \lambda x \lambda P.$ **unlikely**$(P(x)) >!$ STAND
(where x is in the speaker's memory)

Although the lexical item in (26) allows us to calculate the CI meaning of (25), the combination of the existing compositional rules and the lexical item in (26) does not allow us to capture the at-issue meaning and the CI meaning of (25) in a unified way. This is because in the at-issue dimension the predicate *make* 'lose' takes *Federer* as its argument, but in the CI dimension the predicate *make* is considered to be an argument for

[6] The rules in (24) are slightly different from what McCready (2010) actually proposes. He uses a new type called a shunting type *s* for the mixed contents. The basic motivation for introducing the shunting operation/type is to ensure that the argument of the mixed content (in this case γ) is resource sensitive (i.e. to make sure that it does not pass on to the place above $\alpha(\gamma)$ due to Potts' CI application). For the sake of simplicity, this paper will not use this shunting operation. We assume instead that the rules in (23) and (24) do not interact simultaneously in the course of semantic derivation.

ano(**Federer**). Thus, there is a mismatch between the at-issue and CI levels in terms of the predicate/argument relationship.

In order to resolve the 'mismatch' between the at-issue and CI levels, we propose the following new CI application:

(27) Two-way mixed application (Sawada and Sawada 2010)

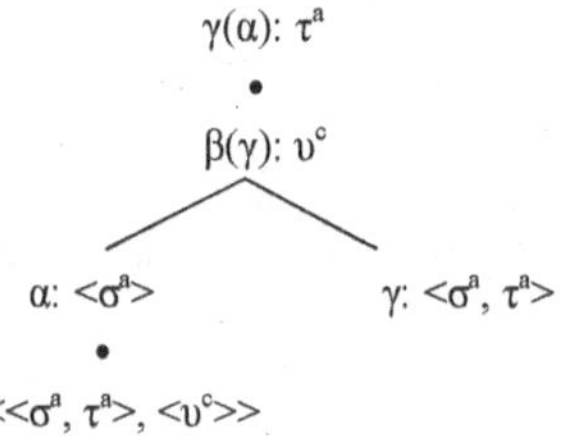

This rule ensures that there is an asymmetrical relationship between the argument and the predicate in the at-issue domain as compared to the CI domain. If we apply this rule to (25), we can analyze the meaning of the sentence as follows:

(28)

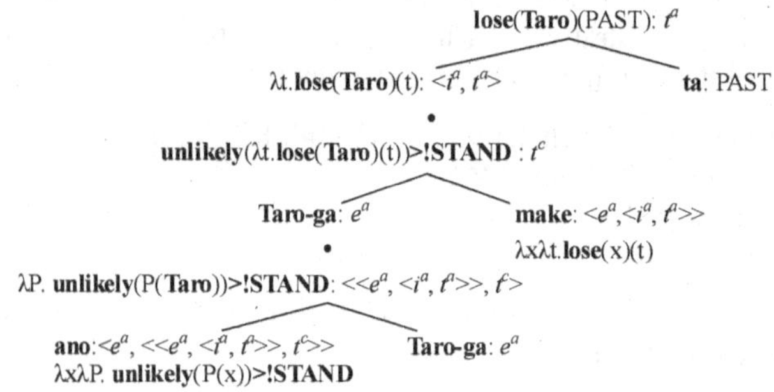

5.3 An Alternative View

Another way to analyze the meaning of sentences with the modal affective demonstrative is to consider the latter to be mixed content, as in (29):

(29) Denotations of modal affective demonstratives (Alternative version)

a. [[ano $_{\text{MOD.AFF}}$]] = λxλP. P(x)♦λxλP. **unlikely**(P(x)) >!STAND (where x is in the speaker's memory)

b. [[kono $_{\text{MOD.AFF}}$]] = λxλP. P(x)♦λxλP. **unlikely**(P(x)) >!STAND (where x is in the speaker's personal space (utterance location))

c. [[sono $_{\text{MOD.AFF}}$]] = λxλP. P(x)♦λxλP. **unlikely**(P(x)) >!STAND (where x is discourse-given)

The advantage of this approach is that we do not have to posit the two-way mixed application. Using this approach, we can analyze the meaning of (25) as follows:

(30)

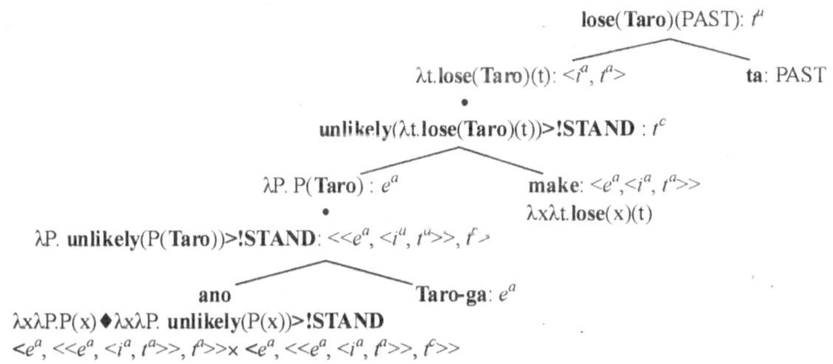

However, this mixed content approach seems problematic because it violates the criteria of mixed content. McCready (2010: 4-5) claims that in order to be mixed content, an element has to satisfy the following criteria. First, a mixed-content element should introduce semantic content in both the at-issue and the CI dimension. Second, mixed-content elements should be monomorphemic. Although the modal affective demonstratives clearly satisfy the second criterion, they do not satisfy the first criterion. They do not have a descriptive content and the truth condition of a proposition with a modal affective demonstrative does not change even if we delete it.

Based on the above discussion, we conclude that the modal affective demonstratives are pure CI triggering expressions. Thus, it is necessary to posit a new CI application—a two-way mixed application—in order to account for the meaning of sentences with the modal affective demonstrative.

6. A Broader Perspective

There are many expressions other than the modal affective demonstratives that morphologically combine with a noun but have to do with the probability of an at-issue proposition; e.g. *even* (Karttunen and Peters 1979), *at least* (e.g. Geurts and Nouwen 2007), and the scalar-use contrastive *wa* (Sawada to appear). For example, in (31) *even* triggers an implication that the target NP Taro is the least likely person to lose among the possible alternatives:

(31) Even Taro lost.
  At-issue: Taro lost.
  Modal meaning: Of the people under consideration, Taro is the least likely person to lose.

Although we need to be careful about the status of *even* (and other possible candidates), it seems that the proposed two-way mixed application can naturally apply to the meaning of those particles as well.

7. Conclusion

In this paper we have investigated the meaning of the modal affective demonstratives in Japanese and considered the semantic/pragmatic mechanisms that can capture their meaning and distribution patterns.

As for the meaning of modal affective demonstratives, we argued that unlike other uses of demonstratives, they conventionally imply that the at-issue proposition radical with a specific target is highly unlikely to be true. We also argued that there are similarities between the modal affective use and other uses of demonstratives (deictic and non-deictic uses) in terms of the semantic properties of the target, and that those similarities affect the selection of the target. As for the theoretical side, we proposed a new CI function application, the two-way mixed application, and showed that it naturally explains the mismatch between an at-issue dimension and the CI dimension in terms of the compositionality of the meaning of sentences with a modal affective demonstrative.

It is theoretically important that the modal affective demonstratives attach to a noun but semantically have to do with the probability of an entire proposition. We hope that this paper provides new empirical perspectives for the study of demonstratives and the semantics/pragmatics interface.

In a future study we would like to consider the question of where the unlikelihood meaning of the modal affective demonstrative comes from. It seems that the unlikelihood meaning is relevant to the general pragmatic property of highlighting that demonstratives inherently have. While the deictic/non-deictic demonstratives highlight something in order to distinguish one thing from another, in the case of modal affective demonstratives, it seems that they are used for highlighting the utterance situation itself. Further investigations need to be conducted with regard to the semantic source of modal affective demonstratives.

References

Davis, C. and Potts, C. 2009. Affective Demonstratives and the Division of Pragmatic Labor. In Aloni, M., Bastiaanse, H., Jager, T., Ormondt, P., Schulz, K. (eds.) *Preproceedings of the 17th Amsterdam Colloquium*, 32-41.

Delancey, S. 2001. The mirative and evidentiality. *Journal of Pragmatics* 33:369-382.

Diessel, H. 1999. *Demonstratives: Form, Function, and Grammaticalization.* Amsterdam: John Benjamins Publishing Company.

Geurts, B., and Nouwen, R. 2007. At Least et al.: The Semantics of Scalar Modifiers. *Language* 83: 533-559.

Gutzmann, D. 2011. Expressive Modifiers & Mixed Expressives. In Bonami, O., and Hofherr, C.P. (eds.), *Empirical Issues in Syntax and Semantics* 8, 123-141.

Grice, H. P. 1975. Logic and Conversation. In Cole, P. and Morgan, J. (eds.) *Syntax and Semantics*, iii: *Speech Acts*, 43-58. New York: Academic Press.

Hoji, H., Kinsui, S., Takubo, Y., and Ueyama, A. 2003. The Demonstratives in Modern Japanese. In Li, A. and Simpson, A. (eds.) *Functional Structure(s), Form and Interpretation: Perspectives from East Asian Languages*, 97-128. London: Routledge

Kaplan, D. 1999. What is Meaning? Explorations in the Theory of Meaning as Use. Brief version. Draft 1. Ms., UCLA.

Karttunen, L., and Peters, S. 1979. Conventional Implicature. In C. K. Oh and D. A. Dinneen, (eds.), *Syntax and Semantics. Vol. 11. Presupposition*, 1-56. New York: Academic Press.

Kennedy, C. and L, McNally. 2005. Scale structure, degree modification, and the semantics of gradable predicates. *Language* 81(2): 345-381.

Kinsui, S. 1999. Nihongo no sizisi niokeru tyokuji yoohou to hi-tyokuji yoohou no kankei nituite (On the Relation between the Deictic Use and the Non-deictic Use of the Japanese Demonstratives). *Journal of Natural Language Processing* 6(4): 67-91.

Kinsui, S. and Takubo, Y. 1992. Nihongo sizisi kenkyusi kara/e (From/Toward a History of Research on Japanese Demonstratives). In Kinsui, S., Takubo, Y. (eds.), *Sizisi* (Demonstratives), 151-192. Tokyo: Hituzi Syobu.

Kuno, S. 1973. *The Structure of the Japanese Language*. Cambridge, Mass.: The MIT Press.

Kuroda, S.-Y. 1979. (Ko), so, a nituite (On (ko), so- and a-). In *Eigo to nihongo to* (English and Japanese), 41-59. Tokyo: Kurosio Syuppan.

Lakoff, R. 1974. Remarks on 'This' and 'That'. *Proceedings of the Chicago Linguistics Society* 10, 345-356.

Lassiter, D. 2010. Gradable epistemic modals, probability, and scale structure. *Proceedings of SALT* 20: 197–215, 2010.

Levinson, S. C. 2004. Deixis. In Horn, L.R. and G. Ward. (eds.) *The Handbook of Pragmatics*. Oxford: Blackwell Publishing.

McCready, E. 2010. Varieties of Conventional Implicature. *Semantics & Pragmatics* Vol. 3(8): 1-57.

Naruoka, K. 2003. Expressive Functions of Japanese Adnominal Demonstratives 'konna/ sonna/ anna.' In *The 13th Japanese/ Korean Linguistics Conference*, 433-444.

Potts, C. 2005. *The Logic of Conventional Implicatures*. Oxford: Oxford University Press.

Potts, C. and Schwarz, F. 2010. Affective 'This.' *Linguistic Issues in Language Technology* Vol. 3(5): 1-30.

Sawada, O. To appear. The Japanese Contrastive *wa*: A Mirror Image of EVEN. *Proceedings of the 33rd Annual Meeting of the Berkeley Linguistics Society*. Berkeley: Berkeley Linguistics Society.

Sawada, O. and J. Sawada. 2010. The Saliency and Scalarity in the Meaning of the Japanese Modal Affective Demonstratives. *Proceedings of the Seventh International Workshop of Logic and Engineering of Natural Language Semantics (LENLS 7)*, 111-124.

Takubo, Y. 2010. Nihongo no Koozoo: Suiron to Chishikikanri (Structure of Japanese: inference and knowledge management). Tokyo: Kuroshio Publisher.
Yoshimoto, K. 1986. On Demonstratives KO/SO/A in Japanese. *Gengo Kenkyu* 90: 48-72.

Part IV

Discourse

Mikan yo Mikan: Formulaic Constructions and their Implicature in Conversation

MAYUMI AJIOKA, MICHIKO KANEYASU, YUMIKO KAWANISHI, AND SHOICHI IWASAKI*
University of California, Los Angeles

1. Introduction

Conversation participants rely on both implicit and expressed linguistic meanings to arrive at the intended communicative meaning. Utterances may be relatively more transparent when the linguistic meanings are richly encoded, but they may be less so when they give little clue for deriving the communicative meaning. In the latter case, the addressee of information

* This paper is the outcome of a graduate seminar offered in the Department of Asian Languages and Cultures, UCLA, in 2010 and the subsequent working group. The four authors of this paper made an equal amount of contribution and the order of the names is completely arbitrary. We acknowledge those who commented on our oral presentations of this paper at the University of Tokyo in August, 2011 and at the Japanese/Korean Linguistics Conference in October, 2011 in Seoul. We also thank Maggie Camp who offered suggestions for both content and form to improve the paper. The four of us share responsibilities for any remaining problems in the paper.

Japanese/Korean Linguistics 21.
Edited by Seungho Nam, Heejeong Ko and Jongho Jun.

must arrive at the communicative meaning through various pragmatic processes, such as referent resolution, missing argument recovery, disambiguation, and inference building. To assist in this process, language provides the conversation participants with various procedural cues signaled by specialized linguistic forms, such as discourse markers, reformulation markers, and pragmatic particles.

The goal of this paper is to examine details of the processes through which conversational participants arrive at mutually recognized communicative meanings. In particular, using actual conversational data, we examine one specific formulaic construction, [N_{i1} (*da*) *yo* N_{i2}], represented by *mikan yo mikan* 'It's tangerines, you know, it's tangerines.' We will trace how this construction operates in conversation by employing concepts developed from relevance theory (Wilson and Sperber 1993, 2002), and show how it functions as a formulaic construction in the framework developed by Fillmore et al. (1988).

2. Background

In recent years, it has been suggested that speakers are heavily dependent on prefabricated formulaic expressions (e.g. Wray and Perkins 2000, Pawley 2009, Corrigan et al. 2009). Formulaic expressions are advantageous to speakers who must perform several tasks simultaneously, such as recalling events, organizing thoughts, producing utterances, and maintaining social relationships with the addressee; they alleviate the task of assembling words according to grammatical rules in order to construct well-formed utterances every time the speaker says something, and instead guide the speaker to select the appropriate form over other well-formed utterances. In other words, formulaic expressions create native-like naturalness in speech, and allow for a smooth production of utterances (Pawley 1985, Pawley and Syder 1983). Some formulaic expressions are completely fixed, e.g. *isogaba maware* 'If (you are) in a hurry, go around (it) (= Walk. Don't run),' or *asameshi mae* 'Before breakfast (= An easy task),' while others are not (see examples in the next paragraph). The meaning of formulaic expression can be either transparent (as is the case with *isogaba maware*) or opaque and idiomatic (as with *asameshi mae*). These expressions are larger than single lexical items, but speakers know their form and meaning/function as a paired unit. The form-meaning/function units, either single lexical items, or larger items, are termed 'constructions' (Fillmore et al. 1988). Some formulaic expressions are context sensitive. *Asameshi mae* (lit. 'before breakfast') as a response to the praise *yoku dekita ne!* 'You did so well!' would be interpreted as 'an easy task' while the same expression used in the sentence *mada asameshi mae da kara chotto matte* 'I haven't had breakfast, so can you wait a little' would be interpreted literally.

While some formulaic expressions are completely fixed, many are not. The English expression 'to break one's back' is one such example. As a formulaic expression, it means 'to work extremely hard,' but the tense and aspect for the verb, 'break' and the possessive pronoun 'one's' are variables; 'He will not break his back for such a low wage,' 'I am breaking my back to put food on this table.' Notice also that as a formulaic expression the possessor must be co-referential with the subject. Thus 'a heavy rock broke his back' is not a formulaic expression, but an innovative sentence created by applying the rule for constructing a transitive sentence. This type of formulaic expression which contains variable slots is called 'sentence-stem' by Pawley and Syder (1983), and 'formal idiom' and 'lexically open idiom' by Fillmore et al. (1988). A similar type of formulaic expressions exists in Japanese. *Hone o oru* literally means 'to break one's bone' (*Taro wa sukii de ashi no hone o otta* 'Taro broke his leg (bone) while skiing') and figuratively 'to work hard' or 'to do a special favor for someone' (e.g. *buji shuushoku dekita no mo oji-san ga hone o otte kureta okage desu* 'The reason why I was able to get a job is because my uncle made a special personal effort for me'). In the latter case, the expression can take several different forms: e.g. *o-hone ori itadaku* (a humble expression '(He) worked hard for me'), *hone ori zon* ('losing despite effort > not worth the effort'). Like in the English example above, this construction has a variable subject, though it remains unexpressed due to liberal use of zero anaphora in Japanese. In addition, the object *hone* 'bone' can be modified by the honorific prefix *o-* as in *o-hone*, and the verb *oru* 'break' can be morphologically modified to *ori*, *otte*, and other forms.

The English and Japanese examples given in the preceding paragraph resemble ordinary transitive sentences in the respective language. There are some constructions which do not appear to be "derivable" from regular grammar. Examples from English include 'all of a sudden,' 'in point of fact,' 'the X-er, the Y-er' and 'let alone,' to name a few. In other words, these expressions are comprised of familiar lexical items, but assembled in an unfamiliar way, according to any normative English grammar rules (Fillmore et al. 1988). The Japanese equivalent of 'the X-er, the Y-er' is X-*ba* X-*hodo* Y, which is an example of a construction made of familiar words assembled in an unfamiliar way. The *-ba* form is one of the four major conditional forms available in Japanese. *Hodo* means 'degree, bounds, extent' and is normally used as a head noun with a modifying verb or adjective; *me ga kuramu hodo mabushii* 'it is bright to the extent that my eyes get blinded.' X may be either a verb or an adjective, but the two Xs must be the same within the construction (e.g. *nome ba nomu hodo genki ni naru* 'X (drink)-*ba* X (drink)-*hodo* Y (becomes healthy) > 'the more one drinks (it), the more healthier one gets'). What is significant about this structure is that the *-ba* conditional cannot be substituted by other conditional forms available in the language; **miru to miru hodo, *mitara mita/ru hodo, *miru/ta nara miru/ta hodo*. In other words, it is not sufficient to independently know how to form a conditional and how to use *hodo* (Okamoto 1994: 390). Native speakers of Japanese know that the [X-*ba* X-*hodo* Y] construction is a formulaic construction with a special local grammar and a specific meaning, and are capable of using it appropriately.

The construction we are examining in this paper, [N_{i1} (*da*) *yo* N_{i2}], is a lexically open construction with N_i as a variable slot for a noun. It has a strong pragmatic force rather than a purely semantic component at its core, which guides the recipient of the construction to arrive at the communicative meaning intended by the speaker. To understand this process, we refer to the framework provided by relevance theory (Sperber and Wilson 1986/1995, Wilson and Sperber 1993, 2002). Relevance theory is an inferential model of communication based on the assumption that human cognition has a tendency to search for relevance. Thus, whenever we say something to someone, it naturally raises expectations of relevance. Inputs are relevant when they make meaningful changes to one's cognitive environment, i.e. positive cognitive effect.[1] According to relevance theory, linguistic items encode not only conceptual information but also procedural information (Blakemore 1990, Wilson and Sperber 1993, 2002). The former encodes conceptual representations, while the latter provides instructions on how to process the conceptual representations through inferential processes. The other crucial concept is the type of assumption communicated by an utterance. According to relevance theory, an assumption explicitly communicated is "explicature,"[2] while any assumption implicitly communicated is called "implicature." Implicature consists of "implied premises," i.e. intended contextual assumptions, and "implied conclusions," i.e. intended contextual implications. That is, upon receiving information through explicature, the addressee must understand implied premises, and based on the premises and the explicature, he/she must attempt to derive an implied conclusion.

3. The [N_{i1} (*da*) *yo* N_{i2}] Formulaic Construction

From the structural point of view, the [N_{i1} (*da*) *yo* N_{i2}] construction is minimalistic with the following six properties: (i) N_i is an open slot; (ii) the cop-

---

[1] Examples of positive cognitive effect include "answering a question [the addressee] had in mind, improving his knowledge on a certain topic, settling a doubt, confirming a suspicion, or correcting a mistaken impression" (Wilson and Sperber 2002: 251).

[2] Relevance theory considers two levels of explicature, the basic and the higher levels; the former is the representation of the complete proposition expressed by an utterance and the latter is the representation of speech act and propositional attitude. For the current study, the higher level of explicature does not come into play and thus is excluded from the discussion.

ula *da* is or can be attached to N_{i1}, but not to N_{i2}; (iii) thus N_i is a predicate, and this suggests that there is a topic that goes with N_i; (iv) the pragmatic particle *yo* is attached to N_{i1}, but not to N_{i2}; (v) N_i is repeated once after the particle *yo*; and (vi) the whole construction is produced in a single intonation unit. From the semantic point of view, as mentioned above, the noun that appears in the slot of N_i is the sole conceptual information that the construction conveys. However, this minimal construction as a whole encodes the procedural information which guides the addressee in his/her inferential comprehension process to reach the communicative meaning. In other words, the whole construction creates specific pragmatic effects in conversations, which cannot be derived simply by combining the functions of each constituent part. More specifically, upon receiving this construction, the addressee constructs the explicature by enriching the logical form provided by the linguistic codes, i.e. TUx *wa* N (*da*) 'TUx is N'.[3] To develop the explicature, the addressee must go through inferential processes, which includes selecting appropriate contextual assumptions (implicature). As we demonstrate below, the procedural meaning conveyed by the construction imposes constraints on both explicature and implicature. That is, the construction guides the addressee through the inferential phase to reach the intended conclusion and communicative meanings.

In the following section, we demonstrate with actual conversation data how the [N_{i1}(*da*) *yo* N_{i2}] construction guides the addressee in the inferential processes to reach the relevance of the utterance. Furthermore, we demonstrate how a successful communication in the use of this construction contributes to a particular cognitive effect of strengthening mutual common ground and trust between the interlocutors.

4. Data Analyses

The data we analyze in this paper come from the corpus of Japanese telephone conversations.[4] In the following phone conversation, two close friends Mari and Kei are talking about how fresh produce is expensive in Japan. Mari now lives in the U.S. but grew up in Japan. Kei used to live in the U.S., but she has returned to Japan and lives there now. The two friends share common knowledge with respect to buying fresh fruits and vegetables in Japan.

---

[3] TUx is an abbreviation of 'Topic Unexpressable.' See Section 4 for an explanation of this concept.

[4] We examined 120 telephone conversations, totaling 18 hours, taken from the following published data: Canavan, A. and G. Zipperlen. 1996. *CALLHOME Japanese Speech*. Linguistic Data Consortium, Philadelphia; Wheatley, B., M. Kaneko, and M. Kobayashi. 1996. *CALLHOME Japanese Transcripts*. Linguistic Data Consortium, Philadelphia.

(1) *Mikan yo mikan*[5]

1. Mari: *yappa serori wa takai.* @@@
as.expected celery TOP expensive
'Celery is really expensive. Ha ha ha.'
2. Kei: *takai no.*
expensive SE
'(It's) expensive.'
3. Mari: *gya::. orenji nante, taberarenai yo?*
INJ orange much.less eat:POT:NEG PP
'Aargh. (We) certainly can't eat oranges, you know?'
4. Kei: *taberarenai.*
eat:POT:NEG
'(We) can't eat (them).'
5. ➔ ***mikan yo mikan.***
tangerine PP tangerine
'Tangerines *yo* tangerines.'
6. Mari: @@@@ (H) *hu::n.*
'Ha ha ha ha. Yeah.'
7. Kei: *un.*
'Yeah.'

Right before this segment, Kei mentions how much she has to pay to buy two stalks of celery in Japan. Then, in lines 1 and 2, Mari and Kei agree that celery is very expensive. In line 3, sympathetically, Mari says *orenji nante taberarenai yo* 'we cannot eat oranges (in Japan because they are very expensive).' Then Kei shows her alignment with Mari's remark in line 4 *taberarenai* 'we cannot eat (oranges in Japan because they are very expensive).' In line 5, Kei then produces *mikan yo mikan* 'Tangerines *yo* tangerines,' the target construction in the current paper. This construction conveys the explicature "(TUx) is tangerines." Then, immediately in line 6, Mari laughs and says *huun* 'Yeah' to display that she understood what Kei meant. In this segment, it is interesting to note that Mari and Kei were first listing what is NOT affordable in Japan (lines 1-3), such as celery and oranges. However, when Kei says *mikan yo mikan,* she actually shifts to what IS affordable in Japan. This newly provided sub-topic, i.e. what is affordable in Japan, is the presumable content of (TUx). This subtle twist, conveyed with this minimalistic construction, amuses Mari, and as a result, she laughs.

[5] The list of abbreviations for glosses is found at the end of this paper.

The procedural information encoded by the construction *mikan yo mikan* places constraints on both explicature and implicature. Among three inferential processes involved in constructing explicature, i.e. reference resolution, disambiguation, and enrichment (Wilson and Sperber 2002), reference resolution is constrained by the construction. That is, *mikan yo mikan* restricts the unexpressed topic to be a complex abstract concept not reducible to any simple linguistic expression. Put another way, the topic is "unexpressable" (TUx) and it must be understood implicitly. While it is possible to insert a presumable content such as *nihon de taberareru no* 'things we can eat in Japan' as a topic, explicitly stating it will destroy the construction, and thus its pragmatic force. In this sense the topic is unexpressable. Simultaneously, *mikan yo mikan* guides the addressee to derive an appropriate implicature, or more specifically, implied contextual assumption. That is, by using this particular construction, the speaker conveys his/her absolute certainty/trust that the addressee is able to understand the (TUx) implicitly, and that the speaker and the addressee share detailed common ground and close personal relationship to make this possible. Indeed, in the present case, Mari and Kei are close friends who share the cultural knowledge about *mikan*.[6] Upon receiving [N_{i1} (*da*) *yo* N_{i2}], the addressee is expected to provide a response which displays that he/she has identified the implied premises, constructed the explicature including (TUx), and derived the implied conclusion. In response to *mikan yo mikan*, Mari laughs. Her laugher is taken as an indication that she understood that 'all fresh produce is too expensive in Japan, except for tangerines,' and 'people can always count on tangerines in Japan.'

Our second example is much more complex, but our analysis can appropriately explicate the process of arriving at the communicative meaning between the interlocutors. In the following phone conversation, two friends Sae and Emi are talking about a brand-name (Gucci) bag that they both have. Sae is the caller from the U.S. and Emi is the receiver who lives with her child in Japan. Prior to the segment presented below, the topic had been initiated by Sae who asked Emi 'I read (in your letter) that you haven't used the bag. Why?' To Sae's question, Emi responded that she did not have a chance to use it because she had to carry things for her child. The dialogue had a couple of sub-topic shifts after that. Just prior to the following segment, Sae and Emi were discussing another sub-topic: Sae had been registered as a special customer at the Gucci boutique because she bought many bags there. In line 1, Sae suddenly shifts the sub-topic again to occasions in which she takes her bag with her, i.e. to lunches with other wives.

6 Cultural knowledge includes tangerines as a popular affordable fruit in Japan.

(2) *Ranchi da yo ranchi*

1. Sae: *kekkoo ranchi toka mo sa:,*
quite.often lunch such.as also PP

2. *[shuu] 1.5 kai gurai ittari shiteru no ne:,*
week (number) times about go:REP do:ASP SE PP
'(I)'m eating out for lunch (lit. going to lunch) about 1.5 times a week.'

3. Emi: [*un.*]
'Yeah.'

4. [[*ranchi::?*]]
'Lunch?'

5. Sae: [[*ippai aru kara*]] *sa, un ranchi toka ne,*
many exist because PP yes lunch such.as PP

6. *hora okusangata to sa:,*
you.know wives with PP
'There are so many (occasions), yeah, like lunch, you know with those wives,'

7. Emi: *a% a%* [*ano:*] *kaado o tsukau tte koto ka.*
INJ INJ INJ card ACC use QT NML Q
'Uh uh u:m you mean you use your card (there).'

8. Sae: [*u:n*].
'Yeah.'

9. Emi: *un?*
'Huh?'

10. Sae: *so- iya cha cha cha cha chau.*
'Righ- no no no no no no.'

11. ➔ *dakara …* ***ranchi da yo*** [***ran***]***chi***.
so lunch COP PP lunch
'You know … Lunch *da yo* lunch.'

12. Emi: [*a%*]

13. *un.* [[*ranchi:*]]?
'Yeah. Lunch?'

14. Sae: [[*un*]]. [*un*].

15. Emi: [*un*].

16. Sae: *ranchi ni: tabe ni ittari:,*
lunch DAT eat to go:REP
'(I) eat out for lunch, and,'

17. Emi: *nani, gucchi [ni] aru wake? ranchi taberu toko ga.*
what Gucci DAT exist PP lunch eat place NOM
'So there is a place to eat at the Gucci boutique?'

18. Sae: *[de-]*
'an-'

19. *e? chiga chiga chiga chiga chigau, daka* (H) *watashi ga tooto o*
INJ wrong you.know I NOM tote ACC

20. *dooyuufuuni tsukatteru no tte, tegami ni kaite-atta kara sa:,*
how use:ASP Q QT letter LOC was.written because PP
'What? no no no no no, you know, because you asked me in your letter how I use my tote bag.'

As evident from Sae's own explanation in lines 19-20, she intended to tell Emi where she would take her bag in lines 1-2 and 5-6 as a response to Emi's question posed in the letter she had written earlier. However, possibly due to the sudden topic shift (from the immediately preceding topic of Sae's special customer status at the Gucci boutique), Emi has trouble understanding what Sae is talking about, and asks 'Lunch?' in line 4, and further checks her understanding that Sae is talking about her card usage in line 7. Sae's negative response to Emi's understanding check in line 10 'no no no no no no' is followed by our target construction *dakara ... ranchi da yo ranchi* 'You know, lunch *da yo* lunch' in line 11.

The construction *ranchi da yo ranchi* conveys the explicature "(TUx) is lunch." Notably, Emi immediately says *un* 'Yeah' in line 13. As we can see in line 14, Sae takes Emi's response to mean that Emi understood what Sae was talking about and begins to resume her talk in line 16. However, Emi is still not sure and checks her understanding again in line 17: 'So there is a place to eat lunch at the Gucci boutique?' Now, realizing that Emi still has a problem identifying (TUx), in lines 19-20, Sae provides more information so that Emi can arrive at the intended (TUx).

This example is rather unusual in that the addressee is not able to identify the unexpressable topic (TUx) communicated via [N_{i1} (*da*) *yo* N_{i2}] construction. At the same time (or because of this complexity), it provides us with insight into the pragmatic processes involved in the use of [N_{i1} (*da*) *yo* N_{i2}] construction. First, it shows that the content of (TUx), under normal circumstances, remains implicit. In the excerpt (2), the speaker revealed a hint for the content of (TUx) only after she was made aware that the addressee could not identify it implicitly. Secondly, the excerpt demonstrates the pragmatic force of the construction. The *ranchi da yo ranchi* indexes the speaker's complete confidence that the addressee is able to indentify (TUx) implicitly. Although Emi's assumption of how "lunch" was relevant to their ongoing discourse turned out to be wrong, her response *un* 'Yeah' interactionally indicated that she thought she had identified (TUx), and had understood the implicature. This was confirmed by Sae's reaction to Emi's response in lines 14 and 16, as we have seen.

5. Discussion

The formulaic construction [N_{i1} (*da*) *yo* N_{i2}] is minimalistic with only N_i being available for conceptual information. The recipient of the construction must build up the explicature, "(TUx) is N_i," and simultaneously search for implied premises and conclusions. While searching for an implied premise and reaching for an implied conclusion, the addressee must identify (TUx) via 'reference resolution' (Wilson and Sperber 2002: 261), in which a missing relevant argument must be sought through examination of all the knowledge shared by the interlocutors. However, identifying (TUx) for the [N_{i1} (*da*) *yo* N_{i2}] construction is much more complex than performing identity resolution for pronouns because complete ellipsis gives no clue about the referent. Identity resolution for our target construction is further complicated because (TUx) is not reducible to any simple linguistic expressions, but refers to complex, abstract concepts. In case of the *mikan yo mikan* example, (TUx) is reached via a complex chain of related concepts and the shared cultural knowledge: 'celery and oranges' > 'expensive fresh produce in Japan' > (via antonymic reasoning) > 'cheap fresh produce in Japan' > *mikan* (tangerines). This twisted telegraphic reasoning amuses the recipient of the construction, who explicitly shows her appreciation by laughter upon realizing the implied conclusion. In the case of the *ranchi da yo ranchi* example, (TUx) must be identified via personally shared knowledge about the letter. However, in this case there is an apparent gap between the current state of informational knowledge between the two speakers, which creates miscommunication.

What these examples show is that the pragmatic function of the construction contributes to achieving the cognitive effect of strengthening the mutual common ground between the conversation participants. To understand how this works, we first need to consider what is available in this minimalistic formulaic construction. Besides N, which gives conceptual information, two resources are available for procedural information. One is the pragmatic particle *yo* and the other is the repetition of N. The pragmatic particle *yo*, according to Matsui's (2000) analysis based on relevance theory, "overtly encodes a guarantee of relevance," and gives the addressee "additional encouragement to pursue the relevance of the utterance" (p. 161). Matsui (2000: 162-3) also argues that a certain type of repetition encourages "the hearer to 'extend the context and thereby add further implicatures'

(Sperber and Wilson 1986/1995: 221)," which is comparable to the effect of *yo*. Our analysis suggests that a combination of *yo* and repetition in [N_{i1} (*da*) *yo* N_{i2}] is not simply doubling the force of adding further implicature (i.e. 'augmentation'), but indexes specific procedural meanings: 1) (TUx) is not reducible to simple linguistic codes, but 2) the speaker is extremely confident that the addressee can identify (TUx).

The first procedural constraint on the explicature is manifested differently in the two examples. In *mikan yo mikan*, (TUx) was indeed never realized linguistically and yet the two friends were able to come to a mutual understanding of the implied conclusion (through laughing). The *ranchi da yo ranchi* is an example of unsuccessful implementation of the [N_{i1} (*da*) *yo* N_{i2}] construction, and the producer of the construction had to repair the miscommunication by hinting at the content of (TUx).[7] The second procedural meaning concerning the implicature can be observed in the difference between the two examples in terms of interactions around the [N_{i1} (*da*) *yo* N_{i2}] construction. In the example of *ranchi da yo ranchi*, frustration on the part of the speaker is obvious because of the misunderstanding on the addressee's part. On the other hand, in the *mikan yo mikan* example, the speaker is not frustrated, but is giving a challenge to the addressee to make an obvious link between 'tangerines' (i.e. inexpensive fruit in Japan) and 'what we are talking about (i.e. expensive fresh produce in Japan).' What is common between these two cases is that the speaker expects that the addressee can make the implied link between N and some other contextual information (TUx) derivable from either the personally or culturally shared knowledge.

What our two examples have in common is the immediate aligning response by the addressee which displays the interactional relevance of the derived contextual conclusion. Mari's laughter is an appropriate response to the culturally-bound remark *mikan yo mikan* with a twist. In response to *ranchi da yo ranchi*, Emi says *un* 'yeah,' even though she does not completely understand what Sae means at this point. The [N_{i1} (*da*) *yo* N_{i2}] construction conveys the absolute certainty and trust in the addressee's ability to recover the (TUx), and this strong pressure makes the addressee feel obliged to respond and display his/her alignment with the other even though in actuality he/she has not comprehended all that is said. It is also important to note that only upon the addressee's response, the contextual conclusion

[7] This seems to indicate that TUx (unexpressable topic) can be linguistically describable when forced. Our intension is that when the construction is put in use in conversation, the producer cannot express it as it involves complex array of pragmatic encoding, and even if it is expressed, as in the case of the *ranchi da yo ranchi* data, it is a kind of rendition of the intended information.

and the communicative meaning mutually manifest between the speaker and the addressee.

While the independent functions of the particle *yo* and the repetition of N can be observed in the use of [N_{i1} (*da*) *yo* N_{i2}] in conversation, it is the construction itself which is linked to the particular pragmatic processes we have described above. The whole construction represents a fixed unit despite the fact that the structure is grammatically deviant. One type of evidence for the formulaicity of the [N_{i1} (*da*) *yo* N_{i2}] construction comes from comparing the intonation contours of the target construction and of other expressions involving all the components involved in the construction (the repetition of N and the particle *yo*).

All the instances of [N_{i1} (*da*) *yo* N_{i2}] in our conversational data are produced within single intonation units (Chafe 1994) with a downstep contour.[8] Figure 1 and 2 below represent the pitch contours of *mikan yo mikan* and *ranchi da yo ranchi*, respectively.

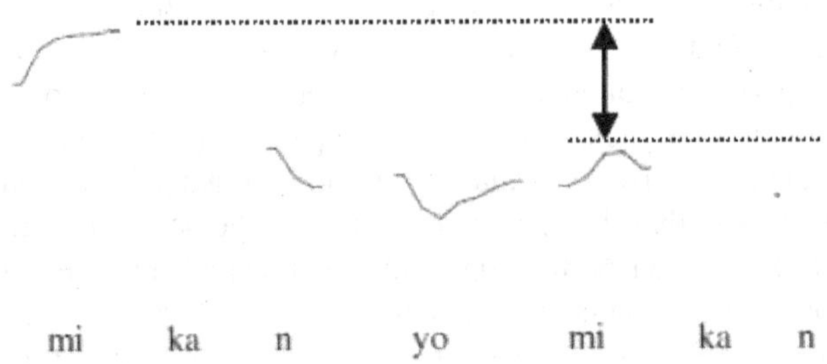

Figure 1: Pitch contour of *mikan yo mikan*

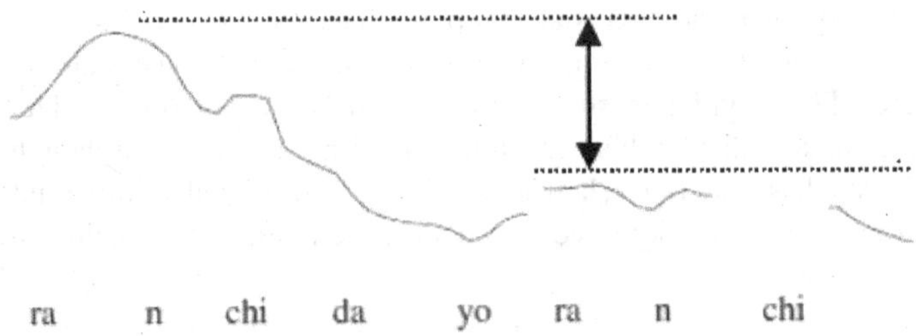

Figure 2: Pitch contour of *ranchi da yo ranchi*

[8] Downstep, also called catathesis (Poser 1984), is defined as the "lowering of the peak pitch of the second phrase within a longer phrase" (Vance 2008:182).

The words *mikan* and *ranchi* are both accented words with the high pitch tone on the first mora (i.e. *mi□kan* and *ra□nchi*). The significant lowering of the pitch peak on the first mora of the repeated nouns (N_{i2}), compared to the pitch peak of the initial nouns (N_{i1}) is observed when the two accented words are produced within a single intonation unit (Poser 1984, Pierrehumbert and Beckman 1988, Iwasaki *to appear*). The sharp downward step from the pitch peak on the first mora of the initial noun to that of the repeated noun, as seen in Figure 1 and 2, illustrates that the whole construction [N_{i1} (*da*) *yo* N_{i2}] is produced as a single unit.

Significantly, other expressions involving all the elements of the [N_{i1} (*da*) *yo* N_{i2}] construction (i.e. the repetition of N and the particle *yo*) do not show the same downstep pitch contour seen in the [N_{i1} (*da*) *yo* N_{i2}] construction. To demonstrate this, we have analyzed the string, N_i *yo* N_i *yo*, which repeats N *yo* twice, and differs from our target construction which has only one instance of *yo*. The following pitch contour (Figure 3) of the utterance *maiku yo maiku yo* 'Mike *yo* Mike *yo*'[9] does not show the steep lowering of the high pitch (*ma□iku*) of the repeated noun although the word *maiku* has the same high pitch tone on the first mora, as do *mikan* and *ranchi*. In other words, *maiku yo maiku yo* is a concatenation of two identical phrases, [N (*da*) *yo*]. In contrast, as this finding supports, the construction [N_{i1} (*da*) *yo* N_{i2}] is a fixed expression rather than a simple composite of constituting elements.

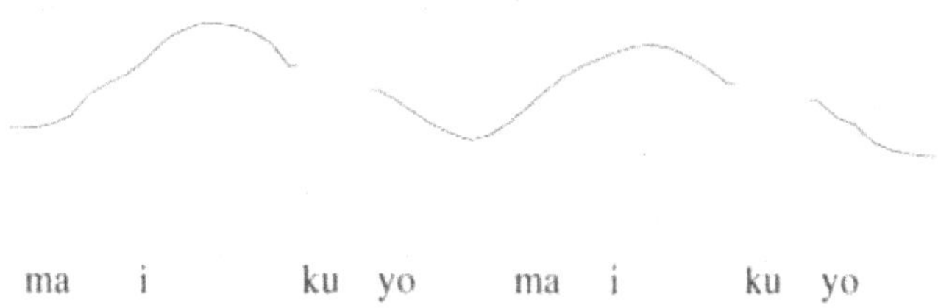

Figure 3: Pitch contour of *maiku yo maiku yo*

6. Conclusion

The findings in the present paper indicate that the native speakers of Japanese have knowledge of the construction [N_{i1} (*da*) *yo* N_{i2}] as a formula linked to the specific pragmatic function. With its procedural constraints on

---

[9] The speaker R is enacting her friend J who said *Maiku yo Maiku yo* to confirm that the man R and J spotted on the street was in fact Mike (their mutual friend) for the addressee F. Unlike the [N_{i1} (*da*) *yo* N_{i2}] construction, the topic is made explicit by the physical presence of the referent Mike and their (R's and J's) mutual attention to his presence.

both explicature and implicature, the recipient of the construction can reach the communicative meaning, and the participants can mutually enrich their cognitive environments. The use of the minimalistic formulaic construction not only helps the speakers cope with the real-time cognitive demands of conversational interaction, but it also contributes to reaffirming the common ground between the interlocutors and strengthening their intimate social relationship. We hope to have demonstrated how the conceptualization afforded by the relevance theory can help in analyzing details of the conversational transactions, while showing a way to take an intuition based theory to a verifiable domain of conversation analysis. We identified the [N_{i1} (*da*) *yo* N_{i2}] formulaic construction through our massive manual search. A corpus-based search may well miss an existence of such a construction with slots and variables. A careful discourse analysis is a key to untangling complex cognitive, interactional operations.

Appendix

Abbreviations

ACC	accusative	ASP	aspect
COP	copula	INJ	interjection
LOC	locative	NEG	negative
NOM	nominative	NML	nominalizer
POT	potential	PP	pragmatic particle
Q	question marker	QT	quotative
REP	representative	SE	sentence extender
TE	*-te* (conjunctive) form	TOP	topic marking particle

Transcript conventions (based on Du Bois et al. 1993)

@	one beat of laughter(H)	audible inhalation	
:	vowel lengthening	[ ]	overlap
%	glottal stop	-	word truncation
,	continuing intonation	.	falling intonation
?	rising intonation		

References

Blakemore, D. 1990. Performatives and Parentheticals. *Proceedings of the Aristotelian Society* 91: 197–213.

Chafe, W. 1994. *Discourse, Consciousness, and Time: The Flow and Displacement of Conscious Experience in Speaking and Writing*. Chicago: The University of Chicago Press.

Corrigan, R., H. Ouali, and K. Wheatley. 2009. Formulaic Language. Volume 2: Acquisition, Loss, Psychological Reality, and Functional Explanations. *Typological Studies in Language*. Amsterdam and Philadelphia: John Benjamins.

Du Bois, J. W., S. Schuetze-Coburn, S. Cumming, and D. Paolino. 1993. Outline of Discourse Transcription. *Talking Data: Transcription and Coding in Discourse*

Research, eds., J. A. Edwards and M. D. Lampert, 45–89. Hillsdale, NJ: Lawrence Erlbaum.

Fillmore, C. J., P. Kay, and M. O'Connor. 1988. Regularity and Idiomaticity in Grammatical Constructions; The Case of Let Alone. *Language* 64 (3), 501–538.

Iwasaki, S. to appear. *Japanese*. (London Oriental and African Language Library). 2nd ed. Amsterdam/Philadelphia: John Benjamins.

Matsui, T. 2000. Linguistic Encoding and the Guarantee of Relevance: Japanese Sentence-Final Particle YO. *Pragmatic Markers and Propositional Attitude*, eds. G. Anderson and T. Fretheim, 145–172. Amsterdam/Philadelphia: John Benjamins.

Okamoto, S. 1994. Argumentative verbal repetitive constructions in Japanese. *Cognitive Linguistics* 5(4), 381–404.

Pawley, A. 1985. On speech formulas and linguistic competence. Lenguas Modernas (Chile) 12: 84–104.

Pawley, A. 2009. Grammarians' language versus humanists' languages and the place of speech act formulas in models of linguistic competence. In Corrigan et al. (eds.).

Pawley, A. and F. H. Syder. 1983. Natural selection in syntax: Notes on adaptive variation and change in vernacular and literary grammar. *Journal of Pragmatics*, Volume 7, Issue 5, November Pages 551–579.

Pierrehumbert, J. and Beckman, M. 1988. *Japanese tone structure*. Cambridge, MA: MIT Press.

Poser, W. 1984. *The phonetics and phonology of tone and intonation in Japanese*. Ph.D. dissertation, MIT.

Sperber, D. and D. Wilson. 1986/1995. *Relevance: Communication and Cognition*. Oxford: Blackwell.

Vance, Timothy. 2008. The sounds of Japanese. Cambridge: Cambridge University Press.

Wray, A. and M. Perkins. 2000. The functions of formulaic language: an integrated model. Language and Communication 20 (1): 1–28.

Wilson, D. and D. Sperber. 1993. Linguistic Form and Relevance. *Lingua* 90: 1-25.

Wilson, D. and D. Sperber. 2002. Relevance Theory. UCL Working Papers in Linguistics, 14, 249–287.

The Use of the -(*su*)*pnita* Form in Korean Language Classroom Discourse

MI YUNG PARK
University of Auckland, New Zealand

1. Introduction

Using naturally occurring teacher-student conversations, this study examines teachers' use of a Korean speech style, the -(*su*)*pnita* form, in Korean as a foreign language (KFL) classroom discourse. The traditional approach to Korean speech styles has established a well-defined descriptive and normative usage in ordinary conversation. These studies claim that Korean speakers select speech styles according to aspects of the sociocultural background of the addressees, such as age or social status (Sohn 1999). However, the function of Korean speech styles is not restricted to merely indicating hierarchical social relationships between a speaker and an addressee. Discourse analytic studies of Korean speech styles suggest that speakers choose speech styles to achieve their interactional goals. Thus, the purpose of utilizing addressee honorifics is not just to conform to social norms and expectations determined by the status of the addressee or other situational factors. Building on recent research, this study examines the functions of the -(*su*)*pnita* form in KFL teacher speech. An analysis of teacher speech reveals that teachers' use of the -(*su*)*pnita* form is prompted by a particular

Japanese/Korean Linguistics 21.
Edited by Seungho Nam, Heejeong Ko and Jongho Jun.

context that requires them to play a role as professionals and carry out various responsibilities.

2. Previous Studies

Korean utilizes an extensive system of speech styles in everyday interaction to indicate social relationships between speakers and addressees. According to Sohn (1999), there are six speech styles in Korean. These speech styles are represented by distinctive suffixes that are attached to the stem of a verb or an adjective. Because these verbs and adjectives are placed at the end of a sentence, they are often called sentence enders. Among the six speech styles, the -(*su*)*pnita* form is the declarative form of the deferential style, which is known as marking the highest level of deference toward the addressee (Song 2005). Traditionally, it has been considered an addressee honorific because it expresses the speaker's politeness toward the addressee. It is predominantly used in speeches directed to a person of higher social status as well as in speeches directed to a large audience, such as news reports and public lectures (Lee and Ramsey 2000; Sohn 1999; Song 2005). Thus, the -(*su*)*pnita* form is often associated with a context of deference and formality.

Although the traditional accounts provide solid explanations of the conditions for the use of the -(*su*)*pnita* form, there are limitations to such an approach because these studies involve elicitation of simple sentences without a context and rely on native speakers' intuitions. Thoughts on speech styles are difficult to articulate because speech style use is a natural and unconscious process to a great extent (Cook 2008a). Studies of Korean speech styles based on native speakers' intuition typically identify one prominent meaning for each speech style. They do not automatically provide us a conscious and comprehensive picture of a speech style in all its contexts of use. Meanings of speech styles are underspecified and uniquely associated with the particular speech context (Cook 2011). For these reasons, a more appropriate research method to examine the complex range of meanings of speech styles is to analyze speech recorded in natural settings (Cook 2008a).

While the traditional grammarians describe the -(*su*)*pnita* form as a marker of deference and formality, discourse-based studies of Korean speech styles have shown cases where speech styles are used as an individual speaker's strategy rather than a social norm. These studies claim that speakers' speech style selections are informed by the speakers' constantly changing feelings, stances, and identities in the course of interaction. Drawing on a large corpus of public speech, Eun and Strauss (2004) claim that the main function of the -(*su*)*pnita* form is to introduce the audience to new information. Strauss and Eun (2005) followed up on this study by looking at the same linguistic phenomenon by utilizing both public speech and informal speech. They state that the -(*su*)*pnita* form indexes a stance of exclusion in relation to addressees whereby the speaker is positioned as neutral, detached, and objective. Additionally, Kim and Suh (2007) examined the use of the -(*su*)*pnita* form within Korean elementary classroom discourse. They demonstrate that teachers use the -(*su*)*pnita* form in order to feature key instructional elements as well as to establish boundaries between classroom activities. These functions cannot be explained by external social factors, which are fixed prior to interaction.

A large body of Japanese sociolinguistics literature looks at speech style use and shifts in a variety of authentic discourse contexts. Shifts between the plain and the *masu* forms have been found to index a variety of social meanings. Examples of these social meanings include multiple voices (Maynard 2008), shifting degrees of empathy or social distance (Ikuta 1983), shifts between a more public versus a spontaneous presentation of self (Cook 1996a, 1996b, 1997, 2008a), social identities (Cook 2008b), and varying degrees of awareness of the addressee (Maynard 1993). The findings from the Japanese speech style literature provide support for the conceptual premise that the use of speech styles is a strategic choice rather than simple observation of social norms (Cook 2011).

Drawing on authentic KFL classroom discourse, this study illustrates a distinctive pattern of the -(*su*)*pnita* form use among KFL teachers and the ways in which the -(*su*)*pnita* form allows them to accomplish their roles as teachers. The results of this study will help explain the complex and multilayered meaning of a speech style, which emerges as a result of its interaction with a context.

3. Data

The data of this study consists of eight hours of naturally occurring teacher-student interactions in four upper-level KFL classrooms at an American university. Each class was taught by a different teacher. The teachers were all in their 30s and had at least three years of teaching experience in the KFL context. All of these courses were designed for students who have finished the third-year Korean courses. The data is transcribed according to the conventions of conversation analysis (Atkinson and Heritage 1984) and romanized using the Yale system. A microanalytic qualitative research approach is used for data analysis because it clearly shows the dynamics that lead to participants' speech style decisions. The procedure of data analysis involves analyzing the presence of the -(*su*)*pnita* form in KFL teacher talk and the roles and responsibilities teachers perform through using the particular form within the particular activity they are engaged in. Most of the students in each class were Korean-American students who had some exposure to the language at home. Each class also had a few students not of Korean ancestry. In the following section, specific examples of the use of the -(*su*)*pnita* form taken from different KFL classrooms are provided.

4. Functions of the -(su)pnita Form in KFL Teacher Talk

The classroom data set exhibits the mixed use[1] of the speech styles among all participants. The teachers mostly use the addressee honorific form, the -*yo* form, which is also called the polite style, in KFL classrooms and only occasionally shift to the -(*su*)*pnita* form. The -*yo* form is the dominant speech style that each teacher employs during instruction. The teachers use this form when providing information, giving an opinion, clarifying statements, and asking questions. Students also use the form to interact with their teachers and fellow classmates. However, teachers sometimes shift to the deferential style, the -(*su*)*pnita* form, that is another addressee honorific form in Korean. This linguistic phenomenon raises two questions about the role of the -(*su*)*pnita* form within the classroom context: (1) In what contexts do the teachers employ the -(*su*)*pnita* form? and (2) What are the interactional functions of the form?

The *-(su)pnita* form is likely to be used in the context in which teachers frame their utterances as formal ones to execute authority and perform their professional roles. Many of the expressions that teachers utter in the *-(su)pnita* form are formulaic expressions. These expressions include *alkess-supnita* 'I understand', *coh-supnita* 'it's good', *swuep sicakhakeyss-supnita* 'class will begin', and *swuko ha-si-ess-supnita* 'you've worked hard'. In the following section, I discuss in detail how teachers play their professional roles through the use of the *-(su)pnita* form in classroom discourse.

4.1 Opening the lesson

One of the important functions of the *-(su)pnita* form is to open the class. The following excerpt[2] shows the use of the form when the teacher begins instruction by saying the expression *swuep sicakhakeyss-supnita* 'class will begin'.

---

[1] All teachers shift their speech styles, rather than strictly using one speech style. In addition, there are variations across speakers in terms of the use of the *-(su)pnita* form; some teachers

[2] In the excerpts, T represents the "teacher," and Ss represents the "students." Two-uppercase letters together (e.g., ET) correspond to the student's abbreviated name.

Excerpt (1) Teacher A: The beginning of the lesson
((The teacher is at the front of the classroom and directs her gaze to the whole class.))

1 T: *ca* *yelepwun* *annyenghasey-yo.*
alright everyone hello
'Hello, everyone.'

2 Ss: *annyenghasey-yo.*
'Hello.'

3 → T: *ney,* *onul* *swuep* *sicakha-keyss* ***supnita***
yes today class start-will-**supnita**
'Yes. Class will begin.'
((Students become quiet and look at the teacher.))

4 *ca,* *onul* *yelepwun-i* *phainel* *nayss-ten-ke*
okay today all of you-NM final submit-PST-thing

5 *ta* *kathi* *pol-ke-n-tey* *ceyil* *mence*
all together watch-thing-RL-place most first

6 *ET-ssi-ka* *ha-n-ke* *po-l-ke-yey-yo.*
ET-Ms.-NM do-RL-thing watch-PRS-fact-be-yo
'OK, today, we are going to watch the videos that all of you submitted as projects for your final. First, we will watch Ms. ET's presentation.'

In line 1, the teacher greets the students by saying *annyenghasey-yo* 'hello', which is the formal way of greeting in Korean. This traditional greeting helps the teacher establish the formal nature of the classroom. Here, the teacher prefaces the forthcoming greeting with a discourse marker *ca* 'alright' and the address term *yelepwun* 'everyone' in the utterance-initial position. These linguistic expressions are used to ensure the undivided attention of everyone in the classroom. In line 2, students return the teacher's greeting. Then, in line 3, the teacher shifts her speech style from the *-yo* form to the *-(su)pnita* form to indicate the formal start of a lesson with an explicit verbal cue, in *ney, onul swuep sicakhakeyss-supnita* 'Class will begin.' The *-(su)pnita* form uttered with a louder voice adds to the formal nuance of the utterance.

The teacher states this class-opening expression in the *-(su)pnita* form to increase the students' attentiveness to the lesson. The use of the *-(su)pnita* form enables the teacher to perform an authoritative persona, allowing the teacher to distance herself from the students. Upon the teacher's formal opening of the lesson, the class looks at the teacher while quietly directing their attention to the teacher's instructions. In this opening statement, we can see that the *-(su)pnita* form serves for more than just expressing politeness or deference. It enables the teacher to successfully manifest her official role as leader of the class. Then, in line 6, the teacher shifts to the *-yo* form to announce the topic to be discussed, that is, watching the students' final projects together.

4.2 Marking the discourse boundary

The second function of the *-(su)pnita* form is to mark the discourse boundary where the ongoing conversation ends and another begins. Excerpt (2), which is drawn from an informal conversation between the teacher and students, exemplifies this usage. In the following excerpt, the teacher goes around the classroom to engage in a short dialogue with each student by asking them what they did over the spring break while stepping out of his teacher role. This informal dialogue is devoted to catching up with students while creating solidarity among the students and between the teacher and students.

Excerpt (2) Teacher B: Spring break

1 T: *eti-eyse ilhay-yo?*
where-at work-yo
'Where do you work?'

2 MI: um… I guess mostly at Banana Republic.

3 T: *mwe ceki Ala Moana Banana Republic*?
well, that Ala Moana Banana Republic
'Well, that Banana Republic at Ala Moana Shopping Center?'
((lines 04–06 omitted))

7 MI: *keyswie hay-yo.*
cashier do-yo
'I'm a cashier there.'

8 T: *AL-ssi-nun?*
AL-Ms.-TC
'How about you, Ms. AL?'

9 AL: *kunyang swi-ess-e.yo.*
just rest-PST-yo
'I just stayed home.'

10 →T: *swi-ess-e.yo? al-keyss-**supnita**. hahaha*
rest-PST-yo know-intend-**supnita** hahaha
'You just stayed home? Oh, I see.'
((walking back to the front of the class))

11 *ca, kulemyen cikum haksayng-tul-i manhi*
okay then now student-PL a lot

12 *eps-ki-n-ha-ntey swuep-ul sicakha-tolok*
be not-NM-IN-do-but class-AC start-to the extent that

13 *ha-l-key-yo.*
do-PRS-PRM-yo
'Alright, even though there aren't many of you here, I'll start today's lesson.'

From line 1 through line 9, students MI and AL reply to the teacher's question by sharing their experiences from their break. In addition to the casual topic of the conversation, MI's use of English in line 2 in response to the teacher's question indicates that the ongoing conversation is informal and off-the-record, as students are encouraged to speak only in Korean during the lesson. In line 8, the teacher uses the *-yo* form to open the conversation with another student, AL. After acknowledging AL's response in line 10 by echoing her response, the teacher uses the phrase *alkeyss-supnita* 'I understand' to end the ongoing social talk with his students. Here, he switches from the *-yo* form to the *-(su)pnita* form to initiate a smooth transition to the main lesson.

The phrase *alkeyss-supnita* 'I understand'[3] is similar to the English expressions *alright* or *okay*, which can be used to signal a discourse boundary where one kind of classroom interaction ends and another begins. Marking the statement with the *-(su)pnita* form indicates its formal nature. The use of *-(su)pnita* in this utterance enables the teacher to extricate himself from an extended informal conversation without appearing rude, and to conclude the ongoing conversation to execute the next agenda item, which is to start the lesson. After closing the conversation in line 10 the teacher walks back to the front of the class to introduce the main activity by reminding students of the discussion questions he passed out during the previous session. Here, the teacher shifts back to the *-yo* form in line 13, which teachers generally use when teaching. Thus, the use of the *-(su)pnita* form indexes a change of situation from informal to formal within a classroom context, rather than achieving politeness goals.

4.3 Giving a positive evaluation

The third function of the *-(su)pnita* form seems to be to evaluate a student's utterance that occurs within an Initiation-Response-Feedback (IRF) activity. The IRF structure, which is a common practice in language classroom discourse, represents three interactional components: an initiation by a teacher, a response from a student, and feedback from the teacher. Students use the *-(su)pnita* form in their responses to maintain a formal tone, but the focus of the discussion that follows this extract is on the teacher's use of the form in his feedback. Uses of the *-(su)pnita* form are likely to occur when the teacher delivers positive feedback to students' speech, emphasizing the teacher's professional role of evaluating students. The on-going class activity occurring in the following student-teacher interaction shows the teacher attempting to elicit a student's response to an episode of *Nay ilumeun Kim Samsoon* "My Lovely Samsoon," a Korean TV drama. The teacher asks all

---

[3] Due to the formal nature of the phrase *alkeyss-supnita* 'I understand', it is often used to index the close of conversation in formal interviews and meetings.

the students to individually describe the settings and actions of the main characters in each important scene in the episode. The focus of the activity is on recounting the sequence of events while using speech styles and descriptive vocabulary properly. In the following conversation, a student, WI, reports to the teacher and the class which characters were in the scene, what actions were undertaken, and what was said.

Excerpt (3) Teacher C: Initiation-Response-Feedback (IRF) activity

1	T:	*open,*	*open-un*	*WI ssi*		
		no. 5	no. 5-TC	WL Mr.		
		'No. 5	As for Scene No. 5	Mr. WI'		
2	W:	*open-ey*	*cinwen.i-nun*	*hyenwu-hanthey*		
		no. 5	Jinwon-TC	Hyunwoo-to		
3		*samswun.i-lul*	*koylophi-ci*	*mal-la ko*		
		Samsoon-AC	bother-NOM	do not-DC-QT		
4		*kulay-ss-supnita.*				
		tell-PST-supnita				
		'As for Scene No. 5, Jinwon told Hyunwoo not to bother Samsoon.'				
5	T:	*ney.*	*kucen-ey,*	*kucen-ey*	*twul-i*	*ettehkey*
		yes	prior	prior	two-NM	how
6		*manna-ss-e.yo?*				
		meet-PST-e.yo?				
		'Yes. Even prior to that, where did the two meet?'				
7	WI:	*yakhonsik-eyse*				
		engagement ceremony-at				
		'At an engagement ceremony'				
8	T:	*yakhonsik-eyse*	*manna-ss-supnita.*			
		engagement ceremony-at	meet-PST-supnita			
		'They met at the engagement ceremony.'				
9		*twul-i*	*manna-ki*	*ceney*	*nwukwu-lang*	
		two	meet-NM	before	who-with	
10		*iyaki ha-ko*	*iss-ess-e.yo?*			
		talk-and	stay-PST-e.yo			
		'Before the two met, who was Hyunwoo talking to?'				
11	WI:	*a,*	*samswun-i-hako*	*iyaki ha-taka*		
		ah,	Samsoon-with	talk-while		
12		*hyencin-i-ka*	*wa-ss-supnita.*			
		Hyunjin-NM	come-PST-supnita			
		'While Hyunwoo was talking to Samsoon, Hyunjin came.'				
13 →	T:	*ney.*	*coh-**supnita**.*			
		yes	good-**supnita**			
		'Yes. Good.'				
14		((moving on to the next student))	*yuk pen*			
			'Scene No. 6'			

Upon the teacher prompt in line 1, the student WI explains what the two main characters discussed in the scene. However, because the student's response does not coincide with the response targeted by the teacher, the teacher asks further questions to WI in the *-yo* form to obtain a more acceptable answer from the student in lines 5–6. In line 7, the student provides a short answer, which is a sentence fragment. In line 8, the teacher changes the student's incomplete sentence into a complete one and then asks another question to elicit missing information. Upon the student's proper response in lines 11–12, the teacher gives a positive evaluation of the student's verbal production by saying *ney. coh-supnita.* 'Yes. Good.' in the *-(su)pnita* form in line 13. In line 14, the teacher asks another student to describe the next scene.

By marking the utterance with the *-(su)pnita* form, the teacher takes on the role of an expert who knows the answers and grants approval of the student's correct answers. While doing so, the teacher displays a rigid, formal teacher-student relationship with the student. When the teacher praises students for giving correct answers, he uses a variety of positive evaluation tokens in the *-(su)pnita* form such as *coh-supnita* 'good', *kcal hays-supnita* 'you did well', and *kwaenchanh-supnita* 'it's alright'. Although the teacher could use the *-yo* form to provide feedback, he tends to choose a more formal and authoritative form, the *-(su)pnita* form, to encourage students to generate correct answers. The teacher does not give negative evaluations in the *-(su)pnita* form because it would sound overly direct or harsh, thereby discouraging students. Rather, he asks a series of questions that can guide the student to give fuller responses. While doing so, the teacher employs the *-yo* form to mitigate the face-threatening effect of negative evaluations.

4.4 Announcing a classroom activity

The fourth function of the *-(su)pnita* form is to announce the next classroom activity in a commanding tone. Consider the next example in which the teacher uses the -(*su*)*pnita* form when explicitly stating what is going to take place next. The topic of the ongoing lesson is the generation gap between Korean children and parents. That day, students were required to individually present on the generation gap they experienced with their parents. After the presentations, the teacher started a class discussion where students had to revisit the issues brought up during their presentations and come up with solutions to overcome the generation gap.

Excerpt (4) Teacher D: Generational Gap

1	T:	*ile-n*	*seyday*	*chai-lul*	*kukpokha-ki*
		this-TC	generation	gap-AC	overcome-NOM
2		*wihayse*	*ettehkey*	*hay-ya ha-l-kka-yo?*	
		in order to	how	do-only if do-PRS-Q-yo	
		'What should we do to overcome this kind of generational gap?'			

3		*kulwup-ul ttalo ttalo nanw-ese ha-l-kka-yo?* group-AC separately divide-by do-PRS-Q-yo Shall we discuss in separate groups?
4		*ta kathi unonhay po-l-kka-yo?* all together discuss try-PRS-Q-yo Shall we discuss as a whole class?
5		*kukey hwelssin caymiiss-keyss-cyo?* that by far fun-think-cyo It is going to be more fun that way, isn't it?
6 →	T:	*ca, seyday chai kukpok pangpep-ey tayhayse* okay generation gap overcome way-about
7		*wuli-ka han pen iyaki-lul haypo-keyss-**supnita**.* we-NM one time talk-AC try-intend-**supnita** 'Okay, we will talk about how to overcome the generational gap.'
8		*ettehkey ha-myen kukpokha-l swu iss-ul-kka-yo?* how do-if overcome-PRS way-PRS-yo 'How can we overcome?'
9		*cokuk-ilato.* little-even 'At least a little.'
10	HY:	*kukpok? kukpok-i mweyey-yo?* kukpok kukpok-NM what-yo '*Kukpok*. What is *kukpok*?'

The excerpt starts with the teacher's question directed to the class, asking for recommendations for dealing with the generation gap between children and parents. Here, using the *-yo* form, the teacher signals the start of the next activity. This question is formulated to invite all students to think about their own ideas about overcoming the generation gap. Then, in lines 3–5, the teacher asks students in the *-yo* form, whether they would like to have a small group discussion or a whole class discussion. Upon the negotiation, the teacher stands in front of the class and, in line 6, delivers an announcement of the classroom activity in a more formal and authoritative manner by shifting to the *-(su)pnita* form. This announcement of the next classroom activity is prefaced by the discourse marker, *ca* 'okay', which signals students to pay attention as well as indicating the end of the prior talk. In line 8, to reinforce the instruction, the teacher formulates an abbreviated version of the same question raised in line 1. In this example, the discourse marker, *ca* 'okay', and the *-(su)pnita* form collaboratively contribute to transitioning the students into the next part of the lesson by firmly announcing the activity with authority.

4.5 Closing the lesson

The fifth function of the *-(su)pnita* form is to end the lesson formally. The following conversation took place right before the end of the lesson. The teacher starts to explain the upcoming oral midterm examination. In the excerpt, a student asks the teacher a question regarding the process of the examination. Upon responding to the student in the *-yo* form, the teacher finishes class by thanking the students in the *-(su)pnita* form for their participation.

Excerpt (5) Teacher C: Oral midterm examination

1	S:	*wuli-ka*	*ssu-ko*	*ilk-ul-swu iss-e.yo?*	
		we-NM	write-and	read-PRS-can-yo	
		'Can we read off from a script?'			
2	T:	*kuke-n*	*an toy-yo.*		
		that-TC	not OK-yo		
		'You can't.'			
3		*yelepwun-i*	*malha-l-ttay*	*ssu-ko*	
		you-NM	speak-PRS-when	write-and	
4		*malha-nun-key*	*ani-canh-a.yo.*		
		speak-RL-thing	not-you see-yo		
		'Because when you speak, you don't read off from what you wrote.'			
5		*yey.* *cengmal*	*khemwunikethipu*	*thaysukhu-yey-yo.*	
		yes really	communicative	task-to be-yo	
		'Yes, it's really a communicative task.'			
6	S:	*ney.*			
		'Okay.'			
7 →	T:	*wwukoha-si-ess-**supnita**.*	*annyenghi ka-sey-yo.*		
		Hard work-SH-PST-**supnita**	peace go-AH-yo		
8 →		*kamsaha-**pnita**.*			
		thank-**pnita**			
		'You've worked hard. Goodbye. Thank you.'			
9	Ss:	*kamsaha-pnita.*			
		thank-pnita			
		'Thank you.'			

In line 1, a student asks the teacher if she can read from a script for her oral examination. In line 2, the teacher responds in the *-yo* form by saying 'no' because it is a communicative task. After the teacher's response, the student who asked the question displays her understanding by saying *ney* 'okay' in line 6. Given no further questions or comments from students, the teacher finishes the lesson by saying the expression *swuko ha-si-ess-supnita* 'you've worked hard', in which the verbal suffix -(*u*)*si* is used to show respect for the students. This expression is followed by another formulaic expression, *kamsaha-pnita* 'thank you'.

Both of these expressions are used in the *-(su)pnita* form in order to thank the students for their participation. These instances of the *-(su)pnita* form index that the teacher is in charge of the immediate goal of the situation, which is signaling the end of the lesson formally. By doing so, the teacher displays his professionalism and gives students the feeling that they are part of the formal instruction. In this excerpt, the teacher's use of the *-(su)pnita* form seems to function to do more than close the lesson. It demonstrates respect toward the students, thereby giving them encouragement to perform at higher levels.

Upon the teacher's expression of gratitude in line 8, the students echo *kamsaha-pnita* 'thank you' to express their gratitude to their teacher. The students' use of *kamsaha-pnita* 'thank you' in the *-(su)pnita* form indexes deference toward the teacher because students, who are of lower status than the teacher, use it for the purpose of showing respect toward him. Here, the students reinforce the teacher's professional persona by displaying their own institutionally sanctioned identity through the *-(su)pnita* form.

5. Conclusion

This study explores the patterns of use for the -(*su*)*pnita* form and its functions in a KFL classroom interaction. The rareness of the occurrence of the *-(su)pnita* form in the teachers' utterances highlights its particular purpose. The *-(su)pnita* form is likely to be used in the context in which teachers frame their utterances as formal ones to perform their professional roles while executing an act with authority. This study describes five uses of the form that were observed frequently in the data: (1) opening the lesson, (2) marking the discourse boundary, (3) positively evaluating students' speech, (4) announcing classroom activities, and (5) closing the lesson. These uses of the -(*su*)*pnita* form differ from those related to a lower-status speaker's deference toward a higher-status person. The analysis shows that complete social meanings of speech styles can be found only when they are analyzed within actual utterance contexts.

Because the data in this study is limited, it is important to extend this research to more KFL classrooms to verify whether other KFL teachers also use the -(*su*)*pnita* form to serve the same purpose. The analysis of larger data sets will also provide a better idea of the language that students are exposed to in KFL classrooms.

Abbreviations

AC	Accusative particle
AH	Addressee honorific
DC	Declarative sentence-type suffix
NM	Nominative case particle

NOM	Nominalizer suffix
PL	Plural suffix or particle
PRM	Promissive sentence-type suffix
PRS	Prospective modal suffix
PST	Past tense
Q	Question marker
QT	Quotative particle
RL	Relativizer suffix
SH	Subject honorific suffix
TC	Topic-contrast particle

References

Atkinson, J. M. and J. Heritage. 1984. *Structures of Social Action: Studies in Conversational Analysis*. Cambridge, UK: Cambridge University Press.

Cook, H. M. 1996a. The Japanese Verbal Suffixes as Indicators of Distance and Proximity. *The Construal of Space in Language and Thought*, eds. M. Putz and R. Dirven, 3–27. Berlin: Mouton de Gruyter.

Cook, H. M. 1996b. Japanese Language Socialization: Indexing the Modes of Self. *Discourse Processes* 22:171–197.

Cook, H. M. 1997. The Role of the Japanese *másu* Form in Caregiver-Child Conversation. *Journal of Pragmatics* 28:695–718.

Cook, H. M. 2008a. *Socializing Identities through Speech Style*. Bristol: Multilingual Matters.

Cook, H. M. 2008b. Style Shifts in Japanese Academic Consultations. *Style Shifting in Japanese*, eds. K. Jones and T. Ono, 9–38. Amsterdam: John Benjamins.

Cook, H. M. 2011. Are Honorifics Polite? Uses of Referent Honorifics in a Japanese Committee Meeting. *Journal of Pragmatics* 43:3655–3672.

Eun, J. and S. Strauss. 2004. The Primacy of Information Status in the Alternation between Korean Deferential and Polite Forms in Public Discourse. *Language Sciences* 26:251– 272.

Ikuta, S. 1983. Speech Level Shift and Conversational Strategy in Japanese Discourse. *Language Science* 5:37–53.

Kim, K-H. and K. H. Suh. 2007. Style Shift in Korean Pedagogical Discourse. *The Sociolinguistic Journal of Korea* 15(2):1–29.

Lee, I. and S. Ramsey. 2000. *The Korean Language*. New York: State University of New York.

Maynard, S. 1993. *Discourse Modality: Subjectivity, Emotion and Voice in the Japanese Language*. Amsterdam: John Benjamins.

Maynard, S. 2008. Playing with Multiple Voices: Emotivity and Creativity in Japanese Style Mixture. *Style Shifting in Japanese*, eds. K. Jones and T. Ono, 91–129. Amsterdam: John Benjamins.

Sohn, H.-M. 1999. *The Korean Language*. Cambridge, UK: Cambridge University Press.

Song, J. J. 2005. *The Korean Language: Structure, Use, and Context*. London: Routledge.

Strauss, S. and J. Eun. 2005. Indexicality and Honorific Speech Style Choice in Korean. *Linguistics* 43:251–651.

Usage of Transitive Verbs in the Depiction of Accidental Events in Japanese and Korean

YUKO YOSHINARI*
Gifu University

PRASHANT PARDESHI
National Institute for Japanese Language and Linguistics (NINJAL)

SUNG-YEO CHUNG
Osaka University

*The experiments reported in this paper were conducted at Osaka University, Hokkaido University, Fuji Women's University and Gifu University in Japan and Chonbuk National University, Kunsan National University and Yeungnam University in Korea. We would like to thank the institutions and individuals for their cooperation. The research reported herein is funded in part by the following research grants: (i) Grant-in-aid No. 21520400 (PI: Sung-Yeo Chung), and (ii) Collaborative research project (Universals and Cross-Linguistic Variations in the Semantic Structure of Predicates, Project leader: Prashant Pardeshi) funded by the National Institute for Japanese Language and Linguistics, Tokyo, Japan.

Japanese/Korean Linguistics 21.
Edited by Seungho Nam, Heejeong Ko and Jongho Jun.

1. Introduction

Accidental events involve a non-intentional act by a human agent (the cause or the causing event) leading to an undesirable consequence (the result or the caused event) such as the breaking of a plate by inadvertently hitting the table on which the plate rested. Prototypical studies on transitivity such as Hopper & Thompson (1980) predict that accidental events are less likely to be encoded using a transitive verb since they deviate from the transitive prototype in terms of absence of volition on the part of the subject. In most languages, if not all, the dominant pattern of encoding an accidental event is by using an intransitive verb (see Jacobsen 1991 for Japanese). However, language-specific linguistic studies such as Alfonso (1971), Ikegami (1982), Teramura (1982), Fukami (1997), Chung (2008) among others show that accidental events can be encoded using a transitive verb in Japanese, Korean and English. In English, for example, the aforementioned accidental event of breaking a plate, can be described in various ways such as 'I bumped into the table and broke the plate' (subject = non-volitional human, verb = transitive) or 'I inadvertently hit the table and the plate broke' (subject = non-volitional human, verb = intransitive) or 'The plate fell and broke' (subject = the entity undergoing a change of state, verb = intransitive) etc. Ikegami (1982) proposes that the notion of 'responsibility' of the subject for having failed to prevent the undesirable consequence motivates transitive encoding of an accidental event.

According to Ikegami (1982: 110), in an accidental event, a de-agentivized (accidental) act is construed as equivalent to an agentivized (intentional) act through the attribution of responsibility to the actor for failing to prevent the consequence (caused sub-event). Since the de-agentivized (accidental) act is construed as an agentivized (intentional) act, the former is encoded similarly to that of the latter using a transitive verb. Ikegami (1982) explains the foregoing *raison d'être* for the use of a transitive verb in the description of an accidental event with the help of the following schema.

(1) Ikegami's (1982: 110) schema

De-agentivized Act	Agentivized Act
X NOT PREVENT something	X CAUSE something (through ATTRIBUTION OF RESPONSIBILITY)

From the aforementioned proposal it can be deduced that the perception of preventability of the result (caused event) dictates the use of a transitive verb when encoding an accidental event.

The past studies that address the issue of the use of a transitive verb for depicting an accidental event are based on the intuitions of native speakers, attested examples, and the analytical power of trained linguists. They contribute to understanding 'possible' grammatical forms. When there are two grammatically possible options (such as transitive or intransitive encodings of an accidental event), purely intuition-based linguistic studies fall short of offering a definite answer as to which expression is preferred or more likely to be used as a spontaneous response.

There are a few psycholinguistic studies related to the use of a transitive verb for encoding an accidental event. These studies are based on eliciting on-line use of language through the use of non-linguistic stimuli. Fausey, Long, Inamori & Boroditsky (2010) explored the issue of the encoding of accidental events eliciting linguistic response through the use of a non-linguistic stimuli such as video-clips depicting accidental event. According to them, English and Japanese speakers described intentional events similarly, using mostly agentive language (transitive verbs), however, in the case of accidental events English speakers used more agentive language (transitive verbs) than their Japanese counterparts. Pardeshi & Yoshinari (to appear) also examined actual descriptions of an accidental event in comparison with an intentional event using a video clip and compared the answers of Japanese and Marathi (Indo-Aryan) speakers. Their results reveal that Marathi and Japanese speakers described intentional events similarly, using mostly transitive verbs while they considerably differed in their depiction of accidental events. For an accidental event most Marathi speakers (almost 100%) use intransitive verbs whereas Japanese speakers use both intransitive as well as transitive verbs. These studies do not, however, pursue the issue of the motivation behind the use of a transitive verb in the description of an accidental event.

In this paper we report the results of a questionnaire-based psycholinguistic pilot study pertaining to the issue of the depictions of accidental events and the motivation behind them by comparing Japanese and Korean, both of which permit transitive as well as intransitive encoding of an accidental event. Drawing insights from Ikegami (1982), our study aims to shed light on the following two issues:

(I) Does the perception of preventability of an accidental event leading to an undesirable consequence vary between Japanese and Korean?

(II) Is there a difference in the use of transitive verbs in the depiction of an accidental event?

2. Design of the present study

2.1 Method

Assuming that the perception of preventability of the result would ultimately depend on the perception of controllability of the cause, we chose the following three causes for the events: (i) carelessness of the speaker, (ii) dizziness of the speaker, and (iii) an earthquake. Intuitively, these three causes seem to differ in terms of the perception of controllability by the agent-subject. Using these three causes as the variable and keeping the result (the breaking of a plate) constant we prepared three scenarios of a hypothetical accidental event in which the speaker happens to break a plate due to these three causes. The scenario description is as follows: 'You are invited to a party at your friend's place (person A). Due to cause X (carelessness of the speaker, or dizziness of the speaker, or an earthquake), you ended up hitting the table. As a result a valuable plate fell off and shattered into pieces. How would you describe this incident to your other friend (person B) who is not the owner of the plate?' As mentioned earlier, both Japanese and Korean speakers display similar behavior in terms of the way they can potentially describe an accidental event—both permit the use of either a transitive or intransitive verb.

Participants read the scenario and wrote down a description of how they would explain the situation to another friend who is not the owner of the plate. After completing their description, the participants were asked to rate the extent to which they felt that the event in question was preventable on a 7-point scale (from 1 = not preventable to 7 = preventable). Seventy-four Japanese undergraduate students (28 males and 46 females with a mean age of 18.7), fifty-five Korean undergraduate students (18 males and 37 females with a mean age of 23.1) participated in our study. The scenarios were presented to the participants in their native language and the descriptions were also elicited their native language. Two points regarding the scenario need to be emphasized. First, the speaker is always the actor (the one who happens to break the plate) irrespective of the cause. Second, the scenario description we prepared contained only intransitive verbs.

2.2 Coding

The undesirable event of the breakage of the plate discussed above can be construed as consisting of three sub-events: 1. the hitting of the speaker's leg against the table, 2. the falling of the plate, 3.The breaking of the plate, which are causally linked as shown in Figure 1 below. Language speakers perceive this causally linked chain of sub-events and encode it as a linguistic expression (see Croft 1991).

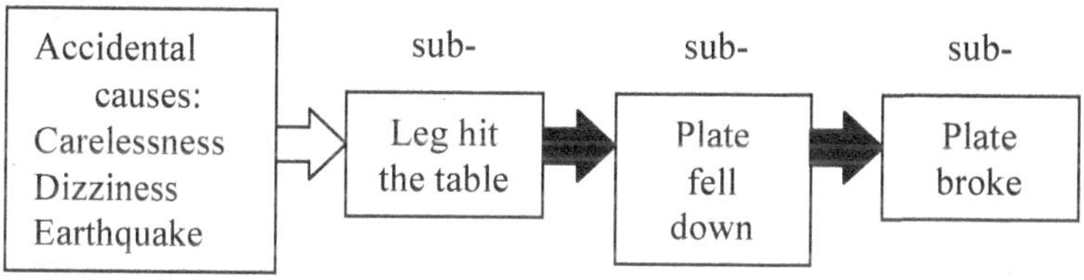

Figure 1: The causal chain of the accidental event of a plate breaking

In this study we are interested in examining the actual use of language in a hypothetical situation such as the breaking of a plate and would like to find out which sub-events are referred to and how they are encoded. In the open ended explanations offered by the participants, we analyzed the descriptions of the three types of scenarios discussed above and classified the verbs used into two groups, namely transitive and intransitive. Representative examples from Japanese and Korean along with coding descriptions are given below.

JAPANESE

(2) *osara* *otoshi-te* *wat-te-shimatta.*
plate(-ACC) drop(tr)-CON break(tr)-CON-finish.PST
'(I) dropped the plate and broke (it).'

(3) *ima-no* *jishin-de* *osara-ga* *ware-chatta.*
now-of earthquake-due to plate-NOM break(intr)-finish.PST
'Due to the earthquake just now the plate broke.'

(4) *ashi-ga* *teeburu-ni* *butsukat-te,* *osara-o* *otoshi-chatta.*
leg-NOM table-LOC hit(intr)-CON plate-ACC drop(tr)-finish.PST
'(My) leg hit the table, and (I) knocked off the plate.'

In example (2) the transitive verb *otosu* (*otoshite*) refers to sub-event 2 while the transitive verb *waru* (*watte*) refers to sub-event 3. Thus utterance (2) encodes two sub-events, and both are encoded using a transitive verb. Example (3) refers to only sub-event 3 using an intransitive verb. Example (4) uses an intransitive verb for describing sub-event 1 and a transitive verb to encode sub-event 2. Korean descriptions are coded in a similar way as Japanese.

KOREAN

(5) *cepsi-ka tteleci-ese kkayci-e-peli-ess-e.*
plate-NOM fall(intr)-CON break(intr)-CON-throw away-PST-IND
'The plate fell and broke.'

(6) *theyipul-ey tali-lu pwuticchi-ese cepsi-lul*
table-LOC leg-ACC hit(tr)-CON plate-ACC
kkay-peli-komal-ass-e.
break(tr)-throw away-CON stop-PST-IND
'I hit my leg on the table and broke the plate.'

(7) *cicin-ttaymwuney theyipul-ey tali-ka pwutichi-ese cepsi-ka*
earthquake-due to table-LOC leg-NOM hit(intr)-CON plate-NOM
kkayci-ess-e.
break(intr)-PST-IND
(lit.) 'Due to the earthquake my leg happened to hit the table and the plate broke.'

As for the coding of the first sub-event (hitting the table) in Korean, there can be different potential opinions on the issue of whether the verb *pwuticchita* should be coded as transitive or intransitive. Morphologically this verb is transitive and it governs an accusative object. In their descriptions, however, some participants used a nominative case marking on the object instead of an accusative (*tali-ka pwuticchi-ess-ta*). Whether *pwuticchita* governing a nominative object should be treated as transitive is a controversial issue. Furthermore, when the object is not overtly expressed, there is no way to judge the case marking of the object. In this paper we coded only those instances of *pwuticchita* as transitive where the object is overtly expressed and it is marked with an accusative. Other instances of *pwuticchita* where the object is overtly expressed but marked with a nominative or comitative, or those where the object is not expressed were treated as intransitive.[1] The following table lists the repertoire of verbs found in the participants' descriptions.

[1] The statistics of the object marking of *pwuticchita* in our data is tabulated as follows:

	accusative object	nominative object	comitative object	object-less
carelessness	3	1	0	1
dizziness	0	1	0	3
earthquake	0	0	1	3

As discussed later, even if we had treated all the instances of *pwuticchita* as transitive irrespective of case-marking of the object or absence of the object, the trend of using a transitive verb would have been the same as that of counting only those instances of *pwuticchita* that take an accusative marked object as transitive. See footnote 2 for details.

Table 1: Transitive (Tr) and intransitive (Intr) verbs in each sub-event

sub-event	verb type	Japanese	Korean
1	Tr	*(ashi-o) butsukeru* 'hit (the leg)'	*(tali-lul) pwutic**chi**ta,* 'hit (the leg)' *(theyipul-lul) chita* 'hit (the table)'
	Intr	*(ashi-ga) butsukaru* '(the leg) bump (against the table)'	*(tali-ka)pwuti**chi**ta* '(the leg) bump (against the table)' *(tali-lul)pwuti**chi**ta* '(the leg) bump (against the table)' *(tali-ka)pwutic**chi**ta* '(the leg) bump (against the table)' *(tali-ka)kellita* '(the leg) get entangled (with the table)'
2	Tr	*otosu* 'drop'	*ttelettulita* 'drop'
	Intr	*ochiru* 'fall'	*ttelecita* 'fall'
3	Tr	*waru, kowasu* 'break'	*kkaytta, kkayttullita, pwuswuta* 'break'
	Intr	*wareru, kowareru* 'break'	*kkaycita, pwusecita* 'break' *phasontoyta* 'get damaged'

3. Result and discussion

As for the description of the accidental event in question, we focused on the perception rating of preventability of the cause (carelessness of the speaker, dizziness of the speaker and an earthquake) and the linguistic encoding (use of a transitive verb). In this section we will discuss the results comparing Japanese with Korean.

3.1 Perception of preventability

In order to confirm the perception of preventability of the three types of causes we examined participants' ratings of perceived preventability for each cause. The cause-wise mean score of preventability ratings is shown in Table 2.

Table 2: Means (and Standard Deviations) of perception of preventability

	Carelessness	Dizziness	Earthquake
Japanese	4.24 (2.16)	3.44 (1.68)	2.25 (1.33)
Korean	4.50 (1.75)	3.24 (1.77)	2.61 (1.77)

The higher the number is, the greater the degree of preventability. We conducted a 2 (language: Japanese, Korean) x 3 (cause: carelessness, dizziness, earthquake) ANOVA (analysis of variance) among subjects for the perception of preventability. The main effect for language was not significant ($F(1, 123) = 0.19$, n.s.), which means that the perception of preventability did not vary between Japanese and Korean. However, the main effect for causes was significant ($F(2, 123) = 12.16, p < .001$). *Post hoc* analyses, carried out with a multiple comparison test using Ryan's method, revealed inter-group differences at $p < .05$ for the causal factors. The statistics indicate that these three causal factors can be arranged in order of preventability: carelessness (mean = 4.37) is rated as the highest on the preventability cline followed by dizziness (mean = 3.34) which in turn is followed by an earthquake (mean = 2.43) which is rated as the least preventable.

3.2 Use of transitive verb

As mentioned earlier, Japanese and Korean rated similarly in terms of the perception of preventability for each cause. So then we must ask, do they behave alike in terms of their use of transitive verbs?

We counted the verbs used in the descriptions of the three sub-events. These scores range from 0 (indicating no use of a verb) to 3 (verbs used to depict all three sub-events) for each participant. The cause-wise mean score of transitive verbs used in the present accidental event is shown in Table 3. The higher the number is, the greater the usage of transitive verbs.

Table 3: Means (and Standard Deviations) of transitive verb use

	Carelessness	Dizziness	Earthquake
Japanese	1.00 (0.80)	0.92 (0.85)	0.42 (0.64)
Korean	0.50 (0.50)	0.53 (0.50)	0.00 (0.00)

We conducted an ANOVA in the same way as for the analysis of perception of preventability. The main effect for language was significant ($F(1, 123)=13.89, p < .001$) and the main effect for causes was also significant ($F(2, 123)=9.11, p < .001$). *Post hoc* analyses carried out with multiple comparison tests using Ryan's method revealed inter-group differences at p

$< .05$ for the causal factors. The statistics indicates that there is no significant difference between carelessness (mean = 0.75) and dizziness (mean = 0.73), but an earthquake (mean = 0.21) is significantly different from the other two (carelessness and dizziness). This means we can divide causes into two groups. Carelessness and dizziness, which are subject-internal causes, fall in one group while an earthquake, which is a subject-external cause, falls into the other group.[2]

3.3 Perception and verb usage in depiction of an accidental event

In the previous sections we have looked at the perception of preventability and the use of transitive verbs in encoding accidental events for each cause. We found that both in Japanese and Korean the perception of preventability was significantly different from one cause to another. As for the use of transitive verbs, the description of causes can be divided into two groups. From these results, we can say that the use of transitive verbs is not precisely affected by perception of preventability. Carelessness and dizziness originate within the subject while an earthquake originates in the external environment. From this, we speculate that the locus of causality seems to be the crucial factor in verb choice (intransitive or transitive).

The results of our study corroborate with the predictions of attribution theory. Social psychologists have discussed and analyzed causal structure in great detail as they are interested in how individuals explain the causes of behavior and events in the attribution theory. The most fundamental distinction between causes, made by Heider (1958), is as follows: "In common-sense psychology (as in scientific psychology), the result of an action is felt to depend on two sets of conditions, namely factors within the person and factors within the environment." Heider's observation, therefore, seems to be in close agreement with our results.

Weiner (1995) proposes a more refined tetrachoric 2 by 2 model: locus of causality (internal, external) and controllability (controllable, uncontrollable). Borrowing from Weiner's insights, we should take into consideration not only the locus of causality but also its combination with controllability. Our pilot study suggests that the locus of causality arguably affects linguistic encoding. We will pursue its combinations with controllability in a systematic way in our future research.

---

[2] Results for the case of treating all the instances of *pwuticchita* as transitive irrespective of the case-marking of the object or absence of the object (See footnote 1) are as follows: Means (and Standard Deviations) of transitive verb use in Korean: carelessness 0.60 (0.58), dizziness 0.77 (0.55), earthquake 0.22 (0.42). The main effect for language is $F(1, 123)=4.12$, $p < .05$ and the main effect for causes is $F(2, 123)=7.42$, $p < .001$. Results of the multiple comparison tests were statistically the same.

3.4 Salient features of linguistic expressions in causal chains

In the use of transitive verbs we found a difference between Japanese and Korean (see Table 3). In this section we will explore the locus where transitive verbs are used.

Table 4: The distribution of encoding patterns in Japanese and Korean

Possible patterns	Possible sub-pattern	Carelessness		Dizziness		Earthquake	
		Japanese % (N)	Korean % (N)	Japanese % (N)	Korean % (N)	Japanese % (N)	Korean % (N)
1	I-I-I	20.0 (5)	15.0 (3)	8.0 (2)	11.8 (2)	33.3 (8)	16.7 (3)
Y-Y-Y	I-I-T	**4.0 (1)**			**5.9 (1)**		
	I-T-I		**5.0 (1)**				
	I-T-T	**16.0 (4)**					
	T-I-I	**8.0 (2)**	**5.0 (1)**			**4.2 (1)**	
	T-T-I						
	T-T-T			**8.0 (2)**			
2	I-I-N		5.0 (1)	12.0 (3)	17.6 (3)		11.1 (2)
Y-Y-N	I-T-N	**4.0 (1)**		**8.0 (2)**		**12.5 (3)**	
	T-I-N	**8.0 (2)**		**4.0 (1)**			
	T-T-N	**8.0 (2)**		**4.0 (1)**		**8.3 (2)**	
3	I-N-I	8.0 (2)	15.0 (3)			12.5 (3)	22.2 (4)
Y-N-Y	I-N-T	**8.0 (2)**	**10.0 (2)**	**12.0 (3)**	**5.9 (1)**	**4.2 (1)**	
	T-N-I		**10.0 (2)**				
	T-N-T	**8.0 (2)**		**4.0 (1)**			
4	N-I-I		5.0 (1)			20.8 (5)	
N-Y-Y	N-I-T		**5.0 (1)**				
	N-T-I						
	N-T-T						
5	I-N-N	4.0 (1)			5.9 (1)		5.6 (1)
Y-N-N	T-N-N			**4.0 (1)**			
6	N-I-N			4.0 (1)			11.1 (2)
N-Y-N	N-T-N			**8.0 (2)**	**17.6 (3)**	**4.2 (1)**	
7	N-N-I		10.0 (2)	8.0 (2)	11.8 (2)		33.3 (6)
N-N-Y	N-N-T	**4.0 (1)**	**15.0 (3)**	**16.0 (4)**	**23.5 (4)**		
total		100 (25)	100 (20)	100 (25)	100 (17)	100 (24)	100 (18)

Table 4 above presents the distribution of encoding patterns in Japanese and Korean. Speakers take liberty in choosing the sub-event to be encoded from amongst the causal chain of three sub-events as shown in Figure 1. As shown in Table 4, there are eight logically possible patterns for encoding the accidental event in question which consists of three sub-events [Y stands for encoded and N for not encoded]: encoding all the sub-events : Y-

Y-Y (Pattern 1); Encodng two sub-events : Y-Y-N (Pattern 2), Y-N-Y (Pattern 3), N-Y-Y (Pattern 4) and Encoding one sub-event : Y-N-N (Pattern 5), N-Y-N (Pattern 6), N-N-Y (Pattern 7) ; not encoding any sub-event : N-N-N (Pattern 8). Pattern 8, although logically possible, did not appear. Furthermore, logically each sub-event can be expressed using either an intransitive (abbreviated as 'I') or a transitive (abbreviated as 'T') verb. For example, if all three sub-events are encoded, there are seven possible combinations (sub-patterns), namely: I-I-I, I-I-T, I-T-I, I-T-T, T-I-I, T-T-I, T-T-T. Table 4 lists possible encoding sub-patterns for each of the seven possible patterns (Pattern 1 to Pattern 7) described above for each cause. Since we are interested in the use of transitive verbs, the patterns wherein transitive verbs are used are emphasized with boldface.

Like the comparison of means of transitive verb use in shown in Table 3, it is also clear from Table 4 that as an overall pattern, irrespective of the type of the cause, Japanese uses more transitive verbs than Korean. For carelessness as the cause, the rate of use of a transitive verb in Japanese is 64.0% while in Korean it is 50.0%; as for dizziness it is 68.0% in Japanese as compared to 52.9% in Korean; and for an earthquake is it 33.4% in Japanese in sharp contrast to 0.0% in Korean. These figures include all the patterns which include at least one transitive verb (some patterns use more than one transitive verb). In Japanese there are many cases where two or more transitive verbs are used in a single utterance (Carelessness: I-T-T=16.0%, T-T-N=8.0%, T-N-T=8.0%; Dizziness: T-T-T=8.0%, T-T-N=4.0%, T-N-T=4.0%) whereas in Korean utterances using two or more transitive verbs were not attested. Thus, even at the level of a single utterance, Japanese uses more transitive verbs than Korean. Let us take a look at some representative examples for each cause.

First, in the case of carelessness, in Korean expressions containing an intransitive verb as exemplified in (8) and those using a transitive verb (9) occur at equal rates of frequency as shown in Table 4. Example (8) represents the I-I-I pattern while example (9) represents the N-N-T pattern.

(8) *nay tali-ka theyipul-ey pwutichy-e cepsi-ka ttelecy-e*
my leg-NOM table-LOC hit(intr)-CON dish-NOM fall(intr)-CON

kkayci-n ke iss-ci.
break(intr)-RL thing exist-SFP

(lit.) 'My leg hit the table, the plate fell and broke.'

(9) *nay-ka* *ilena-taka* *cosimha-ci* *anh-ase* *cepsi-lul*
I-NOM stand up-while care do-not-CON plate-ACC
kkay-mek-ess-e.
break(tr)-eat-PST-INT
(lit.)'When I tried to stand up, since I did not take care, (I) ended up breaking the plate.'

In Japanese as well, although sub-patterns exclusively using an intransitive verb alone are not insignificant (pattern I-I-I, I-N-I, I-N-N), the overall majority of descriptions include patterns using one or two transitive verbs. Further, a transitive verb was most frequently used to depict sub-event 2 or 3 or

(10) *ukkarishite* *tsukue-ni* *butsukat-te* *sara-wo* *otoshi-te*
carelessly desk-LOC bump(intr)-CON plate-ACC drop(tr)-CON
watta.
break(tr).PST
(lit.) 'Through carelessness, (I) bumped against the desk, (I) dropped (the plate) and broke (it).'

As shown in Fig. 1, the accidental event in question consists of three causally linked sub-events: sub-event 1 'hitting the leg to the table' involves a verb meaning 'contact by impact' while sub-event 2 'falling of the plate' and sub-event 3 'breaking of the plate' respectively involve a 'change of position' and 'change of state.' From the data it can be said that transitive verbs are widely used to express a change (of location or state) irrespective of presence or absence of intentionality in Japanese which lends support to Tsunoda's (1985: 393) claim that the affectedness of the object is more crucial to the manifestation of a transitive case frame than volitionality, atleast in Japanese and Korean.

In the scenario where dizziness was the cause, the use of a transitive verb to encode a change (of location or state) was clearly demonstrated. For example, in both Japanese and Korean, the pattern N-N-T was attested as shown in the following examples.

(11) *sara* *wac-chatta.* *katazuke* *tesudaou.to.shitara*
plate(-ACC) break(tr)-finish.PST clearing up tried to help
memai-shita.
dizziness-do.PST
(lit.) '(I) broke the plate. When (I) tried to clear the table, (I) felt dizzy.'

(12)

nay-ka	*selkeci-lul*	*towa-cwu-lye-ko*	*cepsi-lul*
I-NOM	clean up-ACC	help-and-give-intending-CON	dish-ACC

tul-ko	*ilese-ss-nuntey*	*kapcaki*	*ecilew-ese*
have-CON	stand up-PST-that time	suddenly	feel dizzy-CON

cepsi-lul	*kkaythuly-e*	*pely-ess-e*
dish-ACC	break(tr)-CON	throw away-PST-IND

(lit.) 'I thought of helping to clear the table and stood up holding the plate. At that time I suddenly felt dizzy and broke the plate.'

Especially in Korean, a transitive verb is exclusively used to depict a change of location (sub-event 2) or change of state (sub-event 3) [(sub-patterns I-I-T, I-N-T, N-T-N, N-N-T in Table 4].

Finally, in the scenario where an earthquake was the cause, the use of a transitive verb is only found in Japanese. The following example illustrates the I-T-N pattern (Table 4). Note again that a transitive verb is used to encode a sub-event that involves a change.

(13)

sakki	*jishin*	*atta-yone.*	*sonotoki*	*teeburu-ni*
a moment ago	earthquake-(NOM)	be.PST-SFP	that time	table-LOC

ashi	*butukat-te*	*sara*	*otoshi-chatta-yo.*
leg(-NOM)	hit(intr)-CON	plate(-ACC)	drop(tr)-finish.PST-SFP

(lit.) 'There was a earthquake a moment ago, right? At that time my leg hit the table, and (I) dropped the plate.'

Although there is a strong tendency to use a transitive verb to encode a change there are exceptions as well. The patterns T-N-N, T-I-I, T-I-N attest to this. The following example represents the T-N-N pattern.

(14)

kyuni	*memai-ga*	*shi-te*	*teeburu-ni*	*ashi-wo*
suddenly	dizziness-NOM	do-CON	table-LOC	leg-ACC

bustuke-chatta.
hit(tr)-finish.PST

(lit.) 'Suddenly (I) felt dizzy and (I) hit my leg against the table.'

Also, a case of not encoding the change (sub-pattern I-N-N) at all, although rare, was also present. These exceptions merit detailed scrutiny in future.

4. Conclusion

In this paper we focused on accidental events which exhibit variation in their patterns of linguistic encoding across languages. Drawing inspiration from Ikegami (1982) who proposes that 'preventability' of the result as a causal factor affects whether or not a transitive verb is used in the depiction of an accidental event, we manipulated the causes related to the preventability of the result and looked to see if that affects the use of transitive verbs in Japanese and Korean.

Our results suggest that although the perception of preventability of the cause was same in both Japanese and Korean, the use of transitive verbs varied between the two languages. We speculate that the locus of causality might be related to use of transitive verbs in the depiction of accidental events. According to Weiner (1995), natural forces such as earthquakes are external and uncontrollable causes. In such cases speakers should avoid the use of a transitive verb. However, even in this case, the use of a transitive verb was found in Japanese but not in Korean. Korean speakers completely avoided using transitive verbs in the earthquake situation; however, some Japanese subjects did use transitive verbs with 'I' as the subject. Where does this difference come from? The issue warrants further research.

We are aware of the limitations of our pilot study. Our conclusions are based on a single accidental scenario and in order to draw any definitive conclusion, a more comprehensive study is required. An addition of more accidental events as well as the inclusion of more languages is also necessary. Further, taking into consideration Weiner's schema, we need to examine external and controllable causes such as an actor other than the speaker.

Recent psycholinguistic studies, such as Fausey, Long, Inamori & Boroditsky (2010) and Pardeshi & Yoshinari (to appear) show that languages differ in terms of the freedom they enjoy in permitting transitive encoding of accidental events. Drawing inspiration from these studies we would like to carry forward our research and explore various unresolved issues.

Abbreviations

ACC: accusative	CON: converbal marker	DEC: declarative
IND: indicative	LOC: locative	NOM: nominative
PST: past tense	RL: relative	SFP: sentence final predicate
intr: intransitive verb		tr: transitive verb

References

Alfonso, A. 1971. *Japanese Language Patterns: A Structural Approach 2*. Tokyo: Sophia University.

Chung, S-Y. 2008. Piuytocek satayuy thatongsaey tayhaye: Hankwukewa ilponeuy kwancemeyse (On the transitive expression depicting nonintentional situation: From the perspective of Japanese and Korean). *Satanpepin Hankenehakhoy 2008 nyento kyewul hakswultayhoy calyocip (Proceedings of the 2008 winter meeting of the Linguistic Society of Korea)*, 129-141. Seoul: Satanpepin Hankwukenehakhoy.

Croft, W. 1991. *Syntactic categories and grammatical relations: the cognitive organization of information.* Chicago: The University of Chicago Press.

Fausey, C. M., Long, B. L., Inamori, A. & Boroditsky, L. 2010. Constructing agency: the role of language. *Frontiers in Cultural Psychology* vol. 1: 1-11.

Fukami, K. 1997. Non-Intentional Transitive Constructions in Japanese and Korean. *Contrastive Studies of Japanese and Foreign Languages* IV, 213-226. Tokyo: The National Institute for Japanese language.

Heider, F. 1958. *The psychology of interpersonal relations.* New York: Wiley.

Hopper, P. & Thompson, S. A. 1980. Transitivity in grammar and discourse. *Language* 56: 251-299.

Jacobsen, W. M. 1991. *The Transitive Structure of Events in Japanese.* Tokyo: Kurosio Publishers.

Ikegami, Y. 1982. Indirect Causation and `Deagentivization': The Semantics of Involvement in English and Japanese. *Proceedings of the Department of Foreign Languages and Literature, College of Arts and Science*, 29-3: 95-112. Tokyo: University of Tokyo.

Pardeshi, P. & Yoshinari, Y. to appear. An investigation into the interaction between intentionality and the use of transitive/intransitive expression: A contrastive study of Japanese and Marathi. *Journal of Japanese Linguistics* vol. 28.

Teramura, H. 1982. *Nihongo no shintakkusu to imi I (Japanese syntax and semantics I)*. Tokyo: Kurosio Publishers.

Tsunoda, T. 1985. Remarks on transitivity. *Journal of Linguistics*, vol.21, no.2: 385-96.

Weiner, B. 1995. *Judgments of responsibility: A foundation for a theory of social conduct.* New York: Guilford.

Part V

Language Acquisition

Second and Heritage Language Acquisition of Korean Case Ellipsis

EUN SEON (EUNICE) CHUNG*
University of Illinois at Urbana-Champaign

There has been a growing interest in how bilinguals acquire linguistic phenomena involving the integration of syntactic, semantic, and discourse-pragmatic information since bilinguals were found to show persistent difficulty in such domains (Sorace & Serratrice 2009; Hopp 2006, 2009). However, few studies have examined bilingual language development of Korean case ellipsis, whose full grasp requires modulation of highly complex and abstract linguistic and extra-linguistic principles. If the results of previous research are on the right track, this phenomenon is predicted to pose many learnability problems for the learners. By examining how different types of bilinguals (early vs. late) acquire Korean CE, this paper seeks to identify differences between second language (L2) and heritage language (HL) acquisition and investigates how and whether bilingual populations can ac-

*I would like to thank the National Science Foundation for funding this project (NSF dissertation improvement grant: Award # BCS-1122163). I would also like to thank Dr. James Yoon and Dr. Silvina Montrul who have provided invaluable feedback and guidance on this study.

Japanese/Korean Linguistics 21.
Edited by Seungho Nam, Heejeong Ko and Jongho Jun.

quire sensitivity to multiple cues and attain a native-like implicit knowledge in a linguistic phenomenon like case ellipsis that requires modulation of multiple interfaces, both within and outside of grammar.

1. Korean Case Ellipsis

In most transitive sentences in Korean, nominative case marks subjects (*-ka, -i*) and accusative case is used for objects (*-lul/-ul*). However, omission of case markers is allowed in certain contexts, especially in informal casual speech as seen in (1).

(1) a.	Na-*ka*	pap-*ul*	an-mek-e
	I-NOM	food-ACC	not-eat-DECL
b.	Na-Ø	pap-*ul*	an-mek-e
	I- Ø	food-ACC	not-eat-DECL
c.	Na-*ka*	pap- Ø	an-mek-e
	I-NOM	food- Ø	not-eat-DECL
d.	Na-Ø	pap- Ø	an-mek-e
	I- Ø	food- Ø	not-eat-DECL
	'I don't want to eat'		

Korean case ellipsis (CE, henceforth) bears many similarities to CE in Japanese, and both linguistic and nonlinguistic factors have been found to affect the phenomenon—stylistic factors such as formality of the extra-linguistic context and familiarity among interlocutors (Ko 2000; Lee & Thompson 1985), idiomatic, figurative, or metaphorical meanings (Lee, S-B 2006), discourse/semantic factors such as specificity and definiteness (Enç 1991; Lee, D. 2002), focus and information structure status of nominals (Kwon & Zribi-Hertz 2008), morphophonological or syntactical weight of the noun phrase (NP) (Mori & Givon 1987), and syntactic factors such as construction type (e.g. question, idiom) and adjacency of the NP to the predicate (Watanabe 1986; Fry 2001). While many investigations have identified various factors that are involved in CE, few studies have provided a satisfactory framework for Korean CE that integrates the various factors involved.

In a series of corpus and experimental studies, Lee, H-J (2006, 2007, 2008) provides a close to comprehensive analysis of Korean CE in which the variables of contrastive focus, animacy, and definiteness simultaneously and independently determine object CE with contrastive focus having a greater effect than animacy or definiteness. The results of Lee's experimental studies show that the high-prominence value of each variable (i.e. contrastive focus, animate, and definite) favors overt marking of objects whereas the low-prominence values (i.e. noncontrastive focus, inanimate, and indefinite) favor CE. Using Lee's framework and experimental design,

Chung, E (2010) examined the effect of the same variables in subject CE and found that all three factors simultaneously and independently determine subject CE, with contrastive focus having a greater effect than animacy or definiteness which was the case for object CE. High prominence values in animacy and definiteness and low prominence values in contrastive focus were most conducive to subject CE. As such, Lee's framework successfully integrates both information status and markedness status of arguments into a unified functional account for both object and subject CE and shows how the interplay of component factors yields judgments on CE that are not categorical but are gradient preferences. Therefore, this framework was used in the present study to examine bilingual acquisition of Korean CE.

2. Second Language vs. Heritage Language Learners

The two bilingual populations of interest in this paper are adult second language (L2) learners (i.e. late bilinguals) who start learning the target language after puberty and heritage language (HL) learners (i.e. early bilinguals) whose first language (L1) is not fully acquired in childhood (Cummins 2000; Valdes 2000). While some studies have found similarities in linguistic features and developmental characteristics in the two populations (Montrul 2008; Polinsky 2006), others have shown that HL learners possess more native-like knowledge than late bilinguals in certain linguistic domains like phonology (Au et al. 2002) and morphosyntax (Montrul, Foote & Perpinan 2008; Montrul 2010). Moreover, task and knowledge effects further distinguish the two bilingual groups: Montrul et al. (2008) and Hakansson (1995) found that L2 learners are more accurate than HL learners on untimed written tasks that test explicit metalinguistic knowledge while heritage speakers are more accurate than the L2 learners on time-sensitive oral narrative tasks that measure automatic and implicit knowledge.

Despite such differences, both types of bilinguals were found to encounter persistent difficulty in interface domains that involve the integration of syntactic, semantic, and discourse-pragmatic information. Heritage speakers exhibited L1 attrition and developmental instability when they were required to integrate syntax and pragmatics/discourse even though their abstract syntactic features and the computational system largely remained intact (Sorace 2000; Tsimpli et al 2004; Bolonyai 2007; Montrul 2004, 2008, 2010). Similarly, L2 learners experienced difficulty in such domains despite possessing native-like grammatical representations and constraints (Slabakova 2008; Sorace & Keller 2005; Sorace & Filiaci 2006). The acquisition of discourse/interpretative properties was found to be problematic even in L2 end state grammars of near-native speakers (Tsimpli & Sorace 2006; Belletti et al. 2007; Valenzuela 2006). However, others have argued that such domains can be acquired over time (Ivanov 2009; Rothman 2009).

Moreover, Keating, Jegerski, and Van Patten (2011) have suggested that HL and L2 learners differ in how they process and acquire linguistic phenomena that involve the integration of syntactic and discourse-pragmatic properties. The present paper will thus further examine and compare L2 and HL acquisition by investigating a phenomenon, Korean CE, whose properties are similar to those that were claimed to be challenging to bilingual acquisition.

3. Previous Studies

While L2/HL acquisition of Korean CE has not yet been investigated, L2 acquisition of the same phenomenon in Japanese, which is almost identical to that of Korean, has been examined under different theoretical frameworks. Kanno (1996) assumed the phenomenon of CE in Japanese falls under the Empty Category Principle (ECP) with subject nouns being assigned case only when there is a case particle, and object nouns automatically receiving case by the adjacent verb, even without the case particle. Oversimplification of the theoretical assumptions led Kanno to prematurely conclude that adult L2 learners can easily acquire CE. Kanno used an offline written questionnaire and asked the participants to indicate the *naturalness* of the sentence on a scale of three (*unnatural, in-between, natural*) and to correct unnatural sentences. The results showed striking similarity between the scores of the native speakers of Japanese and L2 learners, leading Kanno to conclude that adult L2 learners can acquire CE even at very early stages of L2 acquisition. Many others have since failed to replicate Kanno's findings, casting doubt on Kanno's ECP-based hypothesis, as even advanced L2 learners were subsequently found not to be sensitive to the constraints on case drop (Kellerman & Yoshioka 1999; Mazzotta 2005). This led Kellerman and Yoshioka (1999) to entertain an alternative functionalist account called the 'one-noun hypothesis' in which at least one noun needs to be case-marked in a sentence. However, the 'one-noun hypothesis' is too simplistic and fails to capture the complexity of the linguistic phenomenon in question. In Yoo, Kayama, Mazzotta, and White (2001)'s examination of case drop in L2 Japanese, different theoretical assumptions were used based only on the syntactic positions of NPs where the accusative case particle is optional in immediate preverbal positions but where the NP must obligatorily receive nonspecific interpretation when lacking the case particle. This is also an oversimplification of the phenomenon, as we shall see, and this explains why no significant difference could be found across conditions for all participant groups in the study (native speakers of Japanese, L1-English intermediate and advanced L2 learners).

Taken together, the findings in previous studies of Japanese CE seem to have resulted from overly simplistic theoretical assumptions and a rather limited range of phenomena tested. The proposed study thus re-examines bilingual learners' acquisition of Korean CE under Lee's (2006, 2007) comprehensive framework that has been validated by robust empirical evidence.

4. The Study

4.1. Research Questions

An experimental study was conducted to investigate whether L2 and HL learners can successfully acquire sensitivity to multiple cues that would lead them to acquire target-like competence in Korean CE. More specifically, the following research questions were asked in the study:

a) Can bilingual learners attain implicit knowledge of Korean CE?
b) What are the similarities and differences between L2 and HL learners?

4.2. Participants

Fifteen native speakers (NS) of Korean, 14 HL learners, and 13 L2 learners of Korean completed a language background questionnaire, a written proficiency test, and a written elicited production task. The participants were first asked to fill out a language background questionnaire about the age of acquisition, naturalistic versus instructional exposure to the language, language use etc. Heritage learners completed an additional questionnaire that asked them about their parents' language use as well as other biographical variables pertaining to early bilingualism. All HL learners came to the US before the age of three and were raised in Korean-speaking homes but were schooled in English since childhood. All L2 learners were native speakers of English who had started acquiring Korean after puberty and had received instruction in Korean as a foreign or second language. The participants were graduate or undergraduate students at the University of Illinois at Urbana-Champaign or students enrolled in university language programs in Seoul, Korea. All participants, including the native speaker controls, took a written proficiency test consisting of a cloze test and multiple choice questions with a maximum score of 30. The participant profile is summarized in Table 1 below:

Table 1 Description of participants

Groups	Number	Age of Exposure	Age		Proficiency Score	
			Mean	Range	Mean(St.Dev)	Range
NS	15	Birth	30	25-43	29.73 (0.6)	28-30
HL	14	Birth	24.5	19-32	21.21 (5.78)	14-30
L2	13	17-45	30	23-50	16.46 (5.41)	8-25

As can be seen in Table 1, native speakers were at ceiling in their proficiency while the learners showed varying proficiency scores with HL learners displaying a higher mean than L2 learners.

4.3. Written Elicited Production (WEP) Task

After taking the proficiency test, the participants were given instructions on a written elicited production task that was similar to that used in Lee H-J (2006, 2007) where the participant has to choose a case-marked or a bare NP within the context of a short conversation. The same variables of contrastive focus (CF), animacy, and definiteness were examined. The three variables generated eight experimental conditions, and there were six items per condition for subject and object noun phrases (NPs), resulting in a total of ninety-six test items. The experimental conditions are shown in Table 2, together with the abbreviations used to refer to the distinct test conditions.

Table 2 WEP Experimental Conditions

Object		Subject	
OCHD	CF, Human, Definite	SCHD	CF, Human, Definite
OCHI	CF, Human, Indefinite	SCHI	CF, Human, Indefinite
OCID	CF, Inanimate, Definite	SCID	CF, Inanimate, Definite
OCII	CF, Inanimate, Indefinite	SCII	CF, Inanimate, Indefinite
ONHD	Non-CF, Human, Definite	SNHD	Non- CF, Human, Definite
ONHI	Non-CF, Human, Indefinite	SNHI	Non-CF, Human, Indefinite
ONID	Non-CF, Inanimate, Def	SNID	Non- CF, Inanimate, Def
ONII	Non-CF, Inanimate, Indef	SNII	Non- CF, Inanimate, Indef

The degree of definiteness (proper noun vs. nonspecific NP) and animacy (human vs. inanimate) was controlled, and contrastive focus involved selecting an entity within a limited set of alternatives with contrastive effects. There was no NP modifier, no NP in the beginning of the sentence, no semantic incorporation, no previous mention for contrastively focused NPs, and all sentences were in the present tense.

The context of the conversation was given in English for the learners and in Korean for the NS. The participants were asked to select one answer that sounds more natural in the context of the conversation as quickly as possible and were told that there is no right or wrong answer for these questions in contrast to the written proficiency test. A sample item is shown in (2).

(2) [Object NP: +CF, Inanimate, Indefinite]
(Mina is getting a present for her niece)
Mina: Mwe-l sacwu-ci? Kulimchayk-ul sacwu-l-kka?
WH-ACC buy? picture book-ACC buy-fut-Q?
'What should I get? Should I get her a picture book?'
Youngsu: (pro) acik eli-nikka ________ sacwu-e.
(s/he) still young-CAUS ________ buy-DECL
'Get her a ______ since she's still young'

Answer options: cangnankam-ul (toy-ACC) vs. cangnankam (toy)

The whole procedure could be completed in one sitting (took approximately twenty minutes for native speakers and forty minutes for learners) using an online survey tool called SurveyGizmo.

4.4. Results

The two groups of bilinguals were not native-like in their responses but were also quite different from each other in how they process and acquire the phenomenon of Korean CE. Participants' answers were coded as '1' when the chosen NP was case-marked and '0' when it was bare.

4.4.1. Object CE

The mean and standard deviation values of the participants' performance in object CE are displayed in Table 3 and Figure 1 below.

Table 3 Mean and Standard Deviation (SD) of Judgments on Object CE

	NII	NID	NHI	NHD	CII	CID	CHI	CHD
NS	.17	.09	.42	.31	.40	.60	.49	.78
	(.38)	(.29)	(.49)	(.47)	(.49)	(.49)	(.50)	(.41)
HL	.51	.42	.60	.56	.48	.52	.56	.67
	(.50)	(.49)	(.49)	(.49)	(.50)	(.50)	(.49)	(.47)
L2	.50	.49	.64	.59	.45	.49	.58	.53
	(.50)	(.50)	(.48)	(.49)	(.50)	(.50)	(.49)	(.50)

The large SD values in all three groups indicate a wide range of answers, which is suggestive of the optional nature of the present phenomenon. However, the overall pattern of mean scores was different among groups as illustrated in Figure 1 below.

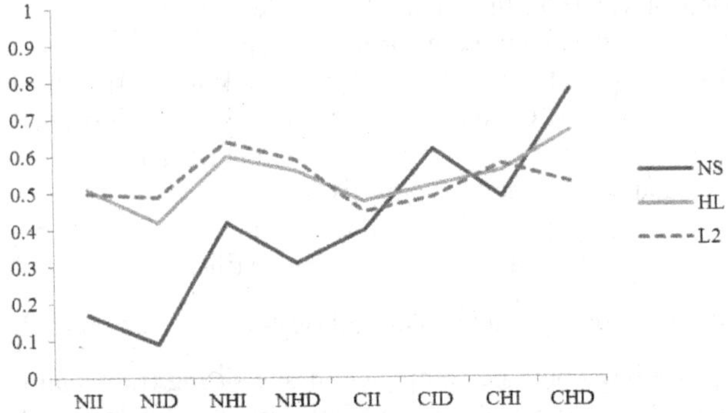

Figure 1 Mean scores of Object CE

A distinctive gradient pattern can be found with native speakers who use case-markers more in [+CF] than [-CF] conditions, in [+Animate] than [-Animate] conditions, and in [-Definite] than [+Definite] conditions, a pattern which confirms the results of previous studies. Both learner groups on the other hand hovered around 0.5 for almost all conditions with no discernible pattern. While the learners also exhibited slight differences in their rate of case-marker suppliance in different animacy and definiteness conditions, contrastive focus did not play a significant role in their judgments.

Statistical analyses of Binary Logistic Regression (BLR) and Generated Estimating Equations (GEE) were conducted on SPSS 19.0 to better understand the above results. Both tests revealed that all three factors of contrastive focus, animacy, and definiteness are statistically significant in NS judgments ($p < .001$, $p < .001$, and $p = .01$ respectively), while only animacy played a significant role in HL and L2 judgments (HL: $p= .003$, L2: $p= .01$). GEE was also used to observe interactions among factors, and more factors displayed significant interactions in NS judgments than in those of HL and L2. In NS judgments, there were significant interactions between CF and animacy ($p = .010$) as well as between CF and definiteness ($p < .001$). HL judgments also showed a significant interaction between CF and definiteness ($p<.001$), but no significant interaction was found between these factors for L2 judgments.

The relative strength of the factors was examined for each group using a nonparametric test—the chi-square test. CF was the strongest factor for NS followed by definiteness then animacy. HL also showed a similar pattern in strength of factors although the contrasts were relatively weaker. For L2 learners, however, there was no significant strength contrast among the factors. The results described above are illustrated in Table 4 below.

Table 4 Statistical Analyses of Object CE Judgments

	NS	HL	L2
Main Effects	CF (p < .001) Anim (p <.001) Def (p = .018)	Anim (p = .003)	Anim (p = .010)
Interaction	CF x Anim (p = .010) CF x Def (p < .001)	CF x Def (p < .001)	NONE
Relative Strength	Def < CF (±Anim) Anim < CF (± Def) Anim < Def (-CF)	Anim < CF (+Def) Anim < Def (-CF)	NONE

When the groups were compared using post-hoc tests on Univariate Analysis of Variance with group as a fixed factor, NS judgments were significantly different from the learners' judgments while HL and L2 learners' judgments were not significantly different from each other.

In sum, native speakers displayed a distinctive and gradient judgment pattern of object CE in which all three factors identified in previous research played a significant role. Among the three factors, CF had the strongest influence, and CF as the strongest factor displayed significant interactions with the other two factors. On the other hand, the two learner groups only relied on animacy. Interactions and strength relationships among factors were almost nonexistent in L2 judgments. While both bilingual learner groups failed to show native-like judgments in object CE, HL learners seemed somewhat aware of the roles played by factors other than animacy as shown by the limited presence of factor interactions and strength relationships in their judgments.

4.4.2. Subject CE

In subject CE, HL judgments closely mirrored those of NS while L2 judgments were significantly different from the others. The mean and standard deviation values are shown in Table 5.

Table 5 Mean and Standard Deviation (SD) of Judgments on Subject CE

	NII	NID	NHI	NHD	CII	CID	CHI	CHD
NS	.61 (.49)	.50 (.50)	.90 (.30)	.24 (.43)	.98 (.15)	.98 (.14)	.82 (.38)	.97 (.18)
HL	.67 (.47)	.68 (.47)	.82 (.38)	.55 (.50)	.86 (.35)	.90 (.29)	.77 (.42)	.85 (.36)
L2	.58 (.49)	.64 (.48)	.71 (.45)	.65 (.47)	.55 (.50)	.50 (.50)	.71 (.45)	.82 (.38)

While the SD values were quite large across all groups and conditions in object CE, there was less variance in NS answers in subject CE, especially in [+CF] conditions. That is, NS had a strong tendency to choose the case-marked NP in [+CF] conditions. A similar pattern was found for HL learners although they showed more variance than the NS, but the L2 learners showed a large degree of variance across all conditions. NS and HL learners displayed a similar judgment pattern in which CE occurred most frequently in the NHD condition, but L2 learners showed much ambivalence across all conditions as can be seen in Figure 2.

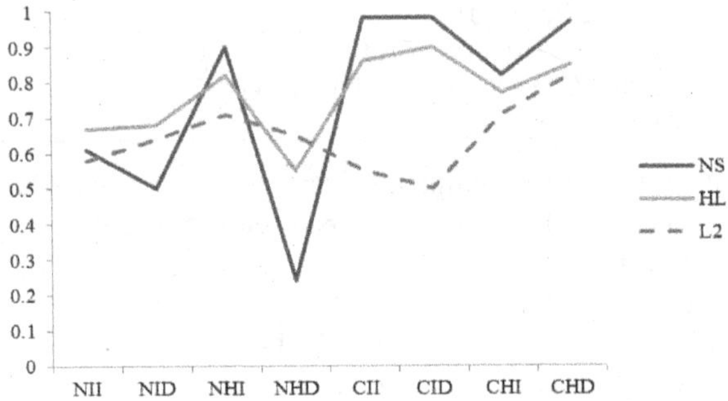

Figure 2 Mean scores of Subject CE

According to statistical tests of Binary Logistic Regression (BLR) and Generated Estimating Equations (GEE), NS took CF ($p < .001$) and definiteness ($p < .001$) into account but disregarded animacy. The bilingual learners, on the other hand, depended on a single factor to guide their judgments: HL relied only on CF ($p < .001$) and L2 only on animacy ($p <.001$). It is interesting to note that CF, which was a significant factor for both NS and HL learners, had close to no effect on L2 judgments ($p=.99$), and that animacy, which was the only significant factor for L2 learners, was insignificant for the other groups. The results of GEE showed robust interactions among all three factors in NS and HL judgments as well as a fair amount of interactions in L2 judgments also. The chi-square test results also showed a similar pattern in strengths of factors for NS and HL in which CF is strongest followed by definiteness and animacy, but animacy was stronger than definiteness in [+CF] conditions. L2 learners found CF to be a stronger cue than animacy in [+Def] conditions and definiteness to be stronger than animacy in [+CF] conditions, which is the opposite of what we find for the other groups. The statistical test results displayed in Table 6 show that HL judgments are quite similar to those of NS in many respects unlike the L2 learners who exhibit divergent patterns. When the groups were compared using a post-hoc test, NS and HL judgments were not significantly different from each other, but L2 judgments were significantly different from the others.

Table 6 Statistical Analyses of Subject CE Judgments

	NS	HL	L2
Main Effects	CF ($p < .001$) Def ($p < .001$)	CF ($p < .001$)	Animacy ($p < .001$)
Interaction	CF x A x D ($p < .001$) CF x A ($p < .001$) CF x D ($p = .015$)	CF x A x D ($p = .043$) CF x A ($p = .011$) CF x D ($p < .001$) A x D ($p = .007$)	CF x A x D ($p = .018$) CF x A ($p = .006$)
Relative Strength	CF > Def (Inanim) CF > Anim (Def, Indef) Def > Anim (-CF) Anim > Def (+CF)	CF > Def (Inanim) CF > Anim (Def) Def > Anim (-CF) Anim > Def (+CF)	CF > Anim (Def) Def > Anim (+CF)

Summarizing the results of both subject and object CE, we see that NS took multiple factors into account while the two bilingual groups predominantly depended on a single factor: L2 learners depended on animacy regardless of NP type and HL learners depended on animacy in object CE and CF in subject CE. While both learner groups were significantly different from native judgments on object CE, HL learners closely mirrored native judgments on subject CE, suggesting a possible advantage for HL learners over L2 learners.

4.4.3. Proficiency Effects

One might view the advantage HL learners have over L2 learners as a reflection of their higher proficiency (see Table 1), instead of any other group variable. That is, the different behavior in the written elicited production task could be an effect of proficiency rather than group. Therefore, the learners' judgments were re-examined after controlling for proficiency. Analysis by proficiency suggests that proficiency affects HL judgments but not L2 judgments. HL and L2 groups were divided into two proficiency levels (high vs. low) as shown in Table 7 to control for proficiency effects and to compare proficiency-matched learners.

Table 7 Proficiency levels in learner groups

Group	Proficiency	N	Proficiency score (out of 30)	
			Mean	SD
HL	High	7	26	2.6
	Low	7	16	1.4
L2	High	4	22	1.9
	Low	9	14	4.3

Table 8 and Figure 3 present the mean scores of object CE judgments by different proficiency levels within each group.

Table 8 Mean of Object CE Judgments

	NII	NID	NHI	NHD	CII	CID	CHI	CHD
NS	0.17	0.09	0.42	0.31	0.40	0.62	0.49	0.78
HL-high	0.29	0.21	0.43	0.50	0.33	0.43	0.36	0.74
HL-low	0.74	0.62	0.76	0.62	0.62	0.62	0.76	0.59
L2-high	0.58	0.54	0.67	0.71	0.46	0.54	0.75	0.50
L2-low	0.48	0.46	0.67	0.50	0.48	0.50	0.50	0.56

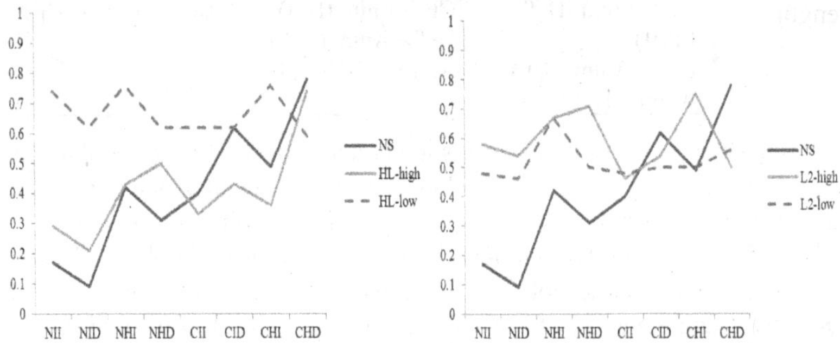

Figure 3 Object CE judgments by proficiency levels within groups

The mean values show a distinct proficiency effect for HL learners as high proficiency learners closely followed native speakers' gradient judgment patterns and low proficiency learners gave similar ratings across all conditions with no discernible pattern. L2 learners, however, displayed patterns that are divergent from that of NS regardless of proficiency. Both high and low proficiency L2 learners' ratings were similar across all conditions like those of low proficiency HL learners. Likewise, proficiency effect was found for HL learners but not L2 learners in subject CE judgments as shown in Table 9 and Figure 4.

Table 9 Mean of Subject CE Judgments

	NII	NID	NHI	NHD	CII	CID	CHI	CHD
NS	0.61	0.50	0.90	0.24	0.98	0.98	0.82	0.97
HL-high	0.71	0.60	0.79	0.45	1	1	0.88	0.95
HL-low	0.62	0.76	0.86	0.64	0.71	0.81	0.67	0.74
L2-high	0.54	0.58	0.67	0.75	0.50	0.38	0.79	0.83
L2-low	0.56	0.67	0.71	0.56	0.58	0.56	0.67	0.83

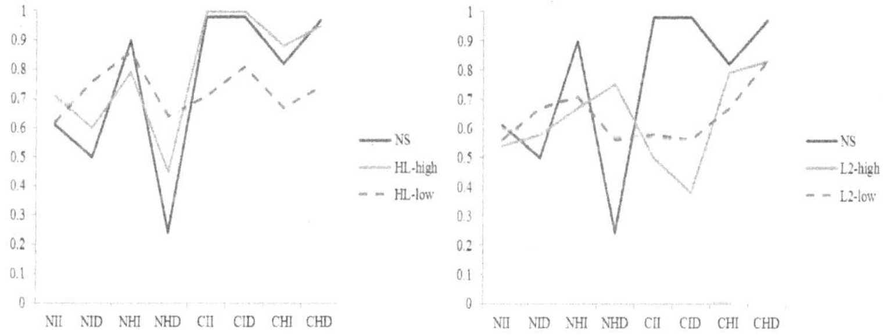

Figure 4 Subject CE judgments by proficiency levels within groups

No inferential statistical analysis was conducted due to the insufficient number of participants in each group, but the judgment patterns shown in each proficiency level within the groups suggest that HL learners might indeed have an advantage over the L2 in the present linguistic phenomenon. High proficiency HL learners' judgments on both object and subject CE patterned with those of the native speakers, but L2 learners exhibited divergent patterns of judgment regardless of proficiency.

5. Discussion

The present study examined bilingual acquisition of Korean CE and has found that while both L2 and HL learners exhibited difficulty, HL learners showed a better understanding of Korean CE in their judgments than L2 learners who exclusively relied on animacy regardless of NP type to guide their judgments. In fact, high-proficiency HL learners were found to be capable of reaching native-like judgments and were similar to NS in their knowledge of interactions and strength relationships among factors.

In object CE, NS judgments formed a distinctive gradient pattern with all three factors of CF, animacy, and definiteness playing a significant role and displaying significant interactions and strength relationships. The two learner groups, on the other hand, only relied on animacy and showed ambivalence in their judgments. The two learner groups displayed judgment patterns that were similar to each other, but there were significant interactions and strength contrasts in HL judgments while L2 judgments showed none. That is, although both learner groups face difficulty in their acquisition of object CE, HL learners were somewhat cognizant of the interaction between different factors that determine object CE whereas L2 learners were not aware of such interactions. HL learners also exhibited a better understanding of subject CE than L2 learners as their judgments mirrored those of NS and displayed equally robust interactions and strength contrasts among factors. HL learners seemed to intuitively understand the nature of subject CE that is less gradient and more strongly influenced by information structure than object CE. L2 learners, on the other hand, treated both types of CE similarly. Moreover, when controlled for proficiency, high proficiency HL learners showed almost an identical judgment pattern to that of the NS, but L2 learners gave similar ratings across all conditions regardless of proficiency.

Overall, the results are suggestive of qualitative differences in the underlying linguistic knowledge of the two bilingual groups. While it seems possible for HL learners to attain implicit knowledge of Korean CE with increasing proficiency, such mastery is questionable for L2 learners. Regardless of proficiency, L2 learners seem to have developed their own analysis of CE that is predominantly determined by animacy with close to no interaction with other variables. That is, an unmarked and unlearned pattern that is independent of both L1 and L2 grammar seems to be emerging as the analysis of CE for L2 learners. Animacy, which is an inherent semantic feature of what an NP denotes, is predicted to be a more accessible and an easier cue than definiteness or focus that are context-inferred. While the results of the present study cannot account for the reason why animacy is the most prominent cue for the learners, it can be speculated that this is due to an effect of universal principles of markedness

The qualitative differences found in the two bilingual groups indicate that proficiency matched HL learners have an advantage over L2 learners in acquisition of Korean CE. Such advantage could be due to various reasons such as the age of acquisition (early vs. late exposure), type and frequency of input, and context and mode of acquisition that differentiate the two populations. HL learners who were exposed to aural naturalistic input in the home since childhood may find it easier to acquire context-inferred subtle discourse-pragmatic properties of Korean CE than adult L2 learners whose exposure to the language mainly occurs in the classroom. As it is, HL learners' language background in age, context, and mode of acquisition seem to better equip the learners in acquiring Korean CE.

To conclude, different types of bilinguals were found to process and acquire the phenomenon of Korean CE differently with HL learners having an advantage over the L2 learners. HL learners were sensitive to multiple cues and attained a certain degree of implicit knowledge of Korean CE whereas L2 learners developed their own pattern of judgment that exclusively depends on animacy with almost no interaction with other factors. Therefore, it seems highly possible for HL learners to attain native-like implicit knowledge of Korean CE with increasing proficiency but L2 learners' limited understanding of Korean CE even in high proficiency level questions their ability to acquire the phenomenon.

References

Au, T., S. Knightly, J. Jun, J. Oh, & L. Romo. 2002. Overhearing a language during childhood. *Psychological Science* 13: 238-243.

Belletti, A., E. Bennati, & A. Sorace. 2007. Theoretical and developmental issues in the syntax of subjects: Evidence from near-native Italian. *Natural Language & Linguistic Theory* 25: 657-689.

Bolonyai, A. 2007. (In)vulnerable agreement in incomplete bilingual L1 learners. *The International Journal of Bilingualism* 11: 3-21.

Chung, E-S. 2010. *Challenging a Single-factor Analysis of Case Ellipsis in Korean.* Paper presented at the Seoul International Conference on Linguistics (SICOL). Korea University, Seoul.

Cummins, J. 2000. *Language, Power and Pedagogy, Bilingual children in the cross-fire*. Clevedon: Multilingual Matters.

Enc, M. 1991. The semantics of specificity. *Linguistic Inquiry* 18: 633-657.

Fry, J. 2001. Ellipsis and 'wa'-marking in Japanese conversation. Doctoral dissertation, Stanford University.

Håkansson, G. 1995. Syntax and morphology in language attrition: A study of five bilingual expatriate Swedes. *International Journal of Applied Linguistics* 5: 153-171.

Hopp, H. 2006. Syntactic features and reanalysis in nearnative processing. *Second Language Research* 22(3): 369-397.

Hopp, H. 2009. The syntax-discourse interface in near-native L2 acquisition: Off-line and on-line performance. *Bilingualism: Language and Cognition* 12(4): 463-483.

Ivanov, I. 2009. Pragmatic effects of clitic doubling in L2 Bulgarian: A test case for the Interface Hypothesis. Paper presented at GASLA 10, University of Illinois, Champaign-Urbana, IL.

Kanno, K. 1996. The Status of a Nonparametrized Principle in the L2 Initial State. *Language Acquisition* 5(4): 317-334.

Keating, G., J. Jegerski, & B. Vanpatten. 2011. Who was walking on the beach? Anaphora resolution in Spanish heritage speakers and adult second language learners. *Studies in Second Language Acquisition 33*(2): 193-221.

Kellerman, E., & K. Yoshioka, 1999. Inter- and Intra-Population Consistency: A Comment on Kanno (1998). *Second Language Research* 15(1): 101-109.

Ko, E.-S. 2000. A discourse analysis of the realization of objects in Korean. *Japanese/Korean Linguistics* 9: 195-208.

Kwon, S.-N., & A. Zribi-Hertz. 2008. Differential Function Marking, Case, and Information Structure: Evidence from Korean. *Language* 84(2): 258-299.

Lee, D-Y. 2002. The function of the zero particle with special reference to spoken Japanese. *Journal of Pragmatics* 34: 645-682.

Lee, H. 2006. Effects of Focus and Markedness Hierarchies on Object Case Ellipses in Korean. *Discourse and Cognition* 13(2): 205-231.

Lee, H. 2007. Case ellipses at the grammar/pragmatics interface: A formal analysis from a typological perspective. *Journal of Pragmatics* 39: 1465-1481.

Lee, H. 2008. Processing Efficiency and Object Case Ellipses in Korean. *Korean Journal of Linguistics* 33(1): 159-179.

Lee, H. S., & S. A. Thompson. 1985. A discourse account of the Korean accusative marker. *Studies in Language* 13: 105-128.

Lee, S-B. 2006. A Pragmatic Analysis of Accusative Case-Marker Deletion. *Discourse and Cognition* 13(3): 69-89.

Mazzotta, M. 2005. L2 Acquisition of Japanese Case Drop. *McGill Working Papers in Linguistics* 19(2): 1-19.

Montrul, S. 2004. Subject and object expression in Spanish heritage speakers: A case of morphosyntactic convergence. *Bilingualism: Language and Cognition* 7(2): 125-142.

Montrul, S. 2008. Incomplete Acquisition in Spanish Heritage Speakers: Chronological Age or Interfaces Vulnerability? *Proceedings of the Annual Boston University Conference on Language Development* 32(1): 299-310.

Montrul, S. 2010. Dominant language transfer in adult second language learners and heritage speaker. *Second Language Research* 26(3): 293-327.

Montrul, S., R. Foote, & S. Perpinan. 2008. Gender agreement in adult second language learners and Spanish heritage speakers: The effects of age and context of acquisition. *Language Learning* 58: 3-54.

Mori, T., & T. Givón. 1987. *Zero object-marking in colloquial Japanese: The pragmatics of optional deletion.* Eugene: University of Oregon.

Polinsky, M. 2006. Incomplete acquisition: American Russian. *Journal of Slavic Linguistics* 14: 191-262

Rothman, J. 2007. Pragmatic solutions for syntactic problems: Understanding some L2syntactic errors in terms of discourse–pragmatics deficits. *Romance languages and linguistic theory 2005*, eds. Baauw, S., F. Drijkoningen, & M. Pinto, 299–320. Amsterdam: Benjamins.

Slabakova, R. 2008. *Meaning in the Second Language,* (Studies in Language Acquisition Series.) Berlin: Mouton de Gruyter

Sorace, A. 2000. Syntactic optionality in non-native grammars. *Second Language Research* 16: 93-102.

Sorace, A., & F. Filiaci. 2006. Anaphora resolution in near-native speakers of Italian. *Second Language Research* 22: 339-368.

Sorace, A., & L. Serratrice. 2009. Internal and external interfaces in bilingual language development: Beyond structural overlap. *International Journal of Bilingualism* 13: 1-16.

Tsimpli, I. M., & A. Sorace. 2006. Differentiating interfaces: L2 performance in syntax-semantics and syntax-discourse phenomena. *Proceedings of the 30th annual Boston University Conference on Language Development (BUCLD 30),* eds. D. Bamman, T. Magnitskaia, & C. Zaller, 653-664. Somerville, MA: Cascadilla Press.

Tsimpli, I. M., A. Sorace, C. Heycock, & F. Filiaci. 2004. First language attrition and syntactic subjects: A study of Greek and Italian near-native speakers of English. *International Journal of Bilingualism* 8: 257-277.

Valdés, G. 2000. *Introduction. Spanish for Native Speakers* (Vol. 1). New York: Harcourt College.

Valenzuela, E. 2006. L2 end state grammars and incomplete acquisition of Spanish CLLD constructions. *Inquiries in linguistic development: In honor of Lydia White*, eds. R. Slabakova, S. Montrul, & P. Prévost, 283-304. Amsterdam: John Benjamins.

Watanabe, Yasuko. 1986. Two kinds of ellipsis in Japanese discourse: A quantitative text study. *Studies in Language* 10: 337-51

Yoo, M., Y. Kayama, M. Mazzotta, & L. White. 2001. Case Drop in L2 Japanese. *Proceedings of the Annual Boston University Conference on Language Development* 25(2): 825-834.

The First Language Acquisition of the Korean Imperfective Aspect markers *-ko iss-/-a iss-*

JU-YEON RYU & YASUHIRO SHIRAI
Tohoku University & University of Pittsburgh

The acquisition of tense-aspect morphology has shown an interesting universal pattern in both first and second language acquisition (Andersen and Shirai, 1996). This universal tendency is referred to as the Aspect Hypothesis (e.g. Andersen and Shirai, 1994), which predicts that past tense forms start with achievement verbs, and progressive forms start with activity verbs.

Correlations between tense-aspect markers and the inherent aspect of verbs have been verified in the first language acquisition of various languages (e.g. Bloom *et al.* 1980 in English, Antinucci and Miller 1976 in Italian, Bronckart and Sinclair 1973 in French, Weist *et al.* 1984 in Polish, Stephany 1981 in Greek, Aksu-koç 1988 in Turkish). However, only a small number of studies have been conducted on the L1 acquisition of Asian languages, including Shirai (1993, 1998) and Shirai and Suzuki (in press) for Japanese, Li and Bowerman (1998) and Chen and Shirai (2010) in Mandarin Chinese, and Gökmen and Lee (2002) for Korean. Gökmen and Lee (2002) found that both Korean and Turkish children use past marking predominantly with accomplishment and achievement verbs first, which is

Japanese/Korean Linguistics 21.
Edited by Seungho Nam, Heejeong Ko and Jongho Jun.

consistent with the Aspect Hypothesis. However, they only focused on the acquisition of the past tense marker *-ess-*. Further research is still needed to verify the Aspect Hypothesis, including the acquisition of the imperfective aspect marker.

This study tests whether the universal developmental pattern proposed by Andersen and Shirai (1996) holds true for the L1 acquisition of Korean, and also discusses what determines children's acquisition of aspect: universal predisposition, the distribution bias hypothesis or individual variation.

1. The Imperfective Aspect System in Korean

Imperfective aspect markers in Korean can denote two meanings: the progressive and the resultative state (Martin 1992). When denoting an action-in-progress meaning, Korean takes *-ko iss-* as the progressive marker. Meanwhile, when expressing a resultative state meaning, Korean takes *-ko iss-* or *-a iss-*. Syntactically, when expressing a resultative state, both *-ko iss-* and *-a iss-* are used, depending on the transitivity of the main verbs: *-ko iss-* with transitive verbs, and *-a iss-* with intransitive verbs (Lee 1991).

Table 1 Imperfective Aspect Markers *-ko iss-* and *-a iss-*

	Intransitive verbs	Transitive verbs
progressive meaning	*-ko iss-*	
resultative meaning	*-a iss-*	*-ko iss-*

-Ko iss- has been generally treated as a progressive marker as in (1a), but unlike the progressive *be -ing* in English, it is not obligatory in describing an ongoing event. The simple present form in Korean can encode an ongoing event at a reference time, just as in Romance languages:

(1a) Pap-ul mek-ko iss-e (JOO 3;3)
lunch-Acc eat-Prog-Dec
"He (or She) is eating lunch"

(1b) Pap-ul mek-nun-ta
lunch-Acc eat-Prs-Dec
"He (or She) is eating lunch"

In addition to its progressive meaning, *-ko iss-* can also describe a resultant state with some transitive verbs, such as verbs of wearing, carrying, and body posture (Ahn, 1995; Lee, 1991). In (2), *-ko iss-* can denote either an ongoing event or a resultant state. This is because in the case of transitive verbs, only *-ko iss-* can be used as the imperfective aspect marker for both progressive and resultant meanings.

(2) Wangkwan-ul ssu-ko iss-eyo (JONG 1;11)
crown-Acc wear-Resl-Dec
"He/She is wearing a crown." or "He/She is putting on a crown."

-A iss has been referred to as the resultative marker in Korean (e.g. Ahn 1995, Martin 1992). Whereas *-ko iss-* is compatible with all transitive verbs, *-a iss-* can only be used with intransitive verbs in describing a persisting state resulting from a completed action, as in (3) (Lee 1991).

(3) Khokkili anc a iss-e (JONG 1;11)
elephant sit-Resl-Dec
"The elephant is sitting."

2. Previous Studies on the Acquisition of Aspect

Previous research claimed that the acquisition of tense/aspect markers is strongly influenced by the inherent lexical aspect of the verbs (Vendler 1957) to which the tense-aspect markers are attached. This hypothesis, generally referred to as the Aspect Hypothesis (e.g. Andersen and Shirai 1994, 1996, Shirai 1991), claims that (1) learners use (perfective) past marking on achievement/accomplishment verbs, eventually extending use to activity and stative verbs, (2) in languages that encode the perfective/imperfective distinction morphologically, the imperfective past appears later than the perfective past, and the imperfect past marking begins with stative and activity (i.e., atelic) verbs, then extends to accomplishment and achievement (i.e., telic) verbs, (3) in languages that have a progressive aspect, progressive marking begins with activity verbs, and then extends to accomplishment/achievement verbs, and (4) progressive marking is rarely incorrectly overextended to stative verbs (in L1 acquisition) (Li and Shirai 2000: 50).

Although researchers generally agree on this descriptive observation (e.g. Shirai, Slobin and Weist 1998), the explanation for this observation is not fully understood. One important hypothesis appeals to a universal predisposition (e.g., Bickerton, 1981), which postulates that children have a bias to map tense-aspect markers with particular semantic content. Bickerton argued that children use past tense marking to denote punctuality, or telicity in aspectology, and progressive/imperfective marking to mark the lack of telicity, because the Punctual-NonPunctual Distriction (PNPD) is a distinction that has a special status in his Language Bioprogram Hypothesis. Meanwhile, the Distributional Bias Hypothesis (e.g. Andersen 1993, Shirai and Andersen 1995) argues that children make particular associations based on input frequency. It suggests that associations in acquisition are based on a skewed distribution of such combinations in input, which was supported by analyzing the input data of mother-child interaction in English (Shirai and Andersen 1995).

Gökmen and Lee (2002) investigated the development of tense-aspect morphology in L1 Korean acquisition from three Korean children (in addition to Turkish, which we will not discuss here). They found that (1) Korean children use past marking predominantly with accomplishment and achievement verbs first, (2) the same children frequently used telic verbs (i.e. achievements and accomplishments) in their past references. Their results suggested that acquisition of past marking *-ess-* in Korean follows the Aspect Hypothesis. However, there have been no studies focused on the development of Korean imperfective aspect markers.

In Japanese, which is known to be very similar to Korean, this predicted developmental pattern has not always been observed (Shirai 1993, 1998, Shirai and Suzuki, in press). Shirai (1993) investigated whether the universal acquisition pattern holds true for the Japanese progressive *-te i-* and past tense *-ta*. He found that the Japanese child (Sumihare, Noji 1976; 1977) analyzed in his study followed the same universal pattern found in previous studies. However, Shirai (1998) reported different results from Shirai (1993). Shirai (1998) investigated the emergence and later development of three tense-aspect markers in Japanese: *-ta* (past), *-te i-* (durative), and *-ru* (non-past) by analyzing data from three Japanese children. He found that the emergence of tense-aspect morphology in Japanese does not necessarily follow the prediction of the Aspect Hypothesis, but is mediated by typological factors of Japanese, and that there was individual variation in the acquisition of the morphology. Shirai and Suzuki (in press) investigated the acquisition of *-te i-* in four Japanese children, including an analysis of the caretaker's speech data. The results indicated that there is no preponderance of activity verbs in the acquisition of Japanese imperfective *-te i-*, and thus progressive meaning does not occur more frequently. For all three children, the use of *-te i-* with achievements was more frequent than with activities. They suggested that frequency is more important than universal predisposition in the acquisition of tense-aspect markers, which is in concurrence with the distributional bias hypothesis and the usage-based model of language learning (Tomasello 2003).

The present study contributes to the existing literature by helping to add detail and explain what has been found thus far. Foremost, we look to offer a wider range to the current research, as the majority of it thus far has been on the L1 acquisition of the tense-aspect morphology of Indo-European languages. Though the current data mostly seems to support the Aspect Hypothesis, Shirai and Suzuki (in press) reported results that conflict with this hypothesis, as mentioned above. In order to truly test the claims of the Aspect Hypothesis, more data from non-Indo-European languages is needed, and this study helps to provide that, being the first to attempt to clarify the developmental process of the imperfective aspect morphology for L1

Korean and offering information about how the Korean tense-aspect system is acquired, which has not been studied in depth until now. Furthermore, our study provides evidence addressing the issue of explaining what has been found and attempts to answer the question of where tendencies in tense-aspect acquisition can be attributed to universal predisposition or to input. In this paper, we investigate not only the children's use of the imperfective markers *-ko iss-*/*-a iss-*, but also the caretaker's use of them, in order to verify the validity of the Distributional Bias Hypothesis as proposed by Shirai and Andersen (1995).

The research questions addressed in this study are:

1 How does children's use of imperfective markers *-ko iss-* and *-a iss-* develop over time in relation to the meanings they denote (progressive and resultative) and lexical aspect (state, activity, accomplishment, achievement)?
2 What are the frequencies of the imperfective markers *-ko iss-* and *-a iss-* in relation to the meanings they denote and lexical aspect in child-directed speech?
3 What is the relation between child-directed speech and children's speech in the distributional pattern of imperfective aspect markers?

Although this is the first study to investigate the acquisition of the imperfective aspect in Korean, we can make some predictions based on previous research in other languages. First, the Distributional Bias Hypothesis predicts that progressive marking with activity verbs will be acquired earlier than resultative *-ko iss-* or *-a iss-* because the progressive *-ko iss-* is more frequently used in native speakers' discourse. According to Lee and Kim (2007), in the Seyjong Written Corpus (http://ikc.korea.ac.kr/cgi-bin/kwic/kwic.cgi), the frequencies of the imperfective aspect exhibited the following trends: the progressive *-ko iss-* (57.0%) was most frequent, followed by the resultative *-a iss-* (28.3%) and the resultative *-ko iss-* (15.7%). However, this hypothesis is tentative, as there is no guarantee that frequency observed in written corpora is also observed in caretaker speech.

Bickerton's prediction for Korean would be that children would map atelic verbs to imperfective markers because in Korean, the punctual side of the Punctual-Non Punctual distinction is already marked by the past tense marker *-ess* (Gökmen and Lee 2002). Children would therefore mark the non-punctual side of PNPD using imperfective markers with activity verbs.

3. The study

3.1 Method and Participants

The Korean data collected consists of longitudinal video-recorded speech samples of adult-child interaction from three children, taken every two weeks for 30 minutes at the children's homes (see Table 2).

Table 2 Children in the Longitudinal Data

Children	Age range	Sex and Sibling	Length of Data
JONG	1;3~3;5	M, no siblings	31hr 37min
JOO	1;9~3;10	F, one older sister	29hr 2min
YUN	2;3~3;9	M, no siblings	20hr 36min
Total			81hr15min

This data set covers an extended period of acquisition, and includes relatively early stages of development, which is essential to see the emergence and subsequent development of aspectual marking in children's speech. The child-directed speech (input) includes the utterances from all of the caretakers. In total, about 81hr 15min of data were analyzed.

3.2 Data Analysis

The three children produced 163 predicate tokens with the imperfective aspect markers *-ko iss-*/*-a iss-*, and their caretakers produced 2,092 tokens (see Table 3). In total, 2,255 tokens were analyzed, excluding immediate exact repetitions of the same utterance in the same turn.

Table 3 Tokens of *-ko iss-*/*-a iss-* Produced by Children and Caretakers

	child	caretaker
JONG (1;3~3;5)	62	582
JOO (1;9~3;10)	36	853
YUN (2;3~3;9)	65	657
Total	163	2,092

We also analyzed the MLU (mean length of utterance) and age of emergence for each child, as shown in Table 4. JONG was 1 year 11 months old when the imperfective aspect first emerged in his speech, while JOO was 3 years 3 months old and YUN was 2 years 7 months old, showing a large difference in the age of emergence. Very small differences were also found in the MLU for each child's first use of the imperfective aspect. It appears that Korean children start to use the imperfective aspect markers when the MLU is around 2.6 to 2.8.

Table 4 Emergence of *-ko iss-/-a iss-*

	Age	MLU	Utterance	Marker
JONG	1;11	2.78	nakksiha-ko iss-e fish-Prog-Dec "He is fishing."	Progressive *-ko iss-*
JOO	3;3	2.66	mek-ko iss-e eat-Prog-Dec "He is eating"	Progressive *-ko iss-*
YUN	2;7	2.68	tha-ko iss-ciyo ride-Prog-Dec "is in" (lit. he is riding)	Resultative *-ko iss-*

All verb tokens with imperfective markers included in the analysis were classified according to the meaning they denote (Progressive or Resultative), and for lexical aspect based on the operational tests by Kim and Lee (2006).

4. Results

4.1 RQ1: Children's Use of *-ko iss-/-a iss-*

Table 5 shows the use of the two imperfective aspect markers by the children and caretakers. *-Ko iss-* is further divided into progressive and resultative, depending on the meaning it denotes. We also separated the caretaker usage into "pre-emergence" and "post-emergence" to see if any difference could be observed before and after children start using imperfective markers.

Table 5 Use of *-ko iss-* and *-a iss-* by Children and Caretakers (token count)

JONG	Pre-emergence		Post-emergence							
	Child	Caretakers	Child							
	1;3-1;10	(%)	1;11	2;0	2;1	2;2	2;4	2;7	2;8	2;9
PRG-*ko iss-*	N/A	51 (64)	2	1	2	0	2	0	0	0
RSL-*ko iss-*	N/A	9 (11)	2	1	1	3	0	0	0	1
RSL-*a iss-*	N/A	20 (25)	1	3	2	1	2	3	1	2
Sum	0	80 (100)	5	5	5	4	4	3	1	3

JONG	Post-emergence									
	Child									Caretakers
	2;10	2;11	3;0	3;1	3;2	3;3	3;4	3;5	sum(%)	(%)
PRG-*ko iss-*	2	3	3	0	0	2	0	1	18 (29)	203 (40)
RSL-*ko iss-*	1	4	0	0	0	1	1	1	16 (26)	66 (13)
RSL-*a iss-*	4	0	0	1	1	1	1	5	28 (45)	233 (46)
Sum	7	7	3	1	1	4	2	7	62(100)	502 (100)

JOO	Pre-emergence		Post-emergence									
	Child	Care-	Child									Care-
	1;9-3;2	Taker (%)	3;3	3;4	3;5	3;6	3;7	3;8	3;9	3;10	Sum (%)	Taker (%)
PRG *-ko iss-*	N/A	401 (62)	2	1	0	3	3	3	1	0	13 (36)	133 (63)
RSL *-ko iss-*	N/A	90 (14)	0	0	0	1	2	2	0	0	5 (14)	15 (7)
RSL *-a iss-*	N/A	152 (24)	1	0	2	9	1	1	0	4	18 (50)	62 (30)
Sum	0	643 (100)	3	1	2	13	6	6	1	4	36 (100)	210 (100)

YUN	Pre-emergence		Post-emergence														
	Child	Care-	Child														Care-
	2;3-2;6	takers(%)	2;7	2;8	2;9	2;10	2;11	3;0	3;1	3;2	3;5	3;6	3;7	3;8	3;9	sum(%)	takers (%)
PRG-*ko iss-*	N/A	35 (42)	1	3	3	1	1	2	1	6	0	1	7	3	0	29 (45)	289 (50)
RSL-*ko iss-*	N/A	15 (18)	2	0	0	2	2	0	2	0	0	0	0	0	0	8 (12)	79 (14)
RSL-*a iss-*	N/A	33 (40)	0	1	0	0	2	2	0	0	2	9	2	9	1	28 (43)	206 (36)
Sum	0	83 (100)	3	4	3	3	5	4	3	6	2	10	9	12	1	65 (100)	574 (100)

Note. PRG = Progressive, RSL = Resultative. Percentages are followed by token frequency in parentheses. The data of 2;3, 2;5, 2;6 for JONG and 3;3, 3;4 for YUN was not observed.

According to the overall distribution of the use of imperfective aspect markers over time, all three children used the resultative *-ko iss-/-a iss-* more frequently than the progressive *-ko iss-*. JONG and JOO used the resultative *-a iss-* more frequently than the progressive *-ko iss-*. Thus, it does not appear to be the case that children generally resist using imperfective markers to denote resultative meaning because the punctual side of PNPD is already taken by the past tense *-ess-*.

In order to see the usage patterns at the earliest stage, we analyzed the first 10 samples of imperfective aspect marker usage by each child, following Diessel and Tomasello (2000). Table 6 shows that JONG and JOO use not only the progressive *-ko iss-*, but also the resultative *-ko iss-/-a iss-* from early stages. However, YUN uses the progressive *-ko iss-* predominantly more than the resultative *-ko iss-/-a iss-*. Thus, YUN's data is consistent with the bioprogram hypothesis, while the other two children's are not.

Table 6 First 10 Imperfective Markers Used

	JONG	JOO	YUN
PRG-*ko iss-*	3	4	7
RSL-*ko iss-*	3	0	2
RSL-*a iss-*	4	6	1

Let us now examine whether or not children's use of *-ko iss-/-a iss-* is associated more with activity verbs than with achievement verbs (see Table 7). It should be noted that stative verbs were not used with imperfective markers *-ko iss-/-a iss-* in the present study. Table 7 shows the following trends: (1) *-a iss-* is almost exclusively used with achievements by all three children, except for YUN who used accomplishments quite frequently (11 out of 28 tokens) and (2) the use of *-ko iss-* shows a great deal of individual variation.

Table 7 Distribution of Lexical Aspect with *-ko iss-* and *-a iss-*

		JONG	JOO	YUN
-ko iss-	activity	13(21%)	12(33%)	16(25%)
	accomplishment	5(8%)	1(3%)	10(15%)
	achievement	16(26%)	5(14%)	11(17%)
-a iss-	activity			
	accomplishment	1(2%)	3(8%)	11(17%)
	achievement	27(43%)	15(42%)	17(26%)
Sum		62(100%)	36(100%)	65(100%)

Table 8 shows the results of the first 10 tokens. *-A iss-* is almost exclusively used with achievements while *-ko iss-* shows individual variation. JOO's usage mostly occurred with activities and thus supports the bioprogram hypothesis, while JONG and YUN used it with telic verbs quite extensively (JONG in particular only used *-ko iss-* with telic verbs), which goes against the bioprogram hypothesis.

Overall, the results indicate that there was no common pattern in the three children's acquisition. Only one child (YUN), especially at the early stage, associated imperfective aspect marking more with progressive marking and activity verbs, while the others used both *-ko iss-* and *-a iss-* quite frequently with telic verbs.

Table 8 Distribution of Lexical Aspect for First 10 Tokens

		JONG	JOO	YUN
-ko iss-	activity		3	4
	accomplishment	3	1	3
	achievement	3		2
-a iss-	activity			
	accomplishment		1	
	achievement	4	5	1

4.2 RQ2: Caretaker's Use of *-ko iss-/-a iss-*

Table 9 shows the caretakers' usage of the two imperfective markers divided by the meanings they denote. YUN and JONG's caretakers use the progressive *-ko iss-* and the resultative *-ko iss-/-a iss-* equally (use of the progressive *-ko iss-*: 49% for YUN and 44% for JONG). However, JOO's caretaker uses the progressive *-ko iss-* more frequently (63%) than the resultative *-ko iss-/-a iss-*. The results indicate that there was no clear common pattern in the three caretakers' speech, though their frequency count is similar to the Sejong written corpus in that the progressive *-ko iss-* is used most, followed by the resultaive *-a iss-* and lastly the resultative *-ko iss-*.

Table 9 Use of Imperfective Markers by Caretakers

	JONG	JOO	YUN
PRG-*ko iss-*	254 (44%)	534 (63%)	324 (49%)
RSL-*ko iss-*	75 (13%)	105 (12%)	94 (14%)
RSL-*a iss-*	253 (43%)	214 (25%)	239 (36%)
Sum	582 (100%)	853 (100%)	657 (100%)

Table 10 Distribution of Lexical Aspect by Caretakers

		JONG	JOO	YUN
-ko iss-	activity	222 (38%)	489 (57%)	275 (42%)
	accomplishment	37 (6%)	40 (5%)	36 (6%)
	achievement	70 (12%)	110 (13%)	107 (16%)
-a iss-	activity	1 (0%)	3 (0%)	
	accomplishment	44 (8%)	9 (1%)	20 (3%)
	achievement	208 (36%)	202 (24%)	219 (33%)
Sum		582 (100%)	853 (100%)	657 (100%)

Table 10 shows the usage patterns divided by lexical aspect. *-A iss-* is mostly used with achievements, while there is great deal of variation for *-ko iss-*, which is predominantly used with activity verbs as expected, but is also quite frequently used with achievements. JOO's caretakers' use of *-ko iss-* is most frequently used with activities than the other children's caretakers.

4.3 RQ3: The Relationship between Caretakers and Their Children

Although RQ 1 and RQ 2 address the issue of bioprogram vs. input, the real test of these competing accounts must come from an examination of the relationship between caretaker speech and children's speech. If there is a bias to map imperfective marking to atelic verbs because the past tense marker *ess* is already mapped onto telicity, then in the acquisition of imperfective marking *-ko iss-* and *-a iss-*, children should use activity verbs (to denote progressive meaning) more than their caretakers. We test whether or not this will really occur here, along with the validity of the distributional bias hypothesis by comparing each child's pattern of use with his/her caretakers'.

Figure 1 shows the children's and caretakers' use of *-ko iss-* and *-a iss-*. JONG uses the resultative *-ko iss-* twice as much as his caretaker. Thus, JONG's usage of imperfective aspect markers leaned more towards resultative markers than his caretakers'. JOO used the resultative *-a iss-* most frequently (36%), even though his caretaker used the progressive *-ko iss-* more than any other form (63%). These results contradict the bioprogram hypothesis, which would predict that children would inflate use of progressive meaning with imperfective markers. In fact, their usage decreased. Meanwhile, YUN's usage closely reflects that of his caretaker.

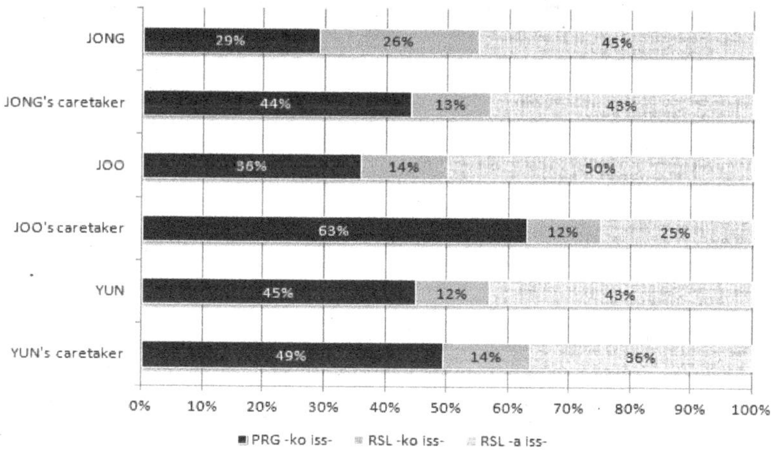

Figure 1 Children's and Caretakers' Usage pattern

With regard to the Distributional Bias Hypothesis, two patterns can be observed in our data. One pattern is that of YUN and JONG. They resemble their caretakers in their overall use of the imperfective markers. The other pattern is JOO's, which does not resemble the frequency of their caretakers. Thus, our results indicate that input in the child-directed speech is not the only determining factor in the distributional pattern of imperfective aspect marking in the children's speech.

Figure 2 shows the same comparison with respect to lexical aspect. As with the analysis based on the meaning denoted by the imperfective markers, all children use less activity verbs with *-ko iss-* than their caretakers. For example, JONG's caretakers use *-ko iss-* with activity verbs 67% of the time, while JONG only did this 38% of the time. This goes against the bioprogram hypothesis, which predicts that children use imperfective markers more with activity verbs than their caretakers.

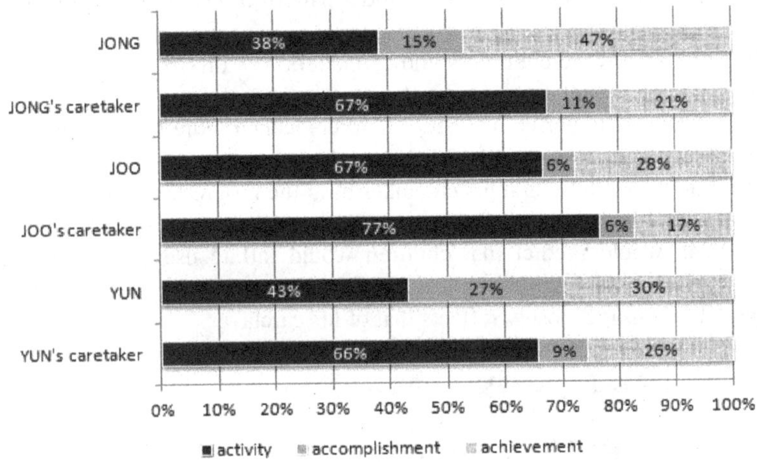

Figure 2 Children's and Caretakers' Usage pattern of *-ko iss-*

5. Discussion

The results obtained in this study answer the research questions stated in section 2 with the following.

1. There was no clear association found between children's use of *-ko iss-/-a iss-* and progressive meaning or activity verbs.
2. There was no clear association found between caretakers' use of *-ko iss-/-a iss-* and progressive meaning or activity verbs.
3. The caretakers' input from the child-directed speech does not determine the distributional pattern of imperfective aspect marking in children's speech. There is no evidence that children use atelic verbs with imperfective markers more than their caretakers.

We hypothesized that progressive marking with activity verbs would be acquired earlier than resultative marking with achievement verbs. However, our results show that there was no common pattern in the three children's acquisition. Two of them (JONG and JOO) associated imperfective aspect marking with achievement verbs early on, but one child (YUN) associated imperfective aspect marking with activity verbs in the early stage. Our results indicate that Korean does not seem to follow the universal pattern predicted by the Aspect Hypothesis. It was also found that Korean children do not seem to associate imperfective marking with atelic verbs, i.e. they do not inflate the frequency of atelic verbs (i.e. Bickerton's non-punctual verbs). Rather, children's imperfective marking was less strongly associated with atelic verbs than their caregivers', which suggests that the acquisition of the Korean imperfective aspect cannot be explained by the bio-program hypothesis.

We also observed that the results regarding the influence of input (i.e. the Distributional Bias Hypothesis) are a little less clear. According to our data, two of the children used patterns similar to their caretakers, but one did not. Thus, it is difficult to say that the distributional bias hypothesis can fully explain the acquisition of the Korean imperfective aspect.

Two of the children were not observed to associate the progressive marker *-ko iss-* with activity verbs at the early stages of development, contra the prediction of the Aspect hypothesis, although one (YUN) did. Rather, there appears to be a large degree of individual variation in the acquisition of imperfective aspect markers in Korean, as was reported by Budwig (1996) in her study of pronominal case acquisition in English. Her research showed that of the six children who received similar input, half of the children exhibited a different acquisitional pattern than the other half.

Individual differences have also been observed in Japanese tense-aspect acquisition. Shirai and Suzuki (in press) note that, of the nine children studied so far, three showed some preference for linking activity verbs to the progressive, while five showed some preference for linking achievement verbs to the resultative, and one did not show any preference. In light of this, individual variation seems more prominent than had been acknowledged in the literature, both in Japanese as it was in Korean in the present study.

Therefore, we suggest that L1 acquisition of tense-aspect markers may differ depending on various factors, such as input frequency, learner characteristics, and the nature of the linguistic category to be acquired. In any event, given all of these factors, it is not realistic to predict that all children will go through the same learning process. Multiple factors appear to determine acquisition patterns, not just innate predisposition (if any), or distributional bias in the input.

6. Conclusion

This study investigated the acquisition of the Korean imperfective aspect markers *-ko iss-/-a iss-* to address the issue of whether Korean children follow the acquisition pattern predicted by the Aspect Hypothesis. The results indicate that there was no common pattern in three Korean children we investigated, and that individual variation plays a larger role in the acquisition of tense-aspect markers than previously acknowledged. The results also suggest that Bickerton's (1981) language bioprogram hypothesis cannot explain the acquisition of the imperfective aspect in Korean.

References

Ahn, Y. 1995. *The Aspectual and Temporal System of Korean: From the Perspective of the Two-component Theory of Aspect*. Doctoral dissertation, University of Texas at Austin.

Aksu-Koç, A. 1988. *The Acquisition of Aspect and Modality: The Case of Past Reference in Turkish*. Cambridge: Cambridge University Press.

Andersen, R.W. 1993. Four operating principles and input distribution as explanation for underdeveloped and mature morphological systems. *Progression and regression in language: Sociocultural, neuropsychological, and linguistic perspectives*, eds. K. Hyltenstam and A. Viberg, 309-339. New York: Cambridge University Press.

Andersen, R.W. and Y. Shirai. 1994. Discourse Motivations for Some Cognitive Acquisition Principles. *Studies in Second Language Acquisition* 16: 133-156.

Andersen, R.W. and Y. Shirai. 1996. The Primacy of Aspect in First and Second Language Acquisition: The Pidgin-Creole Connection. *Handbook of Second Language Acquisition*, eds. W. C. Ritchie and T. K. Bhatia, 527-570. San Diego, CA: Academic Press.

Antinucci, F. and R. Miller. 1976. How Children Talk about What Happened. *Journal of Child Language* 3:169-189.

Bickerton, D. 1981. *Roots of Language*. Ann Arbor, MI: Karoma Publishers.

Bickerton, D. 1984. The Language Bioprogram Hypothesis. *The Behavioral and Brain Sciences* 7:173-188.

Bloom, L., K. Lifter, and J. Hafitz. 1980. Semantics of Verbs and the Development of Verb Inflection in Child Language. *Language* 56:386-412.

Broncart. J. P. and H. Sinclair. 1973. Time, Tense and Aspect. *Cognition* 2:107-30.

Budwig, N. 1996. What Influences Children's Patterns of Forms and Functions in Early Child Language? *Social Interaction, Social Context, and Language*, eds. D. I. Slobin, J. Gerhardt, A. Kyratzis and J. Guo, 143–156. Mahwah, NJ: Erlbaum.

Chen, J. and Y. Shirai. 2010. The Development of Aspectual Marking in Child Mandarin Chinese. *Applied Psycholinguistics* 31:1-28.

Diessel, H. and M. Tomasello. 2000. The Development of Relative Clauses in Spontaneous Child Speech. *Cognitive Linguistics* 11:131-151.

Kim, H. Y. and E. H. Lee. 2007. The Development of Tense and Aspect Morphology in L2 Korean. *Frontiers of Korean Language Acquisition*, ed. J. Song, 91-126. London: Saffron Books.

Lee, H. S. 1991. *Tense, Aspect and Modality: A Discourse-Pragmatic Analysis of Verbal Suffixes in Korean from a Typological Perspective*. Unpublished doctoral dissertation, University of California, Los Angeles.

Li, P. and M. Bowerman. 1998. The Acquisition of Grammatical and Lexical Aspect in Chinese. *First Language* 18:311–350.

Li, P. and Y. Shirai. 2000. *The Acquisition of Lexical and Grammatical Aspect*. Berlin: Mouton de Gruyter.

Martin, S. 1992. *A Reference Grammar of Korean*. Tokyo: Tuttle.

Noji, J. 1976. *Yooziki no Gengo Seikatu no Zittai (II)* [The Language Development of a Child, 2] Hiroshima: Bunka Hyoron.

Noji, J. 1977. *Yooziki no Gengo Seikatu no Zittai (I)* [The Language Development of a Child, 1] Hiroshima: Bunka Hyoron.

Gökmen S. and C. M. Lee. 2002. Aspects of the Acquisition of (Past) Tense and (Telic) Aspect in Turkish and Korean. *Language Research* 38(4): 1317-1347

Shirai, Y. 1991. *Primacy of Aspect in Language Acquisition: Simplified Input and Prototype*. Doctoral dissertation, University of California, Los Angeles.

Shirai, Y. 1993. Inherent Aspect and the Acquisition of Tense/Aspect Morphology in Japanese. *Argument Structure: Its Syntax and Acquisition*, eds. H. Nakajima and Y. Otsu, 185-211. Tokyo: Kaitakusha.

Shirai, Y. 1998. The Emergence of Tense-Aspect Morphology in Japanese: Universal Disposition? *First Language* 18:281-310.

Shirai, Y. and R. W. Andersen. 1995. The Acquisition of Tense-aspect Morphology: A Prototype Account. *Language* 71:743-762.

Shirai, Y. and Y. Suzuki. (in press). The Acquisition of the Japanese Imperfective Aspect Marker: Universal Predisposition or Input Frequency? *Japanese/Korean Linguistics, 20*, eds. B. Frellesvig and P. SellsStanford. CA: CSLI Publications.

Shirai, Y., D. Slobin and R. M. Weist. 1998. Introduction: The Acquisition of Tense-Aspect Morphology. *First Language* 18:245-253.

Stephany, U. 1981. Verbal Grammar in Modern Greek Early Child Language. *Child Language: An International Perspective*, eds. P. S. Dale and D. Ingram, 45-57. Baltimore, MD: University Park Press.

Tomasello, M. 2003. *Constructing a Language: A Usage-Based Theory of Language Acquisition*. Cambridge, MA: Harvard University Press.

Vendler, Z. 1957. *Linguistics in Philosphy*. Ithaca, NY: Cornell University Press.

Weist, R. M., H. Wysocka, K. Witkowska-Stadnik, E. Buczowska and E. Konieczna. 1984. The Defective Tense Hypothesis: on the Emergence of Tense and Aspect in Child Polish. *Journal of Child Language* 11: 347-374.

L1 Acquisition of Japanese Transitive Verbs: How Do Children Acquire Grammar in the Absence of Clear Evidence?*

NOZOMI TANAKA
University of Hawai'i at Mānoa

YASUHIRO SHIRAI
University of Pittsburgh

The acquisition of verbs involves the discovery of agent-patient relations. The major determiners of agent-patient relations are word order (Dryer 2005), inflectional morphology including case marking (Comrie 2005), and various forms of verb agreement (Siewierska 2005). Animacy is also considered to be helpful information, and many researchers claim that very young children favor animate agents and inanimate patients (Bowerman 1973; Brown 1970; Brown, Cazden and Bellugi 1968; Chapman and Miller 1975; de Villiers and de Villiers 1974; Kail 1989; Slobin 1968).

Japanese speech often lacks information that tells the listeners about grammatical relations. First, although the basic word order of Japanese is SOV, it

* This research was supported by grants from the Japan Iron and Steel Federal and Mitsubishi Endowments at the University of Pittsburgh and by grants from the Heiwa Nakajima Foundation to Tanaka. We thank Brian MacWhinney and Na-Rae Han for valuable comments on the paper.

Japanese/Korean Linguistics 21.
Edited by Bjarke Frellesvig and Peter Sells.

allows reordering of major constituents. That is, it exhibits the phenomenon often referred to as 'scrambling' (Shibatani 1990). Secondly, Japanese is a pro-drop language (Shibatani 1990), and therefore allows missing constituents, unlike English, where constituents such as subject NPs and direct object NPs are obligatory. Lastly, case markers can be omitted. The Japanese case marking system is realized in terms of postpositional particles and follows the nominative-accusative pattern, with the subjects of both transitive and intransitive clauses being marked by the nominative particle *-ga*, which we refer to as the subject marker in the present study, and the object of a transitive clause by the accusative *-o*, which we refer to as the object marker. These case markers are optional and allow ellipsis, especially in casual speech (Tsujimura 2007); child-directed speech is not an exception (Aida 1993; Miyata 2008; Rispoli 1989).

These characteristics of Japanese make the input sentences heard by children acquiring Japanese indeterminate. This is in contrast to languages like English, where the verb is heard in a sentence with unambiguous indication of the syntactic and the thematic role (Rispoli 1989). Scholars have sought to find out how Japanese children discover argument structure from such impoverished input (Hakuta 1982; Ito, Tahara, and Park 1993; Miyazaki 1979; Noji 1985; Rispoli 1987, 1989; Suzuki 2005).

While Bates and MacWhinney (1989), based on the work of Kilborn and Ito (1989) and others, viewed case marking as the major cue to sentence interpretation for adult native speakers of Japanese, studies on child language acquisition of Japanese found different results. For example, Miyazaki (1979) and Noji (1985) reported that Japanese children do not produce the subject marking *-ga* correctly until at least the age of three. Ito et al. (1993) further examined children's acquisition of case marking by conducting an experiment where the participants listened to auditory stimuli and then demonstrated what they heard by using toys and dolls. The children did not show adult-like comprehension of the subject marking *-ga* until the age of ten and of the object marking *-o* until the age of seven. According to Suzuki (2005), Japanese children start understanding single-argument sentences with case markers *-ga* and *-o* (e.g. *Koara-ga oshi-ta* 'koala-NOM push-PAST') around the age of four, but their performance does not reach an adult-like level until around the age of 5 to 6.

Rispoli (1987) also claimed that Japanese children classify transitive and intransitive verbs without the benefit of a case marking system or syn-tactic configuration of the noun arguments. He collected data of children's production from the conversations between two Japanese children from 22 to 24 months of age and their caretakers, which was made into a corpus of sentences that include action verbs, i.e. verbs that refer to events of change in the physical state of objects or the bodies of animate beings. The cluster analyses of the 9 to 10 most frequent action verbs in the production of each child suggested that the children use two kinds of semantic information—the planned nature of an action and the animacy of theme referents—in order to classify verbs into transitive verbs and intransitive verbs. He concluded that Japanese children separate transitive and intransitive verbs based on semantics and do not use case marking to guide their comprehension. Rispoli (1989), based on a corpus analysis on the distribution of 300 action verbs in the speech of six caretakers of four Japanese children from 22 to 24 months of age, concluded that two-year-old children use the intentionality (roughly corresponding to animacy) of the figure-patient referent and the expression of intentional, planned action realized as verb suffixes or auxiliaries (e.g. -*tai* 'want to') and adverbs (e.g. *joozu ni* 'skillfully') (Soga 1983: 87–98). Such information helps them assign an action verb to a semantic causal type, which ultimately leads to the classification of transitive and intransitive action verbs.

On the other hand, Hakuta (1982) did experiments to test production, comprehension, and imitation (i.e. delayed production) of simple sentences by children between the ages of 2 and 6, and showed that Japanese children at this age do not show a strong reliance on either word order or case markers alone. He claimed that the children use a combination of case marking and word order for both comprehension and reproduction. A similar study was conducted by Matsuo, Kita, Shinya, Wood, and Naigles (2011), where they investigated how Japanese two-year-old children assign causal vs. non-causal meaning to a novel verb. The results of their experiment demonstrated that children assigned causal meaning to the verb when the verb was heard in a two-argument transitive frame with case marking. They claimed that, despite the omission of noun arguments and case marking in most input, Japanese children can utilize the number of overt noun arguments and case markers to infer the meaning of novel verbs.

Overall, there are conflicting views toward first language (L1) acquisition of Japanese verbs. Whereas adults use case marking as the strongest cue (Bates and MacWhinney 1989; Kilborn and Ito 1989), Rispoli (1987, 1989) stated that Japanese children do not use case marking to learn verbs and instead they use semantic information like animacy. Ito et al. (1993), Hakuta (1982), and Suzuki (2005) share views similar to Rispoli's, although Suzuki (2005) indicated that children at the age of 3 to 4 seem to start understanding the role of case markers. The study by Hakuta (1982) suggested that, while children do not process case markers by themselves, they comprehend sentences using the information from both word order and case marking.

The problem here is that different researchers have looked at different cues separately and argued over which information was important or not. For example, the stimulus sentences used by Hakuta (1982) and Matsuo et al. (2011)

only contained animate nouns and therefore animacy contrast was not included in their discussion. Rispoli (1987, 1989), on the other hand, did not look at word order or noun ellipsis in his studies. The purpose of our study is to provide a comprehensive account of Japanese verb acquisition by taking all cues investigated so far (i.e. word order, case marking, and animacy) into account.

In addition, most of these previous studies except Hakuta (1982) and Rispoli (1987) only looked at children's comprehension, that is, how children interpret input. In the current study, we investigated how the cues in input are used by children by looking at both input frequency and production frequency in order to better understand how children learn from the input and establish their linguistic knowledge about argument structure that can be used in their own speech production.

For this purpose, we conducted a corpus analysis of transcribed data of mothers' and children's production and examined the interaction between the available cues based on the constructs proposed in the Competition Model framework (Bates and MacWhinney 1989).

The Competition Model tries to capture language in a two-level structure, with a functional level concerned with meanings/functions, and a formal level concerned with surface forms (Bates and MacWhinney 1989). Therefore, language learning is viewed as a process of acquiring coalition of form-function mappings.

There are four core concepts in this model: cue strength, cue validity, conflict validity, and coalition between forms and functions. Cue validity refers to the information value of a given linguistic device as a cue that signals an underlying meaning. Under ideal conditions, the value of cue strength converges on the value of cue validity; therefore, cue validity is the major predictive construct in the Competition Model (Bates and MacWhinney 1989). Cue validity can be analyzed into three components: availability, reliability, and conflict validity (MacWhinney 1978; MacWhinney, Pléh, and Bates 1985; McDonald 1989). Cue availability is the extent to which a cue is present when needed, and cue reliability is the degree to which a cue leads to the correct interpretation when you count on it. Conflict validity is the number of cases in which the cue leads to a correct interpretation when two or more cues conflict. Overall validity is the product of cue availability by cue reliability. For example, in the case of Japanese, the word order cue is an available and reliable cue when it is in SOV word order, and the animacy cue is available and reliable when there is an animacy contrast between an animate subject and an inanimate object. An example of such a sentence is *Otoko-ga ringo-o tabe-ta* 'man-NOM apple-ACC eat-PAST'. In a sentence such as *Ringo-ga otoko-o tabe-ta* 'apple-NOM man-ACC eat-PAST', these two cues conflict because, while SOV word order indicates that *ringo* 'apple' is the subject and *otoko* 'man' is the object, the animacy of the nouns tell us that *otoko* is more likely to be a subject/agent of the sentence because it is an animate entity.

While cue validity is mainly concerned with the relationship between a single cue and a single function or meaning, such one-to-one mappings are not common in natural languages. The subsystems comprised of many-to-many mappings are referred to as coalition (Bates and MacWhinney 1989; Sasaki and MacWhinney 2006). For example, Chan, Lieven, and Tomasello (2009) examined Cantonese-, German-, and English-speaking children's comprehension of word order and animacy contrast as cues to the agent-patient relations in transitive sentences, and showed that the children understood transitive sentences better when agent and patient were cued redundantly by both word order and animacy contrast.

While there are studies of cue strength of each cue in Japanese in both adult comprehension and child comprehension (Bates and MacWhinney 1989; Ito et al. 1993), there has not been a study that examined the combination of these cues within the framework of the Competition Model. As mentioned above, Hakuta (1982) indicated that Japanese children from the ages of 2 to 6 understand sentences using the combination of word order and case marking. On the other hand, Rispoli (1987, 1989) stressed the importance of animacy and argued that Japanese verb acquisition is done without syntactic specification of noun arguments, but he did not take word order into consideration. It is necessary to examine every combination of these three cues.

1. The Study

The purpose of the present study is to examine how Japanese children acquire the argument structure of Japanese transitive verbs. More specifically, it investigates what kind of cue distribution they are exposed to, how children learn the relevant cues from the input they receive, and how they use such information in their own production. In order to answer these questions, we analyzed transcribed data of conversation between child Japanese L1 speakers and their caretakers. The speech produced by the caretakers was essential to investigating the importance of the input in children's first language acquisition. We also analyzed children's production in order to examine what children actually learn from the input and how they manipulate the information in their own speech production.

Our prediction is that children use the coalition of SOV word order and animacy in order to identify as well as to express the agent and the theme in transitive clauses. This is because, first, as shown in previous studies (Aida 1993; Ito et al. 1993; Rispoli 1987), case markers are frequently dropped in both input to and production of children (e.g. in an utterance such as *Taroo ringo tabe-ta* 'Taroo apple eat-PAST'). A second reason is because it has been shown that the coalition of word order and animacy is useful for children to understand transitive sentences in other languages (Chan et al. 2009).

2. Method

2.1. Data

The data were taken from the Child Language Data Exchange System (CHILDES) database, which contains transcripts and media data collected from conversations between young children, their playmates, and their caretakers (MacWhinney 2000; Oshima-Takane et al. 1998). We conducted the analysis using the corpus of a Japanese girl, Arika (Nisisawa and Miyata 2010a), and a Japanese boy, Asato (Nisisawa and Miyata 2010b). In this study, we chose data from the age of 3;0, 4;0, and 5;0 for both children. We analyzed the utterances that contained transitive verbs in the children's speech and the speech of their mothers, which added up to a total of 1,101 utterances produced by the mothers and 736 utterances produced by the children.

2.2. Analysis

We examined the availability, reliability, and validity of the word order cue, the case marking cue, and the animacy contrast cue as well as the coalition of two or more of these cues based on the criteria proposed in previous Competition Model studies (Bates and MacWhinney 1989; Chan et al. 2009; Kempe and MacWhinney 1998).

The word order cue was counted as present when there were two overt nouns as seen in (1) and (2), because two nouns are necessary to determine relative ordering of noun arguments. The word order cue was counted as not available when at least one noun was missing from the sentence. Therefore, the word order cue is considered as absent in Example (3):

(1) Arichan aka mikke-ta.
Arichan red find-PAST
'Arichan found the red (toy).' (Arika, 5;0)

(2) Kore zembu Fuuchan-ga kat-tanda.
this all Fuuchan-NOM buy-PAST
'Fuuchan bought this all.' (Arika, 5;0)

(3) Kore-ga mot-te kuru no
this-NOM bring-CONN come FIN
'This (= the tanker) brings [the gas].' (Asato's mother, 3;0)

When the word order cue was available, it was counted as reliable when the sentence follows the canonical SOV word order, but not otherwise. If we look at Examples (1) and (2), both of the sentences have two noun arguments. However, (1) follows the canonical SOV order, while the word order of the sentence in (2) is OSV. Therefore, only (1) has a reliable word order cue.

Animacy of the noun was evaluated based on the context, even when the noun was not realized.[1] When we were not able to retrieve the nouns from the context because of lack of information, the animacy was coded as 'indeterminate' and these data were excluded from the analysis. The animacy contrast cue was considered available when an animate subject and an inanimate object are denoted as in (4), and also when an inanimate subject and an animate object were present, as in (5) (Chan et al. 2009). On the other hand, when the animacy of the two nouns was the same, we considered that the sentence had no animacy contrast. The sentence in (6) shows such a case.

(4) Arichan obento tsuku-ru kara.
Arichan bento make-PRES CONJ
'Arichan will make a bento.' (Arika, 3;0)

(5) Mikan-ga yattsuke-ru no hebi-o?
tangerine-NOM defeat-PRES Q snake-ACC
'Does the tangerine defeat the snake?' (Asato, 3;0)

(6) Neko-san-wa hiyoko-san-o tabe-chau kamoshirenai.
cat-HON-TOP chick-HON-NOM eat-PRES possible
'Cats might eat the chicks.' (Asato, 3;0)

The animacy contrast cue was counted as reliable when the subject is animate and the object is inanimate, as seen in Example (4). This means, in a sentence like (5), where the subject is inanimate and the object is animate, the cue was considered as not reliable.

The case marking cue was counted as present when either the subject or the object was marked in sentences with two arguments (some of these sentences contained noncanonical markers such as the topic marker *-wa* and a few kinds of focus markers including *-mo*).

(7) Asatokun-ga eki kai-te-age-ru.
Asatokun-NOM station draw-CONN-give-PRES
'Asatokun will draw the station (for you).' (Asato, 3;0)

In Example (7), although the noun eki 'station' is not case-marked, the case marking cue was counted as available because we can tell that *eki* is most likely to be an object because the other noun argument *Asatokun* is case-marked with the subject marker. When either of the nouns is case-marked, the cue is only reliable when the case marker marks what it is expected to mark, that is, when *-ga* marks the subject and/or *-o* marks the object.

[1] This is because, while word order and case marking are linguistic notions, animacy is real-world knowledge that is often obvious from what is available in the setting where the conversation between children and their caretakers takes place, especially because such conversations tend to be about the 'here and now'.

3. Results

Based on the criteria described in Section 2.2, we calculated the cue availability and cue reliability of each cue, as can be seen in Table 1–3.

TABLE 1 Availability and reliability of the word order cue

	Mothers		Children	
	frequency	percentage	frequency	percentage
Cue availability	53	6.1%	73	8.6%
Cue reliability	62	85.5%	62	84.9%

Table 1 shows the cue availability and reliability of the word order cue. We can see that noun arguments were often dropped in child-directed speech and children did the same in their own production. Only 6.1% of the input and 8.6% of the production had two nouns in one sentence. But when two nouns were present in a sentence, the word order was canonical SOV about 85.5% of the time in input and 84.9% of the time in production, even though Japanese allows flexible word order.

The cue availability and reliability of the animacy contrast cue is shown in Table 2.

TABLE 2 Availability and reliability of the animacy contrast cue

	Mothers		Children	
	frequency	percentage	frequency	percentage
Cue availability	945	93.5%	697	94.7%
Cue reliability	943	99.8%	697	100%

The animacy contrast cue had high availability and high reliability both in input (93.5%) and in production (94.7%). This means children were able to come to the correct interpretation if they were paying attention to the animacy contrast, and that was reflected in their production. They did not produce many sentences that did not involve an animacy contrast, i.e., they produced few sentences like (6). They also did not produce a sentence where the subject is inanimate and the object is inanimate, such as (5).

As Table 3 shows, case markers were used only about 17.5% of the time by the mothers and 17.7% of the time by the children, but when they were used, they were 100% reliable. That is, mothers never produced a sentence where *-ga* or *-o* marked something else, and children did not either.

Figure 1 shows the validity of each cue. Cue validity predicts the overall information value of each cue, and it is calculated by multiplying cue availability and cue reliability. The animacy contrast has the highest validity, fol-

TABLE 3 Availability and reliability of the case marking cue

	Mothers		Children	
	frequency	percentage	frequency	percentage
Cue availability	11	17.5%	11	17.7%
Cue reliability	11	100%	11	100%

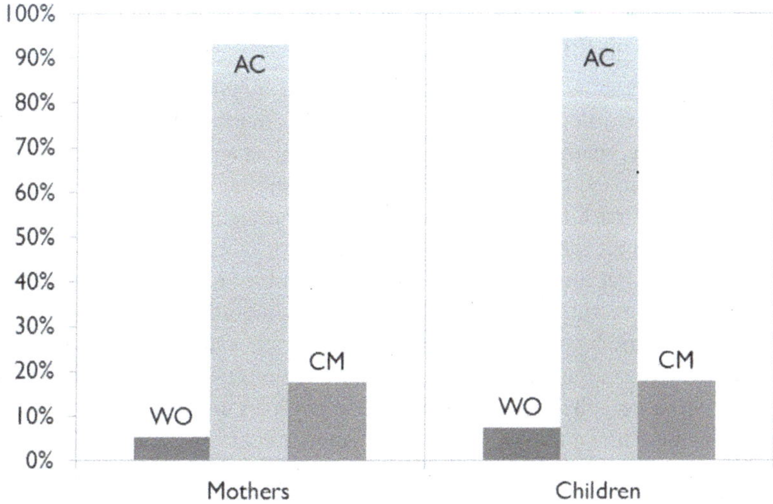

FIGURE 1 Overall validity of each cue (WO = word order; AC = animacy contrast CM = case marking).

lowed by case marking and then word order. That is, if we look at the cues one by one, animacy has the highest information value, followed by case marking and word order.

The results that we have discussed so far are based on the appearance of each cue. We also need to look at how these cues interact with each other. In other words, we have to see if any of these cues appear at the same time or stand alone as a single cue. This is necessary in order to discuss the possibility of multiple cues leading to a single interpretation in combination.

First, we look at the sentences with two noun arguments, which take up 5.5% of mothers' speech and 7.9% of children's speech (Table 4).

Examples (8) through (11) show different instances of cue appearances:

(8) Taroo-ga ringo-o tabe-ta.
Taroo-NOM apple-ACC eat-PAST
'Taro ate an apple.'

(9) Taroo ringo tabe-ta.
Taroo apple eat-PAST
'Taro ate an apple.'

(10) Ringo-o Taroo-ga tabe-ta.
apple-ACC Taroo-NOM eat-PAST
'Taro ate an apple.'

(11) Taroo-ga Jiroo-o tatai-ta.
Taroo-NOM Jiroo-ACC hit-PAST
'Taroo hit Jiroo.'

Example (8) shows a case where all three cues are present and reliable. The sentence has two noun arguments that are both marked with case markers, follows SOV word order, and has an animate subject and an inanimate object. The sentence in (9) follows SOV word order and has the animacy contrast, but lacks case marking. This is the pattern we predicted would be dominant in children's input and production. Example (10) has the animacy contrast and case marking, but the word order cue is not reliable since it has a scrambled word order. The sentence in (11) follows SOV word order and both the nouns are accompanied by correct case markers, but there is no animacy contrast.

Table 5 shows the percentage of appearance of cues in combination and alone. We can see that when there were two overt arguments, word order was agent-theme with an animate subject and an inanimate object about 69.8% of the time in input and 72.6% of the time in production. Other cue combinations were minimal. This means that the word order cue and the animacy cue, but not the case marking cue, worked in combination to help children discover the agent and theme in their input. These two cues were also used in their own production to express the agent and the theme.

We can also see that animacy and word order appeared alone, and the animacy cue stands alone more frequently (7.9% in input, 9.7% in production) than the word order cue (4.8% in input, 1.6% in production). However, this was not the case for the case marking cue. Mothers did not use the case marking cue as a single cue and children did not either. This means that case marking alone cannot lead children to a correct interpretation when they are

TABLE 4 Sentence types

	Mothers		Children	
	frequency	percentage	frequency	percentage
NNV	56	5.5%	58	7.9%
NV/VN	489	48.4%	363	49.3%
V	460	45.5%	310	42.1%
Others	6	0.6%	5	0.6%

hearing such input. Because of this, they did not use case marking alone to express agent-theme relations in their own speech. Earlier, we saw that the case marking cue had higher cue validity than word order, but it in fact cannot be a valid cue when it is present by itself, unlike animacy or word order. This suggests that the case marking cue has lower information value compared to the animacy cue or the word order cue.

We now turn to the sentences with only one overt noun. Since these sentences lack one of the noun arguments, they do not have the word order cue, but we calculated the appearance of the animacy cue and the case marking cue. Table 6 shows the frequency and the percentage of cues in combination and alone. We can see that animacy is the most reliable information in sentences that lack one of the noun arguments.

The appearance of case marking in single-argument sentences is marginally higher than in the two-argument sentences, where it was 0.0%. This suggests that children do mark noun arguments when it is the only way to express the agent or the theme, although the frequency is very low. But here again, the case marking cue is hardly reliable by itself and it is much more likely to occur with the animacy contrast cue. That is, case marking is almost always just an additional, redundant cue, so children could understand the sentence even without case markers.

4. Discussion

The results supported our prediction that the coalition of the word order cue and the animacy contrast cue was used in both input and production.

Although there were sentences with the word order cue alone and sentences with the animacy contrast cue alone, neither the mothers nor the children produced sentences that only contained the case marking cue. The case marking cue had high cue reliability but was only used in a redundant context, which suggests why it is hard for Japanese children to acquire case marking.

TABLE 5 Cues in combination and alone

	Mothers		Children	
	frequency	percentage	frequency	percentage
WO + AC + CM	6	9.5%	6	9.7%
WO + AC	44	69.8%	45	72.6%
AC + CM	5	7.9%	3	4.8%
WO + CM	1	1.6%	0	0.0%
WO	3	4.8%	1	1.6%
AC	5	7.9%	6	9.7%
CM	0	0.0%	0	0.0%

However, as we saw in the analysis of sentences with only one argument, children do make use of case marking to some degree, although the frequency was extremely low.

The current study suggests that animacy is the most useful and important information in Japanese input, based on the analysis of the validity of each cue and the percentage of cues standing alone. This is not only because the animacy contrast has the highest validity but also because the information of animacy is always useful when the word order and case marking is not canonical or when the sentence lacks one of the two noun arguments. This can be seen in Bates and MacWhinney's (1989: 44–45) study, where animacy is in a higher position for children than for adults in the comprehension of most languages. This is also reflected in children's own production: children use animacy to denote agent-theme relations in their own speech.

5. Conclusion

In conclusion, the results indicated that the word order and the animacy cues work in combination to help children interpret transitive sentences, and this coalition was also used in children's production.

Based on these results, we propose the following order of cue strength for Japanese children's sentence comprehension and production:

(12) Animacy > Word order > Case

The animacy contrast cue appears to be the strongest cue because animacy has the highest cue validity and also because it is the most likely of the three cues to appear by itself. Moreover, the information of animacy was always present when the word order was noncanonical or when the sentence lacked one of the two noun arguments. We also determined that word order is a stronger cue than case marking. This is because the results suggested that the word order cue can appear as a single cue and the case marking cue did not. The case marking cue was only used in a redundant context, which suggests why it is hard for Japanese children to acquire case marking in spite of its high cue reliability. This order of cue strength differs from the order of cue strength for adult comprehension proposed in previous studies (i.e. Case > Animacy > Word order; Bates and MacWhinney 1989; Kilborn and Ito 1989). Whereas

TABLE 6 Reliable cues in sentences with single overt argument

	Mothers		Children	
	frequency	percentage	frequency	percentage
Animacy + Case	102	20.9%	46	12.7%
Animacy	365	74.6%	298	82.1%
Case	4	0.8%	2	0.6%

there were sentences with the word order cue alone and sentences with the animacy contrast cue alone, neither the mothers nor the children produced sentences that only contained the case marking cue.

The current study left some questions unanswered, which should be addressed in future research. For example, if case marking is not used as a single reliable cue in input or in production, what is children's motivation to use case markers at all? And how do they manage to learn how to use case markers?

For example, the sentence in (13) shows an OSV sentence without an animacy contrast. Such a sentence needs case marking to specify the agent and theme. If there is no case marking, as in the sentence in (14), the sentence will be ambiguous or sometimes not interpretable.

(13) Jiroo-o Taroo-ga tatai-ta.
Jiroo-ACC Taroo-NOM hit-PAST
'Taroo hit Jiroo.'

(14) Jiroo Taroo tatai-ta.
Jiroo Taroo hit-PAST
'Taroo hit Jiroo.'

This kind of sentence was not seen in the actual data analyzed in the current study. We need to examine if children are able to interpret sentences like Example (14) based solely on the information of case marking and when they start to produce such sentences.

We also need to see if the results of behavioral experiments support the results of the current study. In particular, it would be important to examine how children interpret transitive sentences that only have one overt argument. Although a few Competition Model studies have measured children's comprehension of transitive clauses, there has been no study that has looked at how children interpret single-argument sentences in the framework of the Competition Model, and such a study would help us understand the mechanism of verb learning since children are exposed to many single-argument sentences, including intransitive sentences, which we did not look at in this study.

List of Abbreviations

ACC	Accusative	NOM	Nominative
CONN	Connective	PAST	Past
CONJ	Conjunction	PRES	Present
FIN	Final particle	Q	Question particle
HON	Honorific	TOP	Topic

References

Aida, M. 1993. Omission of Postpositions in Japanese Mothers' Speech to One-year-old Children. *Sophia Linguistica* 33: 313–31.

Bates, E., and MacWhinney, B. 1989. Functionalism and the Competition Model. *The Cross-linguistic Study of Sentence Processing*, ed. B. MacWhinney and E. Bates, 3–73. New York: Cambridge University Press.

Bowerman, M. 1973. Structural Relationships in Children's Utterances: Syntactic or Semantic? *Cognitive Development and the Acquisition of Language.*, ed. T. E. Moore, 197–213. New York: Academic.

Brown, R. 1970. The First Sentences of Child and Chimpanzee. *Psycholinguistics: Selected Papers*, ed. R. Brown, 208–231. New York: Free Press.

Brown, R., Cazden, C., and Bellugi, U. 1968. The Child's Grammar from I to III. *Minnesota Symposia on Child Psychology*, ed. J. P. Hill, 28–73. Minneapolis: University of Minnesota Press.

Chan, A., Lieven, E., and Tomasello, M. 2009. Children's Understanding of the Agent-Patient Relations in the Transitive Construction: Cross-linguistic Comparisons between Cantonese, German, and English. *Cognitive Linguistics* 20: 267–300.

Chapman, R. S., and Miller, J. F. 1975. Word Order in Early Two- and Three-Word Utterances: Does Production Precede Comprehension? *Journal of Speech and Hearing Research* 18: 355–71.

Comrie, B. 2005. Alignment of Case Marking. *The World Atlas of Language Structures*, ed. M. Haspelmath, M. Dryer, D. Gil, and B. Comrie, 398–495. Oxford: Oxford University Press.

De Villiers, J. G., and De Villiers, P. A. 1974. Competence and Performance in Child Language: Are Children Really Competent to Judge? *Journal of Child Language* 1: 11–22.

Dryer, M. 2005. Order of Subject, Object and Verb. *The World Atlas of Language Structure*, ed. M. Haspelmath, M. Dryer, D. Gil, and B. Comrie, 330–33. Oxford: Oxford University Press.

Hakuta, K. 1982. Interaction between Particles and Word Order in the Comprehension and Production of Simple Sentences in Japanese Children. *Developmental Psychology* 18: 62–76.

Ito, T., Tahara, T., and Park, W. 1993. *Bun no Rikai ni Hatasu Joshi no Yakuwari* (The Role of Particles on Sentence Comprehension). Tokyo: Kazama.

Kail, M. 1989. Cue Validity, Cue Cost, and Processing Types in Sentence Comprehension in French and Spanish. *The Cross-linguistic Study of Sentence Processing*, ed. B. MacWhinney and E. Bates, 77–117. New York: Cambridge University Press.

Kempe, V., and MacWhinney, B. 1998. The Acquisition of Case-marking by Adult Learners of Russian and German. *Studies in Second Language Acquisition* 20: 543–87.

Kilborn, K., and Ito, T. 1989. Sentence Processing Strategies in Adult Bilinguals. *The Crosslinguistic Study of Sentence Processing*, ed. B. MacWhinney and E. Bates, 257–91. New York: Cambridge University Press.

MacWhinney, B. 1978. The Acquisition of Morphology. *Monographs of the Society for Research in Child Development* 43 (1).

MacWhinney, B. 2000. *The CHILDES Project: Tools for Analyzing Talk.* Mahwah, NJ: Lawrence Erlbaum.

MacWhinney, B., Pléh, C., and Bates, E. 1985. The Development of Sentence Interpretation in Hungarian. *Cognitive Psychology* 17: 178–209.

Matsuo, A., Kita, S., Shinya, Y., Wood, G. C., and Naigles, L. 2011. Japanese Two-year-olds Use Morphosyntax to Learn Novel Verb Meanings. *Journal of Child Language* FirstView: 1–27.

McDonald, J. 1989. The Acquisition of Cue-Category Mappings. *The Cross-linguistic Study of Sentence Processing*, ed. B. MacWhinney and E. Bates, 375–396. New York: Cambridge University Press.

Miyata, S. 2008. Input Frequency and Case Acquisition in Japanese. *Journal of Medical Welfare* 4: 108–17.

Miyazaki, M. 1979. *The Acquisition of the Particles wa and ga in Japanese: A Comparative Study of L1 Acquisition and L2 Acquisition.* Los Angeles: University of Southern California. Unpublished manuscript.

Nisisawa, H. Y., and Miyata, S. 2010a. *Japanese: Arika Corpus*. Pittsburgh, PA: Talk-Bank.

Nisisawa, H. Y., and Miyata, S. 2010b. *Japanese: Asato Corpus*. Pittsburgh, PA: Talk-Bank.

Noji, J. 1985. *Yoojiki no Gengo Seikatsu no Jittai* (The Language Development of a Child), vols. 1–4. Hiroshima: Bunka Hyoron.

Oshima-Takane, Y., MacWhinney, B., Sirai, H., Miyata, S., and Naka, N. (eds). 1998. *CHILDES Manual for Japanese*, 2nd ed. The JCHAT Project Nagoya: Chukyo University.

Rispoli, M. 1987. The Acquisition of the Transitive and Intransitive Action Verb Categories in Japanese. *First Language* 7: 183–200.

Rispoli, M. 1989. Encounters with Japanese Verbs: Caregiver Sentences and the Categorization of Transitive and Intransitive Action Verbs. *First Language* 9: 57–80.

Sasaki, Y., and MacWhinney, B. 2006. Language Acquisition Research Based on the Competition Model. *The Handbook of East Asian Psycholinguistics: Vol. 2. Japanese*, ed. M. Nakayama, R. Mazuka, and Y. Shirai, 307–14. Cambridge: Cambridge University Press.

Shibatani, M. 1990. *The Languages of Japan*. New York: Cambridge University Press.

Siewierska, A. 2005. Alignment of Verbal Person Marking. *The World Atlas of Language Structure*, ed. M. Haspelmath, M. Dryer, D. Gil, and B. Comrie, 406–09. Oxford: Oxford University Press.

Slobin, D. I. 1968. Recall of Full and Truncated Passive Sentences in Connected Discourse. *Journal of Verbal Learning and Verbal Behavior* 7: 876–81.

Soga, M. 1983. *Tense and Aspect in Modern Colloquial Japanese*. Vancouver: University of British Columbia Press.

Suzuki, T. 2005. Tan-itsu Koobun no Rikai kara Saguru Yooji no Kakujoshi Hattatsu (The Development of Japanese Case-markers Observed through Children's Comprehension of Single-argument Sentences). *Gengo Kenkyu* 132. 55–76.

Tsujimura, N. 2007. *An Introduction to Japanese Linguistics*. Malden, MA: Blackwell.

Index